The Light of One Star
By Anne Fischer Juhlmann

Spy Press LLC
Rehoboth Beach, DE 19971

Cover Design by Crystal Heidel

Zach and Sam

I deeply believe there are always stars and we owe it to ourselves - if no one else -to find those stars and share them with others. I believe that seeing and sharing the stars is why Zach and Sam lived as long as they did. You see, along the way I learned that when we take the time to point out a beautiful star we see, we suddenly develop a little following. Before long the light of one star -sometimes one that is incredibly dim to the human eye -reflects and radiates from one person to the next. Sometimes it felt as if the sky itself had opened up and all this warm and amazing light was raining down on us. It is as if there is a wonderful energy - Zach and Sam energy - wrapping itself around all of us. When they were alive it gave me such a sense of community and shared purpose--it inspired me to never stop looking for the stars. And after they died it gave me the same.

So I hope it is clear that I am committed to star gazing. But I also must be honest and say I am working really hard to see stars and have been for some time.

Anne Fischer Juhlmann, November 11, 2011

2003

TO ALL OF SAM'S DONORS – THANK YOU

The month before my 4th child was born, my blood counts began to drop dramatically. In the hours that preceded his birth I was given oxygen because my blood did not have enough red cells to carry the oxygen that my baby and I needed. I heard doctors refer to my baby as "distressed." I worried about what that meant as nurses gave me the blood that I desperately needed. Samuel was born blue, though the hospital staff quickly and expertly helped him to breathe. I fell asleep holding Sam, too weak and exhausted to fully know the joy of his birth. Two days later, on Mother's Day, I brought Sam home, thankful for the lifeline of blood that now flowed. A precious moments that marked Sam's first weeks at home.

When Sam was 14 months old he was diagnosed with a metabolic disease that makes it difficult for his body to produce enough energy to grow and thrive the way that it should. At the age of 2, his bone marrow, starving for energy, stopped producing the blood cells that his body needs. In the beginning it was just the red cells but the disease has progressed since then. He is now dependent on red cells matched platelets, plasma, and cryoprecipitate transfusions. Without them he would die.

That is what Sam has. That is what Sam needs. Yet none of that tells the story of who Sam is. Sam is six years old - a child with blond hair, big brown eyes and long eye lashes that lay softly against his cheeks when he lies sleeping. He is considered tiny for his age yet his presence is enormous. He loves to tell jokes – none of which are funny. Yet to hear his uninhibited laughter at his own jokes is to step into the sunshine from the shadows – so we ask him to tell the jokes again and again just to hear his laughter. Sam is a study in contrasts: Strong, independent and resilient, his eyes twinkle with pure joy whenever I kiss him. "Ha! Ha!" he proudly announces with his hands on his hips, "I wiped your kiss off again!" and he bursts into laughter. At nighttime I revel in his loving and sensitive nature. "Climb in Mama Puppy and snuggle with your little Sammy Puppy for a minute," he says as he pats the mattress beside him. I climb in with him and approximately 30 stuffed dogs. I lay beside my little boy

1

while he tells me about something he did that day, about how he wants to be the Yellow Power Ranger for Halloween and how he can't wait to go to Kindergarten so that he can have recess "just like the other kids." He tells me that when he grows up he will be Buzz Light Year and catch all the bad guys, or maybe he'll be an ambulance. "You mean an ambulance driver?" I once made the mistake of asking. "No." he said with disgust. "Don't you know about an ambulance? It goes really speedy and it helps people get better. That's what I might want to be." As I walk out of his room at night, I hear him say, half asleep, "I love you Mama. I love you 500! And I love you 700!" Sometimes my eyes fill with tears. I know that I am blessed to have this blond haired boy as my child, even if it is only for a short time. I marvel that he has a profound disease of energy production because Sam is all about living and loving.

Still, my life is impossibly marked by what he has, by what he needs. On my daughter's 10th birthday, he bled too much and she asked, "Will Sam die if the blood center runs out of blood?' Fear grips my heart--after all only 4% the population in the Midwest donates blood. 4% does not sound like a lot to me. She persists, her voice quivering. "Will Sam die if I do not give him my platelets?" I realize I have to reassure her. I begin, falsely at first, but then my own words have the unexpected effect of comforting me. I tell her that Sam's dependence on blood products is scary. It underscores our interdependence on one another in a day and age when individual strength is placed on a pedestal. Yes, I tell her, Sam will die without the blood. Yet day after day it is there for him and because of that I believe anew in the goodness and compassion of our community.

I increasingly wonder who are these people in our community, these 4% who volunteer to give a part of themselves so that my child may live? Day after day, week after week, year after year, they are faithful. I have ascribed names and faces, jobs and lives to these people that I have never met. Still I wonder who are they. I have days that are so busy that I cannot imagine adding one more task —then I stop and think about the person who donated blood during the only free hours they had. "Date collected" is stamped on each bag of each blood product that Sammy receives. I take note of these dates. Date collected - June 14: Sam and I finished planting his garden on a beautiful sunny Saturday while his donor gave platelets matched just for him. Date collected - April 18: It was Friday before Easter. Sam and his 3 siblings painted Easter eggs while his donor gave the whole blood later made into cryoprecipitate. Date collected - May 9: Sam's birthday. He requested and helped make a purple cake with orange frosting while his donor gave the red cells that he can no longer make himself. Who are these people who give to someone they have never met, expecting nothing in return?

Last night, while reviewing my son's social studies curriculum, the answer came. I read that a family is the basic unit of social organization. It is a group of people bound together by blood. Could I count the ounces of blood binding Sam to those who have given it to him? A family is multigenerational – I think of the grandmothers and young mothers, college students, and middle aged men who donate their blood and its components. A family is a vital source of strength and compassion. They give assistance in time of need. I read about the "fabric of family life" and think of a patchwork quilt – each piece unique but interdependent - together creating a whole. A family is a network. As I think of a net and it's intricate weaving designed to catch something so it does not slip away, I realize I have finally found my answer. Who are Sam's donors? They are a part of his family; tirelessly giving a piece of themselves, without whom there would not be a story of who Sam is. Bound together by blood, vital to all he is and will be –that is who Sam's donors are.

A SPECIAL NOTE:

Three times a day Sam needs cryoprecipitate (a blood product that comes from the liquid part of blood and helps blood to clot). Without it, he bleeds uncontrollably. Three times a week he needs plasma, which also helps his blood to clot. Four to seven times a week he needs platelets, which are one type of cell that is in our blood. He cannot receive Platelets from just anyone because of his immune disease. Sam reacts against 92% of the population's platelets. Therefore, he needs platelets that are matched exactly for him. There are only a handful of people in the Milwaukee area who have platelets matched exactly for him. These people faithfully donate week after week for Sam so that he does not bleed. Every few days Sam needs red cells which are another kind of cell that is found in blood. Every month he needs a five-day infusion of immune globulins--a protein in the blood that helps fight off infection.

This is all for just one little boy. His needs are more intense than most any other child but there are many children and adults throughout the United States who depend on donors for their very life. Sometimes they only need your gift once, as I did when Sam was born. For others, they depend on donors once a month like Zachary or for their day-to-day existence like Sam. Please consider donating blood or plasma for others in your community who are in need. You may never know who you help but I guarantee that your gift will be one that is priceless!

2004

Happy New Year!

We've had a very relaxing week and I will be sorry to see the kids go back to school next week. It has been nice to drop bed times, let the kids stay in PJs all day and not worry about homework for a week.

Sam has had a tough week with his heart. Though he has had heart failure for about one year now, he has done pretty well with his various medications. (Most of which are continuous intravenous drips). It is easy to forget sometimes that his heart is barely hanging in there and that these medication drips have never been used outside of the ICU setting as far as our doctors know. I know in my brain he has heart failure but how easy the heart forgets!

On Monday his sodium levels started dropping, which means that he is nor getting rid of as much fluid as he should be. This is something that happens with people that have congestive heart failure. At first he was very agitated, but then became very tired. His heart had a sound that is called a gallop – never a good sign when I hear it. His breathing was very rapid and he was working very hard to exhale. Every day I have drawn blood for testing and tinkered with his medications. Fortunately I can draw his blood though his permanent IV line (CVL) so he does not mind. This morning his blood work looked a bit better and his heart did not have a gallop anymore so his doctor and I decided not to change anything. I gave him a unit of blood, which was a little hard on his heart, but he needed it.

I am hoping that this is the beginning of him compensating better for his heart failure. All of this has reminded me once again of how close to the edge he is. Our anesthesiologist has said that it is like Sam is on a promontory, which gets more and more narrow as times goes by. It makes me feel frightened to hear that but I also appreciate the truth. I am thankful that our primary doctor (and many others) continues to stand with us on that promontory. I firmly believe Sam would not be here without his doctor's dedication to Sam, his trust in me, and the enormous amounts of time he has spent teaching me and trying to figure out what is right for Sam.

Sam is doing great wearing his hearing aids! I am very very proud of him. No complaining ever. The audiologist says that they must be helping him if he is not ripping them off. I agree. When I ask Sam if he hears better he says that he does. He also is sure that the hearing aids make him stronger! Funny. Today he had fun typing rhyming words on the computer (bat, cat, hat, etc.) and then we read them together. I think with the hearing aids he may very well be able to read soon now that he can hear the difference in some of the consonant sounds.

Zach is doing well. He is very happy with me because I began my "Yugio" lessons today. Zach loves this character called Yugio and there is a card game that one can do. No one in the family knows how to play though Sam thinks he does. At any rate, I told Zach that I would learn. I had no idea - it was probably the most challenging thing I did all week. I honestly am impressed that Zach knows how to play this game and remembers everything to do. I think if his teachers could figure out a way to link grammar and social studies to Yugio, he'd have no problem with memory.

Happy week. Thank you for stopping by to see how we are!

Thursday, January 8, 2004 9:44 PM

Tomorrow I have an early morning school meeting for Sam to add the label "hearing impaired" to his IEP (Individualized education plan). It seems unreal to me. He has a sensory-neural hearing loss, which means there is not a surgery that can fix it. He hears but cannot hear the differences in high frequency sounds like s, f t, z, etc. This is why he has been having trouble with phonics/reading and of course partly why his articulation is poor. His hearing loss has been progressive since we first noted it in October - I hope and pray it stabilizes. He wore the aids to school this week, as it was his first week back. He told me that he thinks the kids are all "jealous of me." I'm glad he is so proud of them. His audiologist has his permanent ones in now and we will get them next week. He picked purple and blue – typical Sam – he sure will make a statement with those colors.

I spoke too soon about his heart doing better. Monday he turned gray and developed an arrhythmia during physical therapy. He then had significant chest pain the rest of the day. When he says, "my heart hurts" it breaks my heart. It is all so scary to me. Talked with Peter at length on Wednesday about this. (Peter is his primary doc) and we both feel that it would be wrong to limit Sam's activities even if they are a strain on him. He loves PT. He loves gym and if he wants to do them – well then he should do them. I always said I would do anything for him as long as he has quality of life and I am not going to start wrapping him up in a bubble now just to keep him alive. He deserves better than that.

When I kissed him tonight he said "yuck -girl germs!" I told him "no they are mother germs and boys need mother germs for the rest of their lives!"

Zach is still sick – has been for a few weeks. Peter did not think he would get over it on his own so we have him on intravenous antibiotics. I hope it helps, as Zach just feels miserable.

Tired this week. Still trying to get over the flu and it is not happening as quickly as I would like. Sunday night (1-11) the boys will be admitted for their monthly immune globulin treatment. We'll be there until Friday. Sam will also get his infusion of pamidronate which helps stop the breakdown of his bones which he have been seeing.

Thursday, January 15, 2004 2:06 PM

Our hospital week is almost at an end! It has been a LONG week. Nothing acutely wrong. I just find that with each admission I am getting more and more antsy.

The boys have been having fun playing unlimited Game Boy and computer games, watching movies and odering room service (really - our hospital has room service for kids - they can call any time, for practically anything – very very nice!).

Yesterday was a reality in-your-face day for me. Our surgeon came by to check on Sam and once again gave his opinion that Sam really needs to have major GI surgery. Our primary doc and anesthesiologist all feel Sam would not survive. Our surgeon feels that while Sam would be in ICU for some time - that in the end he would be better off for having the surgery. I just don't seem to be able to get to a place of peace on this. I thought I was but the what ifs are so endless. There is no glass ball to know what is right or wrong and I just don't know. It would be wonderful if all the doctors agreed but I also respect that each of them has their own opinion and perspective and that they are willing to share that with me. They are every respectful of the other's perspective. I try to remind myself that they don't really know any better than I do...it's just a guess for them too. I know that in the end I need to make a decision; making no decision is a decision in and of itself. I just wish I felt some peace but I don't. I wonder if a mother ever stops second and third guessing every decision she makes.

The other piece of news from our surgeon is that Sam's newest central line is slipping out of place. He has not formed scar tissue around it and the cuff is showing. This is potentially catastrophic as a new line requires surgery (devastating for Sam). It was a miracle that they were able to place this line as he has clotted all of his major blood vessels that can support a line. We don't need to do anything today - but the chances of him keeping this line are very slim now. That was a pretty devastating piece of news for us.

Child Life just gave us free tickets for Disney on Ice Saturday night -really awesome seats. Hopefully everyone feels well enough to go! It's Toy Story and Sam LOVES Toy Story.

Sunday, January 18, 2004 9:33 AM

We went to Disney on Ice last night!!!!!! It was Toy Story 2. The hospital gave us free tickets and the seats were awesome. The Child Life Dept has been given a few free tickets and knowing how much Sammy loves Buzz Light-year they gave them to us. Now how perfect is that?????

Sam loved it! Zach loved it! Abby and Brittany liked it, but are too cool to admit it. Sam said his favorite part was seeing Buzz fight Evil Zurg!

Do you know what I loved? Seeing my little boy's face. I think I watched his face more than the show. He was in awe. The look on his face is engraved in my heart. I woke up many times last night and thought of his eyes shining and heard his little hands clapping, saw his head resting on Zachary when he got tired and his hand in mine throughout the show.

Do you know what else I loved? Going somewhere with my entire family. I feel sorry for people who take these things for granted and never know how special it is to just go somewhere - anywhere with the people that they love. We rarely can do anything together as a family because of Sam's needs (and Zach's). But this worked out and it was so worth all of the hassle with med schedule changes to get there.

Many times medical providers ask me (or more often ask Peter: our doc) why we do what we do for Sam. Is it really worth it when there is no hope they ask? Last night was why we do everything that we do. So that Sam can live and do all the things he wants to accomplish in his life for however long or short that may be. And hope? My hope is infinite.

Saturday, January 24, 2004 11:30 PM

This has been a busy week with work and activities and what not for the kids. Zach has had some pretty profound episodes of fatigue. He could barely function Monday and Tuesday but seems to be finally back to himself today. It is hard to see him like that. I guess the hardest is that he is at an age where it is starting to really frustrate him when he is so tired and unable to do as much as other children can do. I want to be sensitive to it – lord knows I am. It breaks my heart. But I also want to help him find a place of joy - not just acceptance but true love of himself.

My brother and sister in law – Elaine and Mike – came over tonight. They picked up pizza and Elaine made brownies. Yum! It was so nice to see them and so effortless on our part which is always a treat. Elaine said she has been reading a book with her high school students (can't recall the name) that talked about the acceptance of each other and oneself versus loving others and one. It was so ironic as I have been thinking about that a tremendous amount lately myself. Acceptance is not enough. I want my children to love themselves for the wonderful and unique individuals they are, to love their weaknesses which only give rise to their strengths. As Zach struggles with all these coming-of-age issues and the chronic illness issues on top of it - I just hope and pray I can mother him through it so that he comes out seeing himself the way I see him – as one very incredible person with so many strengths that I am inspired almost daily by him.

As I am by all my children. Brittany will be 17 on Friday the 30th. How in the world did that happen????? She and one of her best friends are planning a party for Saturday night – at our house of course.

Should be…. Hmmmm, LOUD! She had exams all week and did a banner job studying. She is also busy shopping for the perfect outfit for a school dance in a few weeks. Such is the life of a teenager. She brings a tremendous amount of life and humor to our home.

Abby joined Future Problem Solvers this week. The topic this year is artificial intelligence. I know little about this but Abby and I plan to read a bit tomorrow. I think it will be exciting to learn more about this. Thank you Peter, Dad, Mom, Kris and everyone else who helped us find some information to start our AI education.

Sam…good days and bad. Heart was struggling early this week but we caught the decompensation sooner this time than we did a few weeks ago, added some more diuretics (which help get the fluid out of his body since his heart cannot pump it very well anymore) and his heart is sounding better. He sounded out the spelling of BAT today - so proud of how hard he is trying to listen and learn. I am especially thankful this week for the children in his kindergarten class. They clap when he comes - still - after all these months. One little girl has been asking for him to be her partner in gym and saves seats for him each day. He played blocks with some boys on Tuesday and they had him laughing so hard I was afraid he was going to pass out. When he leaves they all hug him. Sweeter children I cannot imagine.

Tuesday, February 3, 2004 9:27 PM

We're in the hospital this week. Everything has been okay so far.

We just found out that Zach has developed another metabolic problem. I don't really understand it as of yet but it is a fatty oxidation defect. I do not know what this means exactly except that it is considered a worsening of his disease. Will find out more in the next few weeks I'm sure. In the meantime Zach is recovering from the illness he had last week with high fevers. He had a head MRI today as it seems he may have had a minor stroke or stroke-like event in the last few weeks. Not sure but something is amiss cognitively and everyone involved in his care is concerned with the subtle but pronounced changes. The MRI probably will not show anything because mitochondrial stokes are different than typical strokes. They are not caused by a problem with blood flow to the brain -rather they are caused by a dramatic decrease of energy to the brain. We felt it

11

wise to get an MRI anyway though just to make sure we are not missing something more treatable.

Sam is doing well! His heart sounds good this week. He has been in very good spirits, reading, playing with his best doctor and nurse and therapy friends and enjoying the attention that he always gets when he is here in the hospital. The highlight of his day was when our nephrologist paid a visit and juggled Sam's stuffed dogs for him.

Brittany's 17th birthday was last Friday! She and her close friend, Prissana, had a party for a mere 60 friends in our house. Fun! It really was not that bad at all to be honest. I get a kick out of the kids though it makes me feel old.

I'm reading a good book right now called *Undressing the Moon*. It is nice to have time to read a bit. I also read 6 back issues of *Newsweek* yesterday – wow I feel like I have re-entered the world!

I am thinking a lot about Samantha - our sweet little friend who died 2 years ago today. She was Sam's exact age friend - they grew up at Children's together and she died while waiting 18 long months for an organ transplant. If you don't have it noted on your license to be an organ donor please think about doing that today -in honor of our sweet Samantha Rose who we hold so dear in our hearts.

Saturday, February 7, 2004 10:20 AM

We are leaving the hospital, walking through the skywalk.

Zachary says to me, "Do you think there will ever be a cure for Sam and me?"

I want to say, "Of course there will be," but I know I can't.

My heart hurts when I say, "I don't know Zachary. But I hope there will be."

He is quiet.

I think he has gone on to a new subject when he says, "I am not going to be a scientist when I grow up. I am going to be a doctor."

"Yes I know that," I tell him. "You'll be a wonderful doctor too!"

"But scientists are the ones who find cures aren't they? Do doctors ever find cures?" he asks.

"Yes many do," I answer. "Many doctors are scientists."

12

He looks confused but then all of a sudden his eyes light up with understanding. "Like Doctor Havens! Right?" he exclaims. "He's a scientist isn't he? He finds little cures for me and Sam all the time!"

"Yes he does"

Zachary is quiet again. We are outside in the garage now – almost to the car. "I'm going to be like him. I'm going to be a surgeon AND a doctor like Dr. Havens. I'm going to find little cures for me and Sam just like Doctor Havens."

I wish that Peter could have heard that.

"Zachary – I don't have any doubts about that!" I tell him.

He seems at peace with the subject now -as if his fate has been decided.

We're in the car driving home. I look back and he is holding Sam's hand and Sam is asleep leaning over his booster seat so that his head rests on Zach.

"I'm going to find a cure for us, Sam" I hear him say.

I tell him that I love him more than he can ever understand.

I know he is scared.

I know he wonders what the future holds.

I am scared - I try not to think too far ahead.

I try so hard to have hope and courage and I think I have some.

But it is Zachary's hope and courage that I envy.

Saturday, February 14, 2004 9:49 AM

Happy Valentine's Day!

Sam has been very sick this week. On Tuesday he began to have fevers up to 104. The fevers persisted all week although they are finally down this morning. This was very stressful on his heart and on him in general. By Thursday, tests showed that the reason he was so sick was an infection in his blood. Blood is supposed to be sterile but tests showed that he has both yeast and bacteria in his blood.

Mitochondrial disease is a disease of energy production – the person cannot make enough energy to keep their body functioning normally. Illness and especially fevers increase the body's demand for energy. Yet a person with mitochondrial disease cannot respond to the increased need for energy. This is how it has been for Sam and his body has been struggling intensely to deal with the illness.

13

I have been doing everything I can to try to help his body do what it cannot do: infusions of blood products, extra fluids, bicarbonate, antibiotics and antifungals are helping. Even though he has a bleeding problem he also has a problem with clotting too much – this makes him so hard to treat sometimes. This problem with too much bleeding and too much clotting has been much worse this week. He has needed extra medicine to break up some of the clots. Bacteria and yeast like to "hide" in clots so we have to try to get rid of the clots aggressively.

Yesterday Sam missed his kindergarten Valentines Day party. It was heart breaking for me because he was just devastated. He cried for so long and begged me to call the teacher and ask her to change the party to Saturday. He could not understand why that could not happen. The kids and I promised him that we would have a family Valentines Day party today and that made him smile. All morning he keeps asking me when the party will start.

I think he'll be just fine but it has been a very scary week. My hope now is that the medications we are using for the yeast will work. If they do not clear his blood we will have to use amphotericin, which for Sam would be devastating. The last time we had to use it, he went into acute kidney failure. I don't think his heart can handle that.

Tuesday we went to our neurologist. He has been their doctor since they were babies. He does feel Zachary had a stroke and perhaps has been having little stroke like episodes all fall. He had some ideas - mainly medication changes and some testing. We'll try. Zachary had a good week and made it to school all three days and even back Friday afternoon for his Valentine Party.

Things and People I am especially thankful for this week:
Brittany – On Thursday night I realized that I was responsible for the Girl Scout snack on Friday for Abby's troop of 25 kids. Without my asking her, she went to the store, bought snacks, brought them to the girls on Friday and picked up Zachary from the school party. Brittany, I love you.

The boy's doctor – as always – who has spent inordinate amounts of time talking me through this illness of Sam's so that I can keep him at home. Even while away at a conference he was available to me – I think I paged him 6 times on Thursday and even though he had been up the entire night before he patiently guided me on what to do.

14

It was 100 day in Kindergarten on Tuesday! I was unsure whether to take Sam to school Tuesday morning because his heart was not doing well. Our doctor encouraged me to take him and I was thankful beyond thankful that we went. When we arrived we found out it was 100 Day! (The kids have been in school 100 days!). What a sense of joy and celebration in that classroom – it felt like it was Christmas. Sam stayed 2 hours and loved all of the 100-day activities. It reminded me that each day has the potential to be a holiday – find joy however you can, whatever you can, whenever you can.

Janet -my very dear friend! Thank you for listening to me and caring, praying, hoping, laughing and advising. You are a gift to me.

Thank you to everyone who cares so much for us. We're lucky to have you all in our lives!

Thursday, February 19, 2004 9:04 PM

Sam's blood cultures are all coming back negative now! Looks like he has snuck by this time and will not need to have the medication that has not served his kidneys well in the past (amphotericin).

All in all, he is doing rather well for having been so sick. His biggest issue now is pretty significant sleepiness. He was a little better Monday and Tuesday but by Tuesday afternoon started getting profoundly tired. Today I think he was asleep virtually all day except for a few hours in the morning.

I feel worried about this but I know from experience that this is his body's way of recovering. Still my heart worries.

The kindergartners have a letter of the week each week. On H week they were asked to answer this question:

What makes you happy?

Their responses were things like:

When my mom cuddles with me,

When my Daddy tickles me

When my mom reads to me (that was Sam's)

When I see my friends

Coming to school and seeing the teachers

Coming to school and learning

When Sam comes to school (Really, that was what one little boy said!)

Not one of the 25 responses was about material things. Not one said being the best reader or the best at anything for that matter. Not one response was about money. Just family, friends and learning...that was what all 25 children said made them happy. When do we lose that understanding and begin to think that things make us happier than people?

Here I thought that I would set aside my time to go to school with Sam so that he could have the opportunity to learn and make friends. The surprise has been how much I am inspired by these children.

Saturday, February 28, 2004 11:27 PM

Well, Sunday is admission day for Zachary and Sam. This is every fourth week admission for IVIG (intravenous immune globulin). Admit Sunday and hopefully home on Friday – or as Dennis – our hospital pharmacist says: "five and out!"

We had a pretty uneventful week – how nice is that for a change?

Last Friday Bethesda Elementary, where Zach, Abby and Sam go to school had their annual Sock Hop. Woo-Hoo! Did we have fun? Sam did not last terribly long but the sight of him dancing with a bunch of kindergarten girls was a sight worth seeing! Zach and Abby had a fun time too. The theme was Pirates of the Caribbean. Before we left Zachary said, "Anyone who is anyone is gonna be there!" Glad I was there!

The kids only had 3 days of school this week – Winter Holiday. A lot of parents hate that but I have to say it was so nice to slow down a little. School days and schedules keep us all so busy. On Friday I took the girls shopping at the mall. The boys said "no thanks!" and stayed home. The girls got clothes, Abby and I got a few more George Winston CDs (he's coming to Milwaukee in May!) and we had dinner at the Olive Garden.

Today Abby, Sam and I had time to go to the library and gets lots of books and movies for the hospital. We also got a few books on tape, which we have never done before. I was so glad we did because Zachary has been listening to one all day – he loves it. Reading is such a strain on his eye muscles, and then he gets tired and loses attention.

He absolutely loves the book on tape so maybe this will be a nice new thing for him to do.

Sam is still on a few extra medications for his yeast blood infection. I have been able to stretch him back out to every other day plasma instead of every day and that has been going okay. I am concerned that he is still running fevers. They are low grade but it is worrisome. The blood cultures we did on Thursday still have not grown anything but Peter wants me to draw some more when we get to the hospital Sunday night.

Sunday, March 7, 2004 9:00 AM

Home from the hospital! So wonderful to have a cup of coffee without first having a shower, getting dressed, putting on make up and dealing with 5 people in my room. A woman is not made to function without having one cup of coffee- alone and in silence - first. I am trying to get over John Edwards losing out to Kerry but it is tough. I really like Edwards!

My Dad (lives in Florida) visited in the early part of the week. Thanks Dad! I missed the Starbucks cappuccino and the discussions about our "love" (gag) for George Bush Jr. after he left.

Zach had a perfect admission! He played a lot of chess with Gramps as well as Dr. S. He beat Gramps most of the time but Dr. S was a harder opponent. Anne, the art therapist came 3 days, which is always the most wonderful treat for Zachary. He loves spending time with Anne and we love her. He actually looks forward to the admissions so he can create things with Anne. He did need a unit of blood and got a rash with the transfusion (a first) but was able to get the whole unit in. Hoping it will give him a bit more energy! Home in time to start a science class on Saturday through our Park and Rec. Abby is taking it with him. He is also busy researching Jackie Robinson for a reading project. I am so incredibly proud of how industrious he has been, waking up early to do the research without anyone telling him to - and doing most of it independently.

Sam did not have a perfect admission. He persisted with his fevers and his blood tests showed that he has another bacteria strain in his blood. He's on some strong IV antibiotics for that and I hope and pray that this time it will sterilize his blood. I am pretty worried that his

17

central line is the source of these infections. Peter (our MD) reminds me to have hope – we have a good chance of clearing this up.

Sam's heart continues to struggle. He is on more medications and they are helping but it worries me so, how each month his heart seems less and less able to deal with anything. Just the low-grade fevers seem to have thrown his heart into a tailspin. As Peter says, fevers to Sam are like running marathons back to back for us. The stress is incredible for him and his heart, try as it does to compensate, needs more and more help to do so.

While sick, he began to gag and retch. He cannot vomit due to a surgery he had when he was younger. Even though we aggressively gave him medication to stop the gagging and retching, he still has a small GI bleed. Sam is just so fragile and bleeds so easily. Thus, he had quite a few transfusions of blood in the last 6 days and needs a lot more Factor 7a. The bleeding persists but it is not getting worse. Thankful for that!

The rehab and fitness doctor consulted as something is not right with Sam's left leg. In the last few months he has taken to standing/walking on the outside of the foot. Though we cannot know for sure, the docs think he likely had a stroke (common with this disease) because his left arm is weaker too. They will observe him in PT next week and then make some sort of a brace/splint. Our concern is that he is quite unstable the way he walks on the foot now and certainly cannot afford to fall and either bleed or break something.

College looking time for Brittany! She is making a list of where she wants to go and then we will plan out the visits. I won't be able to go on the overnights given Sam and Zach's needs but hopefully Lou will do that. She likes UW Madison, Marquette, U of NC, UW LaCrosse, Northwestern, Penn State, U of Minn and Washington (in St. Louis). I would like her to look at some smaller private colleges as well to see if she might like that better so she is going to research that. I told her we will look at them then worry about the money (yikes!)......this is a whole new chapter in our lives! She wrote a wonderful essay this week as part of her application to National Honor Society. She is an awesome girl!

Abby is busy with piano, soccer, Future Problem Solvers, Art Club, science class, Battle of the Books, Student Council, Girl

Scouts....how did she get this busy? But she loves every minute of life so it obviously suits her.

Thursday, March 11, 2004 10:12 PM

I can't believe it is only Thursday – this week has been so long. It should be Friday already. The wind is howling outside – I need spring.

Zach is sick. The only problem is I don't have any clue what exactly I can do for him. I just hate this disease. It is sucking the energy and spark out of Zachary - little by little - and I am really angry about it this week.

He is fine when he is in the hospital or at home and just playing. But as soon as he goes to school or therapy or walks a little too much he becomes exhausted. His head hurts, he's dizzy, he cannot think or go to school or therapy, etc. In the last few months he has even taken to running fevers when he is tired, and though we always test his blood to make sure he does not have bacteria in it, (as the cause of the fevers)...he never does. It's just the stress that comes from exhaustion, from not having enough energy to do much more than stay home anymore.

On Tuesday he woke up exhausted. It was a school day (he only goes for three ½ days a week). I told him it would be fine if he wanted to stay home. He said he was really tired but he also really wanted to try to go to school. He stayed until 12:50 – his usual time to be picked up. But he has been feeling awful ever since he came home. Fevers and now high blood pressure. The kicker was that today it was high enough that we actually had to give him meds to bring it down. This is exactly how the blood pressure problems started with Sam a few years ago. There is nothing comforting in walking these same steps again.

He is frustrated and wants to go to school tomorrow. I so hope he can do it.

I know in my head that there are not any better treatments out there, no more answers to be found...but it is just inconceivable to my heart that it has to be this way.

I don't feel sorry for myself. I don't even feel sorry for Zachary because there is absolutely nothing to pity about him – he is such an amazing person. But it hurts – it hurts a lot to watch this happen to him. I know I can't stay in this place I am at right now – dwelling on this will not help me or Zach…but I guess I just need to say I'm mad. I hate how this disease slowly sucks the physical life out of my children. At the same time I do know – I really do – that it is not sucking their spirit, not their heart, not their joy…and I guess in the end that is what really matters and what I have to continue to focus on.

Tomorrow is another day! (And it is Friday!)

Saturday, March 13, 2004 9:19 AM

Zachary did go to school Friday – so many of you have asked and I just wanted to make sure you knew he was able to go! Thank you so much for asking and caring. The sun is shining in Wisconsin this morning although still cold. The wind has died down.

Zachary's BP is still too high and he continues to require medication for this. On Monday I will talk to his doctor about finding a medication that might last a little longer as right now he requires medication just about every hour. For now I do not want to jump to that in the hope that his BP will stabilize itself.

Wednesday, March 17, 2004 9:23 PM

Sammy went on his first class trip to the Educational Environmental Center, which is part of our school district. He was ever so excited to take his very first school bus trip. His sweet little friend Josie asked him to sit with her and so he did. God could not have imagined a more wonderful little friend for him than she is. All of the kids are sweet but she slows down and adjusts her play to include him, constantly moves in order to sit by him and makes him just laugh. What she does for Sam reminds me so much of how Abby has always been with Zachary.

Once at the Center Sam was brave enough to touch a live snake and live turtles and even a dirty old Salamander. (Mom was NOT brave at all). He went into a very dark cave with his friends and looked for the bats that the taxidermist had prepared in there. He played several games, and touched bones, feathers and furs. He really loved it all and stayed awake through the entire trip back to the school. Once home he was exhausted but so proud that he had gone on a class trip just like the other kids.

He is identifying a few words finally when we read: *No, I, A, Sam, yes* and *Is*. This literally happened overnight! Yeah for Sammy!

Zachary has found a wonderful pen pal this week – also named Zachary and also 11 years old. Pretty cool for the boys. He seems to be feeling fairly well this week. Tomorrow he has a kidney ultrasound as he still has this high blood pressure and some bleeding. He has a clotting disorder and so the thing we need to rule out is whether the bleeding and high blood pressure are a result of a clot in the blood vessels that connect to his kidneys. I certainly hope not. A few labs are a wee bit off, suggesting he may be having some heart dysfunction. In any event we did start him on a medication for the blood pressure that lasts a bit longer than the one we had been using. The added benefit is that the medication not only improves blood pressure but heart function too.

My sister Maribeth is here visiting and the kids are enjoying all of the extra attention and love that comes when a special guest is in the house. I am so lucky to have such a wonderful family.

Happy Saint Patrick's Day!

Friday, March 19, 2004 8:20 PM

I have not seen the dictated report yet for Zachary's kidney ultrasound but I do know that Zach does not have any clots in the renal blood vessels. This is very good news. It does not take away the bleeding in the urine or the high blood pressure but I am relieved that we are not dealing with a clot that could damage his kidneys. I am sure he has some degree of kidney disease but it is what they call "medical renal disease" which means that the function is not perfect but there are no clots or narrowing or anything else anatomically wrong. Zach had a fine old time with the ultrasound, as he was able to lie on the table and still play Game Boy Advance! What could be better than that?

I talked with his doctor and unfortunately, Zachary's labs in the last week together with his symptoms of profound fatigue, inability to walk without shortness of breath, and increased BP all add up to heart failure. Today he went to empty the dishwasher for me and got so winded that he ended up not going to school. He tried several times but was dizzy and fatigued each time he tried to get himself ready. He laid down most of the day. Right now he is in his glory because Daddy rented him a Game Cube game.

He is on enaliprilat now to vasodilate (make his blood vessels bigger). This helps in this way: imagine pumping fluid through a tube that is narrow versus pumping fluid through a tube that is wider….it is of course easier to pump the fluid (in this case blood) through the wider tubes (blood vessels) and that adds up to less work for the pump (heart). The enaliprilat also should help keep his blood pressure down. He is already well past the pediatric dose....next we'll add a drug that has been good for Sam called labetalol (a beta blocker).

I'm sad but somewhat expected this - his sodium levels have been dropping for a week now and that with the difficulty with any activity tells a story I am familiar with by now. I so hope the right drugs help - I'm trying to focus on that as my positive...that maybe his terrible fatigue will improve if we can help his heart and that we are recognizing it before we did with Sam (not until he was in the ICU really). We also realize that we have to be very careful with fluids (something that he could handle fine in the past). So in many ways we are much smarter and catching it much earlier and I just hope with every beat of my heart that he will not end up with the significant heart failure that Sammy has.

Sam was MAD that he could not go to school today – but there is no way for me to be in two places at once. I had to be at home with Zach, which left no one to take Sam to school. He did get over it and has actually been as sweet as can be all day. Though I felt bad for Sam, part of me loves seeing and hearing how much he loves school. Last fall one of the doctors I know who works with dying children (palliative care) told me that he thinks that Sam's love for school may very well be what keeps him alive. There's no way to know of course but I do think of it often and feel so thankful for our school and the teachers and kids…..giving him something to look forward to and take pride in as his very own thing.

Saturday, March 27, 2004 9:42 PM

Spring is trying to come to Wisconsin. We even had one day that was 65!

I have not felt great this week and now have some virus or who knows what. I feel like I have been run over by a truck and probably look that way too. I am a bit better today than yesterday though I am losing my voice. This, no doubt, probably makes my kids happy.

Zachary has actually felt really well this week – he made it to school all three days and on Friday he even stayed until 2 PM for an assembly on science. The odd thing is that his heart failure did not improve as we hoped it would with the decrease of fluids and increase in medication. In fact he has developed an intermittent gallop (a heart sound that sounds literally like a horse galloping - not a good thing. Still, I cannot get over how much less tired he is now that he is on these medications. Perhaps a coincidence, for as I said, his heart does not necessarily seem better by objective measures, but either way it is so nice to see him have energy. He spent most of the week working hours each day on his research project: Jackie Robinson. I have never seen him so motivated. I think having his own laptop and not depending on adults to dictate his work to makes a huge difference. I am very proud of him. He is planning to have a friend over tomorrow – something he rarely does – so I hope he continues to feel well for that.

I did call Make A Wish for Zach this week. It is a hard call to make even though I know they will add joy upon joy to his life. Hard because it brings reality right to the forefront -this is a child that may not see his 18th birthday (that is the criteria that the doctor has to sign off on for Make A Wish). But my motivation remains Sam. I put off calling for him and when I finally did we had to cancel several times because he was so ill. Finally his wish came true (to go to Disney World and meet Donald Duck). 6 months later he started bleeding all the time and our traveling days were over. I am so thankful for the memories we have of that wonderful trip with and for Sam. I can never say enough about all the good things that organization does for children like mine.

Zach's wish is for his own arcade/pool hall/TV viewing area in our basement. I'm not sure there will be room left for him if he gets all that he wishes for….but I'm sure the wish granters will work with him and he'll end up with a wonderful place to enjoy his own company as well as that of friends and family. His inspiration for "game room" came from another Wisconsin wish child, Michael K. Michael passed away from cancer but not before he also wished for a game room and then went on to raise thousands of dollars for Make A Wish. When Zach heard about Mikey, his eyes literally lit up and he said "that's exactly what I want – a game room."

Prior to reading about Michael, Z was struggling with the whole Make A Wish thing because he wanted to go to Hawaii but we cannot travel with Sam. The day he read about Michael it was so perfect – Zach just got so excited and started planning out his game room…and really there would not be a more perfect wish than that for Zach. He loves electronics and he is so tired all the time so that a piece of heaven right in his own home that he can enjoy for as long as he is able is going to be wonderful for him. I know Michael's mom slightly - she works at CHW with me so I told her about it. I wanted her to know that even now her son is touching the lives of others. He certainly touched my Zach's life and Abby's too. Abby is on student council at her elementary school and is proposing that they raise money as a school for Make A Wish. She was so impressed with how we were treated for Sam's wish and also with Michael and his efforts to raise money, despite having such a horrible illness. I thank Michael up in heaven for the inspiration he is to my children.

This is getting long so I'll just say a few more things. Sam is riding the train tracks – which Peter always says is what we want for him – nice and even, steady, no surprises. He had a good week at school but is mad because the gym unit has been dance and he "hates dancing."

Please keep Brittany in your thoughts. She is playing soccer and struggling so much with fatigue and leg cramps. She feels that she is hurting her team (she is not) and cannot understand why there is anything anyone can do to make her better. She knows she has excellent technique and that the fatigue of the disease holds her back and I can only imagine, never fully know, how frustrating and heart breaking that must be to someone who loves soccer and is as good as she is. I admire her so much and hope she will find the strength to deal with this - it is so hard.

Saturday, April 3, 2004 10:26 PM

Home!

Tonight we spring forward even while it is windy and cold outside. This is the part of Wisconsin I do not like – the lack of spring! Sammy keeps asking when we can plant flowers again. We had so much fun doing that last year.

Zachary has been in the most wonderful, happy mood for over a week now. It is pure joy to see him so engrossed in life. He spent hours making these very intricate mosaic pictures at the hospital, humming and whistling while he worked, laughing at his TV shows, joking around with the staff – just completely engaged in life again! I can only attribute it to the medicine that he is on for his heart and blood pressure. I wonder how long did he need it…..all those months this fall and winter of barely getting through the day. This is a joy to savor seeing him LIVE again.

Sam did not have such a good week. He has been so irritable and has had a fever, headache, increasing abdominal pain for days now. Today his labs suggest the beginning of pancreatitis – something that used to make him critically ill month after month, though he has not dealt with it in almost two years now. Oh how I hope he does not go down that path again. His bleeding remains much worse than usual. "Too many red cells to count" in his urine, and blood constantly oozing from his GI tract. He is asleep now with the help of narcotics and sedatives and on oxygen. But oh his spirit…he was mad even through the haze of narcotics that I did not have all the ingredients to make him a pizza crust to eat at 8 PM tonight (which is when we arrived home from the hospital).

I'm looking forward to the next few weeks. So many Easter seasons have been spent in the hospital…it has only been the last two that we have been home. Its silly but I love dying Easter eggs and all the excitement that goes along with a holiday. The kids will be off from school and though we cannot take any overnight trips with Sam's blood product dependence issue….I am hoping for time to slow down a bit during their vacation, which always helps me gain perspective.

Perspective…I desperately need to climb "the hill," to view my life from a different vantage point. The ocean has always been my "hill," my solace, even since I was little. I have always been convinced that a week of bare footed walks on the beach – the part where the waves meet the sand – cures any illness of the soul, renews a tired mind, restores hope, grants perspective. I almost cried this week when someone told me he had been surfing at the ocean recently. I felt so envious knowing how unlikely it is that all four of my children and I will ever play on the beach together, unlikely that I will ever rise while they are still sleeping and walk for hours. The envy is my warning that somehow I have to find a new ocean….one in Southeastern Wisconsin. My hope tells me there is one.

Thursday, April 8, 2004 10:18 PM CDT

Hyper, hyper kids. They woke up full of it. Their poor teachers on this last day before Spring Break.

Everyone has given me their list of what they NEED during Spring Break. I love how kids use the word need.

Sam NEEDS to go to McDonalds for French fries. He NEEDS to color the eggs for the bunny.

Zach NEEDS to rent a Game Ccube game and he and I NEED to plan a late April Fool's Day at home (as he was in the hospital on the true fool's day). I think he just wants to have a license to drive his sisters nuts.

Abby NEEDS to go to the Egyptian exhibit at the Museum, she NEEDS to shop at the outlet mall and she SHOULD have lunch at the Rain Forrest Café (after all everyone in the entire 5th grade has done that).

Brittany NEEDS to shop at the same outlet mall - with me (or anyone who has money I suppose). She NEEDS clothes because of course she does not have any – poor kid.

Lots to do to get ready for the Easter Bunny!

Tuesday, April 13, 2004 10:26 PM

Love spring break! Love the laziness of mornings at home when the kids do not have to be at school or therapy or practice….we had that this morning.

The Easter bunny was busy and when we woke up Sunday he had left many goodies. The girls and I maxed out on chocolate and my personal favorite – PEEPS! I feel the need to eat salad the rest of the week. The Bunny brought Sammy a newborn dog named "fudge" who with the help of batteries, opens his eyes, whines, barks and moves his baby puppy head when talked to or petted. Too cute!

Easter dinner with Mike and Elaine. So nice to watch my brother play chess with Zach, do puzzles with Sammy, even talk politics with Brittany. (How can that girl like George Bush???). Mike and Elaine brought Abby her birthday present EARLY - on May 4 they are taking Abby and me to the George Winston concert. So cool. Abby can hardly wait.

Museum today with Abby. Loved the time with her. We have to get a membership as even with an afternoon there we only got through the Egyptian and Rain Forrest exhibit. So much to see and learn.

I recently found a picture of Sekhmet, Mother Goddess of Love, Fire, Shadow, the End and th Beginning. I LOVE this lady! She has a lion head and is dancing on crocodiles, while holding the symbol for everlasting life in both hands. I decided she must actually be the symbol for all mothers.

What mother does not become a lion when need be for her child?

What mother does not dance with ease and grace on the crocodiles which represent the conflicts in life?

And especially meaningful to me, this goddess holds the symbols for everlasting life. Reminds me of how my children will live forever, whether here on earth or not.

Thursday Brittany and I are off to Madison to take a 2 hour walking tour of UW campus and then she has an interview. She was asked to the prom last night! (Shhhhh).

Zachary's blood pressure remains hard to control which in turn affects his heart. Thank God for our doctor who is being quite proactive and aggressive in treating this so that we can try to prevent some of the issues we have now with Sam. He is so careful with their care and without him they would not be here.

Sam is doing fairly well. I thought he was getting sick Sunday and Monday he looked really bad. Tremoring when he walked or moved, chest pain, fatigue and then low grade fevers at night. Today he seemed ok. One day at a time.

Sunday, April 18, 2004 9:51 PM

Brittany and I had a nice time walking around UW-Madison campus. She liked it a lot – it certainly is impressive as to size and resources. In many ways it reminded me of Rutgers - of my own experiences there. She still has a lot of looking to do but I was thankful to spend part of a beautiful day in such a pretty and invigorating place with her.

Friday to the library with the boys – fun but once again I felt overwhelmed with how tired Sammy gets from the littlest of excursions. He was barely able to stand after walking from the car to the library and was having trouble breathing after that. I really need to get a wheelchair for him.

Thurs and Friday Abby got to go to Chicago with her friend Kaitlyn overnight. They took the train and went shopping on Michigan Avenue – the American Girl store was the highlight I think. I'm thankful for all of Kaitlyn's sweetness as well as that of her family. It is so nice for Abby to get to go somewhere and impossible at this time for me to do Chicago with her. Earlier this week, she bought Abby a candle that smells like the ocean. She told Abby that she wanted her to have it since she knew Abby could not go to the beach this summer! I was so touched by that.

Outlet shopping with the girls Saturday. I'm tired but had fun with them.

I'm scared tonight. Sam woke up in a pool of blood from his nap - all from his G tube (a tube that goes into his stomach). It was pretty bad. Cleaned him up, gave him a bolus of novo seven (factor 7a) which helps him to clot - he cannot clot on his own anymore. He also got other blood products: plasma, cryo and platelets and he seemed ok.

7 pm we're watching the movie "snow dogs" and he starts choking and when I turned to look at him he had blood coming out of his mouth. I cleaned him up as best as I could, gave him a drink of water but even with a flash light in his mouth – I can not tell at all where the blood is coming from. He continued to choke so I gave him another bolus of factor 7a.

Meanwhile blood is hanging on the IV pole as he is getting a blood transfusion – I watch the blood go in and think he is bleeding it all right back out. Mouth bleeds terrify me – especially when, like this one, I cannot even see where the bleeding is coming from even if I could get in there and apply pressure – it would be a blind guess where to apply it – if even in his mouth. It could be his throat for all I know.

I called Peter (Dr.) and he says if it is not stopping to give a 3rd bolus (extra dose) of 7a, turn up his continuous drip of the 7a and I can give one more bolus right before I go to bed at midnight.

Bleeding makes me feel so out of control. ...There is rarely a warning. He is not sick. He did not fall. I laid him down for a nap and he wakes up like this. I hate the feeling of not understanding why he bleeds, how to make it better.

Tuesday, April 20, 2004 6:49 AM

Sam is doing so much better. Thank you everyone for your kind thoughts and messages. There is comfort for me in knowing that others hold his life dear. He is so precious to me and I don't think I will ever get used to the terrible bleeding episodes. The day-to-day bleeding I can deal with but it is frightening when it gets out of control. Enough, though, of that because thank God that once again we have stopped it.

Today is Zachary's birthday!!!!!!!!! He is 12 years old today. Something I can hardly believe. He hates when I tell him how I recall so many moments of his infancy – but I do and I treasure each one. Birthdays are so precious - a celebration of a special person and all they are and all they will be!

Thursday, April 22, 2004 10:08 PM

Tired today and I'm cold. Zachary asked me if there would ever be a day I did not say I was cold. Nope!

Zachary had a wonderful birthday. Thank you so much to everyone for your prayers, happy birthdays, cards, gifts....you are all so wonderful and you made the day even more special for him. Zachary had made himself a little schedule for his big day. It went something like this:

29

6 am: wake up.

7 am: Mama makes me sugar cookies for breakfast

8 am : open 1 present

10 am: eat ice-cream treats with my class

1:30 pm open presents

2 PM ice cream sundae (he listed each topping),

etc etc etc

Very touched that our Dr. H called Zach for the purpose of singing Happy Birthday to You! Zach laughed and laughed. I love when Zachary laughs.

I spent the day thinking about Zachary. My pregnancy, his infancy and finding out he was ill, watching his personality grow and define itself despite the challenges he faced. I thought of his little baby smile, how he used to say "mama hold you" when he wanted me to hold him. His little hands working at puzzles, always so intent on whatever he was doing. Pictured the way Brittany could always calm him when he was little, how his smile and laughter grew by leaps and bounds when Abby was born, his pride and careful ways and love towards his "best brother" Sammy. I remembered some of the very painful things he endured as a baby and little boy as we searched for answers for his elusive disease and marvel still at the person he has become. I am so blessed that he is part of my life.

Hospital next week. Hoping for some help for Sammy. He has been having some extreme mood swings that are beyond the realm of normal. They come on suddenly and he becomes very combative and "manic." Afterwards he cries and wonders why he was "like that." This follows the left leg problems that are progressing faster than I can stomach. His leg is weaker and weaker and because of that he is becoming very tight. More concerning is that last week his right leg became much weaker. The splints he was just casted for last month will not be supportive enough now - that is how fast it has progressed. His PT is very worried about it. He is really very unstable on his feet which poses a huge risk given his bleeding disorder. Peter talked to our neurologist today and the plan is a head MRI on Monday and then the neuro will come by to help us out.

Saturday, May 1, 2004 7:53 AM

We are home from the hospital – it was a fairly busy hospitalization. We had quite a few consults with some of our specialists and I guess the general consensus is Zach and Sam remain difficult to figure out.

Zach – his primary nurse came the day he was admitted to bring him birthday gifts. We have some really wonderful nurses at Children's – I am always humbled by how much they want to do for us. He spent most of the admission playing this game called "The age of Empires – the age of kings." He is very engrossed at the moment in this game. He did manage to get a few chess games in though with Dr. S. We all had a fun time teasing Zach that he is almost a teenager. Zach is sure he is going to stop the clock and not become an adolescent. He is determined his brain will not get "infected" - how he describes the mix of adolescence and Brittany.

Peter and I talked with L, our nephrologist and we all agreed to start Zach on atenalol, which is a beta-blocker. It should help his blood pressure and also should even out his autonomic nervous system so that his heart stays "happier." The cardiology people finally got back to us and Peter talked some more with them and finally we have a plan for this exercise test for Zachary. We'll get that done in the next few weeks.

Sam – not sure I am ready to write much about him. The neurologist was pretty worried about the changes since February. A few more neurological issues began in the hospital. Briefly he thinks that Sam has a progressive peripheral neuropathy (nerves are being affected now) - we all have to do some more talking but they think De-Toni Fanconi syndrome is what is going on here. Dementia is part of it. He has not been diagnosed for sure. Treatment is symptomatic and I think they are doing all they can for Sam and we will continue to as long as he has meaning and quality of life. We started Sam on a new anti-seizure med – lamictal.

When the neurologist came Sammy was bright and interactive. Sam told him jokes, cooperated with everything that Dr. I asked of him. Sam was playing computer games with Zach at the time and just full of energy and intelligence. The next day we had to sedate him out of a manic episode. Dr. I said that seeing Sam so full of life is what

31

makes this so heart breaking. If Sam's life were miserable decisions would be easier and very different. The neuro said we'll just keep trying.

Reading *The Bridge of San Luis Rey* by Thornton Wilder:
"How often as she turned the pages with her hands she would ask herself, whether the constant pain at her heart had an organic seat. She wondered whether a subtle doctor cutting through to that battered throne, could at last discover a sign and lifting his face to the amphitheater cry out to his students: "This woman has suffered, and her suffering has left its mark upon the structure of her heart."

I don't like to dwell on sorrow but I do like that passage. I want there to be a mark on my heart….not just a mark of the sorrow I have felt but a mark of the love and the thankfulness, the hope and the fear and the relief. Shouldn't my heart be stretched out from loving these children more than I thought anyone could love? Shouldn't there be new cracks and old healed-over fractures for all the times I cried? The healed fractures as a tangible sign of hope – there is morning, there are rainbows. Shouldn't my heart have ceased to beat in a normal rhythm by now but rather beat to the tune of the road we have walked?

Wednesday, May 5, 2004 10:53 PM CDT

Abby and I went to the George Winston concert last night. It was her birthday present from Uncle Mike and Aunt Elaine so we had the pleasure of sharing the night with them as well. Wow can that man play the piano! His hands were a flash at times they were moving so fast. I am inspired to say the least! Sure makes me wish I had the time to play more though I doubt I'd ever be that good. Abby loved it! We really had such a good time.

Zach has a fever and a terrific headache poor kiddo! Home from school and simply tried to keep him comfortable all day with medication and love. He did not want me to go to work even though we had a nurse in the house ….I had a lot to do but it is kind of nice to be so wanted and appreciated by him. So I was happy to stay home with him although I wish he could feel better. I drew blood cultures to see if he has a blood infection. Hopefully not but that is always the fear when someone has a central line. A central line is basically a permanent IV that goes into the vein leading to the heart. While the line gives him life, it is also a direct route for infection to travel to his blood and heart. Thus, any fever has to be taken seriously. He is on IV antibiotics around the clock until we know that his blood is not infected – probably about 2 days.

Sammy is going to be 7 on Sunday -Mother's Day. He generously told me that he would share the day with me after I assured him he would get more presents and cards than I would get. I cannot believe he is going to be 7! Such a miracle and a gift – There is not one day I take for granted with him. He has been so happy. For one thing he is thrilled that Grandma came back from Florida. Today was the one day she could not come see him but he stood at the window, nonetheless waiting for her for 30 minutes. He sure does love Grandma. He went to school Tues and Wed and lasted about 2 ½ hrs each day. I look at him sometimes in school and he just has this look on his face like "I am so thrilled to be here!" It makes me feel like everything we are doing is worth it for this. He has been so good with his homebound teacher as well. He told her yesterday that "two little letters are trying to trick me but I'm not going to let them do it anymore!" (he was referring to *b* and *d* and his confusion with them).

Friday I have to talk to a group of pediatricians, nurses and parents at a Wisconsin Medical Home Learning Collaborative. I had asked Abby if she wanted to drive up to the Dells with me where I am presenting. I thought it would be nice to have the ride together and go out to lunch. The more we talked about what I would be presenting, the more interested she became and guess what? She is going to talk a little bit with me from her sibling perspective and the importance to her as a family member that her brothers are receiving coordinated, comprehensive care. I am shocked she wants to do this but I guess the apple does not fall far from the tree. I really like speaking myself. And whom do you think I got that from …..Dad? Gramps? Mike?

Thank you everyone who has written such kind words in the guest book. Thank you as well to those who email or simply take time to think of us. It is heartening to know how many people love my children in this world and it surely makes the world feel like a smaller, safer place. Thank you

Saturday, May 8, 2004 10:59 PM

May 9! Happy Birthday Samuel Patrick!

Your birthday is the most wonderful Mother's Day present to me!

I brought Sammy home from the hospital on Mother's Day 1997 in an outfit that the kids had picked out for him before he was born.

His first birthday - he was in the hospital for one month preceding his 1st birthday. He woke up on May 9 and they discharged him. The next day was Mother's day - he was home – my wonderful mother's day child.

His second birthday - we celebrated in the hospital because Zachary was inpatient. He could not talk yet but he could sign, *Mama, I love you*, and so many other words and phrases. He had just learned how to walk. I'll never forget his pride as he showed me how he could walk when he came to visit me in the hospital one day during Zach's long admission.

On his third birthday he was very ill. I am not sure he even woke up on his birthday. We celebrated a few days later. Blue's Clues was the theme. It was a wonderful day of celebration even if it was not on his birthday. It was one of many reminders that I have had over the years that holidays do not have to be on the day that the calendar says they have to be on. Sam's birthday was something to rejoice in and celebrate whether we did that on May 9 or May 12.

Four! A month or so before he turned 4 the transplant team in Madison told me that he was too ill for a transplant. They told me that without a transplant it was doubtful that he would make it until his fifth birthday. Those were the darkest days I had ever lived up until that time. I wondered, as I shopped, if it would really be his last birthday. By the time he blew out his candles on May 9, I had realized that there was no way that anyone could predict what his life span would be. Perhaps he would not have another birthday and perhaps he would have 40 more. I had to learn to not only live with that but to LIVE and LIVE and LIVE.

We went to Ocean City for 2 weeks that year – the first time we took a vacation since he was a baby.

We took him on his Make A Wish trip to Disney World

On his fifth birthday he told me that he was not a baby anymore – but "I will still be your baby!" He wished that he could be a birdie and he wished that his tummy would not hurt anymore. Unbelievably he did not need medicine for his stomach for months after he made that wish.

Ocean City again – this time for almost 3 weeks and the sun shone every day!

Then the bleeding got out of hand - he bled and he bled and he bled. His heart got worse. I could not imagine his little body could sustain much more.

He turned six! The entire house was full of Buzz Light Year presents and he insisted on a purple cake which turned gray when I baked it. He did not mind. I thanked God for his blood product donors who keep him alive with their gift of life. He made a wish that he would go to Kindergarten – to the same school and Zach and Abby. I begged God to please grant that wish for my little boy. Peter added a comment on his medical summary – "our goal for Sam is for him to stay alive long enough to go to kindergarten." It was all that any of us wanted for him.

There were not any trips to Ocean City last summer. His health too precarious now. I felt and feel thankful for the times we did go away when we could.

The whole world shone on that day in September when he went to kindergarten – at Zach and Abby's school. The acceptance of the staff, the children, Sam's eyes and smile….continue to brighten the world every day that he goes to school.

And now …He is seven! I don't know what lies in his future but I know that whatever he does, forever as long as he lives, he will continue to add meaning and love to my life.

Sam, I love you! Happy Birthday.

Saturday, May 15, 2004 12:54 AM

I was asked to speak to a group of pediatricians, nurses and parents last Friday as part of the Wisconsin Medical Home Learning Collaborative. I was asked to give the perspective I have as a mother who has seen the difference that this type of care has made to my children. An easy task for me because life before Peter was infinitely harder and more overwhelming than life after Peter - the boy's most wonderful doctor. I talk quite frequently to groups about these types of things. But I had a brainstorm last week. What if Abby spoke with me? Sure the thought of speaking to 70 people when you're only 10 might be daunting but I knew she could do it if she wanted to.

I asked her on Wednesday night – the talk was Friday. She jumped at the chance and she was awesome. She was poised, looked at her audience, spoke with expression and feeling ...in short she was better than many adults I have seen.

I was very touched by what Abby had to say. Some of it came from an old essay she wrote which some of you may have seen. The story of that essay is that her 4th grade teachers did not believe she really wrote it. When I asked them why I was told that she had talked about anticipating death and used big words like "mitochondrial" and therefore she must have had help. Well, they sure do not understand siblings of children with special health care needs now do they? And they sure did not understand the depth and breadth of my daughter's feelings and emotions.

We presented in a back and forth format. I talked and told about some things and then she took off of one of my points from her perspective or I took off from one of her points from my perspective. It worked very well. Below are some of the things she said:

Abby began with introducing herself....

Hello. My name is Abby and I am almost 11 years old. I am a 5th grader at Bethesda Elementary in Waukesha. I am going to talk a little bit about our family today....

My brothers, sister and I have a mitochondrial disease. Mitochondria are supposed to turn food into energy. We all need energy to live so it can be a big problem if your mitochondria do not work.

Even though we all have the same disease my sister and I are much healthier than my brothers. Zach and Sam's mitochondria do not work correctly no matter how much food or medicine we give them – they just cannot make energy. Because of that they have a lot of medical problems.

On what she knows about when she and Zach were little:

When I was little I was very sick just like Zach. My mom used to take Zach and me to therapy 5 days a week. I got stronger and healthier and by the time I was three I did not have to go to therapy anymore. But Zach did not get stronger. My parents took Zach to see a lot of doctors because my mom knew something was really wrong. Zach threw up all the time. The doctors told my parents that it was just a stage that kids go through and that nothing was really wrong with Zach. But Zachary did not get better – he just kept getting worse. I guess it was not just a stage.

Remembering when Sam was born:

When I was four years old my baby brother Samuel was born. I remember that the day Sammy was born I made him a card and put it in his bed while he was sleeping. I thought that he would read it when he woke up. Sammy was born healthy but he got sick when he was a few weeks old and his problem were worse than Zachary's were. I did not really notice though – he was just my baby brother and I loved being his big sister.

On hospitalizations:

My brothers have had a lot of surgeries and have had to stay in the hospital a lot. I don't like it when they are in the hospital. I have to wake up early and go to my friends' houses. I miss my Mom, Zach and Sam and I get tired of visiting the hospital. One time when Zach was in kindergarten he had to stay in the hospital for 5 months. We were in kindergarten that year and he was my best friend. I missed him so much. Sometimes I would sleep in his bed at night because I missed him and I would eat cheerios in the morning even though I hated them because he liked them and it reminded me of him

On honesty:

One night my mom had a talk with us. She told us she wanted us to be prepared that Sam might die. It was hard for us to hear and I started crying. I felt like I was choking and I could not say anything. Sam and I have a really good relationship together. I love him so much. It is very scary to think of him being gone forever. When he is in the hospital that is okay but for him to never come back is too sad. I'd miss his voice and his little face and I think I would cry if anyone said orange because it is his favorite color.

It was horrible when my mom first told me that he might die and not grow up to be an adult. But I am glad that she told me so it won't be a surprise if anything happens. I think my heart would be totally stricken. I don't think about him dying very much. Sam is very strong and he has the best doctors. He has been close to dying before and he has not. I try to hope for the best for him. Every night I pray for him to get better or at least not to get any worse.

On how nice it is to have her brothers at home:

Until a few years ago I felt like my mom lived at the hospital with my brothers. They were always in the hospital and I never knew when I'd come home from school and they would not be home. Last year my mom spent almost every day at the infusion clinic with Sam. I hated that. I felt like I was being sucked in and trapped and it was hard to have hope. Now that Sam can get his blood products at home it is so much nicer. My mom is very busy taking care of Sam and Zach and sometimes I get jealous but at least she is at home. I never feel like we are a normal family but when everyone is at home I feel like I can forget about the disease for a while and we can just laugh and have fun.

On Dr. Havens:

When I think about my brother's doctor I think about how much he loves them and wants them to be happy. He listens to my mom and he always helps her figure out what to do. He always has new ideas and He spends a lot of time with my mom and brothers. I can tell they like him a lot. My brother Zach says his doctor is his friend. He called my brother on his birthday. I think it is cool how comfortable my brothers feel with him. I can't imagine if he did not take care of my brothers

Sunday, May 23, 2004 10:29 PM

The boys and I are going to the hospital. They need their IVIG and I need help taking care of them. I fell down the stairs on Thursday night. Sam had awakened screaming, I went to comfort him, walked back to my room (in the dark unfortunately) and instead of walking into my room I stepped into the air of our stairs and fell down.

It terrified me - I still feel scared when I see the stairs. Lou was out of town and all I could think as I fell was "who will take care of the kids." I have never fallen like that before…it probably only takes a few seconds but it felt like a long time going down.

Thank God it was not a lethal fall. I did manage to break our wall though I am unsure what hit it – my head, my shoulder, who knows… my left side is pretty torn up.

Brittany was wonderful. I crawled up the stairs to her and she was so calm. She called our neighbor, Mary, who is a nurse. Actually, I think Mary is an angel. She came over at 2:00 a.m. and got us all back to bed – even Sam who through it all was whining "where's my benadryl?" Poor baby had no idea what was going on. The next day she brought dinner over for us. Just having her come over that night gave me a sense of peace…to have such good neighbors that will do anything for us when we need it is a blessing.

My mom, Ione, my family….have all been very helpful and after I somehow got the kids' meds into them on Fri am., I think I slept the rest of the day thanks to everyone pitching in.

I don't think anything is broken. But it is not feeling much better and I am so exhausted and nauseated still from the fall. The bed at the hospital leaves a lot to be desired but it'll be ok. The pain and fatigue are too limiting right now to do much of what I do for the boys and though I still have my right hand, it is unnerving how weak it is when I have only one hand to use. It's scary how much of taking care of them depends on physical fitness and manual dexterity.

The boys are fine….this and that but really okay. Brittany went to prom last night. I managed to stay on my feet while her friends were here and I think we got some great pictures. She looked beautiful – because she is of course. Meanwhile, Abby was at Great America for the day with the Girl Scouts. She is so proud that she went on a lot of the roller coasters. She had a fun day.

Thank you for all the sweet messages in the guest book.

Sunday, May 30, 2004 8:29 PM

We are home from the hospital. Sam has pancreatitis (inflammation of his pancreas), which can be painful. He is not in pain because we have the medicines we need at home.

I remember all of the heart break I felt when he was younger and first began to have his migraine headaches. At the time we had doctors that were afraid to prescribe the drugs he needed to be free from pain. I felt so helpless and it hurt so deeply that there was nothing I could do to comfort him. The world seemed so dark those days. Today he was hurting for about 10 minutes until his pain medicine started working and I realized that I have begun to take his freedom from pain for granted. 10 minutes is about the longest he is ever in pain anymore thanks to our doctor who trusts me to have the medications he needs at home.

Zachary has spent the last few days playing with a neighbor friend of his. I told a few of my friends that the rain has become a rainbow for me....this is a friend that normally does not call Zach to play because he is a fairly active (typical) 11 year old and Zach can not keep up with that type of activity. To hear the phone ring for Zach, to know he is over another child's house, to watch them play chess and game cube over at our house.....these are the things that make me feel that every moment and ounce of energy spent on caring for these boys is worth it. Zachary is EXHAUSTED and asked to go to bed at 7 Pm tonight but the exhaustion is worth the light in his eyes.

My arm, shoulder, neck hurt still.... I went to the ER and nothing is broken. I rested at the hospital but coming home has made it all much worse. I have an appointment at the orthopedic doctor on Tuesday. I hate taking time for stuff like this but I feel frozen with fear when I think of how limiting this will be if I do not get someone to help me make it feel better.

Tomorrow is Abigail Nicole's birthday. Abby will be eleven! I am amazed at how fast my children are growing up. There is a small part of me that wants to keep them little forever....I just want to go back to when they were babies and toddlers and little kindergartners and have MORE of those moments and further and more deeply imprint those times on my heart so that I never ever forget any of them. But a larger part of me is so proud of who they are, who they continue to grow into being and I love watching them and learning from them. Abby my little girl....11 tomorrow. I cannot imagine my life without her. I cannot imagine our family without her. Sometimes I think the burden on her must be so heavy....to be so loved and needed by all of us. But she continues to flourish - she is so full of joy and unselfishness, her soul is so deep and so wise and when I think of life I think she IS life.

I know this is Zach and Sam's page but they are who they are because of all the lives that have touched theirs – most of all their wonderful sisters. Tonight I'd like to close with an essay Abby wrote for school about piano – I think it is a window into Abby's soul – my birthday girl.

MY FLESH and BLOOD

Piano is my life.
It is my thing.
Every time I play a note or push the pedal down,
it makes me happy and cheerful.
Every song has a different mood
and a different feeling.
I love to open the top of the piano
and see how it works.
When I grow up,
no matter how much money it is,
I'm going to buy a piano and use it every day.
Piano opens my mind
and makes me feel good.
It's a warm feeling, even if I'm alone.
If I'm stressed, it calms me down.
Piano is my path, my guide.
Every "A" on the piano is different,
no matter how you make think it is the same.
The high keys are little, sometimes curious.
But sometimes they are just the opposite.
They are shy and quiet.
Piano is magic.
It is all magic.
The notes, the hammers, the strings,
the beautiful black and white keys.
Piano is always pretty,
no matter what the notes you play.
The piano is like my best friend,
carrying me away and occupying me for hours and hours.
The notes have their own language.
It is such a different language than any others.
If I am mad,

the songs and notes I play are mad.
If I am tired,
the notes are tired.
The notes are me and I am the notes.
We are a family all stuck together.
Their personality is MY personality.
When I have to shut the piano for the day,
my imagination doses until -
I have another special moment to touch
those beautiful, delicate, special keys.
They are alive.
As long as I live
The piano will live

Wednesday, June 9, 2004 8:22 PM

Life is crazy.

The presentation for the CATCH Conference (Community Access to Children's Health sponsored by the American Academy of Pediatrics), in July, in Chicago, was due Monday night.

Missed that deadline - fortunately the AAP extended the deadline until today. I have been working on it every spare moment I have (which aren't many). I'm presenting with a few others and was the elected one to put it all together. The slides look really nice. What a great feeling to hand it over to the Fed-Ex people today though. Tomorrow I have to talk about the rotation to leadership at the hospital and then I hope to forget about all of it for a few days.

I love my job but I have been somewhat overwhelmed with all I have going on lately. Meg and I are planning a Care in the Community Conference for September. It is for parents and health care providers or anyone who is interested in finding ways to improve care and opportunities in the community for children with special health care needs. It will be good but lots of "deadlines" with that right now too.

The scoop on my shoulder:

I did go to the orthopedic doctor last week. He agreed nothing is broken but said my shoulder is very badly sprained. In addition he said my muscles are terribly weak - he is unsure if I injured the muscles or if I am just in too much pain to use them but he was taken aback with my weakness. He felt the best choice is for me to do 4 weeks of PT to see if they can make it more functional. After that he will reassess. If my arm is still as weak or if I am still in as much pain then we will have to do more muscle testing. He prescribed a stronger painkiller – thank GOD!

Zachary: tired this week. Having issues with one of his blood pressure medications so we need to wean him off of it and start a new one. Things are not looking great with this blood pressure issue. He has been very motivated, however, to do his New York state report. He even got up at 5:30 a.m. on Saturday because he wanted to work on his poster board sized map. He really loves this type of independent, hands on type of work although the last day it got too rushed and he got too stressed from it all.

Samuel: Kindergarten will be over in a few days. I don't think he really is taking it in that he will not have school for several months (he'll have home bound school but not classroom school). I love his little friends and hope we have some of them over this summer. Struggling with the autonomic seizures. He had a GREAT day all day yesterday, then had a seizure, bumped his head terribly hard in the process…..it is all so scary how fast it happens and how little control I have to do anything for him. He is also having blood clotting issues with his central line so he has a line study scheduled for Friday.

Kids are out of school on Friday. We really need the break. Been running way too much. I can't believe all the work they have had for the end of the year. Soccer will be over for Abby and Brittany's is already over. I have no goals this weekend except to go outside and take the kids to Shrek II if it is raining.

Happy Birthday Mom! Today is my Mom's birthday. I feel a little guilty that she took Brittany and me to the club to celebrate but it was nice to go out. Thanks Mom!

Monday, June 14, 2004 10:18 PM

School is out!!!! No 8:00 PM bed times - so less rushed at night - with the 3 younger kids. I love that the most. Much more relaxing mornings. Sam will still have homebound school 2 days/week but it will be so good for him. He is so close to reading I think! Zachary does not have social studies during the school year to try to prevent school overload. It's nice but the tradeoff is that he and I do the year's worth of social studies during the summer. What is nice is that the district gives me the freedom to teach however I want as long as he ends up knowing the core competencies for that year. So I try to make it very hands on learning for him.

Nice weekend with the kids. Enough rain to spend some time inside and get some things done that desperately needed to be done. Still, lots of sunshine to be outside. Sammy told me Saturday, "I think I am going to be shy with Zach and Abby's friends" but he is sure doing a good job talking to all the various and a sundry kids that we accumulate in our house. He used to hide when they came and now talks and even plays with them (if they let him) so this is fun to see!

Sam's line study was bad or at least not perfect depending on who is talking. The radiologist that did the study told me that the line is up against his vein wall and actually sucks in the vein wall when I try to draw blood from it. He told me it is a matter of time until it is infected or clotted and felt we needed to discuss the risks versus benefits of changing the line. (Huge risk because of anesthesia, bleeding….). I cried.

The next day Peter talked to a different radiologist who said this is the position lots of lines are in (against the wall) and kids keep the lines in and do not have problems. Ok. Well, that is a night and day answer. So one day I cry, the next I feel hopeful and then just frustrated to realize that once again it is all a matter of educated guesses and experience and never ever a crystal clear answer of do this or that will happen. The burden of trying to do what is right feels so heavy sometimes.

Today Peter and I met like we do every month to go through their care, assess goals we have made for them, evaluate current treatments, decide on treatment for the next month, etc. I don't know why but I just felt so overwhelmed with so many emotions. I don't understand how it happens – I have been doing so fine, even knowing the reality of 2 boys who are having a harder time but I felt my heart in my throat the entire time we talked. Actually I had a hard time even talking because I thought I would cry. Actually I did cry the whole way home.

We talked about Sam and his upcoming surgery next Thursday to repair his G and J tube sites. All of a sudden I just felt panicked about doing it, remembering last time how much he bled after that surgery

44

(on Thanksgiving weekend). We talked about Sam struggling to walk some days, to get up from a sitting position. About how he is getting pancreatitis again after 18 months or so without it.

Seeing everything on paper…..Well it tells the story of the course of the illness – a story I don't always appreciate when I am in the middle of my own little world just trying to take one day at a time and have moments and memories to hold in my heart.

On to Zachary and then it hit me terribly hard.

Our Goals: We added a goal that his care will not be limited as long as he has good quality of life. We took off a goal about increasing his muscle mass with growth hormone. That goal was made years ago, when increasing his muscle mass mattered to me. I realized today that I could care less what his muscle mass is. I just want him to grow up.

So Peter drew a red line through the old goal, and wrote in the new one. To me all that red was an outward sign of my heart breaking, as I try to accept that this IS progressive for Zachary. I don't know if I am there yet to be honest. How do I reconcile progressive with a kid that is so alive?

I think that right now I like the summary the way it looks with the big red slash through the old goal and the new one written in by Peter. It draws attention to the story of Zachary. The finished summary will just have the new goal and not the old one…as if it never existed, as if there was never a time in Zach's life that he was healthy enough that increasing his muscle mass was an important goal.

Don't get me wrong – it was an important thing to work towards but as Peter said "he is in a different phase in his life now" and what we are dealing with his that he can not climb the stairs without fatigue, he is on multiple meds to control his hypertension in a matter of months, his heart cannot compensate as it should with all of this.

I know it could be worse. I really do. Our little friend Kyle, who has Mito disease and a central line like the boys, became septic (multi-organ failure from a blood infection) a few weeks ago. Until then he was healthier than my 2 boys. Now the infection has "burned" 40% of his body and he will probably lose parts of each of his legs and fingers.

My friend Lynne has 2 beautiful children, Angus and Allie; both died from Mito. How does she wake up every day and still be there for me and for so many others when we need her?

Laura's Samantha died after living a year in Pittsburgh's ICU waiting for organs she so needed, the ones that never came.

There was a note in our hospital newsletter about a sleep lap technician who was killed in a traffic accident on the way home from work, leaving behind 2 young teenage children and a husband.

I don't understand any of this...only that our lives can change in a moment and somehow I have to find hope, and run one mile at a time.

Tonight it was quiet in our house (really it was for once!) and I sat on the couch to read with Sammy. He asked me, "Are you cold?

"No," I said. "But I can put the blanket on you if you are."

"OK," said Sam. "But please get under it with me." Of course I did.

A few minutes later someone else got under the blanket with us – Zachary. And there we were, just us three, reading and laughing and reading some more. I needed that time with them. No one else in the house and I could just be their mother for a while.

Now that you all think I've completely lost it...I am ok. I am not depressed. I am sad. But I am ok albeit sad – I hope that makes some sense.

Thursday, June 24, 2004 8:54 PM

"I want people to know that in every life, there are storms. But we must remember to play after every storm and to celebrate the gift of life as we have it, or else life becomes a task, rather than a gift. We must always listen to the song in our heart, and share that song with others." --Mattie Stepanek

Sam is hanging in there. He is home - Not doing great but I should not be surprised I suppose. He has fevers and is swollen from head to toe. The swelling is because the fluid in his blood vessels is moving into his tissue instead – it is called systemic inflammatory response syndrome (SIRS) and Sam gets it when he is especially stressed like an infection or surgery. He is getting daily platelets, daily plasma, 2x daily cryoprecipitate and his Factor7a infusion (24 hrs a day) to try to prevent bleeding. Today he did start bleeding from the surgery site though. Not good.

46

He has a Foley catheter in his bladder and we hope to leave it in for at least a week. He has been losing sensation in his bladder and consequently it is very stretched which can impact the kidneys if the urine backs up into them. We hope that by keeping a catheter in, it will keep his bladder empty, shrink it down some and therefore protect his kidneys.

As for the CT scan the dentist still has to look at it. However 2 radiologists and peter reviewed it and they believe that the large, moveable, fluid filled masses are not infectious because they do not seem to have done any damage to his bones. Of course the only way to know for sure would be to put a needle in and take out some of the fluid but no one wants to do that with Sam. The general consensus is that he bled at some point – maybe when his molars came in or maybe just bled for no reason at all. The result is he has these masses that are on the insides of both of his cheeks. They are fairly large. The hope is they will recede. If they don't I do not know what we will do. We'll see the dentist again this week so we'll know more.

Both boys were evaluated for wheelchairs on Friday when we were at the hospital. We hope insurance will approve a power wheelchair for Zach, and for Sam it will be one that I push. I think it takes months and months for this process of getting approval and then getting them made. Sam also had his new leg braces made (AFOs). We should pick those up this week and the orthotist said he would make them within a few days given how unstable Sam's left leg has gotten.

Finally, Mattie Stepanek, a courageous, ALIVE, wise and beautiful 13 year old, who was born with a type of mitochondrial disease, passed away on Tuesday. This wonderful child was wiser than most adults I know. He became well known throughout the world as the National Goodwill Ambassador for the Muscular Dystrophy Association (MDA). He had a message of hope and peace that he spoke of and wrote about throughout his short life. Mattie's choice to not be bitter, to live his life with hope inspired me for the last 4 years since I first read about him.

A champion is an optimist,
A hopeful spirit...
Someone who plays the game,

Even when the game is called life.
There can be a champion in each of us,
If we live as a winner,
If we live as a member of the team,
If we live with a hopeful spirit,
For Life
--Mattie Stepanek

Saturday, July 3, 2004 9:45 PM

My mom and I took the kids to see Shrek 2 this week! It was even funnier than Shrek 1and just such a wonderful message. The kids laughed and laughed – I did too. Sam has been repeating lines from the movie all week.

That's my prelude to telling you how Sam is feeling. Really well compared to last week!

The bleeding is particularly bad, though, as I pretty much knew it would be. Yesterday and today he has bled through countless dressings and shirts and all week has needed blood every other day. Our next-door neighbor's big retirement party is going on right now but Sam and I are at home – the bleeding makes it difficult to take him anywhere at all. I wish I was able to go. I love my neighbors and rarely get to talk with them anymore.

I am worried that we are using way too many blood products for Sam to handle but Sam seems oblivious to it all. Thank God for that!

We did manage to get to the infamous Waukesha Parade today. Woo Hoo – must have been some major budget cuts in Waukesha this year. This is never a big scale parade--mainly it consists of fire engines, police cars and kids on decorated bikes but it is always lots of fun for the kids. This year the mood was almost sedate....very little music, no real dogs, no dump trucks and they must have cut out the kids on decorated bikes. But the kids still loved battling other kids for the candy thrown in the streets.

Zachary has developed more bleeding issues this week. We are unsure if it is due to one of his medications (I doubt this but his hematologist thinks maybe) or if it is just a development of bleeding similar to Sam. I don't really want to believe that either so for now I am trying not to think about it. Next week we'll do more medication levels but I think it will be a "time will tell" situation and to be honest I am not in any rush to think or know any more about it. The thought of another child with a severe bleeding disorder is not something I can even bear thought of right now. I will deal with it if I have to and until then I just cannot.

I want to share a wonderful Zachary story. A few weeks ago I started making a calendar on a dry erase board for the week for our whole family. It has what everyone is doing every day, who has what jobs that week, what we need if anyone goes to the store, etc. My attempt to de-stress life a little bit. One thing I decided was that during the summer we would rotate dinner responsibility, (because Lord knows I can never think of what to make!). Each of the kids has one night they are responsible for "making dinner.". The thought was that they would talk with me and decide what we would eat, make sure we had the ingredients and make it with my help.

Well, all of them have pretty much relied on me to tell them what to make – which is fine - and we have made it together. However, Friday am I found plates and bowls of food all over the refrigerator and counter. It was only 6:30 am. Come to find out Zachary got up at precisely 5:17 am and made a terrific fruit salad, sliced bagels for sandwiches, made a salad with everything anyone could want on it, made layered Jell-O, an Oreo milkshakes and popcorn. Who could want a better dinner than that? This is my child who receives calories intravenously - he does not eat what we eat for the most part. He could eat normally until he was 7 and the loss of eating has probably been the hardest thing for Zach about this illness. Yet here he planned an entire meal and made sure it would include things he could eat (milk shake and Jell-O). And even though I would not have picked that particular dinner to make, I will say that it was an absolutely wonderful thing to not have to think about what to make or even make it for that matter. Thank you, awesome Zachary!

Please keep sweet Sarah and Francis in your thoughts and prayers. Last Saturday night we had dinner with this wonderful couple, who have befriended my Mom in Naples, and had come to Wisconsin to visit. They have prayed and loved my children from a distance. This week, back in Naples, Sarah had a stroke. She is doing better but I am sure the road will be long. Tomorrow is their 50th anniversary! Happy anniversary Francis and Sarah. We love you!

My sister, Dad, Dad's wife and their 2 kids (my baby brothers aged 12 and 10) are coming to see us and my brother Mike and his wife Elaine this week so it will be a Mountain Dew busy week!

Happy Independence Day.

Tuesday, July 6, 2004 10:35 PM

Sam is on the add-on OR schedule for tomorrow (Thursday) afternoon. The surgeon would like to look at the site under anesthesia to see if there is anything that can be done surgically. I trust our surgeon so much- but I feel unsure if this is the right thing to do. It could be but it could also make things a lot worse. I don't know what I'll do but for now he is on the schedule.

Sam is still bleeding too much and I am scared for him. While, he has had some pretty major bleeding episodes in the past, nothing has ever lasted this many days.....I am scared it is not going to stop.

The Factor 7a does work miracles if he gets it every 3-4 hours. But he cannot get it forever - the side effect of that much factor is too much clotting and he could easily have a stroke.

He is crabby and sick of lying down. But if he sits or walks...he bleeds. He cannot walk actually - I don't know why but he can barely bear weight on his legs. This is new since the weekend.

Our hematologist talked about Sam to his hematology colleagues today. They wondered about using a drug that is normally used for bleeding during heart bypass surgery. There is no experience using it in a case like this. That was pretty much the only stone left unturned. I don't know if we'll try it or not...I need to know more about it and talk with everyone some more.

My sister is staying with us and thank God for her presence. She has helped to not only distract Sammy but to give the other kids the attention and time they deserve. I'm tired and Peter has been very clear that we can come to the hospital any time we want. I know that and appreciate it. Part of me wants to go - to not be alone taking care of him. But I know Sam is happier at home for now. And so many of the nurses are overwhelmed with Sam - I just can't deal with the stress of nurses feeling overwhelmed and having to be the one to calm them down. For now I think we need to stay as long as I can safely care for Sam.

Friday, July 9, 2004 2:34 PM

Sam did not go to OR yesterday. He woke up Thursday am with relatively little blood on his dressings. We hope that maybe he had begun to form a clot and felt that moving him from home to the hospital would likely precipitate a bleeding crisis.

Our preference all along has been to treat him medically and not surgically.

We decided to put him "to sleep" for a few days. With the help of a lot of drugs he has been relatively immobile and asleep. He wakes up sometimes and that makes me either laugh or feel bad. The funny part is he is just so darn mad and has no idea why we are all in such a tizzy about his bleeding. He says "just put some 'pwessure' on it." And "Come on – what can we play!?" I miss him but if this makes him better, it is what needs to be done.

He is getting boatloads of Novoseven (Factor 7a) and it seems to be helping but it is a lot.

Yesterday (Thursday) he did not need blood. Today is Friday and he does. One day at a time.

He had a major gushing episode at noon today. Our surgeon called during it and was encouraging that there may be some other things to try to put on top of the wound. He was very kind yesterday when I cancelled Sam's surgery. He said he supports whatever we choose to do – medical or surgical.

Blood bank is re-testing his blood to see if they are getting the most perfectly HLA matched platelets for him. Right now he is a hard person to match for and he has very dew donors. He has a PRA of 93% which means that he reacts against 93% of the platelets in the population. They fear that he has developed new antibodies in the last year since the testing was done. If that is true we will have to find new donors for him and it will be even harder to find matches.

His BUN was 49 and his creatinine was 0.8. For Sam this is astronomical. His sodium is low, making it look like a picture of some degree of kidney failure/heart failure......we'll try more diuretics today and lots of hope. He has very mild pancreatitis. Peter says that finally Sam will have to be admitted and I know he is right.

I am going to pack some stuff...perhaps if I do that, his labs will look better and his bleeding will stop.

My sister is gone, it is rainy here and kind of cold. It does not feel like summer at all.

He is so worth fighting for. His spirit is something I just marvel at. That he can be so full of it, even with his body falling apart is my inspiration. Sam I love you! I carry your heart in my heart.

Thank you to everyone who has called, left messages, emailed, said prayers......it means everything!

Sunday, July 11, 2004 9:40 PM

Miracles

Webster says miracles are a wonder – a wonderful, marvelous thing that we cannot explain, seeming to contradict all scientific laws.

Sam – a miracle – my miracle!

Friday was a very bad day of bleeding.

Saturday morning in the shower I thought of Samuel in the bible. His mother promised God that she would give her son to God, if God would only grant her heart's desire – for a son.

But how could I give my son to God if God granted my heart's desire? (My heart's desire is more time with Sam, to stop the bleeding. Give me time with my son!!!!) I have been fighting so hard NOT to give my son to God. I am not ready for Sam to go to "a better place." I don't know if I ever will be.

I told God something like this. Nothing is working anymore for Sam. We have tried everything medically, surgically...he is still bleeding. If he gets better now I will know it is you. Not me, not anything I have done. I will tell him that. I will make sure he knows that even though I do not understand why God allows this illness in his life...God loves him.

Then darkness came. Saturday was a day I will never forget. I did not know a day could be so black. I have never felt such an absence of hope in all of my life.

He bled and bled and bled and nothing I did or said or prayed for stopped it. I gave him 2 units of blood and he still bled. Factor 7a in such grossly huge amounts, praying he did not stroke from it, platelets, cryo, plasma...I could not see straight through the tears that filmed my eyes all day long

For the first time since this all started he felt sick, he looked sick, he was so weak. He vomited blood and blood drained from his tubes ounce upon ounce. I bathed him 10, even 15 times trying to wash it away.

I wondered if I wanted him to die at home or in the hospital. I did not know. I wondered when I tucked him in to bed if it would be the last time I would kiss him good night and I almost strangled on the thought. I laid his blanket on him – blood stained despite my best efforts to get the blood out of the blankets and sheets he has been bleeding all over. Sam's blood.

At 10:00 at night I called Peter. He told me to give more Factor 7a to Sam. He told me it was ok to stay home if I wanted to but Sam should come in first thing in the morning. He told me that I had done everything I could for Sam but sometimes it is beyond our control. I just cried – because my everything had not been enough. The world was so black last night.

This morning, I woke up and the sun was shining. Sam's dressings were white – dry. He had not bled from the surgical site all night long. He was still bleeding internally but not like yesterday. I wondered how long it would last. I was, I am, so scared of it all being a dream and waking up and he is bleeding everywhere again.

To the ER as Peter and I had decided last night. Sam was so excited. He hoped they would say "911 it's an emergency!" when he walked in the door, just like his play emergency phone does. Still no bleeding. Peter tickled him and pressed on his stomach. No bleeding. We made jokes about mothers that bring their kids to the ER for no reason. Peter asked me if I wanted to keep him in the hospital but we both knew I would not say yes. We agreed that if Sam needs 2 units in one day again, that will be the time for admission.

There were stars on the ceiling in the ER. "Lets make wishes, Sam and I said. "I wish that you will stop bleeding." I said. Sam looked at me like I was silly. "That's your wish?" he said. I could hear him internally saying, *Humph –what kind of a wish is that?* I asked him, "Well what is yours?" "To be the yellow Power Ranger," he said quite definitively, with his big smile. That's what I love about Sam. The illness is a sidebar – not the main event of his life. It's a given but certainly not something to be focused on.

Home – he is of course still bleeding and did need a unit of blood again today. His BUN is up to 60 now and that is very worrisome to me, although the nephrologist thinks he needs to compensate with a high BUN right now in order for his heart to work. His labs indicate that he is developing pancreatitis. But the sun is shining again. It is so true that true hope only comes when we come face to face with the darkness.

I asked him tonight if he remembered my wish and he said "yes – for me to stop bleeding." "Did it come true?" I asked him. "YES!" he shouted. "Thank you God for making my wish come true," I said. He smiled and then, "I sure hope he does not forget my wish to be a power ranger!"

Miracles do happen. Wonderful, marvelous things that we cannot explain but we surely do learn from. Wonderful, marvelous people who happen into our lives. God, I still do not understand why you allow this to be. But I do know that Sam is a miracle every day.

Saturday, July 17, 2004 10:55 PM

May I just say thank you for all of your messages and emails while Sam was so ill. One of the only blessings I can see in going through a critical illness such as Sam just did, is that there is a great intimacy that builds and builds between the people that share in the fear, the worry, the care, and hopefully the recovery. To know that the world is full of people loving and hoping for us is what will remain in my heart - forever.

Sammy is doing really well! Chris, one of our home nurses said, "Sam is a cat!" and that is so true. Although it seems he has had more than 9 lives! His bleeding is actually quite minimal today. His kidney/heart function seems to be dramatically better. The only truly concerning thing is that he has incredible weakness of his legs, difficulty walking more than a few steps, tremors because he is weaker, and something called clonus of his left ankle, which is a neurological thing.

On Tuesday I took him to get his new splints. I'll have to take a picture of them. They go from his feet up to the area below his knees. On one he has Bugs Bunny and the other he has Roadrunner. The man who made them, (Jim), had only casted Sam for them 2 weeks prior but in that 2 weeks Sam's left foot has gotten significantly worse so that if we had waited another week, Jim felt he may have had to make new splints all together. As it is, we have a lot of difficulty getting Sam's left foot into that splint. Because it stretches the foot into a better position, it is not the most comfortable thing right now for Sam. However, we hope that with time, it will help improve his function or at the least, prevent this very rapid deterioration in walking that he has had since February.

Zachary has been busy with our across the street neighbor. They have become such good friends and it is wonderful to see. What I love about this friend of Zach's is that he just takes Zach's issues in stride. He is so accepting of Zach's differences and he adapts his play as needed to adjust to Zach's fluctuating energy and endurance.

I went to the American Academy of Pediatrics CATCH conference in Chicago on Friday and Saturday. This was a conference looking at the care of children with special health care needs within the community. How can we do a better job of caring for children like Zach and Sam (medically fragile) as well as those with developmental disabilities, mental health issues, learning issues, etc.?

I gave a presentation on TEAM, which is the special health care needs rotation for pediatric doctors in training that I (and some others) developed. I don't know how many of you know this but the resident program was born out of my incredible frustration and almost mental collapse after years of carrying everything on my shoulders. (pre-Peter of course). A few months after Peter started caring for the boys I was so awed by the difference that I wanted to do something that would help other children. I could not clone Peter so I figured the answer was education. Education of young pediatric residents, because you can rarely teach old dogs new tricks. I went to the director of resident education and pitched the idea. He loved it and that was the beginning...

It was so wonderful to go to all these talks with people who believe in what we believe in (better care for children with special health care needs). My head is spinning but in a wonderful way. What I loved about the people at this conference is they are all willing to share their research, their ideas and their tools. They believe so strongly in moving our nation towards the ideal of providing excellent care to children like mine, that they release ownership. That is RARE in medicine. The energy was inspiring!

It was a major accomplishment for me to leave the boys to go to this conference, but we all survived and I actually had a lot of fun palling around with some of my colleagues that I never get to see outside of the hospital.

On Monday the boys will be admitted to the hospital for their IVIG infusions – we'll be there all week as always.

Please keep dear Francis in your heart right now. His wife of 50 years passed away, after suffering from a very severe stroke days before their 50th anniversary party. The love so apparent between the two of them is what I will always remember and I know Francis and his family will as well.

"But soon we shall die…but the love will have been enough. All those impulses of love return to the love that made them. Even memory is not necessary for love. There is a land of the living and a land of the dead and the bridge is love, the only survival, the only meaning."
Thornton Wilder - *The Bridge of San Luis Rey*

Tuesday, July 27, 2004 7:25 AM

The boys had a pretty uneventful week in the hospital – uneventful is always nice.

Dad – at the hospital they got to meet Fellipe Giaffone, who is a racecar driver and the current spokesman for Racing for Kids. Fellipe brought his car and the kids were able to sit in it and wear his helmet. They got baseball caps signed by him as well. I actually found it all very interesting – must have been all those endless, (I mean wonderful), Saturday nights at the East Lansing Race Track with Dad.

Sam has yeast growing in his blood again. Yeast in the blood has plagued Sam since he was about 2 years old. He is actually not sick at all – some mild fevers. This is amazing as it can be a lethal type of germ to have in the blood. I'm glad he is feeling fine but we have to clear it out of the blood quickly. My biggest concern right now is that often yeast will cling to foreign objects in the body. Sam has the 2 central lines in his chest, which he depends on to be alive. (They are like permanent intravenous lines). If the yeast clings to one of the

56

lines, it will have to be pulled and a new one put in. That requires surgery and post surgical bleeding is something all too fresh in my mind. Thus, we're treating it aggressively even though he does not seem ill at the moment.

Zachary had a great time in the hospital. We happened to be assigned to a resident who actually knew how to play Yugio cards! I'm more impressed with this doctor's cognitive abilities that he knows how to play that then the fact he finished medical school. Many residents are very overwhelmed in their first few months and it is hard for them to take time to connect with children. This resident, however, actually kept Zachary up until 11:30 PM playing Yugio cards the night he was on call. Every time he got called out of the room because a patient needed him, Zach would lament why in the world the patients couldn't just behave and not need medical attention! A few days later, when the resident could have left for the day, he stayed and played cards with Zach for another hour!! Zachary also had the pleasure of playing chess with Dr. G and Dr. S. (he beat Dr. Greenbaum!) Such good people in this world to take time out of very busy days!

Meanwhile, Sam had a ball trying to knock Peter over by giving him five as hard as he could. His favorite was asking Peter to sit on his bed with him and then pushing the button to make the bed go up and make Peter fall off. Now Sam tells everyone how he did this to Dr. Havens and he can't even get through the story without laughing hysterically, which makes us all laugh. Sam laughs so hard and it fills the room with joy to hear it.

Sam's leg seems marginally better. He can bear weight on it now without pain. We did x-ray it to make sure it was not broken given his poor bone health, but as expected it is not broken. My guess is that the IVIG and daily PT helped his nerves and muscles. His PT and OT modified his splints so that his foot does not have to be stretched quite so much. We figure we'll do this in stages, and not ask his foot to be in perfect position right now. It's too painful. Chris, his OT made him a new nighttime splint as well so he should be splinted almost 24 hours/day and I think that will help a lot to get him walking better or at least not with pain.

Had a big scare yesterday. Abby woke up unable to move. As she describes it she could not move her head or arms. She said her head felt huge and very big and heavy and it hurt terribly. Her neck hurt very badly and when she tried to use her arms to get herself out of bed she had excruciating pain. She started screaming for Zach and me to come for her because she literally could not get out of bed. This is a child who stays at school when she is sick without telling anyone because she does not want to worry me so if she is screaming for help something is very wrong.

I got her up and she seemed fine neurologically in that she could walk. The inability to move her arms was pain related...if she moved them her neck and head hurt but the arms themselves were fine. If she yawned or talked her neck hurt. She did not have a fever and looked way too good for meningitis.....and the doctor agreed with me later when she saw her.

At the pediatrician's they could not find anything wrong - no swollen anything or tight muscles. The pediatrician said she was very concerned because the story was so strange and not the typical story of someone who slept on their neck wrong and had a crick in it in the morning.

She ordered a cervical spine MRI to be done this week, quiet play only until then and to give ibuprofen around the clock. If it gets worse then she needs to go right in. The pediatrician said her concern is that this is a manifestation of mitochondrial disease, although admittedly is unsure what it could be. Abby is scared and sad she can't play soccer until the MRI is done. Her biggest fear is that she needs to have an IV put in for the MRI. Abby is petrified of needles and even a blood draw will send her heart rate up over 200. I feel so bad for her. I honestly think they will not find anything wrong – perhaps it was a migraine and Abby just never had the type of pain before. But I do agree with getting the MRI and making sure we are not missing anything more serious. I could not bear to hear that Abby's disease is kicking back into gear – she has been so healthy since she was three.

Sunday, August 1, 2004 9:38 AM

Abby is doing okay and moving without any difficulty. She has not awoken with any further episodes this week. The stat MRI that the pediatrician wanted is not scheduled until August 9. I guess the radiologists did not think Abby needed to come in as soon as our pediatrician did. Funny, how the radiologists can make that decision when they are never even saw her…our pediatrician was NOT happy, nor am I but we are thankful that Abby is doing fine. Hoping it was a fluke episode and nothing else.

Zachary and Abby just finished a summer art class. The art teachers did a very nice job with this class and they seemed to really enjoy it.

Brittany has been un well all week and Friday she went to our pediatrician. Turns out she has a terrible case of strep and possibly mono. She has been home and in a lot of pain (throat and ears). I feel so bad for her as nothing seems to take away the pain. I will have to call Sunday if this persists, as she cannot even sleep. It's strange having her home so much and I wish she felt better.

Sammy: Oh I love his spirit. He is having a little trouble with his heart failure right now. We had tried to wean his diuretics a tiny bit and his heart just could not handle that at all. He has been fairly tired all week and working very hard to breathe. I am hoping that tomorrow is a better day for him as we are supposed to go to "Gwandmaw's" to celebrate my birthday and he has been so looking forward to that.

My birthday was Saturday! Glad to be alive and so privileged to be Brittany, Zachary, Abby and Samuel's mother. The first half if the day was a very sad one for me as I attended a funeral for my friend's 3 year old who died very unexpectedly on Tuesday. He did have a mitochondrial disease and certainly had his share of medical issues but death was the last thing that any of us saw as happening in his near future. The shock has been overwhelming for me so that I cannot fathom the shock for his loving family.

I think I held life pretty dear before this child died so quickly but I must confess that I have lingered at my children's bedsides longer this week, cleaned my house much less, felt joy at their antics even more and thanked God for their very breath and heart beat each night. I have been left with this feeling that I could just blink and they could be gone…. I don't feel this in a pessimistic sort of way but just an even sharper awareness that life is so fragile and never – absolutely NEVER – to be taken for granted.

Beautiful cards and gifts from my family. I used my birthday to beg the girls into consenting to watch Sense and Sensibility with me. I've been long wanting to see it, having bought the video a year or more ago. They actually liked it, as did I.

And finally – (Don't I know this will bring a slew of comments) - isn't John Edwards just awesome???!!!???!!!!

Thursday, August 5, 2004 8:01 AM

Sam is bleeding profusely again.

It started in his mouth and just when that got better his gastrostomy site on his stomach started gushing.

It is as bad as it was a few weeks ago only this time I cannot blame surgery.

I don't have anything to point to and say this is why he is bleeding – as more often is the case I just don't know.

The blood center does not have enough Factor 7a for him. They cannot get it drop shipped until today at noon and then it has to be driven to a pharmacist's house to be "dispensed" and then they can get it to us.

In the meantime we borrowed several vials from the hospital but we can't really borrow anymore because then their inventory is depleted.

The problem is that it is so expensive that no one wants to keep an inventory of it.

It is frightening how hard it is to obtain this stuff when supplies run low.

So please hope and pray that nothing happens and we can get a delivery mid- afternoon. We don't really have enough until then but we can give some smaller doses and I pray that something works to stop it.

I feel like some of our doctors and nurses are tired of this…I think it is just me being so tired and miss understanding their non-verbal language, but I just can't bear it if they give up on Sam.

Sam has been so unsettled, manic and agitated for days and ever since yesterday afternoon he has been so much more calm – right when the bleeding started. It makes me wonder what in the world goes on inside his body that leads to the bleeding.

Please keep my little boy in your thoughts. I love him so much.

Thursday 10 PM Update

Sam's bleeding stilled to nothing all afternoon with the help of his Factor 7a. He even played "Bat Man Mobile" and Bat Man action figures with Zachary.

Then tonight it started up again. He had fallen asleep on the floor while we were eating dinner. I went to pick him up to take him to bed and the carpet was all red.

He is so good and patient about these dressing changes. It is tedious to peel off all the old gauze, clean his little body up and then fix all the layers of things that go into making that new dressing. But he is very still for the most part and he lets me do this. One time today he got very exasperated with me and said, "I'm frustrated!" and immediately after he said "what does that mean - frustrated?" I said, "well it means you're feeling a little crabby about things" and he said, "Yes, I am FRUSTRATED CRABBY!"

Thank you to everyone for your prayers and hope and thoughts for Sam. The Factor 7a arrived in record time thanks to the most awesome Blood Center in the world. Initially when I spoke with them this morning, our support person there told me she would drive the 7a to the appropriate place to expedite the process that it has to go through to get checked in on their end. I was really touched by that. But about 30 min. later Katie called to say that actually their manager, wanted to personally bring us the factor 7a. He and one of his colleagues from their distribution center drove all the available vials out to us this morning. Sam had his factor in the house before he even needed it thanks to them.

Sometimes I am so startled by the kindness and goodness of the people that surround us. There are hundreds of people who help to keep Sam at home…I don't know that I even know all of their names because maybe they work night shift or do something behind the scenes that I am unaware of or perhaps they are one of our many donors for Sam's blood products. But my heart knows them. I realize that sounds quirky but, the impact of what these people do for us strikes me so deeply at times and their actions have been imprinted on my heart, telling me that there is still so much goodness left in this world. They wanted to bring Sam his Factor today!

61

Other staff from the Blood Center started calling in donors so that Sam can go back to getting his platelets every day, rather than 4x /week which does not seem to be cutting it at the moment.

So for now we're just doing all we can do to stop the bleeding.

One hour at a time.

Thank you Ione and Chris, (our 2 nurses that come on Mon, Wed and Thursday)!! Thank you for your patience with Sam, for treating him like a child and playing with him, for your careful assessment and meticulous care. I know things are crazy and sometimes scary around here with the boys and their increasing needs - thank you for being there for our family. We love you!

Sunday, August 8, 2004 9:30 PM

Sam is doing better thankfully. The Novoseven (Factor 7a) is such an effective drug for the most part. Sometimes it is hard to figure out how much he needs – it seems to vary but in general he certainly seems to need more than he used to. At any rate, once I get the dose and frequency right, it works and for that I am so thankful.

With a lot of factor 7a on board I actually took him out on Friday to the pet store. The original purpose of the trip was to buy one gold fish for Zach's friend, Kevin. Kevin had asked Zach to watch his ONE gold fish for 3 days and of course we killed that ONE gold fish within 12 hours. (Perhaps less – not sure of time of death). So off to the pet store we went. We picked out THREE gold fish. I figured it would be good insurance that there would be at least one left on Sunday when Kevin came back for his fish.

Of course Sammy just loved seeing all of the puppies. So did I. They were ever so cute. Sam LOVES dogs and has at least 100, probably more, stuffed dogs. He knows each one by name too. Sam has pretty much resigned himself to the fact that Daddy says NO DOGS so he did not ask for one. However, the whole time in the pet store he kept asking if he could please have his own pet…."please. I'll do anything if you buy me my own pet." Ok, big brown eyes and little hands folded together up at me…would you be able to resist? I think not. I tried to talk him into a baby bird but he saw the hamsters and fell in love with them. As for me, I fell in love with the look on his face when he watched the hamsters play.

That is the story of how we came to have "Pancakes." Yes, that is his name. Or hers. Sam says he wants Pancakes to be a boy but actually I think "he" is a girl. The whole way home Sam was laughing saying, "Daddy is going to fire us for buying a pet." Zach said, "I'm not taking the fall for this. It wasn't my idea." Oh sure. And when their Dad finally did come home they all pointed at me and said it was my fault. For someone who grew up with pets, he really does hate animals and he is sick of us staring at what he calls a glorified rat but we do love Pancakes. I love him because Sam is so enthralled with him. I have not seem Sam have so much energy and interest in anything in months. He just watches him all the time, reads to him, tells him jokes and today was trying to handcuff his cage. He told me yesterday that he wished he was a hamster and when I asked him "why?" he said, "So I could get in his cage and be his friend. DUH!"

Of course we had to go back to the store the next day and buy more things for Pancakes. Today Sam even went outside (something he has not had the energy to do for weeks) in order to find twigs and grass for Pancakes.

In between all of this he has bled but not too badly because we have been giving a lot of Factor 7a. Yesterday, I began to wean the extra doses and today I only gave one extra dose. He is still on quite a high daily drip of the 7a and it will be a long time if ever that we get back to the amount he got before the GI surgery. But getting rid of the extra doses is HUGE. I don't know if he is just doing better or if it is because he is getting platelets every day (versus his usual 4x/week). I don't know if I will wake up tomorrow and he'll be profusely bleeding again but for today he is doing better and I am thankful!

Thank you, Julie, for making such a wonderful dinner tonight. The desserts (yes plural) are heavenly! What a nice surprise. I had time to sit and play a game with the kids after dinner, having saved time from not making it to begin with.

Tomorrow is Abby's neck MRI. She is scared of the IV but I think she'll be fine and just hope that whoever reads it, does so with wisdom.

Brittany is feeling somewhat better. Still exhausted but the Strep throat is gone, and with that the pain.

Oh – and the THREE gold fish were all alive when Kevin came for them today. Not bad, hey?

Saturday, August 21, 2004 9:35 AM

I am sorry that I have not updated in a few weeks. Thank you for checking in on us, despite my lack of writing. It means a lot to me.

Abby's MRI procedure itself went okay. She was absolutely terrified…the top layer of fear being of the IV she needed. But, underneath that I think there were layers and layers of fear about what this MRI meant to her …was this the beginning of her having an illness like her 3 siblings? Thankfully someone with a heart medicated her and she stopped sobbing and was very calm throughout the test. Thankfully, the MRI was read as completely normal. Most important: she has not had any more episodes. We wonder if it was a severe migraine, which she certainly has a strong family history for. I never knew how scared I am about her developing more symptoms like the other 3 until she woke up that morning and could not move. She has been busy playing soccer, creating a magazine with one of her friends for 6th grade girls, going to parties, having friends over…just being a very healthy and happy eleven-year-old. I don't take that for granted.

Brittany is feeling better. She is back to work and probably doing way too much by playing soccer and tennis. She voluntarily stays home enough nights these days that I know she is still not feeling 100% She won't say that. But it is clear she is listening to her body enough to stay home and go to bed early when she starts feeling badly. It is necessary for her survival - not so much because of the mono but because of the Mito disease and I am very proud of her for making what must be a very hard decision. I really cannot imagine how difficult it is for a 17 year old to make that decision.

The boys spent this week in the hospital for their routine intravenous immune globulin (IVIg) treatment. Zachary had a pretty uneventful week except I think he gets very tired of the nurses and me by the end of the week. A 12 year old boy in a room with several females who talk and laugh all the time …no wonder he plays computer and Gameboy all the time. You should see how he has perfected rolling his eyes at us! Poor guy! The nurses and I do get a little silly after a few days in one room together. He had his share of chess matches with Dr. S, Pharmacy Dave, Aunt Maribeth and Uncle David (who were both visiting from their respective corners of the earth this week).

Sammy did not have a good week due to his bleeding. His mouth has been bleeding profusely. It bleeds badly for two days that I can't imagine it will ever stop. My entire world seems to narrow down to giving blood products and cleaning his face, his sheets, his hair. I soak his clothes in Oxy Clean but it never quite gets rid of the stains and sometimes I wonder if I really want to get rid of them. The bleeding eventually stops – so far it always has. There will be a time it does not.

When he is not bleeding I find myself believing that he will be able to go to first grade this year…that he will play with Josie and Jonathon and all the other kids who have loved him so much. Sometimes I wish I did not hope so much ….it makes it all that much harder when the bleeding starts up again. In the hospital, everyone was shocked at how much his mouth bled and I realized how much I have gotten used to. We treated it very aggressively and it stopped on Thursday. This morning it is bleeding. Just a little. Enough to make me realize that the odds of him going to school this year are not in his favor. How will I tell him that he has to stay home? But I cannot expect a school or children for that matter to be okay with a mouth crusted with so much blood that he looks like his lips and gums are black.

The medical director of the blood center came to visit Sam this week. I have not seen him in a while.me. He is the one who allowed us to have blood products at home. At first he didn't want us to but in the end he supported it 150%. He is a good and kind person. He suggested to Peter and me that we have a "hematology care conference" with blood center doctors, hematologist, Peter and I. We had one a year ago. I think it is a great idea to have another one. It is clear to me that everyone is at a loss of what to do, feeling there is nothing left to do, hoping that if we sit down together we'll find a better way to treat Sam. They clearly care a lot about Sam.

However, I know that part of that care conference will involve the question that is rarely spoken – is it is just time to say there is nothing else and is it time to stop some of this treatment? I can't fault them for wondering about that. It is okay to talk about it – Peter and I have a zillion times. But that is with Peter who knows Sam has a life worth living, who understands that my decisions have been thought about endlessly and are not about saving a kid at any cost…. How do I make the others understand, who do not know Sam as well? How do I explain in an hour why we continue to give such complex care to Sam? Right now Sam is handcuffing every member of our family and laughing his head off about it….if they could see that and hear him laugh I would not need any words to explain why it is not time to give up.

Next week Sam's legs are getting casted…he'll get new casts every few days to try to get his feet into a position that he will be able to tolerate wearing his splints and thus maintain his ability to walk.

Thursday, August 26, 2004 7:59 AM

Sam did so awesome getting his casts on. He was very cooperative! We've signed our names and drawn pictures all over them…too bad they have to come off today and he needs new ones. I hope so much this helps him remain able to walk for a LONG time. After the casts and therapy, we went to the gift shop where he picked out another stuffed dog – what a shock! Our house is getting overrun with stuffed dogs.

Pancakes hamster is great. Zach and I brought lunch to Brittany at the sporting goods store she works in on Saturday. The thing is that the Pet store is in the same shopping center. Naturally we had to go into the pet shop and buy another cage and tubes to connect the cages and a few more climbing things for Pancakes. Our $6.99 hamster will soon have a million dollar complex to live in the way we're going.

If all goes well (I don't ever take it for granted that all will go well), 11 year old Abby and I are going out tonight for girls night with a bunch of friends and their daughters. We have tickets to see the show Mama Mia downtown. Before that we are going to have dinner at the Rock Bottom Café. Abby and I can't wait.

Zach has a fever and headache. Typical thing he gets a few days after the IVIG. I sure wish he did not have to feel this way every month. More steroids have helped to a point – the headaches are much less intense but they don't completely seem to erase this post IVIG headache/fever thing he gets.

Sam's central line broke yesterday. Always scary when that happens because a new line = surgery= hemorrhaging for Sam. Thank

God the CVL nurses were able to fix it by cutting off the broken part and re-piecing a new end on.

Sam's Bleeding…well I'll just cut and paste the email I sent to Sam's hematologist and blood bank doctors:

Subject: Sam is NOT bleeding anywhere!

Bet you never thought you'd see that subject line again.

Sam's factor 7a drip is down to 9.6 mg - the lowest he has been able to go in a month!!!!!! and if he does well another 24 hours, I will cut it down again.

He has not needed any 7a boluses since last Thursday!
He is back to 4x/week platelets and 3x/week FFP as of this week.

His gastrostomy has had precisely one quarter- sized spot of blood today on the gauze and his J dressing is spotless!And his mouth!!!!!!!! you saw him so you can appreciate this - it is perfect! not one hint of old or new blood anywhere to be seen. I don't know how long it has been since he has had a mouth that looks like this. He had his picture taken for school last night so I will be sure to show it to all of you when we get it.

Monday, August 30, 2004 6:57 AM

Even railroad tracks.

No run away trains.

Sam's mouth oozing blood – doesn't look too hot but it is not a dangerous bleed. Unfortunately, it is a bleed that will keep him out of school, which starts Wednesday.

Sam is doing well with his casts. At times he is in pain but for the most part he has done really well and seems to be walking more with them on than without. I hope this is because when his feet are in a better position he can actually walk. It gives me hope that if he can keep the splints on he will continue to be able to walk.

Busy busy in our house. Make A Wish called and they are getting everything ready for the Zachary Rec Room. I'm going to wait until we know everything for sure to tell you what will be in there but WOW!!!!! Make A Wish has been so good to our family – first sending all of us to Disney World a few years ago when Sam wished to meet Donald Duck and now this!

The busy stems from the fact that I have to actually clean that basement(aka Zachary's Rec Room) for them to do their part. I am a pack rat. My kids are pack rats. The basement is pretty full!

School starts Wednesday. Abby and Sammy cannot wait. Zachary says he is "fifty percent about school" and Brittany says she is NOT going to be there at 7 am like she is supposed to be.

Tomorrow I am taking the boys to Madison to see a metabolic doctor about some questionable labs the boys have had. I won't bore anyone with the details unless there is something to make of it. We'll see what he says. Peter also called and then faxed the lab results with a letter to the metabolic guy that diagnosed the boys. Hopefully that doctor will help us discern what is concerning and what is not.

Pre-school year meetings for both boys tomorrow afternoon (after we hopefully get home from Madison on time). This is Zach's last year in elementary school – he'll be in 6th grade. Sammy will be in 1st. I so hope Sam gets to school this week or he will be devastated.

Labor Day Sept. 6, 2004

What a rainy day in Wisconsin. However, it is nothing compared to what Grandma, Dad, Patty and the boys have been experiencing in Florida. Thank God for their safety through Hurricane Francis. Dad, hopefully you have been able to get out of the house today ... you were never one to stay inside and in one place for too long!

School has indeed started! WOW! I forget how busy the beginning of the school year is. It took me hours just to fill out the various papers that 4 kids need filled out in order to step foot inside of the school.

Brittany, Zachary and Abby all started on Wednesday. I had to laugh at my oh so cool daughter who had senioritis even before school started. She wore sweats to school the first day and when I asked her why she informed me that she is a senior and does not need to impress anyone! She refused the traditional first day of school picture too. I think it came as a shock to go to school and realize that senior or not, one still has to sit in class and do homework. She seems to like all of her teachers - especially her Honors English teacher. After school she is playing tennis for the school team and soccer for our city club. She continues to work 2 days a week. I guess the mono has been cured. I'd have collapsed by now but she is intent on grabbing all that her senior year has to offer.

Zachary and Abby have a wonderful 6th grade teacher. They are quite impressed that she can speak Spanish, having been born in Puerto Rico. Maybe they'll even learn some Spanish! The day before school I had a meeting with all of the people involved in Zach's education, (specially designed phys-ed, exceptional education teacher, PT, OT, Speech, his aid, his homebound teacher). It is always so heartening to me how they take time before school even starts for him. Anyway, I typically ask the new teacher if they know anything about Zach's diagnosis and they typically say no. I was so touched this year when Mrs. E told me that she had been reading about mito disease. No one has ever done that before.

As always the beginning of the year is hard on Zachary physically. He was exhausted most of the week and on Sunday became very weak even in his arms. He has been taking long naps and looks a bit better today to me. This is good because in science they are making their own rockets and he is so excited to do this.

Abby of course loves school. She was not so happy the first day because of some friendship issues and a new phys-ed teacher. I read her "Alexander and the Terrible No Good Very Bad Day" and she said she was definitely going to move to Australia. But Thursday and Friday were wonderful 6th grade days – she is full of chatter about school and friends. 6th grade is awesome –the oldest kids in the school.

Sam! He did start on Friday! And he lasted from 8:40 until 11:15! That is a record for Sam. When he was done, he was done and it was time to go but he sure liked it when he was there. He loves having his own desk and especially the "drawer" that he can keep things in. Wow he was impressed with that! Having his dearest friend Josie next to him was icing on the cake. This is his friend that I am sure is an angel in disguise - so accepting and empathetic. She stayed in from recess to be with Sam, showed him how to use the library and took him to get a drink of water. Sam went to reading group and lo and behold he LOVED reading group! This is good. On the days that Sam did not go to school, his teacher sent home papers and little notes for him. How thoughtful is that? It really made him feel a part of things.

Medically, Sam is doing ok. Bleeding is the best it has been in months. I keep waiting for the other shoe to drop. But so far he is just not bleeding very much. Last week he went a whole entire week between blood transfusions. That is just amazing. His seizures have been terrible. We increased his Lamictal on Friday and I thought Sunday he seemed better. We shall see. Last night his labs looked like his heart is decompensating again. Sometimes giving him more diuretics than his normal dose helps so we will try this.

The visit to Madison was ok. No big surprises and certainly no cures or amazing treatments. I did not expect that. I just wanted someone to interpret some of the odd results we have gotten back on the boys. It sounds like what has happened is they have developed a secondary metabolic problem called a "fatty acid oxidation defect." In particular something called Methylmalonic Acidemia and Proprionic Acidemia. This represents a worsening of their disease - I knew this but did not want to know it in my heart. They did have some suggestions of things we could try and are supposed to be drawing up a stepwise plan for Peter and me to follow. The doctor seemed to want to drum it into me that none of the suggestions would change things dramatically but they might help in small ways. He was intelligent and very kind but he appeared very overwhelmed with Zach and Sam's complexity. I think he figured he needed to make me understand this is not a curable disease and they are not doing well. That was hard to hear after a while but all in all, I am glad we went and hopefully they follow through with the plan of things we can try in an attempt to tweak things where we can.

I'm sorry this has gotten so long. I need to write more often but life is so crazy in this house these days! Thanks for hanging in there with us.

Thursday, September 9 2004 05:01 AM

Thursday: Sam's labs are getting worse meaning his heart is not compensating very well right now. I'm worried. He is breathing so hard when he does anything at all. We also had to increase his Factor 7a drip back up - bleeding too much again from his mouth.

70

On a good note - Sam just loves first grade even without "playtime" and is working so hard to learn. I am so incredibly proud of him!

Saturday, September 11, 2004 8:29 AM

Sam's labs still "critical" according to our lab. At least they are no worse. His breathing remains very audible and he seems to be spending a lot of effort expiring (breathing out). This is especially notable with any activity. In addition, his blood cholesterol has really dropped. I realize this sounds like a good thing but our bodies do need a certain amount of cholesterol and too low is bad. He only drops it this dramatically when he is about to have or is in the midst of "Mitochondrial decompensation." This means that his body is using more energy than it is able to make and deliver to the various parts of his body. Last night he began to have fresh gastrointestinal bleeding – seemingly out of nowhere.

It is all so concerning but I suppose I have seen it happen enough times that I should not be surprised. What always hurts the most is that it seems to always happen when he is at his best. Here he has been going to school, enjoying learning, not bleeding…last weekend he even went to the library, out to dinner with us, played outside. All these wonderful, normal 7 year old things to do and then without warning he starts decompensating. It is like being on a roller coaster and wondering when the coaster will rush downhill or flip you upside down…never knowing when it will come but always anticipating it, fearing it. I sit here and wonder why – what triggered it? Was it staying up 30 min extra the other night? Was it going to school? What did I do wrong? Could I have seen this coming? The guilt is useless but I'm a mom and I just feel so responsible. At the same time, even if I knew it was from going to school or playing outside, I cannot imagine changing one thing. Those are the things he finds so meaningful and without them, his care would feel so pointless.

At any rate, we decided to increase his diuretics, which should give his heart a break. He will be admitted Monday – or sooner if things get worse - and at that time we can assess his heart pressures. We'll also do a kidney ultrasound, as his kidneys seem like they are struggling as well.

71

Zachary had a pretty tough week. Tired and weak, struggling to walk, climb stairs, even lift his arms. Episodes of dizziness and blurred vision. He missed 1 of his 3 days of school. However, after a questionable start to the day Friday he was able to stay at school until 1 PM. His goal is 1:30 so this was very very good. He told me he had a great day at school! Thankful for this small but HUGE gift.

I went to a good conference yesterday and heard a pediatrician from Massachusetts talk about caring for kids with special health care needs. Inspiring. Work is crazy. The house is over filled with things I need to take care of.

Next week the hospital all week and that "hematology care conference" which is heavy on my mind. (This is a meeting of Peter and me with Sam's hematologist and the 2 blood bank medical directors - all of whom control the Factor 7a and blood supply). Sam's care IS expensive and he DOES use a lot of resources BUT can a dollar limit be put on his life? I don't think so and I so hope they do not ask us to do that.

Pancakes hamster is doing awesome. Sam has given him a middle and last name – Pancakes Waffles Syrup (naturally!)

Saturday, September 18, 2004 9:24 PM

The boys and I are home from the hospital. It seemed like a long week to me, even though it was fairly busy there. I have been pretty tired – not sure why but need to get some blood work done that is months overdue.

Zachary went in feeling pretty weak and tired but after a day of rest in bed he was perkier and by mid-week he sure seemed good. Today he was back to feeling tired again but not nearly as bad as before the hospitalization. He struggled more than he has in a long time with his IVIG infusion – pretty low blood pressures most of the week and in fact we had to hold many of his normal medications for high blood pressure. By Thursday he was back to his baseline though.

Zach had a dexa scan done (a full body bone density study that looks at percentages of lean mass (muscle) and fat as well as bone.). The results were not calculated yet BUT his bone age showed that his bones have only grown 4 months in the last 12 months. I am not sure why this is as he gets nightly growth hormone injections. This may indicate that he has become resistant to the growth hormone – which is not good. I need to call his endocrinologist this week and find out what he thinks.

Zach also had a liver CT scan and still has what is called "Fatty liver" as well as an enlarged liver. But it is not changed from 12 months ago, which makes me feel positive. We give him an infusion 2x/day of another medication to protect his liver and I'd like to believe that this means it is helping.

Today Zachary helped Abby make some signs for her campaign: she is running for student council rep for 6th grade. It was sweet of him to help her. Speaking of Miss Abigail - she had to go to Madison for a soccer game - but worked on her speech after she came home. Abby had a busy week while we were gone. On Tuesday she read the book we had made about Sammy for his kindergarten class last year called "Sam I Am" which explains in very simple language some of the differences about Sam and then points out how he is the same as his classmates. She read it to his new first grade class and brought his bear in with the central line and tubes and answered the kids' questions. I really am proud of her for doing this without me there! On Wednesday she was chosen to be one of the school reps to go to the parade for the Hamm Brothers (Olympic gymnasts). They are from Waukesha. Tuesday and Thursday she stayed after school to help her teacher make a website for the 6th grade – this is a project she will do all year, I think. She loves this project.

Sam is doing well. His bleeding is ok. Not perfect but we are increasing his Factor 7a drip and I have faith it will be perfect for him to go to school on Tuesday. He was such a good boy at the hospital – which is so hard when you are stuck in one bed at the age of 7 for 5 days. On Tuesday he also had a Dexa scan and his bones show absolutely no growth in 12 months. I don't know what to make of that. I told him if he was as still as a statue for the test he could go to the gift shop and so we went and he picked out an orange care bear, which he has slept with every night.

His kidney ultrasound showed the same diseased kidneys he always has. The right kidney keeps getting bigger (not good). We put a Foley catheter in and I think this will help to temporarily reduce the size of his bladder so that urine does not back up into his kidneys. Peter says it can come out Tuesday am so he can go to school without it. He is very excited to go to school. Little by little his labs have improved on the increased diuretics, which help to pull fluid out so his heart does not have to work so hard. His heart continues to need more support but thank God that support helps him. He has new casts on – they should be more durable. They are flexible fiberglass. We are all impressed with the positive changes that have come about from this casting therapy.

The hematology care conference was fine. I should not have been so worried. The main purpose seemed to be that the blood center docs just wanted to go over what we were doing and have a group discussion if we need to change anything. They were very clear that they did not necessarily think we should change anything but they just felt that periodic group dialogue is crucial when someone is on this much support. I agree and feel bad that I allowed myself to think of it as an "us versus them" meeting. It was anything but and I appreciated their ideas and questions. There are some changes we may make based on the talks we had but right now we are not doing anything until we can get Sam to bleed a little less than he has in the past few days.

Brittany got a beautiful dress for her homecoming dance – it is Saturday 9/25. She just brought home 4 pairs of shoes for us to vote on. She will look beautiful as always.

Lou and Brittany almost lost Pancakes while we were away. They put him in his ball per Sam and my strict instructions to exercise him every night and he got out. They told me they were considering setting a mousetrap to catch him to teach him a lesson. MEAN! Fortunately, they found him. Poor baby hamster! I'm sneaking him into the hospital next admission.

Sunday, September 26, 2004 1:41 PM

Another busy week but a fairly good one for both Zachary and Sam. My sister has been here all week, which makes thing extra special for everyone.

Zachary made it to school each day. Tuesday was an exciting day because he was able to launch the rocket he had made. His class had all launched their rockets the week before while he was in the hospital. His teacher – so thoughtful – kept the launcher so that when Zach came back he could launch his for his class to see.

Sam was also able to go to school three days this week and his bleeding has been very minimal. I was not so sure that would happen, as even Monday he was bleeding quite a bit. But Peter had me give him some extra Factor 7a and it did the trick – so off to school Sam went. On his second day day of school his sweet little friend Josie told him, "you look awesome." I asked him what he said. "I told her hi" was his reply. On Friday he reported to me that *he* told Josie she looked awesome. He was very pleased with himself.

On the center of our dining room table is a stalk of celery in water and every day Sam measures to see how much water the celery is "drinking." What I love is the excitement he has for such a simple life event – a plant taking in water. People ask me if it is a burden to have to go to school with Sam, to have to do so much "home" work with him and I say that yes, sometimes I do feel weighed down with it all - I just don't have one more minute to do one more thing. But invariably my time at school and helping Sam with his work causes me to stop and look at life through a child's eyes, learning anew what we adults take for granted. Wow – baby mice are NOT born with fur and isn't it amazing that a tadpole turns into a frog and what a beautiful mind image of a plant reaching out to the sunlight and gathering it in to create the nourishment that the plant needs to grow and thrive. Sam's friends Josie and Ben explained to me a few times (Ok I was a little slow) about a seed coat and the pride they took in teaching ME was humbling. The smallest things become amazing through these children's eyes and many times a week I think how lucky I am to get to go through school again, and to look at life through the eyes of a child – my child, Sam.

Likewise there are the days of thinking, "I just want to be a mom" which translates into I am tired of giving blood products and medicine all day, tired of charting my use of Factor 7a, of practicing the word "the" for the 1000th time with Sam, making sure the school has everything set up for Zach's field trip, calling in refills for prescriptions at 3 different pharmacies, reviewing our weekly home care order, changing dressings, making decisions that have the power to change so little or change so much. I feel guilty about not reading enough with the kids, not taking them to the symphony and art museum, missing the girls' soccer games, too much processed food, not enough outside time.

BUT then it hits me again and again that I AM a mom and no one can take that away from me. No life circumstance can erase that I gave birth to these children. I love them and I am their mom. How exactly does one define mom? I have come to realize that it is defined by the child's needs and just because I have to meet needs that I never imagined my children having, taking on roles that other moms don't have to take on, does not mean I am not a mom. Part of being their mom IS adapting what I imagined being a perfect mom meant to being a perfect mom for what they need and who they are. Part of being Zach and Sam's mom IS all those medical things but does that make me less of a mom?

I have read so many books about having to adjust your dreams and dream new dreams when one has a child with a disability or a chronic illness. But little is said about adjusting your dreams from being the mom that you imagined yourself or were to being the mom that you are. I may never be able to take my girls on overnight trips to Chicago, or take my children to all the wonderful cities and national parks in the US that my dad took my siblings and me to. Sometimes, I have to stay home with one child while my sister and mom watch my other child play soccer. I may never be part of the PTO or be able to help out at the school Ice Cream Social. But this week I got to see my oldest off to her homecoming dance and I had the honor of her asking me to help her with her college application essay. On Sunday I helped Abby with her student council speech and saw her shining smile when she won. At school on Tuesday, I was present to watch Zachary's rocket get launched. I had time to read to Sam nearly every night before he went to bed. So while it is true that I spend a lot of my time being a nurse and a teacher, a researcher and secretary.... in all those roles I am still and will always be a mom to 4 unique, special individuals – Zachary, Abby, Brittany and Sam. They are my greatest gift.

Wednesday, September 29, 2004 10:40 PM

Monday night, while reading Sam a book, one of his central lines just simply broke. I have absolutely no idea how it happened.

Fortunately, I was able to clamp it and thus avoid a trip to the ER that night. On Tuesday morning I took him to the hospital and the central line nurses repaired it. I figured that was the end of that.

Last night he told us he was running away, tried to run a few steps, fell down and smacked his mouth. Bleeding -again.

This morning he woke up with slurred speech. I assumed he had pooled blood in his mouth but even after cleaning it he was still slurring.

His home bound teacher came and we could all see that he was just plain exhausted. He has been doing so well with Judy but today he could barely get through his lessons. He looked awful but he insisted he was GOING to school today. (His homebound teacher comes from 8:10 to 9:10 and then he goes to school at 9:30 and stays as long as he can last).

When his teacher left he started shaking. His temp was 94-95.

Needless to say, blankets were thrown in the dryer and he was bundled inside of them. I called Peter and he had me culture the lines, do labs and start him on 3 new intravenous antibiotics.

The labs looked pretty bad. His body is "third spacing" which means that the fluid that is supposed to be in his blood vessels is leaking into his tissues. This leaves too little fluid in his blood vessels, which makes the blood pressure go down. The heart tries to compensate and of course his cannot be asked to do that. The kidneys do not like this situation because they are not getting what they need. It creates a domino-like effect of problems throughout the body.

My guess is he has a blood infection from the break of his central line. Peter said he could also be septic from the mouth cut when he fell - there are so much bacteria in the mouth that can easily get into the blood via an open wound. Or perhaps he is just sick because he did not get his nap yesterday. Stress of any kind is so hard on Sam. It's hard to know why this happened and in the end I suppose it does not matter.

His temperature is up to 96 now. If there is any way possible for me to get him out of the house tomorrow I am taking him to school, even if for 15 minutes. The fire truck is coming to school and he has been so excited all week. I am hopeful the antibiotics do their job and that he can at least see the fire truck and a fire fighter even if he has to sit in his stroller.

Zach is doing okay but so tired.

Saturday, October 2, 2004 11:20 PM

YES! Sam did get to the see the fire fighters! He is doing a bit better. Not perfect in terms of his heart, lots of gagging and retching but better. Zachary's 6th grade camp trip is on Tuesday and Wednesday. He will not be staying overnight but he will be going (as will I). My hope is that he can do what he wants to do and that he has fun with the kids in a less structured atmosphere. As soon as he comes home we will be off to the hospital for about 5 days so that the boys can get their IVIG. It may be awhile until I update but the below is long enough to be a few weeks worth of writing. It IS long but my heart and mind have truly been overwhelmed in the last few weeks, nearly blinded by the goodness that still exists in every corner of this world. This is for all of you:

Certainty. That value of certainty has been debated for months now between the Democrats and the Republicans. I don't think it is a secret where I fall on this. Albert Einstein has said, "The important thing is not to stop questioning." So I question – a lot--and I place great emphasis on teaching my children to question and not be afraid to change their path. However, there are a few things I am certain of. One of those is that no matter what course this disease may take, no matter how much destruction it continues to leave in its path – Sam and Zach, and indeed our entire family has been loved. That is what I wake up in the morning knowing and what I go to bed at night knowing. It is the light that gives me hope. My certainty is all of you.

Doubt thou the stars are fire;
Doubt that the sun doth move;
Doubt truth to be a liar;
But never doubt I love.
--Shakespeare from *Hamlet*, 2.2.123-6

Bethesda Elementary school staff: So little time for what they need to get done, yet taking the time to make school be all that it can be for not only the boys but Abby as well. I understand that the law says accommodations have to be made, but there is a difference

78

between making accommodations because the law says so and making them because one wants to. Nurturing Abby, rearranging class schedules for both boys, a wall full of cards from classmates for Zach, countless hours communicating lessons and plans so that the boys can be both "homebound" and school placed, finding the perfect toys to use during therapy that will not only help Sam but engage Sam and bring smiles to his face - the message has always been we want you here and we will do whatever we can with you, for you.

Friday, Sam was the student in first grade that got to bring "the bag" with six objects about himself to share with the class. He packed and repacked this bag for 5 days – 2 favorite books, (One his teacher had bought him because it made her think of him!), a picture of Pancakes Waffles Toast Syrup the hamster, Pancake's "hamster car", Sam's baby picture, picture of what he wants to be for Halloween – the Green Lantern, and a stuffed dog that Ione let him borrow. He sat on a chair, at first not sure what to do. I helped him hold up a book he had brought and he showed it to all of his friends. I don't have words to adequately paint a picture of this ....of the sounds of little children asking him questions about his hamster, telling him how they liked Halloween too, laughing at how cute he was when he was a baby ...and Sam looking at the kids with this smile on his face that just shined so bright. After school he said "Mama the kids really liked my stuff didn't they?" "Yes Sam – and they really like you too."

Little Joey - carrying Sam's chair for him to reading group, back to his desk. Hugging him good-bye. How does a child learn such compassion at the age of six?

Judy and Stephanie – homebound teachers. At night Judy makes books for Sam on her computer. She understands him and works with him through his many moods and illnesses. In July she and her daughter Elizabeth brought "Money." Elizabeth's new puppy to visit. Stephanie, rearranging her schedule to come to the hospital and teach Zach when he is inpatient and then rearranging it again when he is home and we need her at a different time.

Peter: His devotion to making life count, to making the phrase "quality of life" actually mean something for the boys is never ending. I cannot write the words or compose music that could ever pay tribute to the difference he has made for my boys. Sam likes to call Peter – usually to say I love you and something he did that day. "Hi Dr. H., I saw a fire truck and I love you. Bye." He leaves it on Peter's voice mail. When Peter answers the message I give Sam the phone to listen and he smiles and laughs. For the next 3 days he repeats back to me what Dr. H said. "Dr. H said he saw a fire engine and he said he loves me too!"

Jackie, Katherine, Chris and Amy T too: Sammy's therapists since he was a baby; Zachary's friends and therapist forever it seems. MY FAMILY in every sense of the word. I could not do this without their love, ability to make me laugh, willingness to cry with me, unending help, support…there is a book I could fill simply with a list of memories I have of them and what they have done for us. Katherine, I mean Kath and Jackie – Sam's very best friends in all of this world.

Shawn S – our intern from July. He finds out when Zach is inpatient so that he can come visit. I can't contemplate that kind of kindness. Interns are crazy busy. Shawn has a wife and a child. But he makes time for Zach – to play Yugio cards, to look at his school books with him, to just talk. The selflessness is overwhelming.

Our many physicians – always willing to help by email or phone – coming to consult in the hospital so that we have virtually eliminated all outpatient clinics visits. Dr. G – juggling Sammy's dogs for him and Sam laughing so hard he gets the hiccups. If Sam is asleep he comes back day after day until he can find him awake and juggle for him. Dr. S, our hematologist - no matter how many times Sam bleeds, each and every time he emails or calls and says, "I am so sorry." Just a few words but in those few words are his heart.

Our IICU Nurses/Staff and Pharmacists who asked the question a long time ago – "How can we do this better?" and have never stopped asking. Every month it is a new thing, a new idea….always trying to make their admissions go more smoothly. They rearrange their own schedules to be there when the boys are inpatient. I watch them care for the boys and it strikes me that this is truly what CARE means – it means doing everything you can possibly do for your patient because you believe that their life and their family are of untold value. I never thought I would say that a hospital felt like home – but in so many ways it does. Not because of the frequency that we are there but because of the people.

Internet friends: I would have laughed six years ago if I read about someone referring to a person they met on the Internet as "a friend."

But I do have friends that I have never met. Friends, who have loved my family without "meeting" us. At least once a month, gifts and cards arrive for the boys, every day there are countless prayers said and every night I read my email: "Is Sam better? Did he see the fire engine? Did Zach make it to school? Did Abby win for student council? How is Brittany feeling? Did you make that appointment at the doctor for you? " And the answers matter – because they really have been hoping and praying that Sam saw that fire engine.

Blood bank staff who have to go through many extra steps in order for me to be able to give the blood products at home. Not once have they complained or made me feel like I was making their day harder, even though it does add more time to their day. Our courier, never complaining no matter what time of day I call, no matter how many times a day I call, surprising us with frozen custard, a new cooler for labs, presents on the kids' birthdays.

Nancy: Piano lessons at home! My friends are all jealous. Who gets to have a piano teacher come to their home these days? We do because a few years ago Nancy decided that was something she could do for us that would make our life a little easier. I cannot imagine Abby's life without piano – she expresses herself minutes and hours each day through her playing which would be impossible without Nancy's gift of time to us.

Janet: The most unselfish person I know in this world. Calling every night when we are in the hospital, encouraging me through some of my darkest moments. My model of friendship, motherhood, love and compassion.

My colleagues at work: It's unbelievable to work with people that understand if I cannot come in or have to leave because of the boys. People who pick up for me when I need help, who never hold it against me when I am in my "focus don't bother me" mood. There has never been a day that they have not asked me how the boys are doing. If the boys come into the center they pile out of their offices to say hello as if two celebrities just walked into the center.

Ione and Chris – angels who care for the boys on the days that I work. I walk away from the boys and I know that they are not just being taken care of but they are being loved. As they're dashing out the door to get to our house, how do they remember to put a stuffed dog in their car for Sam to "borrow"? I marvel when they ask me

81

"what else can I do?" Sometimes I come home and they are sitting on the floor playing a game with the boys. Never have they complained that the dishes are still all over the counter from breakfast or once again, the trash is overflowing. When Sam has a bad day they come back the next day. So careful and so very thoughtful, they make it possible for me to take time away. I think I would sink if I did not have that time.

Katie and Ralph from the Blood Center – they brought Katie's dog out to visit Sam last week! A real live dog for Sam. I wonder what kind of people volunteer to do this at the end of a long day? They don't live anywhere near us at all. They went home late because they wanted to bring a smile to a little boy's face. They did! Ralph brought me some sand dollars and seashells as a reminder of the ocean that I miss so much. He showed me how a sand dollar when opened, has five doves inside. I never knew that. Five tiny little doves, symbolizing the spread of good will and peace – how true.

Donors – Katie told me that Sam's platelet donors ask about him all the time. Very little information can be shared of course. I thought about that all night….these special people, so invested in my child, without ever having seen his sweet face. I hope they know beyond a doubt what life – what joy – they allow for Sam.

My neighbors, my friends, who bring us dinner. Their lives are so busy, they have jobs and families and activities and they bring us dinner! I don't remember the last time I actually went to one of our neighborhood get-togethers, but still they faithfully call, letting me know that they think of me, have not forgotten or given up. It means everything to me. Do all of you know what a gift this is to be able to spend time with my children instead of cooking?

My Family: Where do I begin? Mom, taking the time to visit the kids so many afternoons. Understanding where Sam is at on any particular day, watching Justice League for the 100th time if that is what Sam wants to do. Dad – taking the time from his own children to fly to WI and be with mine. Just sitting in the hospital room with us, bringing me non-hospital coffee, newspapers, playing chess with Zach, taking the girls out to dinner. Frank – taking time to play chess with Zach, surprising the kids with frozen custard. Mike and Elaine and Maribeth and David – taking the time to "just be" with the kids, bringing us pizza, food shopping for me, doing the errands that I am

82

always behind on, taking Abby to the symphony, playing with the boys....the kids adore and love all four of you so much. Sean -sending us our gifts from the ocean ...always remembering what the ocean means to all of us.

And to all those I have not named. Thank you. Thank you for making soup and cookies. Thank you for filling a card with stickers for Sam. Thank you for watching Abby when I am not home, for taking her to soccer and girl scouts. Thank you for donating your money to the hospital and UMDF. Thank you for donating your blood. Thank you for bringing me books and magazines, for sending me flowers.

Thank you for praying and hoping and caring.

To rephrase what Shakespeare so beautifully wrote,

Sometimes I doubt that the stars are fire;
I doubt if the sun doth move;
I doubt truth to be a liar;
But never I doubt that you have loved.

Tuesday, October 12, 2004 9:33 AM

Zachary had a new CVL line placed Monday. It went in easy enough but it was apparently quite difficult to remove the old one. Our surgeon questioned whether there has been some inflammatory process going on, as the old one was literally cemented into his vein and skin. Thus, a few extra incisions had to be made, albeit tiny ones that should not cause bleeding. Unfortunately Zach IS bleeding – not profusely but a quiet ooze. This is disconcerting and I cannot help but be frightened, given Sam's insidious onset of a bleeding disorder that has now become his most life threatening issue. Right now we are home which I regret. I wonder if walking upstairs so soon after surgery is what caused this. He was fine last night after the surgery – thus discharged. The bleeding of course started after we were home. Waiting to talk with the surgeon and see what to do or whether to just watch it and hope it stops. Zachary is worried that he will never catch up on his homework. What a tremendously wonderful kid he is!

By the way he had an awesome time on his 6th grade camping trip. Just awesome! Archery, canoeing, fishing, chemistry, cutting trees with saws.... opportunities that he has never had before. His success and ability to participate in these activities was directly related to the help and support of the teachers and camp staff. I was so sad I forgot my camera because the site of one of his teachers helping him with archery was touching beyond belief.

Sam had a sinus and facial CT scan yesterday to see what is causing the mouth bleeding and if things have gotten worse since June. Some findings were stable from June yet now seem to be in the bone. There were other new findings. A lesion that the radiologist still had not figured out when we left. Sinuses that don't look perfect and everyone assumes to be blood filled. Gums that are so overgrown from bleeding and re-bleeding that they are actually obstructing his ability to take in breaths.

I admit I'm tired of everyone telling me not to worry about this because after all, "there is nothing that can be done anyway." In a "normal kid" they'd biopsy and aspirate all these cysts and lesions. In Sam it is out of the question because of his bleeding issues. I understand that but to not worry ...I think that is a little farfetched for anyone to expect me to take this all in stride and not wonder and worry. It seems to me we're assuming a lot...and again I understand we cannot do anything but assume it is non-cancerous because we can't biopsy. Yet, I am frightened for Sam. More than anything, I hear his speech get less intelligible as does his speech pathologist and I know that whatever these things are in his jaw and sinuses they are interfering with his ability to be understood and that is a huge quality of life issue to me.

Worrying does not make it better. We cannot fix this no matter what it is. But acknowledgement that this is another "attack" on my vibrant child's life, that being helpless to make it better is cruel punishment to a mother, that is what would be nice. I think sometimes there is scant understanding that telling someone not to worry often makes one feel less supported and alone – not more.

Friday, October 15, 2004 8:24 PM

I was scared. But Zach stopped bleeding and even went back to school today!

Sam went to school all three days this week and seems to just be full of energy.

My weekend plans are about as exciting as they come- to try to clean the basement so we can start knocking out walls to accommodate all of the wonderful things that Make A Wish is getting Zachary for the Zach Game Room.

Taking the kids out for Halloween costume shopping is a must do too!

Have an awesome weekend!

Wednesday, October 20, 2004 9:24 PM

Talking with Sam on Tuesday morning:

Sam: "I figured out the one way I can get to ocean city! I can imagine myself there!"

He gave me a hug, "Don't worry Mama- I'll put you in my dream too so you can come with me."

Sam is doing relatively well. He seems like he may be getting sick – just a bit out of sorts for the last day or so. Still, I am thrilled to see some of the things he is doing. Able to walk up the stairs - albeit slowly and with help but up the stairs nonetheless. A few months ago we wondered if he would be walking the next month. The serial casting has worked miracles. He won't be walking down the block anytime soon but to even be able to walk from 1 room in our house to the next is a gift compared to where he was this summer. In school, he continues to try hard. He seems so lost sometimes and then out of the blue he will let me see that he is taking in so much more than he is able to let us know. Yesterday, while watching Power Rangers I heard him tell himself, "1 + 2 + 2 Power Rangers = 5 Rangers and that is an odd number."

Zach continues to struggle mainly with weakness and fatigue. So tired just walking or drawing and I imagine this is hard for him or will be soon enough. His attitude remains so positive and cheerful. I wonder how can someone be so good and sweet. Every night he reads chapter books to Sam. I'm not always sure how much Sam understands but he loves to lay in bed with Zach and listen to his big brother read to him. Zach's patience with Sam is unfailing and his love for him is so forgiving and deep.

85

Brittany continues to work hard on her college applications. She has already submitted applications to University of Wisconsin – Madison, University of Minnesota - Twin Cities and Case Western in Ohio. She and I went to a college fair a few weeks ago and now she is working on apps to Loyola in Chicago, Marquette, St Louis U and U of Illinois. Her diligence and discipline through this process is quite impressive. There has never been a time I have had to tell her to work on this. She has researched the schools, talked intelligently with the admission staff, and made sure she has everything in order. Its hard to believe she is almost 18. I feel like I am still the 1st time, 20-year-old mother I was when she was born. It is amazing to realize that she is practically as old as I was when she was born.

I have not been feeling well again this week. It seems that everyone I know has this virus with chills and achiness and fatigue. Zach told me tonight that the sun shrinks some each year. Maybe that s why I can never get warm!

Next week is a hospital week. Our fall schedule is filled with every 3 weeks hospitalizations. Between the boys' doctor's times out of town and things we wanted to be home for like Thanksgiving and Zach's camp trip and Halloween, it just ended up this way. After Thanksgiving we should be able to get back to our every 4-week schedule for a while.

Saturday, October 30, 2004 9:11 AM

We are home from the hospital! It was really nice to see the girls and sleep in my own bed last night (and to see little Pancakes still in his cage!)

Dinner ended up a Bush v Kerry debate – I hope our household survives until Tuesday night. After that some of us will be in mourning while the others walk around with big smirky smiles on their faces. I sure hope Abby and I are the ones smirking.

Our basement walls were knocked out this past week. Electrician today. Cable Monday. New walls this week! Then we can proceed with all the aesthetic things that need to be done for Zachary's Make A Wish. I think it will be done before Christmas without a doubt!!!!!

Zachary's CVL site had re-started bleeding right before we went into the hospital. It is swollen and bruised. I put a pressure dressing on it and when Peter lifted it up a few days later I was happy to see that it had not changed. Not better but definitely not bleeding any more into the tissue. He continues to get frequent nosebleeds and spontaneous bruises so bleeding is an issue for him now. Thankfully the line site seems to be stopped. They say it may take weeks for the swelling and bruising to go away and it is painful to touch for Zach again -just thankful it stopped.

When we arrived at the hospital Monday am we walked into a room that was decorated for Halloween, courtesy of Carrie, Zach's primary RN at CHW. There were gifts for the boys and even candy for me!!!! It was so neat because I had just finished lamenting that we had forgotten our Halloween lights to decorate the room with and then we walked into this very festive room! So sweet and thoughtful!

On Wednesday Zach had a pass to leave the hospital in order to go to school for the Halloween Parade. He is Reptile Man this year – something he created which is really just so Zach! It took him days to make his mask – Anne the art therapist at the hospital gave some advice but he did all of the work on it. The rest of the time at the hospital Zach was quite busy drawing and writing a comic book story about Reptile Man. He has a list of those who would like to purchase his first issue – what an entrepreneur!

Thursday brought a visit from Zach's 6th grade teacher and really neat books for the boys. I was not feeling well at the time and missed her. Zach told me about 10 times that his teacher came to visit - it obviously meant a lot to him. Friday, Sam's old speech therapist came and played games with him and the speech therapist that took over for her when she left – it was so nice to see Amy.

Sam's doing ok. He scared the nurses a lot on Monday night when he went into his shock mode. Blood pressures very low (60/30 ish), no pupil reaction to light, no pain response, could not wake him up. He does this when he needs to conserve energy – kind of like a bear hibernating almost. His heart just cannot handle a higher blood pressure and he sort of shuts his body down. Peter and I understand this well enough but the staff doesn't - typically that would earn a kid a trip to the ICU. Tuesday he slept most of the day but by Wednesday he was back to himself. Thursday he started running a fever, so who knows what is up with him?

I talked with Sam's anesthesiologist Friday. He is a very honest, straight, forward man and I have come to trust him because he is so careful and wise with Sam when Sam needs anesthesia. The question Peter and I had for him was what options will there be to establish an airway for Sam if he has a respiratory arrest given the swelling tongue and gums that are impacting his airway. We talked about what might happen, whether intubation would even be possible, what other airways might be established, the consequences of all of that, etc.... It's a lot to absorb but as this doctor said, "In an emergency we are probably going to all look at you and say, 'Anne what do you want us to do?' and it would be a horrific thing if we had never talked to you about this and helped you to think about it ahead of time." He is right.

In the meantime, we all agree that prevention is paramount. Mouth bleeding leads to more swelling and choking. Thus we're going to have almost a no tolerance approach to mouth bleeding before we increase Sammy's Factor 7a. In the past we would let his mouth bleed to a certain point before we increased the factor –not anymore.

Trick or treating tomorrow!!!!!! I sure hope Sam decides what to be before 5 PM when we go out.   Remember to vote on Tuesday!

Tuesday, November 2, 2004 1:40 PM

Sunday night while trick or treating Sam asked to get out of his stroller and walk "with the other kids" (Zach, Abby and friends).

When I got him out of his stroller he could not stand on his left foot. Assuming it was a spasm, that night I have him extra Valium. However the pain got worse, not better. He was up during the night crying and by the morning, the simple act of putting his sock on was too painful.

The foot did not have any obvious swelling and there was not an injury or event I can trace this back to. It reminded me of his elbow joint bleed and his calf muscle bleed. This is something seen in kids with hemophilia - not that he has hemophilia - his bleeding problems are far worse it seems than that.

X ray this am shows it is definitely not fractured. He has such a tiny foot and thin bones that a fracture would not hide according to the radiologist. A swelling was seen in the soft tissue on the top of the foot, which is likely a bleed. The radiologist said it would be very painful for Sam to have anything there.

He does not want to do much of anything but lay on the couch. He is not crabby but he hurts to sit or move. My heart aches for him. We thought immobilizing it would be good but the problem is his splint and cast require him to push his foot into a certain position and he cannot do that right now.

Please keep him in your thoughts. I can handle a lot with courage but his pain rips me apart.

Zach came home from school slightly early - his aid said he is exhausted. I hope that is all it is.

Friday, November 5, 2004 10:02 PM

Sam is doing better!

I gave him minimal pain medicine today and he complained very little about his foot hurting. He still is unable to bear weight on that foot. I am not sure if he is just scared or if he really cannot do it. He tried to several times but just could not, so I don't think it is as simple as fear. It will all take some time I am sure.

He's been such a good boy all week. Not too much fun to be on a couch for days on end with your leg up on a pillow but he complained very little about it. Today he was the most ornery and I take that as a sign of feeling better. He misses school so much! His class sent home a wonderful card. It had a picture of the sun and said "Sam's smile is like the sunshine." And "We miss you!" Inside each of the kids drew a tiny little turkey and signed their names. He took it to bed with him "so I can look at it when I wake up."

Zach had one of his tired weeks. Low grade post IVIG fevers and just general feelings of weakness and fatigue along with a lot of blurry vision. Hopefully this weekend will bring rest and a better week ahead for him.

Work is crazy busy right now – I've missed so much with these frequent hospitalizations and am unfortunately bringing too much home. But, on the other hand lots of exciting things. Last week the director of resident education submitted a proposal with my name as first author for us to present a workshop in Washington D.C. in May 2005. It would be about our experiences starting up our special needs rotation for the residents and helping other medical education programs that would like to do the same. Also, Abby and I were asked to give the keynote presentation in April 2005 at the Wisconsin Circles of Life Conference – audience of about 650! She is excited and not one bit scared – what an amazing 11 year old! This coming Friday one of our hospital nurses and I are part of a panel presentation about partnerships. We will be talking about how we have worked together to create a system of care for the boys that really works when they are inpatient. I am so glad that finally these nurses will be getting some recognition for all that they do for the boys.

I am hoping for a productive weekend. No relaxing unfortunately because I have so much to do. But just having Sammy feeling a bit better, being at home and a forecast of sunny autumn days is a lot to be thankful for. On Sunday Zachary and Abby will be playing the piano at their semi-annual recital. I cannot think of anything more inspiring to do. This is a recital that features the students of their teacher who is a music therapist. To watch a child sing who cannot talk very well, to see a child laboriously play a tune on the piano with one finger who cannot walk or talk, to see children who are so often shunned and made to feel different shining and in the limelight and most of all to see their smiles, their joy, their parents' pride and all of our collective tears at times…these music celebrations humble me to my very soul.

Sunday, November 14, 2004 11:06 PM

We will be in the hospital this week.
We increased Sam's Factor 7a drip early last week - his mouth looks wonderful. It does not bleed. He is beginning to walk again – very tentatively but taking steps all the same. He obviously needed this much Factor 7a but I don't think we can keep him on this much forever.

I just wish it were not so expensive. It makes everyone crazy about how much we use. I am disgusted at what the drug company charges to make it and that they do not give any kind of discount for the amount Sam uses. No one uses as much as Sam or for as long as he has. It is unheard of. We have probably sent those drug reps, their entire office and all of their distant family to Hawaii at least several times by now.

I attended Sam's IEP Thursday. IEP = Individualized Education Plan. His entire educational team and I meet once a year and review his progress, his strengths and challenges and set goals for him for the next 12 months. Sometimes it is a little overwhelming to hear all of his challenges but more than anything what struck me on Thursday was that that he is very loved by the staff. One of my biggest fears has been that he would be held back at the end of first grade if he does not know how to read. It was such a relief to find out that they will not do that –they feel it is crucial that he stay with his friends.

Abby and I went shopping for a few hours Saturday. It was so nice to spend some time with her.

It's been a long week. One more week of school and then the kids are off the entire week of Thanksgiving. It will be nice to slow down a little.

Saturday, November 20, 2004 9:28 AM

The boys and I are home and everyone is in pretty good shape and quite definitely very good spirits. School is out for all of next week (a Waukesha school system oddity) so energy is flying high in our house. Although I would love the kids to have a few more school days for educational reasons – I love how having the week off turns Thanksgiving into a much-anticipated holiday on the scale of Christmas sans the presents. It is wonderful to see the kids so excited about simple things - just being home, extended family coming, playing the piano or chess with relatives, decorating the house for Christmas. And truly Thanksgiving should be such a cherished, looked forward to holiday in our house, for we have so many things and people to be thankful for.

My sister Maribeth and brother David will be flying in from their respective homes – Delaware and Colorado. Mike and Elaine will make the great trip west from White Fish Bay. Mom and Frank will be flying home from Florida with Francis and all will join us. Hopefully, Brittany's friend Prasanna will be a part of our family this weekend as well. This is the only time of the year I get to see my brothers and sister at the same time, so I am really looking forward to it. Lots of great political discussions – we thrive on such things, strange family that we are.

Brittany called me at the hospital Friday morning. Her school had early release and she came home to find that the mailman had come early. She was accepted into the honors program at University of Minnesota – Twin Cities! She was on cloud nine. At this time this is her first choice school although we need to visit a few places once she gets her acceptance letters. (I have no doubt she will).

Hospital news: Sam's left leg had to be re-casted as he lost a lot of ground when he had that foot bleed. They will cut it off (the cast – not his foot) on Monday and then make the next and so on until we get it back to where it needs to be so he can walk without pain. His right leg lost ground too but we were able to use his old cast that was cut down the middle when they took it off. He has been a very good boy about this with little complaining.

He is really struggling with expirations again. Such effort to get his breath out – this is the worst I have ever seen it. He does this when ill though he does not seem ill in the usual sense.

Zachary had a very good week – the rest in the hospital seems to do him good. I went to his conference on Tuesday night and heard that he is trying very hard and has a wonderful attitude about learning. One thing that really touched me was one story the teacher told me. Zach read a science fiction book and was asked if he could relate something about the book to himself. He answered by talking about 2 characters in the book who really looked out for each other and acted like a team. He said it was just like him and Sam – they look out for each other and are a team. So true.

I heard Sam screaming last night and went into his room. He was screaming "Zachary, Zachary, where are you. Don't leave me by myself." He was half awake and I asked him what was wrong. "I was having a nightmare that Zachary was gone and I was all by myself."

Wednesday, December 1, 2004 5:00 PM

We had our first snow last night! It looks so pretty outside. I do love snow although I could not find the kids' boots anywhere this morning. Poor Abby had to wear my boots when she walked to school. (She insists on walking to school every day!)

It was good to be with my family for Thanksgiving as well as our friend Francis who was visiting my Mom and Frank from Florida. My brothers and sister all each so different and yet each so special to me and to the kids.

Sam's mouth is not bleeding at all so he remains on the higher dose of Factor 7a. I just wish that his gums would not be so swollen but maybe in time if they do not bleed that will happen – I hope. He has been such a delight as of late. I love just talking with him and hearing what he is thinking about. He is working hard at reading practice and perhaps (I think?) recognizing a few words as a whole rather than just seeing the individual letters. He has his casts changed again on Monday and will need 2 more sets I think…then we'll see.

Zachary, as always, is working so hard on crafting Christmas presents for his family. Every year he spends a lot of time making things for us by hand. I wish everyone had such a sweet, generous spirit like he does.

I have a lot on my mind these days. Health insurance renewal time and wondering how in the world we can continue to afford it. How can we not?

Abby – trying to raise money for Make A Wish by hand sewing these little fabric holders for the recorders that kids have in grade school. So many have ideas…so few act on them. How good and kind she is.

Brittany – off to ring the bells tomorrow night at the mall - again – to raise money for Salvation Army. I was never so community concerned at her age. She got another acceptance – this time University of Illinois in Chicago.

Sunday, December 12, 2004 11:34 PM

Last week I wrote a few of you about an insurance crisis that we are having. It is rather difficult to explain succinctly but I will give it a try because WE NEED YOUR HELP NOW.

We have always had what I believed to be a very good relationship with the company that insures our family. It is true that Zach and Sam's care has been quite expensive but on the other hand we have saved them a lot of money by being very fiscally wise with our health care spending, saving them literally millions of dollars over the last few years.

We have been told that the CEO of the Wisconsin and Michigan Markets has made several personal contacts with the insurance agent that intermediates our policy for the purpose of telling the agent that he does not want our policy renewed and if it is renewed they will investigate my husband's employer for fraud. Now my husband's employer has not committed fraud but as you all know., a big company like Humana could tie up a little company like the one Lou works for, thus leaving us without insurance while the investigation is taking place.

If Zach and Sam do not have private insurance the state of Wisconsin will pay for their care. However, the care they would receive would be far different than the care they have now. For one thing Sam would have to live in the hospital. Sam loves school. He loves his family, going to the library, playing with his hamster. If Sam has to live in the hospital I do not think his spirit will survive.

I will not be home this week. It is the boys' hospital week. On Friday night we are surprising Zachary. A limo is coming to the hospital to pick us up, bring us home and once home Make A Wish is throwing a party for Zachary and about 10 or so of his friends.

I am trying so hard to not let this man ruin our Christmas but I have to say it is hard.

Monday, December 20, 2004 3:21 PM

CHRISTMAS LETTER 2004

It came without ribbons, It came without tags, It came without packages, boxes, or bags. Christmas can't be bought from a store... Maybe Christmas means a little bit more.
-Dr. Seuss

There's an old proverb that says "Christmas comes but once a year" and like most I have always looked forward to that once-a-year event. With the birth of Zach and then Sam, I learned that there is a gift in each day, that holidays are not always to be celebrated on the precise day noted on the calendar. Still...the cards, baking, decorating, partying, shopping, wrapping, often threaten to steal some of the peace and warmth that is Christmas.

A year or so ago, I was reminded of how wrong that old proverb is. A friend surprised Zachary and Sam by celebrating Christmas with them in early November. In witnessing Zach and Sam's laughter and smiles I realized more than ever that Christmas is not a season, not a day, not "the most wonderful time of year", yet "all the most wonderful times of the year." I can't say that I always remember this perfectly but I am trying to do what Charles Dickens wrote: *Honor Christmas in my heart, to keep it all the year.* In that spirit here is a picture of Christmas 2004 for the Juhlmanns.

Brittany has applied to and been accepted to several colleges - she has even been offered a significant scholarship to Loyola in Chicago. In the next few months she will decide where she will continue her studies but no matter what she chooses, we are exceptionally proud of her. Christmas unexpectedly came, not so much with the acceptance letters, but in the times she asked for guidance and help, talked about what she wants to do and be in the future, walked around a college campus with me on a beautiful Spring day…a gift of time with her that I don't take for granted now that she is almost 18 and so constantly in motion between friends, soccer, school, community service, student council, friends, National Honor Society, part time job and did I say friends? Almost 18!

Brittany will play her 4th and final season for the Wolverines Varsity Girls Soccer Team. It does not seem so long ago that she came home with eyes shining - she had made the varsity team as a freshman. In that time she has only become a more accomplished athlete. Yet the gift I cherish most is not that she is so good – it is how the love of soccer and being part of a team has impacted her. This past fall her soccer coach said that although she has had to endure twice as much fatigue as any other player due to her medical condition, she is one of the most selfless, honorable, dedicated, hardest working player he has ever had.

Christmas came on the many days that I attended kindergarten and then first grade with Sam. Sometimes he felt good enough to go three half days a week! Smiles, offers to stay inside for recess with him, fighting over who gets to sit with him, who gets to hug him goodbye first….these are the gifts that the precious children who are his classmates give each day. It is one of my greatest gifts to be reminded by these 6 and 7 year old teachers of the simple joy of riding a bus for a class trip, celebrating "one hundred day," looking up at the stars in the planetarium. To think that 18 months ago Sam blew his candles out on his 6th birthday and wished to go to kindergarten and though we hoped fervently that he would – we wondered, would he? Now he is seven, in first grade, still full of an energy and spirit that defies and defeats his illness day after day.

Christmas in July: for our family it came after a ten-day period of Sam bleeding so much we wondered if he would survive. On a Sunday morning he awoke and the bleeding had stopped. There have been many other times that Sam has survived an illness, a bleed - inexplicably, surprisingly. Each time it feels like the miracle of Christmas. And what of the "strangers" that day after day donate the blood, plasma and platelets that Sam's very being depends on – a gift that infuses life into him several times a day?

Strange to say – Christmas also came in July through Pancakes (the hamster) at a time when Sam had lost some of his spirit after a month of illness and setbacks. For the joy and interest in life that Pancakes, (Sam has recently changed his name to Waffles),brought back to Sam, he is a gift well beyond the $7.99 I paid for him.

Christmas came in November on Election Day, when Abby, now 11 and in 6th grade, went to the polling booths with me. She was more informed this year on the issues than most adults and though neither of us was sure, it felt like Christmas once the votes were counted. It is an awesome experience for me to share the Fischer family love for politics with my daughter.

Abby continues to be a most gifted piano player, and a wonderful writer - sharing those gifts on a daily basis. In May, I made a spur of the moment request to her – would she like to speak with me to a group of physicians, nurses and parents? She moved the audience to tears with her eloquence and honesty about being a sister of chronically ill brothers. This coming May she and I have been asked to give the keynote presentation to a group of 600 or more at the Wisconsin Circles of Life Conference where she will undoubtedly touch many. Like her big sister, Abby is constantly in motion with student council, soccer, girl scouts, piano, homework and time with friends. Thankfully she does not drive yet!

Christmas gifts come in quieter, subtler ways with Zachary. His head bent over an art project or a gift he is making for someone – he remains a creative artist and our house is adorned with his many masterpieces. A most precious gift is watching him with Samuel, five years younger. The patience, kindness and love are overwhelming and a reminder to me to be gentle and unselfish as Zachary is with Sam nearly every minute of every day.

Christmas most certainly came this past weekend when Make A Wish of Wisconsin sent a limousine to take Zachary, Sam and me home from the hospital where the boys had been inpatient for their monthly 5-day admission. Once home Zachary went down to our basement to survey the progress he hoped had been made on installing a carpet. You see, Zach had made a wish in August for our basement to be transformed into a game room, complete with pool table, Batman Beyond pinball game, and wide screen TV with surround sound and a DVD player. Such joy to see his surprise when his friends and family all jumped out – "Surprise!" The game room is complete with so many other little items added in by Make A Wish, that I am truly startled at the efforts, time and money invested to make wishes come true for kids like Zachary. My brother said he has never seen Zach smile more in all of his 12 years of life than he did on that night.

Christmas comes from all of you: It comes every Tuesday when the neighbors of Cone View Lane interrupt their busy lives to bring us dinner and from many others who surprise us with a meal or a dessert. Christmas abounds at Children's Hospital of Wisconsin where I cannot imagine the kids being cared for by a more loving, committed wise group of people. Christmas presents arrive each time a member of our family takes the time to come to us, knowing we cannot travel any more with Sam., it comes when an unexpected post card or gift arrives in the mail from family and friends who are thinking of us or from an email sent to say 'we are thinking of you, we love you, we pray for you." You cannot imagine how timely these gifts of kindness are.

We hope this December finds you and your family well. We wish you many happy moments with the people that matter to you, doing the things that bring you joy in 2005!

Tuesday, December 28, 2004 11:33 PM

Christmas was fun – there are still too many toys and books strewn all over the floor mixed with pine needles from the ailing tree but lots of smiles - so I'll live with the hazardous walking situation in my family room. We are all really enjoying Zachary's new game room. So fun!

Secret Santa surprised the boys last week with a delivery of tiny little Christmas tree adorned with gift certificates for various things. We have a pretty good idea who Secret Santa is but since no one will admit it for sure we'll just have to say THANK YOU – you made the boys' day and they watch the tree daily to make sure their sisters have not removed any of their gift certificates.

My sister is coordinating a fundraiser in honor of the boys. It is a writer's conference and all profits will go to the United Mitochondrial Disease Foundation. I am so touched that she is doing this for us and touched at the generosity of all of these writers, who have never even met us. They are all donating their time. Here are a few links about it. Please visit them. She has quite a line-up of famous writers.

Sammy is not walking again. I brought him to see Peter (Dr.) today just to make sure I was not missing something obvious. Nothing really to see, though. Potentially he has had some bleeding into his muscles, potentially it is purely muscular. For now he has his removable casts that we are trying not to remove. I am discouraged at how little he seems to be able to walk anymore. He is so heavy for me to carry. His wheelchair did supposedly come in – I have to call to arrange a delivery. But I am unsure how well it will work for us in the house given I doubt he can use it independently. Before Christmas we did get a stair life installed which has been nice for going from our main level to the 2nd floor.

Thursday Dec. 30, 2004 10 PM

Zach may be having his first joint bleed. His knee started hurting yesterday. I could not see anything wrong with it. This am it seemed slightly inflamed but so light that I was not sure. By 12 noon it was obviously swollen and now it is huge and he cannot walk.

Because this is Zach (not Sam) we cannot assume it is a bleed. He will have to get it tapped in the morning unless it is better (highly doubtful - it is huge and painful). Differential diagnosis would be a septic knee but he does not have other signs to suggest infection.

I had told the kids that I would take them to the movies tonight. Needless to say he could not go to the movies and no one was happy.

2005

Sunday, January 2, 2005 9:38 AM

Just a quick update about the boys:

Zachary went to the hospital on Friday morning where Peter examined him. By that time the knee just looked awful in terms of swelling. Thankfully, the pain was not too bad as long as he was not attempting to walk on it or bend it.

The interventional radiologist tapped the knee and aspirated about 50 ml of blood. It certainly helped but there was still a lot of blood left in there. We went to infusion clinic to see the on call hematologist -not ours but I like her a lot nonetheless. She had a few ideas and drew labs but mostly everyone was quite puzzled as to why he had such a terrible spontaneous bleed. They infused blood products that help stop bleeding and then let us go home. Labs came back and offer no clue whatsoever as to why he had a spontaneous bleed. I guess this is going to be like Sam – more questions than answers.

By Saturday morning the knee had started to swell a bit again, looked worse after his nap and this morning looks even bigger. He is due to have more infusions but we just do not know what he needs, given the lack of answers, which makes this all so difficult. It also seems obvious to me that the blood center is going to be cautious about what the doctors use because I am sure they do not want to end up with another Sam. That is appropriate but it is also crucial that they remember that not every child goes by the book, that there are not answers for everyone and in the absence of that it is the right thing to do to treat the child empirically.

Sam's heart is struggling, as are his kidneys. This has been a week of daily labs due to him retaining potassium at dangerous levels and his heart quite obviously struggling to compensate with any fluid. We are giving him extra diuretics beyond his usual massive doses and turned up his labetalol (a heart medication) to a rate that would have killed an adult by now. He clearly needs the extra support as yesterday his labs started to look a bit more encouraging. We will do them today to see if that was a fluke or truly a turn towards improvement.

The girls are exhausted – too many late holiday nights. Brittany is quite sure it is wrong that college students get a longer vacation than high school students because college students have it a lot easier than the overworked senior high school students. Some how I think she'll be singing another tune next year.

Wednesday, January 5, 2005 9:02 PM

It's snowing – it's snowing!!!!!!!!!!!! I love snow (but then again I am not the one that shovels it).

Zachary's knee improved after the tap and his first infusion last Friday but it has been slow since then. He did well until Saturday and then it got slightly worse. Monday morning he got cryo again and I saw a definite improvement in range of motion and his ability to walk by Tuesday morning. By Tuesday night it had swelled a bit more and he had some pain. We think that what this is telling us is he clears the cryo faster than 48 hours. (24 hours is supposed to be the shortest ½ life). Today he got an infusion in the afternoon.

Our hematologist came by today and was impressed with the swelling…. he had not seen it last week at its worst but he thought it looked swollen enough now. Given that Zach does seem to benefit from the cryo we are going to continue it to see if we can get the knee to heal and get his mobility and strength back. So we will go Friday after school, Sunday morning and then he will get it every day next week since he will be an inpatient.

I'm mildly annoyed I cannot give this cryo at home to Zach when I give it several times/day to Sam. But I just don't have the energy to fight about it right now. If it looks like he'll have to be discharged and still get it, then I may be a little more advocating.

Sam's heart is so much better!!!!!!! We increased one of his heart meds and it very quickly turned things around. His kidney insufficiency that was being caused by the heart failure is also much better. Thank God!

Of course no sooner did his heart start working better than he started bleeding copiously from his mouth. That was Monday night. He has been getting more factor 7a because of this. The hematologist had me go back up on his drip rate and it already seemed to be making a difference. But he did miss school both Tuesday and Wednesday because he can't very well go to school dripping blood much as they all love him. I hope we can get it good enough so he can at least go on Friday. Next week he will be inpatient and not able to go.

There is no such thing as a "self-made" man. We are made up of thousands of others. Everyone who has ever done a kind deed for us, or spoken one word of encouragement to us, has entered into the make-up of our character and of our thoughts, as well as our success. -- George Matthew Adams

Wednesday, January 12, 2005 10:18 PM

Many of you know that Sam was supposed to go to surgery today for a broken central line. It seemed beyond repair on Monday and Tuesday.

By the grace of God he did not go to surgery today. The general consensus is that the line is significantly weakened but is still functional - more so than we originally thought last night. In any other kid, the line would be replaced but in Sam, the risk of surgery is so significant that the decision has been to not touch the line until we absolutely have to. That may only be a month or it may be longer but we'll take any time we can get.

I think the entire hospital breathed a collective sigh of relief to be able to buy some time. Sam and surgery are a pretty bad mix.

This was also good news because he is really struggling with high blood pressure right now which has been fairly controlled for a long time. Surgery usually makes all of that even worse so we're glad not to throw that into the mix.

Zach is doing well. Knee slowly getting better with the daily cryo infusions.

Tuesday, January 18, 2005 11:15 PM

It's snowing again and very very cold here in Wisconsin. I don't mind the cold but the wind I could do without.

This is exam week for the high school and despite senioritis Brittany is studying for her exams. She informed us at dinner tonight that she received a high honor for a graduating senior. She was voted "Most Likely To Trip At Graduation." Now let's just hope she does not live up to that title. Friday, she has off and we plan to go look at Loyola and if time, University of Illinois – Chicago. We still need to trek out to Minneapolis to see U of Minnesota but that will have to wait a few weeks.

Zach's knee is doing well without the cryoprecipitate infusions. The PT in school told me that he did not even limp in specially designed phys-ed. Tomorrow he gives his demonstration speech - he is going to do a magic trick. He did the speech for us at dinner but the girls made him laugh and then none of us could stop laughing. Poor Zach – he finally did get through it and did a wonderful job. Brittany asked him when it was. He asked her why she wanted to know and she said she would like to come if it was during a time when she did not have an exam. I kept my composure enough not to fall off the chair. Wonders never cease.

Sammy is still not feeling well. He is so out of sorts and tired -I just cannot figure out exactly what is wrong. He definitely has a head cold and that would make anyone miserable. But his stomach is so distended, none of his tubes are draining out anything (not good) and consequently he is having a lot of stomach pain. He is breathing with great effort although somehow he has not needed oxygen - but I have to think the effort to breathe is making him all the more tired. He work up this morning and within 30 minutes took a nap until his home teacher came at 8:15. He did well with her but by the time he got to school he could barely keep his eyes opened. Came home at 11:30 and slept until 4:30. We did some schoolwork and he did very well but within 90 minutes he was exhausted again. I just hate seeing him this way and he must hate feeling this way, as he is CRABBY. He did light up when he got to school as his friends all made a big deal about him being there! Lots of hugs all the way around. He had not been in school since before Christmas so I hope he can stay awake long enough to go tomorrow.

On another, brighter subject – and I do mean brighter – Sammy got his new wheelchair FINALLY. I think we waited 8 months. It is bright metallic orange and black. Very cool and very comfy for him. I already hurt my back lifting the thing though. I need to go back to remedial nursing school I think for a refresher on good lifting techniques. The chair is going to be so much nicer for him though than the stroller and obviously much more age appropriate. I thought it would be hard for me to see him in a wheelchair. After all – it only took me a year from the time it was prescribed to actually have him fitted for it. I just could not bring myself to accept he really needed one. However, I simply felt a sense of relief that it finally came. It was a little bittersweet but mostly okay. I think it will actually enhance our quality of life as a family. One of the first things Abby said was "now we can go more places this summer" and she is right. I just could not carry him anymore and the stroller was too uncomfortable for even a walk in the neighborhood. Once Zach's electric chair comes there will be no telling where the kids and I will be off too!

Thursday, January 27, 2005 9:36 PM

Sam has had a very good week. His bleeding is relatively stable on a lower Factor 7a drip. Not perfect but acceptable I think. We'll have to see how the next few days go and if he will be able to maintain on this drip. He has been sleeping so much better at night with oxygen on. I can barely believe the difference. In the past few months he has woken up on average 3-4 times/night. Often he would wake up in the morning just exhausted and ready for a nap at 7 am. What a new kid with a full night's sleep – he has been so agreeable and good and trying as hard as he can in school. He has gone to school 2 times this week and I am sure he will go tomorrow – Friday.

This is a story he dictated to his homebound teacher:

I wish I had Zach's brain
And Zach had my brain
Then I could talk like Zach
And Zach could talk like me!

Zach said that he does not want to trade brains. Zachary has been doing okay too. Some higher blood pressure and a heart gallop the last few days so we increased his labetalol. He has some minor bleeding in his urine, which I am keeping my eye on. Let's hope it stays minor. He had fun tonight helping Brittany and Prasanna make hats for a party they are going to tomorrow. Other than that it seems to have been a pretty status quo week for him. Today his school staff was going to meet with the middle school staff to start talking about what needs to be done in terms of the building to make it work for Zach. It is 3 levels and has no elevators. We're asking that they have most of what he needs on the main floor and that if he does have to use the stairs that they limit those trips so that he is not up and down, up and down.

Brittany is going to be 18 on Sunday!!!!!! 18 is always such a special birthday. It feels surreal to me to say that my daughter is going to be 18. Time goes by so fast. I am very proud of who she is and I love seeing her become as she chooses her path to walk. But I admit there is a biter-sweetness – part of me wants to hold her at this age forever, though I realize I felt that way when she turned 1, and 4 and 12. At those ages I could not imagine her being 5 or 8 or 16 but she has been all of those and each of those ages yielded memories that I cherish in my heart.

Abby is doing well. She joined Town Hall, which runs the opposite years of Future Problem Solvers. In Town Hall she will learn about the legislative process (I think). This is right up her alley. One morning a week she is playing hockey – it is just a school thing but she seems to enjoy it. Tonight she is at Disney on Ice with Miss Nancy her piano teacher. Sometimes I wonder where Abby gets all her energy.

Sunday, February 6, 2005 11:26 PM

I'm sorry that I have not updated lately. Thank you to everyone who has been checking in on us.

Sammy ended up with a significant mouth bleed at the end of last week. I just don't think he can tolerate the lower Factor 7a drip for more than a few days but we try it when we can and hope for the best. He has not had one of his best weeks. He has had more manic episodes. I'll be interested to see if his medication levels are low. However, he is doing wonderful from a cardiac perspective. He missed one day of school this week but other than that has made every day for the last few weeks.

We are going into the hospital Monday morning for the week. Hopefully the boys will have some time to work on their Valentines since that is right around the corner. Also Sam discovered books on tapes this weekend. We went to the library on Saturday and got quite a few. He has just loved listening to them although he does not seem to be able to hear the beeps to turn the pages even with his hearing aids on. Oh well – he does not seem to care.

Zach and Abby went to see a play last week in Milwaukee with their class – The Confessions of Charlotte Doyle. They really enjoyed it. Zach is doing fair. Lots of stomach pain when he gets his medications. I'm not sure what is up with that but if it continues we're going to have to try to figure out a way to switch the remaining J tube meds to IV.

As far as school goes – the middle school staff met with the elementary staff last week to discuss transition to middle school for Zach. (Waukesha starts middle in 7th). The middle school is not accessible which blows my mind. I guess they have never had a kid that is physically disabled (?? I'm not sure??) However, my understanding is that they were very helpful and really want to make this work for Zachary. We think we can keep him on one main floor and perhaps just one trip to the lower level. We'll have to see. Our doctor is apprehensive about the stairs but no one wants to move Zach to another school and away from his friends. I do know that I have a lot of work to do in the next 5 years because there is no way I am sending Sammy anywhere except where his friends are and an accessible school will not be a choice for him – he cannot walk stairs and never will. I know the district does not have the money but I am going to look into grants that might help fund an elevator. Anyway, it is a whole new phase in Zach's life and it feels scary to me. I am so used to the Bethesda staff "getting it" and it feels overwhelming to start all over.

Brittany went to her Sadie's dance last night. She looked beautiful and her date quite handsome.

Life has been so very busy and complicated these past few months. However, it struck me the other day that the more complicated life gets the simpler it is as well. My children have taught me that.

Wednesday, February 9, 2005 8:36 PM

Something happened to Sammy today. It is probably a metabolic stroke. He has been increasingly perceiving that it is dark and that more lights need to be turned on. That has been for months. At the same time he has seemed to have more and more trouble distinguishing the letters of the alphabet. He knew every letter when

107

he was four. Yesterday he could not tell the difference between an O and a D.

Today he woke up from a nap, asked for a movie and after a few minutes said, "Mama there is something wrong with my eyes. I cannot see the TV." He was squinting and trying as hard as he could but his eyes could not even track. I held my hand in front of his face and asked him to count my fingers. He could not do it - he was trying to feel for them and counted the same finger three times and said I had three fingers (I was holding up all 5). He could not distinguish colors. After about 45 min to an hour he could see again but was having a lot of difficulty - you could just see it taking all of his effort. At the same time he could not hold his head up without support, could not sit independently and kept falling over against his pillows. He fell asleep at 4 PM. He then tried to wake up about 7 pm but could not sit and then said he was tired and went back to bed. I have seen this floppiness before with his previous strokes but not the vision issue.

I feel sick to my stomach right now. He was doing so well - so very very well. This morning he woke up with a bleeding mouth. He slept most of the day except for the above time period. I hope he is not scared. I wonder what it feels like to not be able to see. Sometimes it just feels like he is slipping through my fingers no matter how hard I try to hold on. I do think he'll be ok - he always is. But every hit to his body is worse...I wonder how many he can survive when he is already a miracle to all of us.

Friday Feb. 11, 2005 6 PM

Sam woke up Thursday and seemed perfectly fine. No visual loss and he could sit up. He had a very good day. This morning he woke up fine as well. But while coloring a picture he began to have acute chest pain and said he could not breathe very well. He was breathing close to 60 times/minute. At the same time he could no longer hold his head up. Scary once again. He fell asleep and when he woke he was better but still difficulty independently sitting for long periods of time. I do not understand what is happening to him nor does anyone else seem to.

He is going on his 4th week of low grade fevers. His blood cultures do not show anything. His intestinal cultures show fungus.

108

Because he has a history of getting blood fungal infections we are going to treat him for one for 4 weeks and hope maybe this will help.

I wish I understood what was going on.

Tuesday, February 15, 2005 10:58 PM

Better days. Sam has not had any more loss of vision episodes since Saturday morning. It's amazing how in an instant things change so that what you once took for granted seems like an incredible gift. Every day since last Wednesday that he can see, that he comments on the color of something or says as only he can say "What's that look for?' I catch myself thinking, "Thank God he can see." followed by an arrow prayer aimed straight for God "*Please* don't let him lose his sight." I am taking him to see a developmental eye doctor on Thursday morning. I was so pleased that she could see him so quickly. I hope that she might help us understand what is happening and more importantly have some advice for what we can do to help him to learn despite these struggles.

Zach – struggling still. The pain is intense for he who has such a high pain tolerance. This is very hard for me to watch as I feel completely helpless to do anything for him. It brings back memories of his 5 month long stay at Children's when he was in kindergarten, which led to his dependence on IV nutrition and fluids. The only things that go into his GI tract are some of his medications that do not have an intravenous form. All other meds and of course all of his calories bypass his GI tract and go directly into his blood. Thus there is nothing that can be done for him short of stopping these medications and of course that is not an option. The IV valium helps but unfortunately by the time he needs it, he has already been in pain and the pain makes him so tired-- as anyone who has had chronic pain knows.

On the bright side Zachary has had some really fun days in between the episodes of pain. On Saturday he had a friend over during the day and then at night he and Abby had a small group of kids over. It was really nice to see him just having fun with the other 6th graders. Monday he was able to go to school in the afternoon for his Valentine's Day Party. He is working on his 6th grade research project – "the historical developments that made surgery safer." He made me a beautiful Valentine decoration that must have taken him a lot of time. I love his creations for he puts so much of himself in each one.

Sam, too, went to his Valentine's Party. I was sad to have missed it but I had to be a grown up and go to work. I would much rather be in first grade! I am told that he smiled and smiled through the party and that he was surrounded and hugged by his wonderful friends. Who wouldn't smile with all of that? Right now he is so excited because his angel-on-earth friend, Josie, wants to come over to play with him after school one day and he just thinks that is the neatest thing in the world. Today she stopped by to bring him a tape/CD of stories from *The Incredibles* and he listened intently to it all the way through and then took it to bed with him (With strict instructions not to turn it on at midnight or 5 am – his 2 favorite times to wake up Zach who shares a room with him). He had a wonderful day today both with his homebound teacher in the early morning and then in the classroom the rest of the morning.

What else? Well, Friday is the infamous Bethesda Sock Hop that the kids look forward to all year. Not sure how long Sam will last but he is pretty excited. Of course that does not compare with Abby's anticipation. This is the big event for 6th graders and she can't wait. Abby too is working on her 6th grade research which is "Children with HIV and AIDS in Africa – why is their care so different than in the U.S.?" She plans to interview the doctor and nurse that care for the kids with HIV at Children's and has a whole slew of books she is looking at. My first nursing job was caring for HIV+ kids in Camden, NJ (either the 1st or 2nd poorest city in the US and recently ranked as the most violent) at a time when there was really no treatment …children with AIDS will always hold a special place in my heart and it is inspiring to me that she has chosen this to be her topic.

And then there is Brittany. The kid who is most likely to trip at graduation (as voted by her senior class) got knocked pretty good in the head at her indoor soccer game Sunday. She was dizzy and nauseated for almost 48 hours but seems to be doing better now. Still vacillating between U of Minnesota Twin Cities and Loyola in Chicago. I'm way too smart to put in writing which one I want her to go to. Aside from that - both are really great schools for what she wants and I am sure that whatever she picks will be right for her. Just trying to support her in whatever she needs to do to make this choice.

For Valentine's Day -albeit a little late – this is the poem I have said to Sam since he was an infant. I did not know whether to laugh or cry when I heard him saying to Pancakes the Hamster right before we left for the hospital, "I carry your heart in my heart, Pancakes. I am never without it. You are a sun and a moon and I hope you don't die."

UNTITLED (but Sam and I call it the heart poem)

e.e. cummings

i carry your heart with me (i carry it in
my heart) i am never without it (anywhere
i go you do, my dear; and whatever is done
by only me is your doing, my darling)
i fear no fate (for you are my fate, my sweet) i want
no world (for beautiful you are my world, my true)
and it's you are whatever a moon has always meant
and whatever a sun will always sing is you
here is the deepest secret nobody knows
(here is the root of the root and the bud of the bud
and the sky of the sky of a tree called life; which grows
higher than the soul can hope or mind can hide)
and this is the wonder that's keeping the stars apart
i carry your heart (i carry it in my heart)

Monday, February 21, 2005 8:36 PM

Busy days never end. I am having a hard time believing that March 1 is next week. Of course in Wisconsin that does NOT mean that spring is around the corner.

The developmental eye doctor appointment was very helpful for me and most importantly I hope it proves to be helpful for Sam. Zach used to see Dr. K when he was younger – she is just an incredibly bright woman who puts a lot of effort into each of her patients. She helped Zachary immensely when he was in preschool and I definitely credit his ability to read and catch a ball to her work with his eyes. She has a much more comprehensive approach to vision than most eye doctors. For example, in Sam's case the eye doctor we have been seeing simply tells me that he has 20/25 vision and his eye looks

111

healthy which does absolutely nothing to help us deal with the fact that for whatever reason his vision is poor.

Dr. K also found that his vision when he is not tired is 20/25. However when fatigue set in (which for him happens after about 20 minutes of playing games or school work), his vision completely deteriorated and he no longer could focus appropriately, was missing letters, calling letters by other names, etc. She said his eye movement is very immature – probably a 4 year old level at best – and therefore we cannot expect him to learn in ways that a 7 year old can learn. Reading requires a lot of eye movement - his eyes are not where they should be for reading. The good news is that there are certainly things we should be able to do to help. For one, glasses should assist him so that he does not have to work so hard to keep his eyes focused. She said they may only increase his eye endurance by 10 minutes but 10 minutes is a lot for him. He will only have to wear them for schoolwork and reading. She also has some ideas about what the teachers and I can do to help him – fairly simple things actually. As far as his episodes of blindness she said she will be researching a few things. She is going to talk with some other eye docs to see if they know or have seen anything like this. She did not have the answer but I appreciated her honest "I don't know" along with her attitude that she wants to know and will try to help him even if she does not know.

Thursday Sam had a spontaneous joint bleed – his knee this time. Initially it got worse but by Sunday it was stable and today it is looking less swollen. He is not in terrible pain but we are trying to keep him from walking as he made it worse initially by walking. This has prompted our hematologist to prescribe an increase in one of his blood products, which makes life busier, but it is expected to be temporary – maybe 2 weeks. Even with the bleed he went to the Bethesda Sock Hop. He only danced a few minutes with Josie and Joey but he had a wonderful time I think. The main attraction for him was sitting on the bleachers with Josie, who wanted to sit with him rather than dance with her friends. When he lost his glow bracelet, Joey offered his. His other little friends were all so happy to see him. If the world was full of people who remembered to act as kindly and accepting as first graders it would be a better place.

Zach is doing ok. Some very bad days last week and he continues to have abdominal pain episodes several times/day requiring pain medicine. It's pretty hard to see him look so tired lately. He too is tired of feeling sick. Who can blame him? Still he made it to school every day last week and works so hard – I am so proud of him. Today he and I drove out to see his endocrinologist who is in Madison – about 90 minutes away – at University of Wisconsin Children's Hospital. I always like the drive out there for some reason and the hospital is just a neat place. It is huge and busy - so much going on. The energy there is contagious. We've known some of the staff since Zach was a baby – this is the hospital he went to until he was 6 when we switched to the closer Children's Hospital. Zach had not grown very well, even on his daily growth hormone injections. It appears he has become resistant to growth hormone, which may be a big problem if we cannot overcome it. Dr. A prescribed a big increase in the dose and we'll see what happens in the next 4-6 months.

Tomorrow is Sam's big day. He is having Josie over to our house after she is done school in the afternoon. He has never had one of his school friends over and he is so excited. He was lying awake for some time tonight, because he kept thinking about all the things they will do together. At times like these I could forget so easily that he has all these medical problems. To see him so excited about having a friend over - something that most children take for granted - it is just overwhelming to be honest. As tired as I get, as bad as some days can be, it is so worth it to me to see his appreciation for such simple things. I see this too with Zachary and my prayer each day is to be as content as they are, as appreciative of the smallest joys in life as they are.

Wednesday, March 2, 2005 5:09 PM

Things have not been so great here. Sam's heart failure is bad this week. He is not able to compensate at the moment and his little body is just exhausted. He has not been able to make it to school. It is very hard to see him so tired and not able to do what he loves more than anything. He is just working very hard and because of that can barely stay awake. Today he has been up twice –once for 2 hours in the morning and then again for about 45 minutes midday. When he is awake he is so tired he can barely hold his head up or keep his eyes open. It seems to take a lot of effort for him to talk and when he does it is difficult to understand what he is saying. I am sure it will get better but it is very affecting to see him look so bad.

Very scary to me how fast he goes down. There really was little warning. His knee re-bled on Saturday and so he has needed some extra Factor 7a to clot. Unfortunately he clotted in his central line too so we have had to give anti-clot medicine (TPA) to take care of that.

Zach is doing ok. He had some friends over Saturday night but was exhausted Sunday afterwards. Yesterday I did go with him and Abby on their 6th grade museum/health education field trip. It was fun to be with the older kids. Those 6th grade boys are too much!!!!! Watch out world! Anyway – Zach was great on the trip -he barely needed the wheelchair in the morning. Afternoon was sitting so that worked well. Today he is kind of wiped out but that's ok if he had a good time yesterday.

I have not felt well since last week so trying to sleep when I can and taking lots of cold/flu medicine. I hate winter germs.

The boys are going to be admitted Friday morning for their immune globulin infusion. I think it will be good for Sam to be inpatient so we can see better what is going on with his heart and do the right thing.

We'll go sooner if he gets any worse.

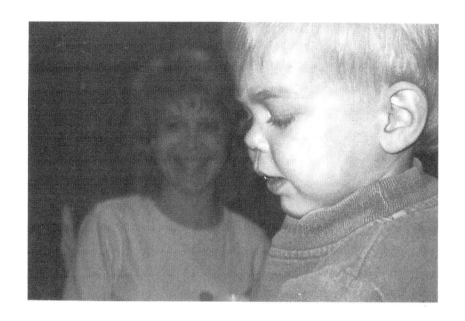

Thursday, March 3, 2005 9:26 AM

My beautiful little Sammy died and went to heaven early this morning - March 3 - at Waukesha Memorial Hospital where he was born. His heart just was so tired. I do not know how to live without him.

Precious Samuel - Mama is with you and you are with Mama just like we always said.

WRITTEN FOR SAMUEL ON HIS SEVENTH BIRTHDAY

May 9! Happy Birthday Samuel Patrick!

Your birthday is the most wonderful Mother's Day present to me!

I brought Sammy home from the hospital on Mother's Day 1997 in an outfit that the kids had picked out for him before he was born.

His first birthday - he was in the hospital for one month preceding his 1st birthday. He woke up on May 9 and they discharged him. The next day was Mother's day - he was home – my wonderful mother's day child.

His second birthday - we celebrated in the hospital because Zachary was inpatient. He could not talk yet but he could sign, *Mama, I love you*, and so many other words and phrases. He had just learned how to walk. I'll never forget his pride as he showed me how he could walk when he came to visit me in the hospital one day during Zach's long admission.

On his third birthday he was very ill. I am not sure he even woke up on his birthday. We celebrated a few days later. Blue's Clues was the theme. It was a wonderful day of celebration even if it was not on his birthday. It was one of many reminders that I have had over the years that holidays do not have to be on the day that the calendar says they have to be on. Sam's birthday was something to rejoice in and celebrate whether we did that on May 9 or May 12.

Four! A month or so before he turned 4 the transplant team in Madison told me that he was too ill for a transplant. They told me that without a transplant it was doubtful that he would make it until his fifth birthday. Those were the darkest days I had ever lived up until that time. I wondered, as I shopped, if it would really be his last birthday. By the time he blew out his candles on May 9, I had realized that there was no way that anyone could predict what his life span would be. Perhaps he would not have another birthday and perhaps he would have 40 more. I had to learn to not only live with that but to LIVE and LIVE and LIVE.

We went to Ocean City for 2 weeks that year – the first time we took a vacation since he was a baby.

We took him on his Make A Wish trip to Disney World

On his fifth birthday he told me that he was not a baby anymore – but "I will still be your baby!" He wished that he could be a birdie and he wished that his tummy would not hurt anymore. Unbelievably he did not need medicine for his stomach for months after he made that wish.

Ocean City again – this time for almost 3 weeks and the sun shone every day!

Then the bleeding got out of hand - he bled and he bled and he bled. His heart got worse. I could not imagine his little body could sustain much more.

He turned six! The entire house was full of Buzz Light Year presents and he insisted on a purple cake which turned gray when I baked it. He did not mind. I thanked God for his blood product donors who keep him alive with their gift of life. He made a wish that he would go to Kindergarten – to the same school as Zach and Abby. I begged God to please grant that wish for my little boy. Peter added a comment on his medical summary – "our goal for Sam is for him to stay alive long enough to go to kindergarten." It was all that any of us wanted for him.

There were not any trips to Ocean City last summer. His health too precarious now. I felt and feel thankful for the times we did go away when we could.

The whole world shone on that day in September when he went to kindergarten – at Zach and Abby's school. The acceptance of the staff, the children, Sam's eyes and smile….continue to brighten the world every day that he goes to school.

And now …He is seven! I don't know what lies in his future but I know that whatever he does, forever as long as he lives, he will continue to add meaning and love to my life.

Sam I love you! Happy Birthday

Tuesday, March 8, 2005 10:02 PM

We buried Sam yesterday. I think we buried my heart too.

SAM I AM

What Abby said right before she played a song that she had written for her best little brother.

This is a song that I wrote a couple of days ago for my precious little brother Sammy Patrick. It is called "Sam I Am." I hope that this song can take you on a brief ride through Sammy's life. Parts of the song are cheerful and happy, like what Sammy brings to me every day. Other parts are slow and sad. They show the challenges that Sammy destroyed with the help of his family, friends, and buzz light-year. I love Sammy more than he loves his dogs. I love Sammy more than he likes to go to school, watch Dr. Green-bomb juggle, and hear what funny things "the red flash" says on "Justice League." I hope that my love will be seen through this song. Of course, this is dedicated to Sammy. Sammy, you are my sunshine and I love you.
    --Abby, your "little sis"

Zachary told some of his favorite memories. This is what he put in Sam's memory book for the service:

ZACH AND SAM

Hello. My name is Zach and I'm Sam's big brother. I miss Sam so much but I do know his spirit lies beside me. I remember that he would always want to play games with me. Sam would often ask, "Zach, can we play Uno?" or Zach, can we play Yu-gi-oh?" Sam and I always called each other best brothers, for a long time now. Sam has looked up to me forever. I feel so proud I made his life good and wonderful. The rest of my life will be really different now that he is gone. I feel sad inside a lot. I couldn't possibly forget him.
Brittany read this poem:

A Heart of Gold

118

Sam, my wonderful baby brother,
I can't begin to express how I feel.
My heart aches from missing you.
Sometimes it doesn't seem real.

But through all the tears and pain,
It's the good times I try and remember.
I was so blessed to be your sister.
You made my life so much better.

With that crazy feisty personality,
Who could ever be mad at you?
I would just sit there, smile, and laugh
At all the hilarious things you'd do

You had a heart of gold and a love for life-
Never letting anything hold you back.
You died like you lived- brave and fighting.
You made the most out of the seven years you had.

I don't know where to stop.
There's so much more I want to say.
But I guess the most important thing
Is that Sam, I will love you ALWAYS

Hundreds and hundreds of people came to the visitation and the service. We had his pictures and his books and toys and creations everywhere. Many people worked hard to inflate orange balloons and they were everywhere. I made sure he had his "Ultimate Hero" socks on. He has his treasured, faithful stuffed dog "chicken food" and his Curious George flashlight. We sang his favorite songs. We showed a slide show of his life that I had put to music with the help of my wonderful friends Kathy, Janet and Neil and my daughter, Brittany.

I never knew how deeply he touched so many lives and even now it overwhelms me. I feel so lost and empty but one thing I do know is that Sam was and is loved. Thank you for your love and support and most of all for sharing your memories of Sam. I did say something about Sam but cannot remember exactly what. The essence of it was

119

this: I love my little boy beyond anything I can ever describe. It was never a burden to be his mother even when his care became so complex. It was simply an honor and I miss him so deeply, so profoundly....words cannot describe this either.

The service: Sam Juhlmann: Remembering a Life

"Sleep Sound in Jesus" (song from Sam's favorite CD when a baby)
Sung by Charity Hoskins

Welcome
Brian McIntyre

Psalm 23
Read by John Fischer, Sam's grandfather

"Sam I Am"
Composed and Played by Abigail Juhlmann, Sam's sister

"Mommy, Please Don't Cry," by Linda DeYmaz
Read by Ashlyn and Carianna Farrell

"Twinkle, Twinkle Little Star"
Sung by Sam's family and friends, accompanied by David Cieri, Sam's uncle

"A Heart of Gold"
Composed by Brittany Juhlmann, Sam's sister

"Jacob's Dream" (originally sung at Sam's baby dedication)
Sung by Scott Pedersen

"He's Got the Whole World in His Hands"
Sung by Sam's family and friends, accompanied by Cressa Serryn

Devotional Message
Delivered by Brian McIntyre

"You Are My Sunshine"
Sung by Sam's family and friends, accompanied by David Cieri

Memories
Zachary Juhlmann, Sam's brother

"My Heart Poem": Memories of a Life
Anne Juhlmann, Sam's mother

Celebrating Sam, Celebrating Life
A presentation prepared by Sam's family and friends

"Swing Low, Sweet Chariot"
Sung by Sam's family and friends

Sunday, March 13, 2005 1:19 AM

Lonely
Hopeless, trying desperately to hope again
Scared
Cold – colder than I think I've ever been
Exhausted
I beg God to see Sam, even if a dream. But those dreams have not come.
Only nightmares. I wake and he is not here. It is so cold.
Nauseated constantly – as if , AS IF, I am carrying my Samuel again, anticipating his birth. But he has already been born and moved on to where I cannot see him or touch him.

I can smile and sometimes I can laugh but it does not feel very real. And Sam was all about being REAL.

I miss his laughter, his defiance, ("I am the boss!"), his eyes, him.

I feel broken. Pieces missing. And I don't know how to glue it back together. Even if I did - what about the holes? What do those get filled with?

I am told that time heals but I don't believe that to be true. How can time replace a child? How can time ease the loss of his laughter and the feel of him snuggled with me on a Sunday morning? He once told his kindergarten teacher that his favorite thing was snuggling with Mama on Sunday mornings.

It would be so dishonoring to Samuel to not live...so I try to wake up and see the sun each day.

But Sam felt everything so intensely and deeply and I know that if anyone understands this grief it is Sam.

Monday Zachary will be admitted to the hospital for his IVIG. I have no idea what that will be like. It was always the 3 of us for those 5 days each month as inpatients and we have so many shared memories – Zach, Sam and me. I don't know how to do this without Sam.

Peter would like to start Zach on nighttime oxygen. We learned, perhaps too late, how much it helped Sammy's heart. Zach's heart already struggles but he is where Sam was 3 years ago. If only we can keep him there.

Zach is quite tired. His IVIG is late - we were to go in for it the day after Sammy died (I hate those words). He probably needs blood. He had friends over and asked them if they could go home early so I know he is really struggling.

There are so many thank yous to be said. I am overwhelmed with the kindness and compassion of so many people -family, friends, community.

The children from Bethesda School make me smile, laugh and yes cry each day. We have hundreds of pictures and letters from these precious children and they are a treasure to me. Their simple faith, their memories through their art work of their simple words, their eternal optimism that it will be okay even though "I miss Sam," "He was my friend," "I cried when I heard ...." What a gift each and every one of those children are.

"The more I give to thee the more I have, for both are infinite."
--Shakespeare
Sunday, March 20, 2005 3:18 PM

Rise up against / multiple meanings,
Trust the trail of tears/ and learn to live.

A dear friend, Mama of 2 beautiful children who died from mitochondrial disease – although they are still alive to many of us - emailed the above to me, written by Paul Celan, a Holocaust survivor. I cannot find any meaning right now in Samuel's death – no hidden blessing. I am not happy he is in Heaven and I don't think God would expect me to find comfort in that right now. I appreciated the above words. I am sure meaning will come someday – or not – but right now I just am trying to learn how to live.

Zachary and I are home from the hospital.

It was a very hard time – very quiet and very sad not only for us but for so many that love Sam. There were times I think my heart ripped in new places to see the pain of some of his "family" at Children's Hospital as well as his own family – my mom, my sister, my brother, and so many others. He was loved -that I will never doubt.

The quiet in the hospital room was unnerving – it is amazing how one little child can so fill a life with noise. Even when asleep, one could always hear him breathing so that the quiet and stillness of the room was and is striking.

Our house is the same – I hardly know what to do with myself but the days do pass. How could it be 21/2 weeks already?

Saint Patrick's Day came and went. Sam always thought it was "Samuel Patrick's Day" and assumed the whole world celebrated him on March 17. I know I always did.

The very hardest part of the week was leaving the hospital. This I did not expect. It was just so hard to walk out without my bubbly little boy. Maybe in a way I was hoping I'd go home and he'd be there even though I of course knew that not to be true. The heart is so slow to learn what the rest of the world knows.

Zachary is on nighttime oxygen now. I am so glad – I just have to believe it will help him. All in all he is doing okay. He misses Sam so terribly yet in his 12 year old mind he is trying to find ways to reach acceptance. Children are so different and all of my children seem to be doing okay, finding comfort in doing the familiar. He is working hard on his research paper – "Advances That Made Surgery Safer." I think the part he enjoyed writing the most was the detailed description of an amputation done in the 1700's without anesthesia. Gruesome to say the least. This morning he went to a friend's, came home and took a nap and is now out with Abby at another friends. He may collapse tomorrow but I am glad he is able to have fun.

Have I said thank you? I'm sure not enough. I know I am poor company. I do cry many times when someone says "I'm sorry" but please know I appreciate every remembrance rather than those that say nothing as if he never existed. Thank you!

My Mom framed Sam's picture of the sunshine. It looks beautiful – I look at it 100 times a day. Today Josie brought me a picture of the sun peering through the clouds. Sam was lucky to have her as a friend.

Below is written by poet, Ralph Waldo Emerson after the death of his son from scarlet fever. I think he was only six.

Threnody - Ralph Waldo Emerson

The south-wind brings
Life, sunshine, and desire,
And on every mount and meadow
Breathes aromatic fire,
But over the dead he has no power,
The lost, the lost he cannot restore,
And, looking over the hills, I mourn
The darling who shall not return.

I see my empty house,
I see my trees repair their boughs,
And he,—the wondrous child,
Whose silver warble wild
Outvalued every pulsing sound
Within the air's cerulean round,
The hyacinthine boy, for whom
Morn well might break, and April bloom,
The gracious boy, who did adorn
The world where into he was born,
And by his countenance repay
The favor of the loving Day,
Has disappeared from the Day's eye;
Far and wide she cannot find him,
My hopes pursue, they cannot bind him.

Returned this day the south-wind searches
And finds young pines and budding birches,
But finds not the budding man;
Nature who lost him, cannot remake him;
Fate let him fall, Fate can't retake him;
Nature, Fate, men, him seek in vain.

I hearken for thy household cheer,
O eloquent child!
Whose voice, an equal messenger,
Conveyed thy meaning mild.
What though the pains and joys
Whereof it spoke were toys
Fitting his age and ken;—
Yet fairest dames and bearded men,
Who heard the sweet request
So gentle, wise, and grave,
Bended with joy to his behest,
And let the world's affairs go by,
Awhile to share his cordial game,
Or mend his wicker wagon frame,
Still plotting how their hungry ear
That winsome voice again might hear,
For his lips could well pronounce
Words that were persuasions.

Now love and pride, alas, in vain,
Up and down their glances strain.
The painted sled stands where it stood,
The kennel by the corded wood,
The gathered sticks to stanch the wall
Of the snow-tower, when snow should fall,
The ominous hole he dug in the sand,
And childhood's castles built or planned.
His daily haunts I well discern,
The poultry yard, the shed, the barn,
And every inch of garden ground
Paced by the blessed feet around,

From the road-side to the brook;
Where into he loved to look.
Step the meek birds where erst they ranged,
The wintry garden lies unchanged,
The brook into the stream runs on,

But the deep-eyed Boy is gone.

Was there no star that could be sent,
No watcher in the firmament,
No angel from the countless host,
That loiters round the crystal coast,
Could stoop to heal that only child,
Nature's sweet marvel undefiled,
And keep the blossom of the earth,
Which all her harvests were not worth?

Perchance, not he, but nature ailed,
The world, and not the infant failed,
It was not ripe yet, to sustain
A genius of so fine a strain,
Who gazed upon the sun and moon
As if he came unto his own,
And pregnant with his grander thought,
Brought the old order into doubt.
Awhile his beauty their beauty tried,
They could not feed him, and he died,

Some went and came about the dead,
And some in books of solace read,
Some to their friends the tidings say,
Some went to write, some went to pray,
One tarried here, there hurried one,
But their heart abode with none.
Covetous death bereaved us all
To aggrandize one funeral.
The eager Fate which carried thee
Took the largest part of me.

For this losing is true dying,
This is lordly man's down-lying,
This is slow but sure reclining,
Star by star his world resigning.

O child of Paradise!

Hearts are dust, hearts' loves remain,
Heart's love will meet thee again

Sunday, March 27, 2005 11:32 PM

Easter

Sam loved Easter though I suppose not more than any other holiday. He simply loved a party – any occasion would do. Orange eggs were his specialty.

It was a sunshine, beautiful day – sunshine, beautiful weekend.

Yesterday Zachary's power wheelchair was delivered – candy red, able to go up to 8 mph (shouldn't he need a license for that?) and capable of doing wheelies and traversing across mud, grass and over hills. His smile was wonderful – such a very real smile. He has been missing Sam so much but his eyes just shone for a time yesterday and that was so good to see.

A bittersweet moment between the vendor (P) and I – or was it shared anger. How dare the state have taken so long to approve this wheelchair? As P said, "Zach should have had it last Halloween." Even now we are still fighting for pieces of this wheelchair. Hours spent writing letters for both his and Sam's - hours during the last few weeks that Sam was alive - stolen from Sam so unnecessarily. It has never been the care of my children that exhausts me but all of the battles that should never have to be fought with people or entities like medical insurance. I told P. how much Sam had enjoyed his orange wheelchair. Then I cried, for Sam too would have had his months and months ago were it not for our state reviewer. P said, "They should be ashamed" and I can only agree.

Part of me so happy to see Zach so free, so fast, so daring, with Abby running to catch up with him, leaving her behind for once. Part of me so grieved - how Sam would have loved watching Zach, getting his own personal ride from "best brother," going to all the places we could have finally gone now that they both had their wheelchairs. And so that is how it goes these days – there is no predictability to any of it. It seems the entire world has become a puzzle that has fallen to the ground, the pieces scattered everywhere and I really have no idea how to put it back together. And of course the picture will never be the same.

Today – a good hour when the 3 older kids and I took a walk (Zach leading the way in his chair). It's good to get outside.

Zachary was very run down and tired earlier in the week but has perked up considerably since Tuesday. He told me that he is sure the nighttime oxygen is giving him more energy because he is having trouble falling asleep at night at his usual bedtime. During the weekend we have been working on switching one of his heart medications that he gets by J tube to an intravenous form. It seems to be going ok. I hope that getting rid of some of his j tube meds will make this increasing GI pain go away.

This week is Spring Break for my kids. It will be nice to have a week of no school although I do think that the structure and consistency of school has gotten them through the last few weeks. Abby is having her sleepover Monday and Zach is having his on Thursday. I believe that the highlight of the week is April Fool's Day. Zachary has been making long lists of what jokes he will play on all of us.

Sam's little friend, Josie, came over this past week to play – by herself. She was very clear to her mom that she wanted to come over alone. We played a few games and I got to hear all the first grade news. I am so glad that she likes to come over to play still. She and her sisters are precious, compassionate girls. On Tuesdays (after Spring Break), I am going to help out in Sam's classroom for Writer's Workshop. I am looking forward to that. School was so important to Sam. I cannot imagine not knowing his friends anymore.

Sam's school (and Zach and Abby's) – BETHESDA ELEMENTARY – is working with Brittany and her friends from Waukesha West High School to have the first ever Walk to Wipe Out Mitochondrial Disease on May 20th. One of the PTO Moms who is planning this walk told me, *"We will never let Sam be forgotten."* You can't imagine how comforting those words felt to me.

Sunday, April 3, 2005 9:48 PM

Spring break is over for the kids and none of them are happy about that. It has been a really warm week in Wisconsin – a nice surprise, since usually it seems like spring does not exist in Wisconsin. Sam's friend, Josie came over to play one day with Abby, Zach and me. What a ray of sunshine she is.

It is amazing how much better Zachary is feeling now that we switched one of his cardiac/high blood pressure medications from a J tube form (going into his intestine) to an intravenous drip (therefore by-passing his GI system). His GI tract functions so poorly that even a tsp or so of medication cases intense pain. This has gotten worse with time - it was not always this way. Until he was almost 7 yrs., he was able to eat like any other "typical" kid. Then, as things got worse he only tolerated some calories by a feeding tube in his intestine (called a J-tube); the rest had to be given intravenously. Many of you will recall that this worsening occurred during his infamous 5-month hospital stay. Thank God we have never seen a hospitalization of that length again. About 2 years ago he stopped tolerating any tube feedings into his J-tube and became dependent on intravenous nutrition for ALL of his "food" and some of his medications. He has gotten worse these last few months in terms of his GI tract function and even his meds were causing a lot of pain when given. This is why we decided to change his Labetalol, which was diluted in about 4-cc and given 4x/day to an IV continuous drip. Thankfully, I think we have done a good thing!!! Just taking away that small amount has made all the difference in the world. He was getting Valium around the clock for the last month or so but since Wednesday he has not even required one dose!!!! It is so nice to see him pain free for the first time in months.

Zach also seems to have more energy on the nighttime oxygen. Time will tell, once he is back in school and busier. I am hoping it is more than just Spring break though and that the nighttime oxygen is improving the amount of energy he has to work with.

Monday begins a hospital week for us. It is just so hard to pack for just one child and prepare just one summary. Sammy LOVED going to the hospital because he could play with his PT, OT and Speech therapist every day, see his favorite nurses and doctors, play a

129

lot more Game boy and watch more TV than usual. AND order french fries as his "rewawd."

Today is April 3. One month since that horrible night and it still feels surreal to me. I was thinking about how when he was a baby I used to count each day and week he was alive. I was one of those moms that always knew how old he was – 19 weeks and 4 days or 38 weeks and 3 days - and I did this until my "babies" were about 2. Now I am counting how many days he has been dead. It hurts so much to know that the number of days since he died will only increase. There are hours when I can barely breathe –

Friday, they brought the death certificate over. I have never looked at a death certificate. It has a question, "Was he ever married?" which was of course checked no. That made me cry the most. It's quite an odd thing what I find to be thankful about these days. Thankful for his doctor, Sam's beloved doctor, signing the death certificate rather than some unknown (to Sam) physician in the ER of a hospital he never received care from. I did not know he signed it but it would have been so wrong to see anyone else's name on there. Thankful that Peter did not simply write that Sam died from cardiac arrest (as the ER doc had written in his report). He wrote that Sam had mitochondrial disease for 7 years and this was the cause of his death. It has just seemed so false and negating of the reality Sam lived with for the ER docs to attribute his death to the cardiac arrest that he had for one hour of his 7 years, 8 months and 21 days. As if Sammy had not fought so hard and with such spirit against the mitochondrial disease that he had been born with.

This is long but I do have to tell you about the most treasured gift I received last night. The story starts when Sam was a baby in the hospital. Sam and I met Laura and her little girl named Samantha who was born with almost no small intestine. Samantha was 3 weeks older than Sam. I so clearly recall the day we all met. Laura and I were good friends and we supported each other through many hospitalizations with our little "Sams." One night, when Samantha was three and 3/4, she was med-flighted to the Pittsburgh Children's Transplant Center from Milwaukee and admitted to their ICU. She survived against all odds for over a year, most of it as an inpatient in their ICU, while waiting for organs (a liver, small intestine and stomach). She never got those organs and died a few months shy of her 5th birthday.

After my Sam died, Tom (Samantha's Daddy) called and told me that he would like to carve a wooden cross for Sam's grave so that he would have a marker up until the time came that he had a more permanent grave marker. I was touched deeply. I pictured a small wooden cross and I knew it would be beautiful and made with love. I did not picture what Tom and the kids brought to me last night. A beautiful, BIG cross hand carved that is attached to a base. Sam's NAME is carved by hand into the horizontal part of the cross. Below that is a carved big heart with many smaller hearts inside. For those of you who went to his funeral, it is a replica of the heart picture Sammy colored that is on his booklet. Sam drew that 3 days before he died. Under that is written "I carry your heart with me." I cannot even describe what I felt when I saw this beautiful, lovingly made cross for Sam. In the last month I have been very distraught about his unmarked grave. I have things there but nothing said his name. I worried incessantly that people would not know that Sam is loved. Now they will know his name – they will know he is cherished. Tom said this would give me time to really choose exactly what kind of permanent marker I wanted that will best honor Samuel. So there we were in the dark last night - Tom and his 3 kids, Abby and me – pounding this cross into the ground. I wished I did not have to be there, I wished Tom did not know enough about a child dying to know that I needed desperately to have that cross there – but it was also so right that Samantha's family was standing there in the dark with me.

Monday, April 11, 2005 11:25 PM

The weekend was very warm and it was nice to be home to enjoy the warmth of spring. I actually got a bit of sunburn on Sunday. I think that is a first - to be sun burned in April in Wisconsin. I wore a winter coat to the hospital when I delivered both Abby and Sam - my May babies.

But before we get to the May babies - Zachary is counting down the days until his birthday. THIRTEEN this year on April 20th! Amazing and wonderful and overwhelming!

We came home from the hospital Friday evening. Zach got his IVIG and a unit of blood so he should be good to go for a while now. He is still pain free – what a gift! Tonight (Monday) he went to bed

131

early – not feeling well at all. He has a low-grade fever, exhaustion, and persistent heart gallop. I hope a night of rest takes it all away.

Last week I went to Sam's first grade class to help out with Writer's Workshop. I wanted to do this but I was very anxious right before I went. I was so afraid I would cry or that it would be too hard. However it was wonderful. Sam's seat is still Sam's seat. I hope he does not mind that I sat in it. I loved hearing the children's stories and being with them. I will go again just about every Tuesday through May.

I found out today that on May 9, Sam's Birthday, a tree will be planted at Bethesda (his school).

A "Sam Tree."

A living, growing reminder of my little boy who lived life and loved life more completely and vibrantly than many people who are far older than he is.

Planted at the place he loved so much, a place that was truly a dream come true for him.

Only the dream he envisioned because of the staff, children and families who fill that school

A "witness tree" - it will grow with the children he loved, who loved him.

Thank you for this beautiful tribute.

Another tree will be planted in our yard from another dear set of friends.

This one with a plaque that was hand made – "Samuel Patrick ~ I carry your heart with me"

Also a "witness tree", to watch over all of us and remind me of all that Sam taught as he grew.

Thank you!

The last week has been very hard – if I lost Sam then why can't I find him? "He is in the pupils of my eyes, he is my body and my soul."

It is time for me to go, mother; I am going.
When in the paling darkness of the lonely dawn
you stretch your arms for your baby in the bed,
I shall say, "Baby is not there!"
- mother, I am going.

I shall become a delicate draught of air
and caress you; and I shall be ripples
in the water when you bathe;
and kiss you and kiss you again.

In the gusty night when the rain patters on the leaves
you will hear my whisper in your bed,
and my laughter will flash with the lightning
through the open window into your room.

If you lie awake, thinking of your baby till late into the night,
I shall sing to you form the stars, "Sleep, mother, sleep."
On the straying moonbeams I shall steal over your bed,
and lie upon your bosom while you sleep.

I shall become a dream, and through the little opening
of your eyelids I shall slip into the depths of your sleep;
and when you wake up and look round startled,
like a twinkling firefly I shall flit out into the darkness.

When, on the great festival of PUJA,
the neighbours' children come and play about the house,
I shall melt into the music of the flute
and throb in your heart all day.

Dear auntie will come with your PUJA presents and will ask,
"Where is our baby, sister? Mother you tell her softly,
"He is in the pupils of my eyes,
he is my body and my soul."

From 'The Crescent Moon' by Tagore

Wednesday, April 13, 2005 10:25 PM

Zach felt pretty bad through Tuesday and stayed home from school. However, he woke up feeling great this morning. His heart sounds good and he is not exhausted anymore.

Tuesday, April 19, 2005 10:05 PM

April 20 – Zachary's Birthday

When I think about Zachary I think about his wonderful spirit of hope. I have never known anyone who is so positive about life and so full of hope. Tomorrow is always a new day for Zachary. It's not that bad days are foreign to him or that he does not feel sadness - it' simply that he knows it will all work out in the way that it should. I marvel at his trust that tomorrow will be better than today considering all of the challenges he has had to deal with.

His sense of humor is like no other. He loves to laugh, to tell jokes and to listen to others tell jokes. April Fool's day is a day he anticipates and makes plans for weeks in advance. He does not always show it to people but once he does it just shines through and makes one smile and smile.

Zachary's inquisitiveness. Perhaps it was all the Curious George books we read when he was little for Zach is curious and this only seems to be growing almost by the month in the last year. He wants to know, he wonders and seeks to understand. He is never afraid to ask why and I find myself wondering and pondering right along with him. There IS so much to wonder about in the world.

His thoughtfulness is inspiring. One of Zach's busiest times of the year is Christmas because for weeks he works during all of his free time to create presents for his family. The poster size Valentine card he made for Sammy is in our family room still – a poster with such detail and care - simply because he wanted to make Sam smile. And it is like that for all of our birthdays. He never forgets, he is always the one who has planned the gift he is going to give weeks if not months in advance. Each morning he asks me, "What can I do to help you?" Every day that Sam was alive he made himself completely available to Sam – even though there were times I know he did not necessarily want to play at that particular moment.

Zach can be quiet and that fools many people. When he was younger he was said to have autism. I believed that to be true yet still there was so much that I could see in his eyes…..I so clearly remember how clear he was even when he could not talk. I used to read him this book when he was a toddler about animals and the sounds they make.

134

Zach was a very silent child – he lost all of his language at the age of 13 months and did not talk again until he was about 2. Even then, he did not like to talk or look at people for a long time. But I would read this book and if I said the Dog says Quack he would give me this look that let me know I was reading it wrong. And if I persisted and perhaps said that the owl says meow he would throw a pillow off the couch. I admit I used to do these things on purpose because I loved to see Zach shine through the silent exterior that he so often showed the world. In the last few months he seems to be showing more and more people who he is and that delights me.

He so rarely complains that when he does, I take it pretty seriously. When he was told that he could not eat by mouth anymore – this told to a 7 year old child that loved to eat – he did not cry. He said "I am sad" and then he asked what he could eat. In the years that have followed, this has been one of the hardest things for Zachary to deal with. There are days he expresses how sad he is that he cannot eat anymore. The week before his birthday he never fails to write out two menus for his birthday. One is for what we will have because he can eat it (ice cream or drinks) and one is what he would have if he could eat (lasagna, sloppy joe, a banana, waffles). But he never whines or complains about this. And it is like this with everything – his need for medications or an earlier bedtime or not being able to run and play sports like all the other boys. This is perhaps the thing about Zachary that humbles me the most.

I always thought that if anything happened to Sam, Zachary would die too. Perhaps not physically but emotionally. So what stands out to me the most about Zach on the eve of his 13th birthday is his resilience and courage. For he has not died. He has had the courage to go on and I cannot imagine how hard that must be. The two boys shared a room, they did virtually everything together – best brothers. As the paramedics took Sammy out the door I will never forget the last words Zachary said to Sammy. *"Hey best brother – we are having a Yugio party Friday night and you will be there!"* Two nights later, on Friday night, Zachary sat on Sammy's bed and played Yugio with Sam. He told me he knew Sam was there but he just needed Zach to move the cards for him. There have been countless nights since then that Zach has played cards with Sam. Sam even wins sometimes! It might concern someone to hear this but the reality is that it simply reflects Zach's resilience, hope, courage and trust. To Zach, Sam is still alive and he has found a way to honor the memory of "best brothers" while having the courage to go on and forge life without Sam's physical presence.

The question he had to answer today for school was "The challenge I look forward to facing in the future is…." Zach's answer: I look forward to going to college, and finding a job that I like – maybe being a surgeon at Children's Hospital or designing games for children. Zach sees clear to a meaningful future for himself and I cannot help but see through those eyes for him as well. Sam taught me to live for today for you don't know what tomorrow will bring and Zachary is the perfect complement to that. I have learned from Zach to hold fast to my hope for tomorrow.

Happy 13th Birthday Zachary Ryan!

Josie came over today and helped me to wrap presents for Zachary. Thank you Josie!! I love when you come over to play with me.

****

From Upcoming Bethesda Newsletter:

PLEASE MARK YOUR CALENDAR FOR
"FIRST ANNUAL WALK TO WIPE OUT
MITOCHONDRIAL DISEASE"
The West High School Senior Board Members, in conjunction with the Bethesda PTO and Student Council, are coordinating a 1 Mile Walk/5 K Run in loving memory of Samuel Juhlmann. Sam, a beloved Bethesda student, is so greatly missed after sadly passing away on March 3 from the devastating effects of mitochondrial disease. All proceeds from this walk/run are to benefit the United Mitochondrial Disease Foundation ("UMDF"), whose mission is to discover a cure for this sometimes fatal disease and be a support system to families affected by it.

Zach had a wonderful birthday. Thanks for all the wonderful birthday wishes, cards, phone calls and visits. I think his favorite present is the bug vacuum I got him – fun stuff to vacuum a wasp I guess!

Abby and Zach played the piano in their semi-annual music celebration on Sunday. Abby played her "I am Sam" song. I cried. But she did a wonderful job. Zach did awesome with "Fur Elise"

Brittany accepted admission to University of Minnesota. She is excited!

I'm exhausted. Abby and I are supposed to give the keynote presentation at Circles of Life on Thursday in Madison to 700 people or so. It would help me feel less overwhelmed if I actually had the talk written and the power point done but I don't. I agreed to give this talk in the fall – when Sam was still with me. Under normal circumstances a keynote address would have prodded even me to begin working on it weeks ago. But this has hardly been a priority the last 7 and ½ weeks. Large crowds do not bother me but it will be my first time giving a talk since Sammy left. I will need to say something about him passing away. The talk is, as usual, about best practice in terms of caring for children with special health care needs – this time with a spin for we are using lessons from children's literature to illustrate our points. The process of going through all of Sam's favorite picture books is painful. Each one holds so many memories of reading it to him. The knowledge I impart has come from my experiences with Zach and Sam so I am used to talking about their past experiences. What feels unimaginable to me is that I will have to speak about my child in the past tense. I am told that going back to work and doing what I have always done – like these presentations - is progress, healthy, going forward. After all I must accept what I cannot change. All of that is true but life is never that black and white – nor is going forward when there is debris all around from the crash ever that easy.

A large part of the debris is from the night Sam died –Our community was ill prepared to handle Samuel the night he died. And I was very unprepared for that – I always assumed he would simply go to his primary hospital where they knew him if we ever had to call 911. And of course I never really believed he would need help so desperately that I would have to call the paramedics. It was not something I even pondered. I guess in my mind I always believed that there would be time for me to drive him to the emergency room at Children's. Although I am not sure that was even a conscious thought of mine….I just did not contemplate this because so many wonderful people cared for Sam so meticulously.

I had no idea what would actually happen when I called 911 - who would respond and what pediatric training and experience they would have. I never knew that 85% of the 911 calls are for adults and therefore adults are the focus of funding and training. I never asked to meet with our fire dept ahead of time – why didn't I? I assumed he would go to Children's. I guess I just got so used to a hospital where everyone knew my children and me, so it never occurred to me that there might be a day when we could not get there. I know better now and perhaps that will help Zach someday -but at what price has this lesson been learned? I'm so tired of learning all these lessons. Depleted.

Move forward? As I said it feels exceedingly difficult. There are things that can be done in our community to move forward and I want that. Zach deserves that. Actually every child deserves that and we have a chance to do what is right so that perhaps Sam's experience will not be re-lived by another child, another family. That would be going forward. There were some things done exceedingly well that night – compassionate paramedics, empathetic ER nurses, Sam's doctor driving out to our community hospital…those all went a step beyond even excellent care. But there were things that were done less well that night and I'm so tired of a world where the people that should say - I messed up, he messed up, I am sorry - won't say those things, are told they shouldn't, or worse don't even see the errors to begin with. Saying those things does not change what I must accept. But does that mean they should never be said?

I will go forward because my children deserve that and because it is one of the ways that I can honor Sam. But it seems to me that going forward would be a whole lot easier if everyone was willing to be a whole lot more honest with me about what went wrong.

There's an older book called *Healing the Wounds*, written by a physician – David Hilfiker. It is a book I am reading right now. One chapter is called Mistakes and the following story was first published in the *New England Journal of Medicine* in 1984 -it was considered a landmark article – written by a physician who is so exceedingly honest about himself, his profession and his limitations. The article was based on real life experiences this doctor had. One such experience he talks about is this: A pregnant woman comes to Dr. Hilfiker. Her symptoms suggest that she has had a "missed abortion" – the baby she has been carrying has been dead for several weeks in utero but she has not had a miscarriage. A procedure is scheduled to remove the dead baby (a D & C). However, he realizes something is very wrong when he is performing the D & C. Later, as he talks to other physicians, he realizes that he has in fact aborted the live baby of his patient – the baby she and her husband desperately wanted. A pathologist report later confirms this.

Dr. Hilfiker sets up a meeting with the parents. He tells them the truth. It is the late 1970's – perhaps lawyers do not advise physicians not to admit their mistakes in the 1970's. Or is it that this doctor simply understands how healing occurs better than most and ignores the advice of his lawyer? I do not know. He tells the parents and the mother asks if an ultrasound would have helped prevent this? Yes. But he failed to order the ultrasound. He cannot say why he made that particular decision but he does take the time to explain to the parents why he made the other decisions that led to his horrible, unimaginable mistake. As the reader I see that the reasons were not wrong even though the decision turned out to be wrong. This is so often the case in life, isn't it? We don't set out to devastate someone's life but sometimes we do.

The family did not sue him. They did not sue him even when they failed to conceive another child for several years. They did not sue him even though I am sure they had periods of grief and anger for the rest of their lives. I can't recall the exact words in the story right now but I do know that this educated family did not sue because he had been honest – and in doing so he allowed them to begin to heal.

A lot of press is given to malpractice suits. Risk management departments in hospitals partly exist to prevent lawsuits. I am not naïve enough to think that a world exists where no one would sue a doctor or a hospital. But I would bet there would be far fewer law suits if physicians and hospitals just took the time to say, "I am sorry. And this is why I did what I did."

139

Human beings are more forgiving than the world gives them credit for. But it is hard to forgive when no one says I'm sorry.

Sunday, May 1, 2005 11:03 PM

Our presentation went well despite the fact that the roof was literally falling in on Abby and me. My Dad had come to the conference from out of town and sadly he ended up missing half of the presentation because he was out in the halls asking the general manager and contractors to stop the roofing work that was going on over our heads (clang – bang – LOUD), drowning us out. He finally had to ask them if he should call Bill Marriott himself and that seemed to finally get them to stop. Later I looked at both my Dad and sister and they had roof debris all over their clothes! If I did not know better I would have thought Abby and I were speaking in the twilight zone. Abby remarkably kept her composure.

This coming week of May 2 is a hospital week. They sure seem to come fast. I will still be in 1st grade on Tuesday morning – I had so much fun with those kids last week. They are so excited about their stories and so proud.

Once we come home it will be Mother's Day on Sunday and Sammy's birthday on Monday – May 9. I miss my little boy so much - so beyond any ability to express it. There are still times of every day that I forget he is gone for a split second. Like today I almost told Abby to be careful around Sam because she has a cold. I hate the realization that comes rushing in that he is not here but I also dread the day that I no longer forget. I have not moved anything of his -his toys are still everywhere, his clothes his school books…I just cannot bear to move anything at this point.

There are many wonderful people who are working very hard on the walk/run in his memory to raise money for mitochondrial disease research.

Friday, May 6, 2005 10:48 AM

Today Zachary should be coming home from the hospital although he needs to get another unit of blood before we can do that.

Cardiology consult was validating even if it did not give us any new information. Basically, his echo shows restrictive cardiomyopathy. The heart is compensating with the medications we have him on and the cardiologist feels that Peter has done an excellent job in treating this issue. Restrictive cardiomyopathy is what Zach's symptoms suggested (Sam's were the same only worse) but previous evaluations have said his heart is "normal." I am thankful that our doctor was able to recognize the limitations of the cardiac echo test and has aggressively treated this problem. (He did the same for Sammy). The damage would be extensive if he had not done so. So a new echo this admission with a different doc reading it, who took the time to look very carefully.....I'm just glad for the affirmation that we are doing all of the right things for Zach and in retrospect we were doing all of the right things for Sammy's heart.

Every day has brought tears here - always unexpected. Someone mentioned a little girl was turning 5 and her mom baked her a purple cake. All I could think about was Sam's purple cake and my purple hands on his 6th birthday. Another day it was walking in the room and seeing one bed and still another time it was eating french fries. Some moments are ok and some are not and there is never a rhyme or reason to any of it. I am told this is normal and I am thankful when I hear others tell me of similar stories.

The days have also brought tremendous acts of kindness. Orange flowers and coffee from one nurse. The flowers are bright and vivid – they are Sam and he would have loved them. A hamster card from another nurse to remind me of Sam and Pancakes. A statue of a little boy holding a golden heart from a nurse who was out shopping and upon seeing it could only think of Sam. It's beautiful, precious. A post card from his homebound teacher who in Paris, stopped at Notre Dame, lit a candle and "thanked God for having had Sam in her life." A beautiful gift basket for Mothers' Day from 3 very special people at the hospital – I am overwhelmed that they would do this. A new "chicken food" (he was Sam's favorite stuffed dog who had been discontinued by the manufacturer). Chicken food is buried with Sam - it only seemed right but when I look at Sam's bed with all of his dogs there has been something missing. It seems chicken food should be there.....a nurse found a new one and brought it to me. A poem sent to me by someone from school, who was imagining how hard Mothers'

Day would be. An email from a doctor who is worried that I may be blaming myself for Sam's death and he just wanted me to know I took such good care of Sam.

I am thankful for these people that I know because of Sam and Zach. I am so thankful when someone remembers that May 9 will be Sam's birthday. I am thankful for people who understand that even though I have 3 other children, they do not make up for the loss of one (just as he would not make up for the loss of any of them). These people understand that Mother's Day is not the same day it used to be for me. I am thankful for people who will talk about Sam and don't avoid saying his name or remembering something about him. I am thankful for people who say "I miss Sam." I am thankful for people who know that this is not an event to get over....that Sam's life changed me and his death has changed me and it will take time to find my way.

This week in first grade - a conversation that is pretty typical for my days there.

Child: "I miss Sam" (they don't beat around the bush or look for the "right words"

Anne: "Me too."

Child: "I think you miss him more because he was your son." (empathy some adults could learn from)

Anne: "I do miss him a lot."

Child: "He was my best friend" (they all claim this status!)

Anne: "He sure liked you a lot. You were a wonderful friend to him."

Child: "Yes, I liked it when he smiled and I was his greeter with a hug every day. He liked that."

Anne: "Yes he did. I hope you always remember what a good friend you were to him."

Child: "I wish he was not born with those medical problems."

Anne: "Me too."

Child: "My mom says that now he is in heaven and he can eat with his mouth and not through a tube."

Anne: "Yes, I think that is true. Maybe he has a dog too."

Child: "Yes, maybe a dead dog (I think he meant a dog that had died on Earth).

142

Then silence.

Then he put his arm around me

Child: "I know he is probably happy but I wish he was here. I miss him."

Anne: "I miss him too."

Child: "I have to go to recess now. I'll see you next week"

Well, I was supposed to be running down for coffee and so I better go. I will be writing again on Sam's birthday if I can. Abby has written a beautiful poem and I will ask her if I can post it on here. Hopefully I will have pictures of the tree that will be planted that day outside of his school. I know the first graders will be a source of sunshine to me on his birthday.

Monday, May 9, 2005 6:18 AM

Today is Sammy's birthday. He would have been 8. It is a day of many emotions. Thankfulness for the beautiful child he is, and that he was my child. Grief - for he did not live to celebrate this 8th birthday here. I have been up most of the night - simply remembering.

What I've written for him reflects the joy and pain of this day. Happy Birthday Sam!

For Sam Love Mama

You would have been 8 years old this May 9th.

I have been thinking a lot about the gifts you have given to me. So many Sam.

You taught me about being real,

for you were real every day of your life on Earth.

Never did you want to be anybody but you.

Nor did you ever pretend feelings you did not have.

You simply were you - and you taught me how to be me.

You taught me that life is to be lived completely and thoroughly.

Like Thoreau, you chose to live deeply, to suck out all the marrow of life.

I have wished endlessly that I had time to say good-bye to you.

143

If only there had been time to hold you and rock you,
To tell you "it is okay to go, Sam. Mama loves you."
But you, Sam, would have none of that nonsense.
I should have known that.
For 7 years, 9 months and 21 days you were never dying.
You were always living –
Until in the space of 77 minutes you died.
And though I selfishly wish it had been slower.
That is my wish – not yours.
It would not have been you.
For you were only about living
And I have no doubt, my darling Sam,
that you are giving God and the angels "a true account of life" in your "next excursion."
I hope only to do the same when I see you again someday.
You showed me what happens when people come together
for a greater good – for one little boy.
Educators, health care providers, blood donors, courier,
administrators, government workers, family, friends and children
The list of those who were a part of your world is unending.
You were mine while you were here, Sammy.
But it is also true that you belonged to many for a while
And I believe you inspired something that I may never witness again -
The power and magnitude of what happens
When we forget our differences and remember what matters.
When I'm tired of trying to make things better
I only must remember to look to you, Samuel
Remembering the strength that everyone who was part of your world felt.
You taught me about love in a way that I have never known before.
Too many times I thought you would not live another day or week.
But miracles happened time after time - your life was spared.
The continual process of being brought to the brink of hell while I feared your imminent death

And then being flung up to the highest reaches of heaven when you survived
Could not help but make me realize how deep my love is for you
And how worth the pain was and still is.
Unbearable, as it is – and it is – yet still it must be borne
If that is the price I must pay for having you come to me
And love me
And change me
Simply because you were mine for a while.
Gladly, I would hand back all the changing and growing wiser
But never would I consider handing back you!
I am so thankful for the gift of you.
I hope that you know that as much as I miss you
As much as your birthday hurts and hurts and hurts without you
It is still your BIRTHday
A day I will always celebrate in my heart.
You truly are my sunshine and my son shine
I do love you Sam – "to infinity and beyond!"

On the Eve of his Birthday
For Sam's 8th birthday

It's the eve of his birthday
Eight full years since he was born
A day of joy
For he is my gift
Yet my heart this day is torn

It's the eve of his birthday
But my son has gone away
Joy of his birth
Crushed, overshadowed
Once Spring, now Winter meets May

It's the eve of his birthday
His voice - "Mama, can friends be there?"
"I want a drum"
There are no plans now

Only heartbreaking despair

It's the eve of his birthday
My beautiful blond boy gone
Remembering
Tears, wishes, please God
Spare me from the break of dawn

It's the eve of his birthday
Remains of the child I knew
A plot of grass
I tend with such care
This is what mothering comes to

It's the eve of his birthday
I can see his playful smile
Light in his eyes
Light of my life
His life joined mine for a while

It's the eve of his birthday
Eight full years since he was born
A day of joy
For he is my gift
Yet my heart this day is torn

Monday, May 16, 2005 0:15 AM

Zachary has not felt well at all this past week. On Tuesday he had a fairly high fever, trouble breathing and increased need for oxygen. It really unnerved me. I am not as calm as I used to be and it is difficult sometimes to trust my judgment in the same way that I used to. Wednesday he stayed home from school and slept most of the day. Thursday he was good for a few hours and then exhaustion, a low grade fever and heart gallop later in the day. Friday morning was rainbow day at Bethesda. He woke and felt great but by 11:30 I was called to school - he was simply exhausted. So back to bed for most of the afternoon.

146

We can't really say definitively what is going on with him. His blood cultures are negative which is good – no blood infection. Earlier in the week it seemed clear it was the aseptic meningitis he gets after his IVIg infusion (aseptic means it is not an infectious meningitis – it's just the swelling but it causes fever and horrendous headache for him). He gets this every month but the last few months it has been getting worse. We're going to try a new 'cocktail" of drugs after he gets his next infusion to see if we can lessen the severity. On Thursday it seemed his "not feeling well" was his heart not compensating but on Friday his heart sounded perfectly fine despite him actually feeling worse than he did Thursday. So who knows? Perhaps he is just overly tired from all the end of the year school stuff.

Everyone is gearing up for the big walk/run in Sam's memory this Friday May 20th. The 1st Walk to Wipe Out Mito. There was a small article about it in *This Week.* Registration can be that day and we'd love to have anyone who wants to come. I think it is going to be a lot of fun. We're counting on Sam to persuade God that the weather should be nothing less than beautiful. We all know how persuasive our Sam can be!

The Waukesha Freeman is coming out Tuesday to do a story – I believe the focus will be on our wonderful community. I hope so for I am simply astounded at the effort, time, and generosity that overflows onto this event.

Thank you for all the birthday messages on Sam's birthday. Thank you for remembering Sammy on his birthday and telling me so. It was hard to wake up the day after his birthday, knowing that 24 hours of May 9th had come and gone and Sam was not here. It has been a terribly hard week. I've cried a lot. Still some special moments.

The rain on his birthday morning that turned into sun by the time we planted the tree.

Walking into the school that day and being hugged and kissed and hugged again by so many of the first graders who were on their way in from recess.

The beautiful wall hangings that our school family had purchased - to hang in the library where he loved to spend time. Arthur, Franklin and Clifford - all favorites of his.

The beautiful, magnificent ginkgo tree – the Sam tree. It is right out in front of the school and very tall. Sam would think it was wonderful.

Wonderful friends and family who traveled to Wisconsin to be a part of the tree planting ceremony. Wonderful friends who were not there, friends that nonetheless made the tree possible. Your hearts were with us that day.

Zachary in his "best brothers" T-shirt while the girls were decked out in orange. Abby, Zach and I to the cemetery with 8 balloons, "the green lantern" (Sam loved this superhero) and of course, "Buzz Light Year." We sat there for a long time just telling Sam stories. It was one of the happier moments on his birthday.

First graders singing Happy Birthday To You – Happy Birthday Dear Sam! I cried but I'd like to think Sam smiled when he heard them. Genesis said she is sure he would eat French fries all day in Heaven.

A Donald Duck Snow globe that lights up and plays the Donald Duck Song! When I pass it I see his smile the day he met the Duck. Orange flowers on his birthday from thoughtful people. Books. Cards. Friends dressing in orange. Thank you.

A card, in which a teacher told me that her youngest had wondered how Sammy would blow out his candles on his birthday. Her 9 year old explained to the 5 year old that when she felt the breeze that day, it would be Sam blowing out his birthday candles.

In school Tuesday the 1st graders had to draw a picture of a favorite day they had. Josie drew her and Sam at the sock hop. And on Sam's desk – pictures made for him by his friends.

Friday – Rainbow Day. I thought of how excited Sam was when it was rainbow day in kindergarten last year. He called Dr "Hanens" voice mail to tell him that it was rainbow day and what was Dr. Havens wearing? Then he told him "I bet you're wearing brown pants!" and he laughed and laughed and then hung up. The memory was so vivid to me - I could hear that laughter so clearly. The doorbell rang late morning. It was his homebound teacher – with the music for "the Rainbow Song" which was one of Sam's favorites and the first one he ever sang with Mrs. C. She did not know it was rainbow day at Bethesda….and after she left I just really heard him singing in my heart. He loved rainbows!

From *This Week* - May 15, 2005

1K Walk/3K Run In Memory of Local Boy

On Friday, May 20, 2005 at 4:00 pm walkers and runners, many of them no doubt wearing orange, will participate in the first "Walk to Wipe out Mito," which begins and ends At Bethesda Elementary School, 730 S. University Drive in Waukesha.

The 1K walk/3Krun is a first in that it is being planned and organized by two groups that don't normally work together: Students from one of Waukesha's three high schools, Waukesha West, along with students from one of its 17 elementary schools, Bethesda Elementary. Plans are already in the works for students at Butler Middle School to join in the planning for next year.

The connection for these students and their schools is seven year-old Sam Juhlmann, a first grader at Bethesda Elementary, whose favorite color was orange and who died suddenly on March 3, 2005 from an incurable disease that robs the body of energy: Mitochondrial Disease. Although many people have never heard of this illness, it is more common than people know, with three children in Southeastern Wisconsin dying of it in the past eight months.

Debby Grabow, the Girl Scout Leader of Sam's older sister, Abby, and a member of the Bethesda Parent Teacher Organization (Sam's brother Zachary also attends Bethesda and both kids will attend Butler next year), came up with the idea. She wanted to do something so that Sam would never be forgotten. She talked to the student council, of which Abby is a member and the idea grew. Simultaneously, students at Waukesha West where Sam's sister Brittany is a senior, wanted to do something in Sam's honor. And so the students combined forces, with the planning, organizing and publication of the event evolving into Brittany's senior project.

Participants can register up until the day of the race, although only those who mail or bring pledge forms to Bethesda Elementary will be guaranteed a T-shirt. ALL profits from the event will be donated to The United Mitochondrial Disease Foundation in Sam's memory.

Monday, May 23, 2005 4:02 PM

The First Run/Walk to Wipe Out Mito was an absolute success!

I don't have the exact figure down to the dollar and checks are still rolling in but as of Friday night net profits were $20,000

What an inspiration and tribute to Samuel Patrick

It was a beautiful sunny day. Just gorgeous!

Orange everywhere – even an orange ribbon tied around Sam's Tree at Bethesda.

Hundreds of people who patiently waited in line to register (we just did not ever expect so many people to come)

The Bethesda kids all wore orange that day to school.

The Sam shirts we gave to participants looked awesome.

I cannot believe that this was pulled together in 8 short weeks! I had virtually no part in making it happen either. The work was all done by friends, Waukesha West Seniors and Bethesda Student Council. On Friday some of those friends put in a 16 hour day to pull this off.

Many people have asked me if we had one big donor – how else to explain so much money. My reply is nope – not one big donor at all– just a community of very generous people who gave with their heart. All I can say is that we have the most wonderful community ever.

Zach and I are in the hospital this week.

The emergency plan meeting went very well. We hope to finalize the last pieces in the next week. Some of "Sam's paramedics" came to the Run/Walk. I was so glad to be able to talk with them and so glad that they were there. What good and caring people.

Tuesday, May 31, 2005

Today is Abby's birthday!

Abigail Nicole born 5-31-93

12 years old!!!

What a beautiful gift she has been to our family!

I can still remember how enthralled Zachary was when she was an infant. He would just stare at her for minutes at a time. Unable to talk, unwilling to look anyone in the eye – it was Abby that unlocked

150

so much. I moved her into his room when they were babies and I can still remember the first time I heard him babble - it was because she was babbling.

Her name means joy. She has certainly been my joy!

Sammy was her baby! She was his joy too!

I remember once he came home from the hospital after many weeks and I found her lying on the floor one night by his crib – asleep. I asked her why and she said she was just so happy he was home. She wanted to be with him.

One day I found a moon and stars on his window. Sammy told me "I asked Abby for the moon and stars and look! She gave them to me." She did -every day of his life.

Happy Birthday to Abby!!

This weekend Abby and Zachary had to make castles for school. It was good to hear them laughing as they worked all day Saturday on them. It is medieval week for the 6th grade and they have a very special week planned. Today King Arthur came to visit and on Thursday Queen Elizabeth will make her appearance. Tomorrow they get to do fun things like stained glass, playing chess and backgammon and I forget what else. Friday is the medieval feast -they dress up and also have a pig roast (YUCK!).

Brittany's soccer team continues to win! Who knows - maybe they'll win state this year! Senior picnic this week, award ceremony for soccer, baccalaureate, exams and then graduation day on June 11! Wow – my little girl is graduating high school! I'm not sure that has really hit me yet. I think she is more than ready to graduate!

Writer's workshop is over. I miss the first graders very much already. It feels wrong that I will not have any kids at Bethesda next year. Sammy is still supposed to be there with all of his friends. They have a birthday calendar at school and they put cupcakes on the days that are kids birthdays - but not names. One of the boys wrote Sam's name in under his cupcake. His teacher said she just saw it one day.

Missing Sam so much. Thankful that summer is almost here and the kids will be home. I don't do well with the silence of the house when they are all at school and I can't seem to concentrate enough to get anything done.

I did read a very good book last week when we were at the hospital called *The Kite Runner*. It was a story about 2 boys growing up in Afghanistan before the Russians invaded and it ended in 2001 when the Taliban were there. It really made me think about a lot.

Tuesday, June 7, 2005 10:29 PM

Tonight was the 6th grade dinner. It's amazing to me that Zachary and Abby are on the brink of leaving Bethesda and starting Butler Middle School. The theme was Survivor and the 5th grade parents did a wonderful job turning the gym into a jungle.

Zachary was given the President's Education Award for Outstanding Academic Achievement. The purpose of this award is to recognize students that show outstanding educational growth, improvement, commitment or intellectual development in their academic subjects. These students demonstrate unusual commitment to learning in academics despite various obstacles. They maintain a school record that would have met the school's selection criteria for the President's Award for Educational Excellence but illness, personal crisis, or special needs prevented the student from maintaining such high standards despite hard work. Bravo, Zachary!!!!

Abby was given the President's Education Award for Outstanding Academic Excellence. To receive this honor, students are to earn a grade point average of 90 on a 100 point scale, (an A on a letter scale or a 3.5 on a 4.0 scale). The primary indicators of excellence must be based on academic achievement. In addition, students must have scored in the 85th percentile or higher on standardized tests in math or reading. Yeah, Abby!

This has been a horrendous spring for all of us and I am so proud of Zach and Abby for continuing to wake up each day and do their best at school. No one would have thought anything of it if they had begun to do worse in school, tried less, been absent more....but instead they went to school each day and tried hard. I have not even been able to continue on with life as they have – I admire them both so much.

I cannot leave out the oldest child either. Brittany was given the Perseverance Award for her Soccer team on Friday night. I can't think of a better award for her to be given for she has certainly persevered with grace and hope. She began playing Varsity soccer as a freshman which tells you how skilled she was at the game. Over the

152

course of the next four years, playing soccer remained a great passion of hers but it became more and more difficult for her physically due to the mitochondrial issues. She is an inspiration to her entire team and we are told a very humorous one at that!

In the 6th grade memory book Zachary wrote: *"I look forward to going to college and getting a job that I like. I may get a job making toys for kids or be a surgeon at Children's Hospital."*

Abby's future goal: *"I know there are many challenges ahead of me. If Hillary Clinton doesn't win, I hope to become the first female president of the U.S. I want to find a cure for Mitochondrial Disease and AIDS, write some books, be a chef and become a paramedic for pediatrics. This is a lot to hope for, but I am convinced at least one of these goals will come true."*

Friday is the last day of school. The 6th graders will spend the day at the zoo along with many of us parents. Meanwhile, Brittany, will be finishing her exams. I do have to agree with her and her friends that the fact they are still going to school is nuts! These poor kids checked out months ago and at the very least should not have to go to school as long as the rest of the district -even a week earlier for graduation would be fair.

Saturday is graduation for Brittany!

Saturday night from 6-8 PM we will be at the grand opening of the Cold Stone Creamery in Waukesha as the celebrity ice cream scoopers (bet you wish you had that title!). Cold Stone Creamery is a wonderful ice cream place that donates a lot of money to Make A Wish of Wisconsin. It will be an honor to be there representing Make A Wish.

And still there is someone missing – I feel it so deeply – Sam's absence. It's easier to think that he has gone away then to think he is not coming back.

Wednesday, June 15, 2005 6:44 AM

Well, everyone is graduated now. What a week! Friday I went to the zoo with Zach, Abby and their class. Despite the 90+-degree weather I was glad to be there. I was a klutz with driving Zach's wheelchair up the portable ramp into the van. Good thing a friend of mine was on the other side of the ramp since I nearly drove it right off. I really need to practice before I take this chair anywhere else.

Josie came over on Friday afternoon. We had a quiet time. Usually we play with Zach and Abby but they were both busy. Instead we made necklaces and bracelets and talked. Josie put a lot of dogs on her necklace. It was nice to sit down with her and just make our necklaces and talk every now and then.

The end of the school year has been difficult. It really hit me that Sammy is not in anyone's class now. Before this I could always go into HIS class – with his friends and his teacher. I could sit at his desk and feel his presence there. But now that is gone. He does not have a teacher anymore. He does not have a class anymore or a desk. These are the things that hurt when your child goes away….things you would not expect to hurt so deeply.

The yearbooks were distributed last week. I had ordered Sammy one and his friends signed it. There he was on his first grade class page, smiling out to me in the midst of all of his friends. They had added a little box at the bottom of Mrs. Brooks' class page that says:

Dear Sam,

We are richer for knowing you. Your love for school and learning will always inspire us. We will always admire your spirit and courage in the face of great challenges. You touched the hearts of so many and will live forever in our memories.

Love,

Your Classmates

Saturday: What a day. I ran to the store in the morning to shop for Sunday's party, cleaned the house a little. Graduation for Brittany was quite an experience. They do not limit the number of guests the seniors can have so it was so incredibly crowded. Thank God it was inside as it was so hot and humid out. I cried of course. She was happy but it was just overwhelming to me that my little girl graduated high school. I am so proud of her and proud to let her fly even if a part of me would like to wrap her up and keep her in the nest forever. She got several scholarships, which were noted in the program booklet. So off to

University of Minnesota in the fall to become a GOPHER! (Couldn't they pick a better name than that?). She plans to study biochemistry and wants to be a physician. Yes, this is my child that even 2 years ago said she was sick to death of medical things and no way would she ever have a job remotely connected to healthcare.

Home from graduation and then we went to the Coldstone Creamery. Zach was too tired to scoop ice cream but he did sell make A Wish bracelets and we all had delicious ice cream treats. Thank you to our friends that stopped by. It was so fun to visit with you and we appreciate your donation to Make A Wish – an organization so special to our family.

Sunday was Brittany's graduation party. It was busy and we worked all day getting ready but it turned out so nice and I did end up being able to spend some time with most of our guests. My grandmother came, which was the ultimate gift!!!! The night before I had pulled out all kinds of pictures of Brittany to make 4 big picture boards of her. That ended up being hard because it reminded me of the last time we made picture boards – for Sam's funeral. But it was also good for me to do this. Each picture holds a memory and it allowed me to focus on Brittany rather than the party details, which so often threaten to overtake the reason for the party. I have a beautiful, intelligent, compassionate, ethical daughter. I don't think I could ask for her to be anything better than that.

Life has finally slowed down a little although the end of the month will be crazy again. I started making a garden in the backyard – a Sam and friend's garden. I've never been a gardener but then again Sam has always inspired me to do all sorts of things. I hope to eventually make it a memory garden for quite few different children who have passed away.

When I came out of work Monday it was thundering so loudly. My first thought was that it would wake Sammy up and he will be scared. My next thought was that I needed to go home to him – he will want me. This of course is all happening in split second time. And then it hit me that he is not at home and it just took my breath away. I literally had to sit down – in the middle of the steps of the parking garage. I felt like I could not take enough air in. I wish I understood grief – it is just not understandable how some moments and even days can be okay and other moments it is as if I just found out he died all over again.

Friday, June 24, 2005 8:34 PM

We have been in the hospital this week – Zachary and I.

We have been trying very hard to figure out what amount of fluid he needs and it has been easier said than done. It seems like it should be easy to figure out but it often is not - heart failure and dehydration can both make his blood work have the same abnormalities. Just when it seems clear that the problem is that his heart is not compensating, we then begin to think the problem is that he needs more fluid. It's frustrating because of course we want to do the right thing.

The good news is that Zachary looks great and seems to feel very well too. He has had a little more trouble with activity in the last week, which again, we think is related to too much fluid. He has now gone 7 weeks without needing blood. It is almost July and he has only had 4 blood transfusions this year, which is amazing. Last year he needed a transfusion every 4 weeks. We're not sure why the improvement. He is actually showing that he is making some new red cells and while I doubt he'll stop needing blood, it would be such a positive sign if he could go back to only needing it every 3 months. So we'll see.

It was nice to spend time with Zach this past week. We had time to play a lot of games that he likes. It's still an enormously difficult thing for me to leave the hospital without Sam every month. For whatever reason walking out without him hits me hard every time. It's also much quieter in the hospital room without him, fewer people in the room and just a far slower pace. I was always ready for him to take a nap but even then the quiet was eerie after an hour or so and I'd wish he would awaken. He certainly knew how to fill the world with light and joy. It makes me appreciate my time with Zachary more, knowing that the presence of my children is not something to be taken for granted – not ever.

Tomorrow (Saturday) Abby and I are going to Chicago for the day with my brother Mike and his wife, Elaine. We are going to see the show *Lion King*, which I hear is phenomenal. Well shop and eat of course too. This was their birthday present to Abby and I am lucky to get to tag along.

156

Monday, Brittany and I leave for Minneapolis for her college orientation (and my parent orientation). I am looking forward to seeing the school and spending some time with her. She went out and looked at it a few weeks after Sam passed away but I did not go that time. We're staying at a hotel right in the middle of the campus. On Tuesday and ½ of Wed I actually won't see her as she has to stay overnight in the dorms. This is all somewhat surreal to me but she is excited to begin this new phase of her life.

When we came home today I had a very touching surprise package from Make A Wish. It was a heavy, shiny, gold star with a little boy's name on it – Caleb. The letter with it said that all the donations to Make A Wish in Sammy's memory were enough to send Caleb on *his* wish to Disney World and on a Disney Cruise. Caleb, they wrote, is 8 years old, loves computers and loved his wish coming true. I hope Sammy got to see Caleb having his wish.

It struck me anew how each of our lives affects another. Sammy's health care providers gave so much to him – especially his primary doctor – to keep him alive far beyond all the predictions. Because of their efforts and because of so many unknown people at Make A Wish (MAW), Sam was able to go to Disney World. Sam's joy during that trip is something engraved on my heart and led to naming MAW as one of the charities people could give to if they chose after he passed away. A lot of money was donated to MAW, by people whose lives had been touched by Sam's life, a life so fully lived because of hundreds of people who gave to him. All of that generosity has in turn affected little Caleb's life and I have no doubt that Caleb's life is affecting others.

It is the same of course with those who donated to UMDF in Sam's name, money that will lead to awareness, better treatment and someday a cure. And there were those who donated to the Pediatric HIV program at Children's – money that will be used to help other children and families live with a disease that is still seen as a stigma and a terrible burden for families to grapple with. So it is in these ways that I can see that Sammy lives on. Not in the way I want at all, not in the way I would choose, but here -in my heart always.

If You Were Coming In the Fall
by Emily Dickinson

If you were coming in the fall,
I'd brush the summer by
With half a smile and half a spum,
As housewives do a fly.
If I could see you in a year,
I'd wind the months in balls,
And put them each in separate drawers,
Until their time befalls.
If only centuries delayed,
I'd count them on my hand,
Subtracting till my fingers dropped
Into Van Diemen's land.
If certain, when this life was out,
That yours and mine should be,
I'd toss it yonder like a rind,
And taste eternity.
But now, all ignorant of the length
Of time's uncertain wing,
It goads me, like the goblin bee,
That will not state its sting.

Tuesday, July 5, 2005 8:11 AM

Busy lives.

Abby and I had fun at *The Lion King* as well as walking around Chicago, shopping and eating with Mike and Elaine. *The Lion King* is amazing – it's almost too much to take in at one show. The message really hit me as well.

Minneapolis was wonderful. The University of Minnesota does a wonderful job with orientation. I was very impressed with the lengths they go to in order to break the large university down into something smaller for these kids. It seems they have done a lot of research in what leads to success for the college student. A lot of it is common sense but it is neat to see it backed up with legitimate research. There are six qualities of the successful college student and one of them was resilience. Well that one is a given for all of my children. They are truly the branches that bend with the storm but do not break.

158

Of course I got teary eyed many times over the days we were there. Yes, I was the one with tear filled eyes when they talked about such mundane things as tuition bills. It's just all so overwhelming. But I'm so very happy for her too. It was great to be able to see where she will be. We walked around a lot the day before orientation and I have a good picture of her there now. She'll be just fine. I talked a bit to the medical people too and we have a plan for emergencies.

The city itself is wonderful from what I could tell walking around. I also took a neat trolley tour one night. Lots of green space! There are 22 lakes right in the city aside from the Mississippi river. It's clean. There's public transportation and it has history. It seems to have all the perks of Chicago but much more manageable.

Zach did okay while I was gone. He had a bit of his IVIg reaction but it was quite manageable. His central line did bleed some and it was red and painful to touch when I came home. Peter thinks it is more inflammation than infection and I agree. The cuff that holds the line in place is partially out and so I think the line is on borrowed time as it is. He seems better without extra fluids but it has also been much cooler in the past week so it is hard to say for sure.

Zach is taking a "build your own website" class through our school district. He has been enjoying it and at some point he will be creating his Spider Man website

Thursday Zach got a new hairdo. How do you know your son is 13? He wants a style for his hair. Spiked. It's very "cool" looking and I am glad he's happy with that and has not moved on to the hair-coloring phase. Afterwards, Abby, Zach, Josie and I went to see *Herbie*. Goofy movie but it's a Disney classic of course.

My Dad, his wife Patty and their 2 boys (which makes them my children's uncles aged 13 and 11) came for a short visit to Wisconsin. We went to the Waukesha parade yesterday, which is pretty much what you'd expect from a homegrown parade. It was hard to go, for Sam loved that parade. His favorite part was collecting all the candy that gets thrown. The kids made him a bag anyway and collected candy for him like in years past. It is at his grave now. I don't know what else you do except keep going on. Sunday was four months since he left. I cannot take that in – how could I have not heard him laugh for four months?

Abby and I were downtown Waukesha on Saturday and stopped into the monument place. I talked with the lady a bit about what I would want for Sam – something very honoring to him and unique – something that focuses on him and not the monument itself. I think I may end up drawing some designs and getting quotes. That will be another four months the way I am going with this. I just can't seem to move any faster with this. Out at Sam's grave, the grass will not grow very well over his coffin. I think this is actually funny and in an odd way it is very comforting. As if Sam would want to blend in with the surroundings. I'm glad that grass is not growing.

Monday, July 11, 2005 8:37 PM

Zachary is in the hospital this week. I am in with him of course.

The beautiful weather has allowed us to enjoy being outside a lot. Of course we could use some rain so I hope it does that this week while I am in the hospital. Friday I took Zach and Abby to Pewaukee Lake. They had quite an education in building sand castles with lake sand (not an endless supply and it is rocky) and no waves of water to fill their moats. I realized they have never spent any time playing at the lake – at least not since they were toddlers. They only know the Atlantic Ocean beaches of New Jersey and Florida. They were not sure about the rocks on the bottom of the lake either. But they still had fun. We'll have to go out to Lake Michigan – I think it may have nicer sand beaches.

At work I am busy getting ready for an expansion of our resident teaching program. Starting next week we will no longer be just a rotation for 3rd year residents but more of a 3 year program. Every year of residency, the residents will spend time on special needs related activities and they will be matched with a family for all 3 of their residency years instead of just the one visit in their 3rd year. We are excited about this.

Most comforting and exciting to me is that we have been given permission to develop a module on emergency preparedness for children with special health care needs – medical emergency preparedness. Sammy taught me of the need for this and I am blessed to be working with others who want to address that need head on. When I emailed the American Academy of Pediatrics staff person that

I work with, she was so enthused. It seems they do not know of any other pediatric programs addressing this need. For me this is one small way that Sam's life can continue to affect others in a positive way.

Monday, July 18, 2005 8:53 PM

Life marches on.

It seems that just yesterday I had baby Sammy, riding in the car to take Brittany and our neighbor kids to school. One of those "kids" is Julia – she's 16 now. She recently participated in her first triathlon along with two of her friends. Her family, upon arriving at the event, was shocked to see the girls' shirts, which indicated that they were dedicating their race to "Sammy J.... Mr. Incredible." Her remembrance of Sam is incredibly meaningful to me.

When I went to Sam's grave Saturday night I found a long stemmed white rose that someone had left. Then I looked and saw that whoever had left it also left one at several of the children and babies' graves surrounding Sammy. I don't know who did that but I was extraordinarily touched by the gesture from a stranger? Or a friend who also left roses for other children? There are many children in Sam's half of the cemetery. Sad and yet it is why I chose that cemetery. When I saw all the children it was the only place I could imagine burying his little body.

Last week was hospital week…

Zachary was so happy that Anne – the art therapist at the hospital – came back to work last week. She is so good for him and such a warm and wonderful person. She gave Zach materials to make some garden decorations for both Sam's garden at our house as well as the one at the cemetery. Abby spent some time with us at the hospital last week and she made some as well.

Zach attended the first Children's Hospital of Wisconsin Teen Advisory group meeting. Marisol, one of his IICU nurses, went with him. Told me he was quite talkative. Zach has years of suggestions and ideas piled up in his head. This will be so good for him. They plan to meet on a monthly basis.

Medically he is grappling with a few things at the moment. He has an infection of his jejunal site (the jejunum is part of the intestine and he has a tube that is inserted into the jejunum. The infection is

161

around the tube). It's painful. He also has an overgrowth of bacteria and yeast in the intestine. Typically, there should not be a predominance of any one type of germ. The risk for Zach is that historically, when things overgrow in his intestine, it leaks into his blood stream and he becomes ill. We're still trying to fine-tune treatment for this.

He also has a very low number of one type of white blood cell – his lymphocytes. We're also waiting for a more definitive count to come back on his CD4 cells (helper T cells). This has been an issue for some time but it seems to be getting worse for reasons unclear to us.

His heart has trouble with the extra fluid last week. He gets about ½ liter extra of fluid each day between his immune globulin (IVIg) and fluid he needs to keep his blood pressure up (which tends to drop with the IVIg). ½ liter is about 16 ounces – not a lot but enough to make his heart work a bit too hard. Getting blood on Friday did not help. Now that he is at home things are better unless he goes up the stairs more than one at a time. The good thing is we recognize this very early on.

As much as all of the above sounds like a lot is wrong – it all seems so minor to me when I compare it to Sammy's issues. It's not minor of course- my view of reality is just so skewed. But the thing is that in the ways that count to me Zach is doing wonderfully. I am continually humbled by not only his resilience but by his joy and optimism, his ability to not just wake up each day (even I can do that) but to find meaning in the day. I admit to struggling but he doesn't. And really none of the kids do. I know Sammy must enjoy watching them continue to live so completely.

I've been staring at an atlas each night and thinking about vacations. Of course some of that is either from nature (my Dad) or nurture (2 month long summer trips touring the USA for most of my childhood with my family). But I recognize some of it as a desire to run and run and run. So there are books about Maine, Nantucket and the Cape, Long Island, Delaware and Maryland beaches, Washington D.C., the Apostle Islands…all over the place. I am trying to work out a vacation, though I think it will be somewhere in Wisconsin – a first for me since I have never taken the kids anywhere aside from the East Coast. Someday I will go back home to the Jersey shore but I don't know if I could do that without my heart breaking even more at this point.

Tuesday, July 26, 2005 11:40 AM

We're all doing well. Zach's infection seems to be improving. His immune studies came back a lot worse than I expected so the fact his infection is resolving is really quite good. According to the report he appears to have some "severe" underlying immune issue, which is far worse than what we already knew he had. He clearly will need to have this looked at further. However, his primary physician is out of town for a few weeks and I do not want to do anything until we can take time to sit down and discuss it. I am perplexed that the test showed such a profound problem and yet Zach is doing quite well from an infection perspective. This could be due to the preventative antibiotics and antifungals he is on all the time in addition to the monthly immune globulin. I don't know – time will tell.

I don't want to jinx myself so I will just say that there is a strong possibility that we will be going to the ocean for a week in mid-August. The Atlantic Ocean – the real thing! I have not seen the ocean in three years. I'm not going to even say where or when because it is not definite. It's a lot to coordinate ahead of time - setting things up with hospitals, home care providers, airlines ahead of time. Yet I think of the times we went away…and then how without warning things changed so much for Sam that even going an hour away would have been impossible to coordinate. I never foresaw a time when Sam would not be able to travel. But it happened and taught me how important it is to do these things when we can, knowing there is no guarantee it will happen tomorrow. His smile. His memories – they were all so precious and worth every inconvenience of going away. Hoping it happens – that the pieces fall in place. Wishing that Sam could come.

That's about all – I have not felt well since last week and the kids have been very patient with that. I hope very much that I can do a bit more with them this week. We're on our way out to lunch in a few minutes.

<u>Native American Prayer</u>

I give you this one thought to keep –
I am with you still – I do not sleep.
I am a thousand winds that blow,
I am the diamond glints on snow,
I am the sunlight on ripened grain,
I am the gentle autumn rain.
When you awaken in the morning's hush,
I am the swift uplifting rush
Of quiet birds in circled flight.
I am the soft stars that shine at night.
Do not think of me as gone –
I am with you still – in each new dawn.

Wednesday July 27 11:30 PM

HAPPY late BIRTHDAY JOSIE!!!! Sam's very dear friend, Josie, turned SEVEN years old on Sunday July 24th! Sam loved Josie - how could he not. I know he must be celebrating her birthday and her life wherever he is. I have never witnessed such quiet understanding between two hearts and souls. I loved to watch them together. She brought him a lot of joy and she continues to bring me joy!!!

Monday, August 1, 2005 9:51 PM

Zach has a fever. I sent blood cultures in.

I really hope he just has a fever and he did not spill all that bacteria and yeast that was in his small intestine into his blood.

With the central line we can't really wait until the cultures come back (24-28 hours) to find out if they are positive or not. If the temp is still up in the morning we'll have to start him on IV antibiotics.

Yesterday was my birthday – the kids really went out of their way to make it special. Brittany cooked dinner – she did an awesome job. Zachary decorated an umbrella and a frame for me. Abby made a very creative pencil holder about my life and filled it with some goodies. They all picked out a bright pink mini Ipod for me. I am so thrilled

164

although Brittany will have to show me how to use it. My mom made a delicious carrot cake. Before that Josie, her sister Jessy and her mom came over. Josie picked out a very rich chocolate mini pie and 3 fish cookies for me. So if I get fat…. well now you all know why.

My sister is here this week – I get a bit spoiled since it is like having a personal assistant. She food shops, cooks dinner, transports the kids and runs errands for me. Aside from that we just love having her here. She is teaching a writing class this week for a few kids – Abby being one of them. (Zach kindly declined the invitation!)

Last night my friend Kris' husband died unexpectedly from a heart attack. He was young and fit – in fact one of his favorite things to do was run 5 k races on the weekend while pushing his beautiful daughter, Kayla, in her wheelchair. Bob and Kayla. Kayla has a mitochondrial disease - which is how I met her wonderful mother, Kris. When Sammy passed away Kris, along with a few others in our small circle of "mito friends" flew into Wisconsin from Boston to attend his funeral. I cannot begin to express what I am thinking or feeling about this small family. Bob, Kris and Kayla are a team – advocating, teaching, showing the world how to really be a friend, supporting, living life so fully and thoroughly…. always a team. My heart has not even figured out how to respond to this…we've worried so about Kayla in the past (though she has been very healthy the last few years) but not Bob. It all makes me just want to go outside and scream and scream and scream.

Wednesday, August 3 will be 5 months – 5 months since Sammy passed away. I am supposed to co-facilitate a workshop for the medical students that day. I have only spoken publicly twice since Sammy passed away…the 1st time was actually easier than the 2nd. I am hoping I can do this. I think I can and I want to – for me it is a way to honor Sammy, a way for his life to continue to teach others.

Tuesday, August 2, 2005 12:35 PM

Zach's temps are spiking up to 104-105 now - they come down to 101 with IV Toradel (Like Ibuprofen. IV antibiotics should be coming this afternoon. I did have some emergency ones that we were able to reconstitute and give him. He's been sleeping mostly. Trying to keep him at home.

Wednesday, August 3, 2005 11:00 PM

Lab still has not identified it beyond gram negative bacilli - oxidase positive (and you thought you did not have to pay attention in microbiology class!). I hope tomorrow they can tell us more so we can assure he is on the best antibiotics. For now he is actually feeling rather good. He did have a lower fever again tonight after not having one all day but nowhere near the 104-105 of Monday and Tuesday. I have a feeling this is going to turn out to be an opportunistic pathogen that he got due to his immune issues.

Sunday, August 7, 2005 8:00 AM

Thank you to everyone for asking about Zach and thinking of him this week.

He is feeling very well and finally had an entire day without a fever. The lab is still having difficulty identifying the bacteria that he had in his blood. They do know it is resistant to one type of antibiotics, which is really not a good sign. He is on three different antibiotics now although I am sure we'll be changing them again when we know more. He is also on a second IV antifungal for the yeast. It's a lot of meds but worth it if he can get rid of this. I don't like hearing anything about resistant organisms.

We're going into the hospital Sunday August 7th. Zach needs his IVIg. He also needs to get a study of his central line and pulmonary function tests. His breathing is labored for such minimal activity in the last 3-4 weeks – it's really very concerning to me because it is such a change. I can hear his shortness of breath in another room if he even walks up one flight of stairs or reaches up to get a glass or gets dressed.

Zach is looking forward to going into the hospital because then he gets much more of my attention. He wants to teach me how to play poker and black jack. His home nurses have taught him this summer and he loves playing with them.

Talking with the medical students on Wednesday went much better than I ever expected. It was actually one of the best experiences I have ever had with that group. A friend and co-worker gave the

166

workshop with me. Eileen is just wonderful. These med students talked A LOT and asked some very direct questions trying to get at how they could talk with families, how they could make a difference for children with chronic illness or disabilities. It was one of the most encouraging things I have done in a long time and truly I felt as if Sam was right there with us.

I have not said much about the night Sam passed away. The treating ER physician was very cold. After Sam died he said, "I'm sorry," shook my hand and walked away. I never saw him again. He may have felt compassion but because he did not show it, I wonder all the time if Sam was anything more than a "case" that did not go well. I just cannot fathom that he walked out of the room – that he could not even stay 2 minutes to ask if I had questions. Thank God Sam's doctor came that night.

In the time that has followed there has been a meeting with the administrator about that night, some letters....one from the ER physician. The subject has been various issue regarding care and emergency services that I won't go into today. At any rate, contact with anyone from that hospital has lacked compassion – so much so that it has been like salt in the wound. The letter from the physician was actually dismissive. Neither the physician nor the administrator I have talked with have ever said "I am sorry Sam died." I guess they are so scared that I will take that as an admission of guilt that they have completely lost sight of anything else. It's sad. Is this what risk management does to health care?

The entire experience makes one wonder about humanity – the arrogance and lack of empathy from these people is just so overwhelmingly potent. BUT THEN....to be around those med students on Wednesday. To be around Zach and Sam's doctors and nurses and all the others who have a role in making that care happen...I am reminded that Sam and Zach are precious people to most of those who have cared for them. The night Sam died is unfortunately one isolated case. The coldness of that physician is something that will likely always torment me but thankfully it is not the overriding story of Sam's medical care. Empathy, kindness, listening, respect, compassion, great wisdom, humility...this is what I remember about the majority of care that Sam received for 7 years, 10 months and 21 days. This is the story I can tell medical students and residents and everyone else I give talks to - so that hopefully they can see the profound impact their actions can make on a family.

One med student told me afterwards that he felt blessed to have seen pictures of such a beautiful boy and to have heard his story.

Wednesday August 10, 2005 8:00 AM

Well, Zachary is still growing yeast from his newest blood cultures. Not a good sign but we're still going to try to treat it. The other option is to pull his line and place a new one but he bled way too much with the last placement...I just am not ready to take the risk of a line placement setting off irreversible bleeding issues. He has septic emboli over most of his lower legs. He did spike a fever on Monday. However, he is on round the clock ketorolac and that keeps him feeling fine and no fevers.

Saturday, August 13, 2005 6:19 PM

I was just about to walk out the door last night when the immunologist called about the immune studies we sent off on Zach. He was working on them and in his words became "increasingly concerned." He wanted to make sure someone knew how bad the test results were before the weekend even though he has not finished working on it. He also wanted to verify that we had a doctor that would address the issues he is finding. When I told him who our doctor was he said he was "greatly relieved" and that "we are in the best hands". I already know that!

But the news was quite dismal so it goes downhill from here. Basically he said Zach's immune system is severely affected and he needs a bone marrow transplant (BMT) soon. He was very blatant about what will happen if Zach does not get a BMT – he told me "the writing is on the wall." I explained to him that I cannot imagine Zach surviving a BMT – we had talked about it extensively for Sammy when he was 2 and 3 and the hematologists and oncologists all said Sammy would not survive it. He told me that Zach needs to be put on this and that drug to try to prevent infection at all costs….(some he is already on). The studies he is doing look at a white blood cell group called lymphocytes. T cells and B cells are 2 types of lymphocytes.

Years ago we found that both boys had some problems with their B cells, which is why they have gotten immune globulin. However, the T cells were noted to be fine at that time. These last few tests show that the T cells are no longer fine and in fact his CD4 count is only 63. (Anything less than 200 is considered severely abnormal). His B cells are also far worse than what they were. The immunologist said he is reporting that Zach has 10 B cells and "that is a generous report" (he should have >100 at a minimum). The immunologist will continue to do some testing but I'm not sure it can get any worse than this. In essence it seems that Zach has a progressive immune failure that is most likely secondary to his mitochondrial disease.

The immunologist asked a lot about Sammy who likely had the same issues (we just never sent the tests off because there would not have been any treatment aside from what we were doing). He was impressed with the drug regimen we had Sammy on and said it likely added years to his life. Another reason to thank God for meeting their doctor.

I have not been able to think or sleep since hearing this news. That call was the last thing I expected last night and I certainly never anticipated news like I was given. I have 1000 questions and I am guessing there will be few answers. I don't know what this means in terms of school, vacation…I need to talk to Zach's doctor who is away until Sunday night to help me understand what this means in terms of everyday life.

I am well aware of the realities of mito disease but even after losing my Sam, I cannot begin to grasp what this doctor told me in terms of Zach's prognosis if we cannot do a bone marrow transplant. I look at Zach and he looks just the same as he did before I heard this news – how can something this wrong be happening inside of him?

We had planned to go on vacation for a week starting Friday to Rehoboth Beach, Delaware. On Thursday Lou made the decision not to go due to some work issues. I still planned to take the kids as my sister lives there and she is always a wonderful help to me. So many people who I have never met have offered things to us while there: wheelchair, vastly reduced hotel suite rate, parking and state park permits, a vehicle to use for the week. The generosity and kindness of strangers is overwhelming to me. I don't know now what we will do – maybe he can wear a mask on the airplane. Or they may tell us we cannot go. I just want to do what is right. I explained the situation to Brittany today, expecting great disappointment. She said, "Don't you even worry about it – Zach comes first." God gave me wonderful children.

Tuesday, August 16, 2005 8:30 PM

Zach's primary doctor – Peter - helped me put it into perspective – this immune stuff. He reminded me that Zach's basic complete blood count (CBC) has shown a worsening problem with the lymphocytes for at least a year. We knew that and accepted it.

We had the lab do some fancy tests to try to understand this better – to understand why he has so few lymphocytes. The tests have come back telling us he has acquired severe combined immune deficiency (SCID). He was not born with it. It carries a pretty horrific prognosis if one cannot get a bone marrow transplant but the fact is that Zach is doing well at this time. Aside from the last month with the blood and jejunal infections he has not had infections for some time. I don't even know the last time he had a cold.

I am reminded of what our neurologist told me after the boys were diagnosed with mitochondrial disease. "A diagnosis is not a verdict – it is only an explanation."

Now we have a better explanation and understanding of what is wrong with Zach (and probably Sam's) immune system - and information can only be helpful. But it does not change anything about Zach. It does not give me a verdict – it is not a glass ball that can look into the future and predict what will happen to Zach from this point on. No one knows.

We know now Zach has severe immune issues but they are not any worse or different than they were last week. One week ago he went over his friend Colin's house. One week ago, knowing he had some immune issue that I did not understand, I had every intention of taking him on vacation. I had every intention of sending him to middle school, which he is looking forward to. Just because he has a label from an immunologist does not mean he is any worse today than last week.

170

So nothing has changed. I AM taking all four kids on vacation – Sam will be in my heart where he always is. Peter said there is absolutely no reason why we cannot go.

When Sam was 2 ½ I took him to an out-of-town physician who told me that Sam would die from sepsis. I cried in the taxi on the way to the airport following that appointment. The taxi driver handed me Kleenexes one after another after another.

When Sammy was four I took him to a renowned metabolic heptologist in Chicago. He wrote a letter after we were there telling Peter that Sam would continue to get septic despite whatever we may do. He predicted Sam would die soon from sepsis. I remember the day I read that letter like it was yesterday.

Sam did not die from sepsis. He did not even have an infection when he died. Yet he was able to do things that mattered to him.

No one knows what tomorrow will bring.

A month or so before Sam went away he said to me, "Mama – I thought of how we can go to the beach this summer – I can just close my eyes and I will be there. Do you want to come with me?" He so loved the ocean and he loved me so much. His love was so honest and real. I was so lucky to have him – so blessed to be his mother. Sam taught me more than anyone about hope. It's the part of his heart that beats inside my own that helps me to remember what matters in life. Right now what matters is putting this medical news away for a time so that I can enjoy a week with my children.

No one knows what tomorrow will bring.

Sunday, August 28, 2005 10:47 PM

We are back from the beach – what a wonderful time we had! We went to Rehoboth and Dewey Beach where my sister, Maribeth lives. It's a wonderfully energetic place. It was raining when we got off the plane in Philly but by the time we got to the hotel it was sunny and not a raindrop fell the rest of the week. Just unbelievably beautiful weather.

It was odd, sad and at times outright devastating to be somewhere that Sam had never been. At times walking I would count the kids and wonder where Sam was. I thought of him endlessly – he would have loved this, he would have laughed at this, he would have said this.

171

Yet, the surprise was the comfort I felt there also. I was somewhere that Sam did not know of yet not in a place where Sam was unknown. My sister's many friends all know of Sam - in fact most participated in small and large ways in the "Writers at the Beach Conference" the weekend after Sam died. The profits from the conference were all given to the Mitochondrial Foundation. Her friends knew Sam through stories and pictures. They knew a precious little boy had once lived with me – it's amazing how much that meant to me.

Zach did very well. The day before we left he had bleeding within the tissue of his foot. It was quite swollen and painful and I was afraid it would keep us from going. However, his doctor and I talked about it and decided he should go. I'm so glad we did. He continued to have soft tissue bleeds while there and is having some pain walking so we need to figure out why and/or what we should do. However, aside from that and poor endurance for walking he really felt quite fine. Tonight I sent in blood to see if he still has the yeast in his blood. Despite a lot of meds I think he probably does and we'll have to address that more aggressively now that we're home too.

School starts Thursday for Zach and Abby – 7th grade which is the start of middle school in our district. Brittany has to be at University of Minnesota in Minneapolis on Saturday. It's all quite overwhelming. Second grade starts on Thursday too. I feel sick whenever I think about the school year starting without Sam. He will always be a first grader – I cannot even describe what this knowledge feels like in my heart.

The kids and I were truly blessed to be able to go away for a week, relax, spend time together, laugh, play, meet wonderful new friends, see my sister and honor the spirit that Sam taught us all to live each day with.

Monday, September 5, 2005 5:54 PM

It has been a long week.

Zachary and Abby started middle school on Thursday. They were both tired – Zach was literally exhausted – on Thursday but seemed to do better on Friday. I think the longer schedule will take Zach some time to get used to. His goal is to be at school 4 days/week versus the three he has always done so this is a new challenge for him.

Medically, his blood still has yeast. We're waiting for one last set of cultures to come back and if they are positive I am afraid we have no choice but to pull his current central line. He will then be without a line for a few days and will need multiple IV lines started in his arms. After a few days, if his cultures are clear they will put a new line in. It's not typically a major surgery but for Zach and Sam there is never such as thing as a minor surgery. I'm disappointed he needs this and worried but at this point it is probably the best choice. We'll be in the hospital this week regardless.

Brittany left for college – ironically she had to be there 6 months to the day of Sammy passing away. It's really starting to set in – her not being here. I miss her a lot but am also very proud of her and happy for her. I keep reminding myself that her leaving is not like Sam leaving – she will come back. It is not forever. She has called a few times and it sounds like she is doing well, meeting lots of new people and walking a lot. Classes start Tuesday for her so I'll be anxious to hear how it goes. Before she left she got presents for everyone. She also wrote a letter to the Mayor and Common Council of Waukesha about the flaws for children like Sam and Zach in the current pediatric emergency response system. On the morning before middle school started she had left little presents and notes for Zach and Abby. They miss her too.

Hurricane Katrina has affected me deeply as I know it has affected so many. There are times I just have to clear my head – I feel so helpless and torn for my fellow Americans. I was asked to provide nursing care for 2-3 weeks. I would like to do this more than anything but I don't think I can with Zach's needs. I have volunteered to give time to our local Red Cross. It all feels so minimal though. I think the story about the little boy who had a dog "Snowball" taken away from him and he cried and cried "Snowball! Snowball!" wrenched my heart the very most.

Saturday September 3 was 6 months since my child died.
6 months seems impossible to me to not hear his great big laugh and see his smile and feel his soft arms around me. I miss him terribly.

The children went back to school, excited about their new teachers and seeing their friends. It is harder than I imagined not having him go forward with his friends. When his class was still in first grade I felt he was still a part of the class. Now it feels as if he will simply be forgotten. I know he won't and a few of the "first grade moms" (now 2nd grade moms I guess) have taken the time to tell me they thought of Sammy on the 1st day of school. I look at his tree and feel so thankful it is there at Bethesda. I just wish Sammy were too.

At the cemetery the grounds keeper planted new grass seed. Sam's is the only plot of grass that is just not growing. Even people buried well after Sam have green grass. I almost hope the grass does not grow, that the area where I laid his body never blends in with the surroundings.

Pancakes is ill. Pancakes is Sammy's hamster. (Actually Sam told us his name is Pancakes Waffles Toast Syrup). I know he is just a hamster but he is Sam's. I know hamsters do not live long but .....He is Sam's.

Saturday, September 10, 2005

We're home from the hospital. Zach still has positive cultures for yeast but we did not pull the line. Instead we started him on a stronger anti-fungal medication. It's not perfect as it can be toxic to the kidneys and indeed he already has had some changes in his labs.

Other than that there is not much going on here. It is hard to get used to Brittany not being here. She is doing well – not too much homework yet but I am sure that will change very quickly.

Sammy's hamster, Pancakes, is doing better. He is only squeaking now and then so I think he must have had a cold or something.

Sunday, September 11, 2005

Zach's kidneys are struggling. After getting lab results last night, we had to stop his TPN (IV nutrition) last and just run fluids. This morning his labs were somewhat better so we're trying 1/2 fluids and 1/2 TPN and we'll do labs again this evening. The medicine for the fungus actually seems to be working but it is also the cause of the kidney trouble. We're definately betwen a rock and a hard place now.

Abby gave me permission to share a poem she wrote for Sam:

TOGETHER FOREVER
by Abby Juhlmann

Your heart still beats next to mine
Your fingers hold me, nice and fine.
I hug you and you hug me back, just as it was,
Though I do feel an emptiness, but only because

You're having fun and my eyes can't see,
I can't see the beauty of all of these.
My heart gives anything to hear your voice,
Still though I don't have a choice.

You need me to be home, do what I can,
I need to hold on, I need to stand.
Though my heart shatters, because I miss you,
I have to wait here, I have to wait it through.

I love you Sammy, I miss you so much,
I would give anything just to touch,
Your silky blond hair, gleaming in the sun,
Your eyes, legs and hands that clung and clung.

It was your turn, you had to leave,
It's not mine though I can't deceive.
I live on Earth with no choice
But to wander alone, without your voice.

I carry you Sam, I carry you in my heart,
We are one piece, we are not apart.
Together we will travel, you and me,
That's the way it is and always will be.

Tuesday, September 13, 2005

UGH! One of Zach's cultures came back positive from last Friday although the one before it and the ones after it still have not grown anything. So - right now we have surgery scheduled for Friday to

175

remove his line and place a temporary central line. However, if no other cultures are positive then we may cancel that.

Kidneys are still very marginal. We had to take out 1/2 of his usual electrolytes and almost all of his calcium from the TPN as his kidneys were not clearing it and it was building up in his blood. We've been doing labs every 12 hours. The last few times it shows that things are staying more stable even if not good. We may be able to go to every 24 hr labs tomorrow if the ones tonight come back without any surprises. Zach has been exhausted - long naps and sleeping 12 hours at night. But he is home! Thank God for Zach's wonderful doctor who guides me in what to do several times/day so that Zach can be at home.

It thundered tonight and my first thought was that Sam was going to start getting scared. It seems impossible that such a vibrant child could be so still now.

Sunday, September 18, 2005 10:07 PM

Zachary did not have surgery on Friday. He has had a few more positive cultures but I was reluctant to send him to surgery. The cultures are not consistently positive which leads me to believe that maybe we are making progress clearing the infection. Also, his kidney function was worsening by the day and without knowing why or how bad it was going to get I was scared to commit him to an elective surgery. He is likely to still need the surgery but I want to do it when he is at his best. His doctor continues to be ever patient with my reluctance. I just keep hoping that things will improve.

Through the week we received results every night from Zach's blood work that indicated his kidneys and then his liver were becoming increasingly dysfunctional. Initially, it seemed it was a direct consequence of the Amphotericin B (medication that treats the yeast) but as the week went on we began to suspect that his heart might be functioning worse and not getting oxygen to his kidneys. Friday night we decided to see what would happen if we increased his Labetalol IV drip (heart med) and gave him more doses of the diuretic in an attempt to unload fluid so his heart did not have to work so hard. Saturday he was not worse, though not better either. Tonight his labs were definitely better – which is just such a relief! He also seemed more cognitively aware – he's been sort of "out to lunch" all week. Of course none of this is good news in the sense that his heart function really got worse in the last few weeks but as long as we can do something about it I need to focus on that. I try so hard not to assume that Zach will follow in Sam's footsteps.

This was Zach's first four-day week of school. He did okay. It's definitely an adjustment for him. He loves his art class - naturally. They put a wireless card in/on his computer this week and he has his own flash drive so technologically he is way beyond me. It's really neat that technology can be such an asset to him. They are able to scan in all his worksheets so he has very little writing by hand to do. There have been a few beginning of the year kinks with school – this is a brand new school with all new staff so I think it is to be expected. Remarkably, there are several on the staff who have gone out of their way to advocate for him and work towards assuring that he gets what he needs. That gives me the confidence to know that this will all be okay. Tuesday I am going in to talk at the staff meeting.

I was devastated to go out to Sammy's grave tonight and find that there has been theft at the cemetery - again. This time whoever it is stole something from Sam's grave. They took Buzz Light Year and the Little Green Men. They were just little plastic figures and they have absolutely no monetary value – but they mattered to Sam – they mattered a lot. How can anyone be so cruel? I just sat on the grass and cried.

I am comforted by a gift from Tanner, one of Zach's friends, who made a ceramic, orange flower for Sammy's grave. It is beautiful!

There are many tears in the heart that never reach the eyes
    ---Anonymous

Sunday, September 25, 2005 10:43 PM

Below is from an Op-Ed piece in the NYT today by John Grisham:
When William Faulkner accepted the Nobel Prize in 1950, he said, in part: "I believe that man will not merely endure: he will prevail. He is immortal, not because he alone among creatures has an

inexhaustible voice, but because he has a soul, a spirit capable of compassion, sacrifice and endurance."

The piece was about the unending hope, perseverance and resilience of people from Biloxi and Southern Mississippi. I think it rings true about so many families who have children with special health care needs – those still here and those who have passed away. I think it describes all of my children and so many siblings of children with special health care needs. It gives me hope that I myself will endure.

Zachary has been talking a lot about Sam lately. He said he woke up this morning and just wished he could see Sam's face in the empty bed across the room. Sammy used to wake up about 5 am. At one point he'd call Zach's name, "Wake up, Zach, Wake up, Zach" over and over until Zach finally woke up. It took a while to convince Sam that he should be quiet when he woke up and not wake up Zach. After that he would just sit up in his bed, sometimes reading and sometimes just singing to himself in a little whispered voice…he did not wake Zach up but he was always waiting for his best brother and he'd yell out "Zachary – you're awake!" when Zach opened his eyes.

Children's grief is so different. Weeks go by and the kids seem to fine. They talk about Sam each day but don't talk of missing him. But then there are clumps of days when their hearts are heavy. They don't say much but it comes out in the things they do. Zach will start playing games that he played with Sam or reading Sam's books. Abby, too, will read Sam's books or play the piano in such a way that I can hear she is trying to cope.

Today we went to Kohls and they have the *Go Dog Go Book* and dog there. *Go Dog Go* was one of Sam's favorite books. He loved to act it out with his stuffed dogs. I had Zach and Abby with me and we all just kind of stared at the display. The kids wanted to buy the dog and we did. It's on Sam's bed with 100 other dogs.

In terms of Zach's health it was another week of daily labs and adjusting his TPN. His heart is struggling to compensate and as a result his kidneys are fairly dysfunctional. He is beginning to regulate things like potassium, magnesium, calcium and bicarbonate himself but it's all quite precarious. On Thursday he needed a unit of blood and the extra fluid tipped him back over into decompensation. We increased his diuretics again. In 2 weeks' time he has doubled his daily dose. It seems to be helping but he is nowhere near to where he was 2-3 weeks ago.

Unfortunately, we had to cancel our trip to Minneapolis this weekend to see Brittany. I was heartbroken about it and she was pretty disappointed as well. Mainly she was just worried about Zach. He is ok…it's simply that it takes close monitoring and daily adjustments in meds to make him ok and that meant we could not leave without the supports and systems we have in our community. I hope that in a few weeks I will be able to get up there. Zach and Abby miss her a lot. Abby made her a care package this weekend and Zach just keeps saying, "I miss Brittany." Who would have guessed -I guess absence does make sibling hearts grow much fonder!

Friday, October 7, 2005 11:04 AM

We're okay. I had no idea how many people read the website until everyone started emailing to express worry that I have not written for a few weeks. I'm sorry I worried everyone. Zach went into the hospital Sunday evening and the days leading up to that as well as this entire week just seemed to fly by.

He did okay in the hospital. I think we pushed him a little hard to get his IVIg done in 4 days. It required more steroids that usual but I guess the trade-off is he was done and home in 96 hours. We'll see how he does weaning down from the steroids. Sometimes that is harder for him so I plan to do it slowly given the boatloads he got over the last 4 days.

I'm not sure we've gotten any wiser about what is going on with his heart but I think we do feel more comfortable that we're not doing the wrong thing. The cardiologist did not have anything to add to Zach's care. I was disappointed but in his defense he is not a "lifer" as one of our longer term docs put it, and does not have the perspective that can only come with time and experience working with my kids. Despite the disappointment at nothing new to offer Zach, I am ever so thankful for the "lifers" – our doctors, who while frustrated that there seems to be so few clear answers for the kids, are still able to accept that medicine often poses more questions than answers. In the absence of certainties all we can do is try to put together the pieces of the puzzle that we do have, be cautious and yet open minded as we forge forward doing the best we can do.

One of our bigger questions was whether the treatment for his heart is worsening his kidneys. The nephrologist put my mind to ease that he thinks we are thinking about this correctly and he trusts that we are careful enough to continue treating Zach in the way we have been.

We did three more sets of blood cultures to assure ourselves that the yeast is really gone from Zach's line. So far all the cultures are negative. He still needs to be treated for another month with the Ampho B. Zach did need another unit of blood and even so, his hemoglobin last night is not where it usually is after a transfusion. For whatever reason his transfusion needs have increased.....I hope that goes away as quickly as it came.

School conferences this week – both Zach and Abby seem to be doing well. Always good to hear. Right now Zach is home for the day, but working on his English essays. I have looked over his shoulder a few times and am impressed with some of the thoughts he has expressed. He is not necessarily grammatically correct but the thoughts are precious.

Abby has been writing for the school newspaper. She so loves to write. Her most recent article is on the nomination of Chief Justice Roberts. Right up there with writing is her love of politics. Last week I was watching the FEMA hearings on C-Span (partisan as they were) and she was right there watching with me. She reminds me a lot of her Uncle Michael at that age.

Brittany has now had three of her four mid-terms. The first mid-terms are always a learning experience but she seems to have done well and certainly has studied hard. I am really proud most of all that she is putting so much effort into making sure her learning experience is positive. I admit I was worried about her going to a large state school and my bias was for her to attend a small, liberal arts, private college. My concern was that she would get lost in the system and would not ask for help. I could not have been more wrong. She has made a connection with either a professor or a TA in every class, goes to office hours when she needs to, asks questions and does whatever she needs to do to understand. She said it is freezing in Minneapolis right now. This weekend she and 2 girls that attended high school with her (and who also attend U of MN) are going to a different university to visit some other high school friends. She is really looking forward to that. On the other hand, she seems to be very connected at U of MN – playing intramural soccer and flag football and participating in her dorm government.

My brother David just got back from recording in New York City. He composed some beautiful pieces and assembled a talented group of musicians to make this recording. "Prayer for Sam" is one of the new songs he wrote – sad but beautiful. He should be sending us the demo copy soon. I have only heard the portion he plays (the piano) so I can hardly wait to hear it with the cello and other instruments added in.

Thursday is the 2nd grade concert. Josie asked me to attend. One song they will be singing is a song that they sang in kindergarten – when Sam was there. I expect that a part of me will feel intense grief on Thursday night but as always that is never a pure emotion. There will be the joy of seeing Josie and the other children and remembering the impact they made on me and Sam. I don't think I could bear to ever lose touch with what those kids are doing or to not watch them grow up. And I just try to believe that Sam will be on that stage - even if it is beyond my vision or understanding or even acceptance.

Sunday, October 9, 2005 2:04 PM

THANK YOU to whoever put the pumpkin at Sam's grave. Sam loved carving his pumpkin each year (or rather telling us how to carve it). Thank you to the friends who made sure he had a new Buzz Light Year!!

Sunday, October 16, 2005 8:51 PM

I spoke too soon. One of Zachary's blood cultures came back positive from last week. If I thought screaming would help, believe me I'd be doing it. So now we're back to drawing cultures every day. Once he has five negative cultures in a row, he will remain on the Amphotericin for one month from that date. Let's hope that happens before he turns 14 in April! Ampho B is just not kind to the kidneys and he cannot stay on it indefinitely.

The 2nd grade concert was a joy to see and heart breaking as well. I loved seeing the kids and how they have grown. They were very animated – dancing and singing - full of the life that always inspired me during the years I went to school with Sam. I realized how much I miss hearing about what they're up to – they always loved talking to me when I was there and I loved listening. They did a very cute version of *Knick Knack Paddy Wack Give A Dog A Bone* – Sam would have loved learning that song. Before I went to the show I thought about how it was going to feel to not see his name in the program brochure. But there between I and K it said (In our Heart Samuel Juhlmann) in bold letters – right where his name belonged. It is impossible to say how I felt when I saw that. I can only say it was a priceless gift to see his name embedded in there.

It has been 7 months now without Sam. Sometimes it feels like it has been 7 years and other times like 7 minutes. Lately I can hear him and see him so vividly – wherever I go. I miss how much he made me laugh. And I miss how much he loved me – how excited he was to see me. In the morning he would sit on the bottom of the steps, refusing to move – "not till I see Mama" he would yell at the kids and Lou.

The marigolds at his grave are still growing and so beautiful – yellow and orange. Thank you to the person that left him the dog. I don't think anyone loved stuffed dogs as much as Sammy did.

I read an article about President Lincoln in *The Atlantic*. It's called *Lincoln's Great Depression* - and is about how what we see as a weakness (depression), Lincoln turned into a strength and used to save our nation. The article was so meaningful to me. So often we focus on our weaknesses as something to be cut out and removed and yet so often our weaknesses are also our strengths. If we try to cut out all of our weaknesses, I think we severely diminish our capacity to be all we can be and do all we are meant to do.

"Lincoln's melancholy is part of a whole life story.."

"With Lincoln sadness did not just coexist with strength – these qualities ran together... His despair lay under a distinct hope"

I thought about Sam – and my sadness since he has died. Missing Sam is part of my life story now.

One verse from Lincoln's favorite poem:

"Yea – hope and despondency, pleasure and pain,
Are mingled together in sunshine and rain;
And the smile and the tear, and the song and the dirge,
Still follow each other like surge upon surge"

Friday, October 21, 2005 10:21 PM

Zach has had a few more positive blood cultures for yeast. We have one last thing we'll try which is called "luminal brushing." Basically the interventional radiologist uses a brush that fits inside the central line, (think of a "rota rooter" job), with an intent to dislodge any yeast that is stuck on the inside of the line. They have to order the equipment so I believe it will be done in about a week. In the meantime we're trying another drip of TPA for 24 hours, which is an anti-clotting drug. It's quite potent and the hope is that if the yeast is "hiding" in little blood clots we can dissolve them and get the yeast out so the anti-yeast medicine can work better. Why do I feel like I am explaining a military technique in Iraq?

In all honestly, I fear he will lose the line at this point. I worry about the effects of surgery on him – it has never done him any favors to go through surgery – but that is probably what we will have to do. I guess I just need to know we have done everything possible to prevent this surgery so that if he suffers negative repercussions, I can know I made the best decision I could make. I feel so much guilt over past surgeries that both he and Sam have had. I always have tried to make the right decisions but without a crystal ball sometimes they are the wrong ones. The burden feels so heavy sometimes. But I think if this last week of attempts with these 2 things does not work (brushing and the TPA), there is not any other choice I can make.

Zach has had an up and down week. Very tired at moments and seemingly fine other times. His arms and legs seem to get tired a lot more easily these days. I think we're going to have to get a chair lift for the basement steps soon. (We have one from our 1st to 2nd floor). He did get a unit of blood again on Tuesday and hopefully that will keep his counts up for a bit. It's odd going to infusion clinic again.

Makes me miss Sam intensely. Infusion clinic was Mama and Sam time. For close to a year Sammy and I spent 3-4 days of the week there until they allowed me to give his blood products at home. Even though it was time in the hospital I have a lot of special memories from our days there.

I attended Zach's IEP this past week. I have to admit I was not looking forward to it. I don't know why – I guess because I don't know the people as well at his middle school – and I just did not know what to expect. IEPs at Bethesda had been so frequent with the 2 boys that it was more like sitting around the kitchen table with your family. So I get to the IEP (which stands for individualized education plan in special education lingo) and of course there are a lot of people there - Learning specialist teacher, Speech, Occupational and Physical therapists, specially designed phys-ed teacher, school nurse, math teacher, psychologist, homebound teacher. Everyone talked about where they see he is at now and goals for the next year…pretty standard stuff. But what was so nice was that everyone had a story to share about Zach – something they appreciated about him or a strength they saw in him…and he has only been in school 6 weeks. I worry (really I know that is a shock!) and so to hear them express such positive things about him really helped me to see that he will be okay in middle school. They see his potential and at the same time they are getting to know him and beginning to understand his needs. I felt, as we talked, that we all want the same thing for him. So it was good.

Tonight was the first Butler Middle School dance for Zach and Abby. They were all dressed up for Halloween. They are home now and seem to have had fun. I asked Zach if he danced with any girls and he said "well not close to any." Abby said she hung out with a bunch of new girls in addition to her old friends - she seems happy there. Right now she is in the shower washing out the red dye she put in her hair – I sure hope it washes out. If it does, maybe I'll try it one day. I always wanted to be a neon red head.

I miss Brittany! But she is doing well. Her room looked way too clean - it was getting eerie. I had to close the door one day. So, in the process of cleaning Zach's room I piled a bunch of things on her floor. Now it's messy again and quite honestly – I feel a lot better about it. I even left her door open this week.

Last weekend when I switched the winter coats from one closet to the one we use I could not help but hang Sam's coat up with all of ours. I put his mittens and hat in the sleeve. Crazy, I know, but I figure its cheap therapy. It makes me feel better to see his little coat there.

Saturday Oct. 22, 2005 9:30 PM

Late last night Zach told me his arm hurt. It was slightly swollen and I assumed that it was the autoimmune swelling thing he gets when it gets close to the time he needs IVIg. When he woke up this morning he could not straighten his arm and it was quite swollen from above the elbow to midway to the wrist. It has increased through the day. He is exhausted and in pain - has slept a good bit of the day and not made it off the couch. It seems he has a joint bleed. His labs showed a high D-Dimer and a dropped hemoglobin from just 2 days ago. It is hard to see him in pain. He will have to be evaluated but I am certain it is a bleed. He had that knee bleed in January and of course Sam had numerous joint bleeds. They're pretty unforgettable once you see a child suffer from one - just terribly painful.

The consensus today is that Zach's arm looks worse. For now he will be getting daily cryo.

THANK YOU to ?? for the Halloween decoration at Sammy's grave. Sam was in the hospital for many of his Halloweens but he loved being at home for the last 2 of his life.

Saturday, October 29, 2005 10:00 AM

Zach's arm measured the same Friday as it did Thursday so finally we believe the bleeding has stopped. It is still nasty looking – very swollen. Zach, ever the optimist, commented that it looks like he has a very big muscle now. He thinks that is very cool. Looks aside, I am glad he appears to be clotting better. Now we just need to keep it clotted. However, he still needs daily infusions of cryoprecipitate. He also needs more packed red cells, which is the 2nd time this week. This is just not typical for Zach at all. We decided we will admit him this weekend. It just seems to make more sense at this point. He is due for his IVIg anyway on Monday and if we're going to pull his central line this week, I'd rather do it sooner than later. However, the last 4 cultures have been negative so I am still hoping that we can avoid that.

Zach has been a very good sport about all of this. School was on vacation Wednesday, Thursday, and Friday and yet he spent most of the week in the hospital. We had tentatively planned to visit Brittany and that was cancelled again. At this point he is not happy about being admitted and I absolutely understand that. But it will be better in some ways just to stay inpatient than all this back and forth. I truly think he'll be more comfortable.

Abby and I went to the craft store last night and got him some special things to do in the hospital and I'll go back if need be. She and I also picked up some books on CD for him at the library. I'm not sure he was as happy about that as he was about the scratch art reptile kit but he did agree it is better than actually reading the book. I honestly don't know how I have a child that does not like to read. I'd say he was switched at birth but he is definitely mine – I'm not giving him back even if he does not like to read! (He does not like politics either. He told me it was torture to have to listen to the Patrick Fitzgerald press conference on the radio as we drove home from the hospital. Poor kid!)

Brittany is doing well. Our neighbors and another neighborhood friend have both been to Minneapolis so she had 2 nice dinners of non-dorm food courtesy of them. Lou also spends a fair amount of time in Minneapolis so he has seen her several times. And finally my sister is the most recent visitor to see her while traveling through the Twin Cities. I'm jealous - I admit it – but glad she has been able to see faces from home. They say she cannot wait to come home for Thanksgiving and I know I cannot wait to see her.

I woke up Friday and there was frost all over the grass. The flowers – so beautiful with their vibrant orange and yellow – all faded, having died during the night. I have not had the courage to go to the cemetery and see the same site but I will today. I refuse to leave dead flowers at a place that is supposed to honor my beautiful, vibrant child. I think I'll buy some more pumpkins – he was always so excited to carve his pumpkin each year.

Shine Your Light--Robbie Robertson

The cry of the city like a siren's song
Wailing over the rooftops the whole night long
Saw a shooting star like a diamond in the sky
Must be someone's soul passing by

Shine your light down on me
Lift me up so i can see
Shine your light when you're gone
Give me the strength
To carry on

Shine your light down on me
Lift me up so I can see
Shine your light when you're gone
Give me the strength to carry on
Carry on

I thought i saw him walking by the side of the road
Maybe trying to find his way home
He's here but not here
He's gone but not gone
Just hope he knows if I get lost

Shine your light down on me
Lift me up so I can see
Shine your light when you're gone
Give me the strength to carry on

Saturday, November 5, 2005 11:01 PM

Zach and I came home from the hospital on Friday night. He had daily cryoprecipitate infusions while there. His arm is still fairly discolored but the swelling is almost completely absent. For now we are going to stop the cryo infusions. I'm not completely at peace with this decision given Zach has had 3 major bleeds in the past 12 months but it is the decision we have made for now.

187

He continues to need way too much blood. He received 2 units again this week. We really do not understand why but are transfusing as needed. For the time being he will have to continue to go to infusion clinic for transfusions even though I was allowed to give Sam his at home. Still I am ever so thankful for blood donors, and blood bank staff who keep my child alive.

On Friday he had the endoluminal brushing procedure of his central line. It took quite a bit of effort to actually get the brushes to the hospital. I ended up talking with the person who invented the brush on Wednesday and he talked with the radiologist doing the procedure as well. This was good as he gave us several helpful hints. We will not know if it helped until we wait many days for many cultures to sit and hopefully not grow anything. If they don't, then it worked.

On Friday, one of Zach's primary nurses worked her last shift at Children's. The month before, Sammy's primary nurse worked her last shift on our unit. Good byes are difficult for me. They always have been but I especially feel it now. I could tell many stories of kindness but the one I am thinking of tonight goes like this: On the night Sam died, Waukesha Memorial nurses tried to do his prints but they only had supplies for little baby hands. In essence they printed his thumbs. I was in too much shock to notice. But Carrie and Rachel noticed when they came to my house the next day. It bothered them immensely. A few days later they brought me a gift – Sam's handprint. Each little wrinkle was imprinted into the plaster – even his little thumbnail. A perfect hand. I was stunned – did they do it before he died? No – they had gone to the craft store and then to the funeral home, they held his little hand and printed it for me so that I would have that remembrance. Such kindness from them – from so many nurses that have cared for my boys over the years.

We received a letter from the fire department. Their records falsely state that Sam stopped breathing before they got there and I gave him CPR. None of that ever happened – he never needed CPR until after they came. They also falsely state that the reason we called was because Sam was unconscious. (We called because his heart rate was slow; Sam being unconscious was hardly a 911 event - otherwise I would have called 100 times before that). I requested an amendment to the record. I figured it would be no big deal - after all, it would not have changed what they did for Sam that night.

But obviously it was a big deal to someone. We got a letter stating that they will not amend the record because the men who came that night say that the records are correct. They had their lawyer review it even. *What?* How can their staff have a clue what happened in our house before they got there? I certainly never would have told them I gave Sam CPR since I did not. Sam's doctor was on the phone –don't you think I might have mentioned it to him if I had given Sam CPR. And does the 911 call not speak for itself – when we clearly stated the reason for the call was his heart rate?

It is such a slap in the face. Perhaps a little thing to them but not to me – they are changing the story of my child's last moments. I don't understand why. I just burst into tears when I got that letter. I cannot even begin to understand how they can tell me they know what occurred in my own house when they were not even there. Every one of my kids stood there and watched those minutes before the fire department came unfold yet they have the nerve to tell my children that what they saw is in fact not what happened? My children are haunted by the truth of what happened. I can file an appeal and I will have my attorney do so but I am sick that I even have to go through this. It's messy and it is such an unnecessary burden. I feel beyond overwhelmed when I think about dealing with this. I have stared at the letter now for 2 weeks. I am so tired and tempted to do nothing but it simply feels all wrong to allow Sam's last minutes to be recorded as fiction and not fact.

Eight months since Sam went away. I wonder what he would have been for Halloween, would he be reading now? What would he want for Christmas? When it thundered tonight he would have snuggled with me – scared but happy to be with his Mama. The "if onlys" haunt me a lot lately. If only, if only I had put him in the car and driven him to Children's that night instead of calling 911. It is so senseless to review this in my mind – as if I could change it, which I cannot. But that does not stop my mind from circling around it over and over.

I adore Anderson Cooper of CNN. (For the record I loved Aaron Brown and am not happy he was fired). At any rate, Anderson Cooper writes a monthly column in *Details* He is a very thoughtful writer – just as he is a thoughtful reporter. This month he wrote about his brother who committed suicide many years ago. I am not suicidal but it did give me pause to read the final lines of his essay:

My brother was a sweet young man who wanted to be in control. In the end, he simply wasn't.
None of us are. We all dangle from a very delicate thread.
The key is not to let go.

Wednesday, November 16, 2005 5:11 PM

It's snowing. Irrationally I worry that Sam is cold. I keep reminding myself he is warm all the time now.

We switched Zach's anti-fungal on Tuesday. I want it to work but even if it doesn't I certainly will know we tried everything imaginable to save this line.

Zach is tired this week. He got blood yesterday and he definitely has better color. Hopefully he'll have more energy for school tomorrow.

Sunday, November 13, 2005 6:11 PM

Brittany came home for the weekend. It was so good to see her. She really just needed a break from school. There is a shuttle that runs from campus to Madison, Waukesha and Milwaukee so she took that home. She looks wonderful and she seems to be doing so well. It's hard to believe that I had not seen her since September 2nd. Many times as a mom I look back and wonder where did the time go? Childhood seems to fly by before you know it. Yet on the other hand – it is so neat to see my daughter in this phase of her life. She will be home again for Thanksgiving and we're all looking forward to that. Still – I feel more at peace now just seeing her for myself and knowing she is okay despite all the ups and downs and newness of her first year at college.

Zach and Abby both received their first quarter grades. Both made high honor roll. Better than that – both received favorable comments about their attitude and effort, which matters most to me.

Zach is doing okay. Labs continue to show dysfunctional kidneys – better some days than others but never too good anymore. He did have a few more positive blood cultures. We will decide on a plan tomorrow. We may try a different medication – even if just to buy

190

time. I really do not want him to have the line pulled until after the holidays.

Work feels too busy lately – I am still playing catch up from the many days I lost with Zach's bleed and then hospitalization. I took a walk at the cemetery Saturday. The leaves have fallen - another season but still Sam is gone. I found myself wishing a wish that can never come true – for him to come home for the weekend like his big sister. If only. Instead I hold his laughter in my heart and it never ceases to make me smile. His spirit remains so strong and his love of life remains my joy.

Tuesday, November 22, 2005 11:11 PM

THANKFUL
When I look at my children
Growing, laughing, learning
I am thankful for all they are
And for all they promise to be

When I read stories, see the pictures
From places like Zimbabwe, Sudan, Pakistan,
I am grieved that this is our world,
That children and families suffer so.
There but for the grace of God
My children are safe and warm.

When I lay awake at night thinking of Sam,
Missing him, heartbroken
I am thankful for his life,
His joy, his fervor, his resolve
How is it that I was chosen to be his mother?
I would not trade that honor for anything.

When Zach gets a blood transfusion
I am thankful for unselfish strangers
Giving their time and a piece of themselves
So that Zach may live
And though there is not a cure for him now

I am thankful that we live in the United States
Where he can be given all that medicine has to offer.

When the nurses take Zach to school,
Or care for him at home, at the hospital,
When I watch Zach laugh during PT or OT
When the driver from home care tells Zach jokes,
When the pharmacists carefully prepare all his meds,
And the doctors carefully make decisions with me,
I am so thankful for what they do,
For the little things that make the difference,
For staying by our side.

When I send my children to school
I am thankful for our school system
A school that has added depth
And breadth to my children's lives,
People who made Sam's wish come true,
People who continue to teach,
Nourish, care for my children.
Are there better schools than here?
I cannot imagine so.

When I see orange
I think of a beautiful day in May
Children dressed in orange shirts with
Sam's face smiling out at me
They ran and walked to "wipe out mito"
And to remember Sam
My community. Sam's community.
I am thankful.

When the 3rd of the month rolls around
And the memories of "that night" come back
I am thankful for the people that were there
In those first early days holding me up,
Near and far they dropped everything and came.
I water the many plants given in Sam's memory,

50 times a day I walk past the baskets of sympathy cards
That remind me of so many people
That love Sam.

When I wake up in the morning
Tired, missing my little boy,
a shattered heart that time does not heal,
I am thankful that I still have hope,
Thankful that my children still have hope,
Allowing us to walk forward
Through this winter of our lives,
That we are still walking,
That we carry Sam with us,
Wherever we go,
Is perhaps what I am most thankful for.

Tuesday, December 6, 2005 2:51 PM

Abby called - Sam's hamster - Pancakes - died this afternoon. Sam said his full name is Pancakes Waffles Toast Syrup. Sam loved him a lot and so I did too. I know he is just a hamster but I am sad.

4 PM: Zach is inpatient this week. We're trying to sort out a few things. As usual the answers do not seem to be very easy to find.

For about a month his endurance has been pretty poor. Not that is has ever been great but when walking a short distance is too much for him - well, that is concerning. He has had to sit through almost all of his PT session and take many many breaks to catch his breath.
Sometimes the amount of oxygen his blood is carrying drops precipitously with activity. But other times it does not.

Last week he began to have dizziness with blurred and double vision. It seemed related to activity. But he has had it here in the hospital - sitting in a bed.

The 2 best guesses are that it is his heart or respiratory muscles weakening. Trying to sort that out. His doctor has talked with him about using oxygen during the day - on the days when his oxygen saturation levels are low. He'd have to take it to school. But perhaps he'd feel better while there.

We're also still trying to figure out why he has not been able to tolerate any calcium in his IV nutrition (TPN) since September. Even with none his blood levels are high-normal. That means it is coming from breakdown of bones. There is an IV infusion he could get to try to drive the Calcium back into his bones. We had to use it with Sammy and we are trying to decide whether to use it with Zach.

Tomorrow he will see the eye doctor to make sure his eyes are ok, given the sudden onset of blurry and double vision. He will also have neuro-psych testing to assess his memory and see if it has changed.

I am feeling better now - just tired. December is hard...
Seeing toys Sam would have loved, watching the Christmas shows with the kids and remembering his delight, wishing for things that can never be.

Abby helped me decorate at his grave on Sunday for Christmas. We had to park quite a distance and walk because it had snowed so much that we could not see the road (it is not paved). So many families have put our wreaths and hung ornaments for their loved ones there. It's incredible - there is so much love and remembrance that goes into making this one small cemetery a place of honor for those who have passed away. I have heard of cemeteries where the plots are uncared for or there are strict rules about what can and cannot be there. Not here - the snow is lit up with stuffed animals, wreaths, Christmas trees, ribbons, Disney figures, wind chimes...It reminds me that love is the bridge between the lives on earth and those in heaven.

Monday, December 12, 2005 10:10 PM

Anyone who enjoys cold weather can feel free to come to Wisconsin – way too cold for me right now.

Zach and I are home now. I'm not sure I have any answers. I have been reminded that there ARE answers – we just don't have them unfortunately.

His pulmonary function tests showed some slight changes but nothing that really explains his difficulty breathing with activity. We have a fancy new, portable pulse oximeter. This measures the amount of oxygen his blood is carrying. Ideally we like him to be above 95 This will help us know what is happening when he gets so exhausted and has trouble breathing with activity. We had a big, bulky, antique machine before - it certainly was not something to just cart around. If we find he is dipping we'll put him on daytime oxygen as needed. Zach seems to accept this will actually help him feel better.

It was very clear last week that his heart tolerates next to nothing these days. On Wednesday he had hospital school (sitting in the playroom), some neuro-psych testing (sat in a chair for this), an eye appointment (rode in a wheelchair to this). Though he did not move much, just being up all day and not lounging in a hospital bed seemed to be the precipitating factor for a much higher CVP (measure of his heart's function) than he had all week. His day on Wed was similar to a day he would have at home so I think we are leaning towards thinking that his heart is the primary problem causing the dizziness and difficulty breathing.

He also had some very intense GI pain at the hospital -required a lot of pain meds and eventually we just had to hold all of his J tube meds for a while. That helped but it shows how the slightest thing (his busy day Wed.) can tip him over the edge.

On Thursday he got a unit of blood and hopefully that will hold him for a while. We did decide to give him the Pamidronate infusion and we'll do it for a 6-month trial per the nephrologist. The hope is it puts the Calcium back into his bones where it belongs. One good news thing is that his kidney function seems to be improving. I'd like to see this over a few weeks as he tends to go up and down but for now it is a bit better. Oh and best of all – no positive cultures - I think we actually saved his line from the infection he battled since August.

His eye appointment was a disappointment. His eyes are "perfect" aside from some far sightedness, which I am told is normal, and does not need to be corrected. This is a disappointment because something is terribly wrong when a kid has acute onset blurry vision impacting his ability to read and write. The doctor had absolutely no suggestions. When I give workshops to the med students I always teach them that it is ok to tell parents "I don't know." I tell them parents do not have a problem with this. Sometimes they look a bit incredulous when I say that. I then explain that it is really ok to say I don't know as long as that is followed up by actions that communicate "But I care and I will help find the answer." What is not okay is to say "I don't know" and communicate "and I really don't care enough to figure it out either." Ignorance is acceptable. Arrogance is not. So I will be taking Zach to the eye doctor that Sammy went right before he passed away. Insurance does not cover her so I was hoping the one they do cover would help but I don't think that will be happening.

Neuropsych testing was okay and not okay. His memory is intact and in fact he has some exceptional abilities (99% with memory). However, he showed consistent deterioration in the way his brain processes information – whether visual or auditory. I don't really want to say a whole lot more about it than that. He is smart and capable so I just need to work with his teachers so we can figure out a way to help him to continue to learn. This will be a challenge as the content in school is more and more abstract and involves critical thinking but we'll figure it out.

I hate giving such lengthy medical updates as the above – because I am always afraid it leaves the impression that his life is one big medical problem. It is not and I know that anyone who knows him knows that. He was busy all week making Christmas presents. On Sunday he played piano in a Christmas Music concert. He enthusiastically helped decorate the entire house for Christmas this weekend (he felt I was dragging my heels with this task – after all it was Dec 11 by the time I got around to it). Today Grandma made cookies with the kids – cut out cookies. You can tell which ones are Zach's because the cookie is about ¼ inch thick and the frosting is ¾ inch thick!!!! And may I just say Grandma is amazing – she has been making cookies with the kids for the past week. I just do not think I could handle that this year but they need to do all the things they have always done. So thank you Mom/Grandma!

Pancakes is in a box laying on a Christmas pillow and snuggled in a Christmas sleeping bag made by Abby. He looks very peaceful. Don't worry – I don't open the box and I'm not keeping him. He is going to be buried in Sam's garden as soon as it is a bit warmer (hopefully this week). I hope he is with Sam right now.

Those who love
death cannot divide
It only provides an extra soul
To watch over us from the other side.
--From Trans Siberian Orchestra Lost Christmas Eve

Tuesday, December 20, 2005 7:38 AM

It has not gotten any warmer here and I complain a lot about how cold I am all the time. I've also had some upper respiratory thing on and off for weeks now. Last night Abby and I watched a story on the Pakistani earthquake victims on The News Hour With Jim Lehrer. Its 10 below zero there and there are still so many without even a tent to live in. So I really have nothing to whine about.

Christmas is harder than I ever imagined (and I imagined it would be hard). Easter was still so soon after Sammy died that I was in shock, on Halloween I escaped to the hospital and avoided seeing kids trick or treating (whoever said avoidance isn't a good coping mechanism), Thanksgiving was worse than Easter and ever since then its been bad. There's always someone missing in everything that we do.

It's hard to imagine I ever believed that time healed grief, or that bereavement was something one got through or over. Did I really say to myself "she is stuck in her grief" about other mothers? Yes, sadly I did. Well, an earthquake could not separate a mother from her grief. Unfortunately we're bonded, grief and I, and anyone who judges that, as I used to, has obviously never had their beautiful child die. A few months ago I asked a friend of mine "so what does a bereavement counselor do?" (She being a bereavement counselor.) She said, "Part of what we do is to assure grieving parents that what they feel is normal." My reply: "Well then maybe we should send all the non-grieving people to you – so that you can tell them that we, the grievers, are normal and it is they that need the bereavement counseling!"

On the record: I am not knocking the benefits of bereavement counseling – I am thankful for my friend, most of all because she gets it.

Zach has been doing well the last few days. Last week he had his typical "aseptic meningitis" (a reaction he gets after the IVIg infusion that includes severe headache and fever) but has felt well since Thursday evening. His blood work actually looks as good as it has since the summer. He remains busy, busy, busy making and wrapping gifts.

Abby played a solo in the 7th grade choir concert last Thursday. She played Lori Line's "Carol of the Bells" on the piano. It was

197

beautiful. Rumor has it that Lori Line is in Milwaukee this Thursday. Abby keeps saying she wishes we had tickets. Instead she and I are going to the Wisconsin Club with some of my family for dinner. She'll be surprised when the shuttle comes to pick us up and takes us ....somewhere.

Zach's Christmas list was categorized this year. One category was "live objects" which included a snake, a lizard, a tarantula, a scorpion and a dog. Well the male Santa in the house says he is not living with a dog (Bah Humbug is the comment that comes to mind) so female Santa is trying to decide which live object to get. I can tell you with near 100 % certainty that it won't be the tarantula.

Brittany comes home tonight!

Friday, December 23, 2005 7:26 PM

Wishing a holiday filled with laughter, peace and joy and a 2006 filled with meaningful, cherished moments for our dear friends and family.

2005 will forever be the year that Samuel passed away at 7 years old and 10 months. That night seems like both a lifetime ago and just yesterday. In the weeks before he died he attended his school sock hop, played with his treasured friends at school and home, went on his favorite outing to the library and McDonalds and spent time with his beloved family and hospital friends. Those are shining days etched on my heart. Sam lived fully - right up until the last few hours of his life – and we find ourselves laughing and smiling about his antics and feistiness nearly every day.

2005 is the year that I learned that the heart has an amazing capacity to feel unfathomable grief and deep joy all at the same time. Watching Zach, Abby and Brittany continue to be a part of life and maintain their hope and enthusiasm has humbled me many a day. I have felt immense pride watching Brittany graduate from high school and make the transition to University of Minnesota in Minneapolis. Zach and Abby both graduated, as well, from their wonderful elementary school. They are now in 7th grade at Butler Middle School.

Soccer, piano, volunteering, School Newspaper, Robotics Club, hospitalizations, medical appointments and work continue to fill our days. Time with our family and friends is cherished. We did manage a one-week vacation to Rehoboth Beach, Delaware. Every day was sunny – it was easy to believe that Sam had lobbied for that to God. Chicago and Minneapolis were also cities that we enjoyed this past year.

Zachary continues to struggle - the mitochondrial disease persists on its maddening, destructive course. Zachary, however, remains resilient, joyful, and courageous – always with the sense of humor so unique to Zach.

The Saturday after Thanksgiving the kids, my siblings and their spouses, my Mom and I went to First Stage Theatre in Milwaukee. It is one of our annual traditions. The play we saw, The Life and Times of Santa Claus invoked Virginia O'Hanlon's 1897 letter to the New York Sun and the now famous reply from the editor.

Yes, Virginia, there is a Santa Claus. He exists as certainly as love and generosity and devotion exist,
and you know that they abound and give to your life its highest beauty and joy.

The world felt depleted of its color and sound after Samuel passed away. And yet, so many family and friends have surrounded us - within our community and as far away as Australia – that we feel encircled by love, generosity and devotion.

A beautiful Ginkgo tree ("Sam's tree") planted outside the doors of his much loved school, another planted in our backyard …both reminders from friends that Sam remains with us though we see him not. A run/walk held in his memory to raise money for research on a beautiful, sunny day in May. Wall hangings of his favorite storybook characters in the school library, lovingly embroidered with his name. A second grade concert program in October, still listing his name with his classmates: *Samuel Juhlmann, in our heart forever.* Surprise gifts, letters, cards, donations in his name, treasures left at his gravesite, and countless other acts of kindness. The love, generosity and devotion from all of you abounds and has helped to give life beauty and joy during some of the darkest, quietest moments.

199

There are some things that cannot be described by words. Thank You is such a phrase – wholly inadequate. I trust you know how much more is meant to be said with those two words.

Friday, December 30, 2005 4:53 PM

Christmas was full of Sammy. I felt him everywhere although I am not sure I missed him any more than I do every day. Still…the sadness was the quiet kind. I did enough crying for a few years in the weeks leading up to Christmas day. I think the kids had a nice day and I did enjoy spending time with them and my mom and Frank. On New Years' we will celebrate Christmas again with my brother Mike and his wife Elaine.

The concert that Abby and I went to – Lorie Line – was amazing. I really have to admit that by the time Thursday the 23rd came around I was dreading it. That morning had been the Bethesda sing-a-long, which I could not bear to attend, much as I always loved it. The thought of listening to some woman play piano for a few hours was not something I was looking forward to. I was wrong of course. It was absolutely wonderful. It was not a boring piano concert but a celebration full of humor and interaction, singing, acting, color and light. I laughed (and cried a little of course) for almost 3 hours.

Zach did not get a lizard or any other reptile since I learned that would place him at risk of becoming chronically infected with Salmonella. Still working on the dog but I don't think that will happen anytime soon.

Zach does feel pretty good. His labs are screwy but what else is new. He has had some significant pain above his knee for the last few days. It is not swollen or dis-colored but it is warm to the touch. I am worried about another bleed and watching it closely. Part of his central line broke today and had to be repaired. Thankfully it did not involve surgery and was a fairly simple repair. He also got his new splints for his legs. He still insists they have Batman and Spiderman on them – he has had the same design since he was four. Talk about someone resistant to change!!! At any rate, I hope these will help him have a bit more endurance for walking as he can stay on his feet for so little time these days. Next week is a hospital week.

I'd like to end 2005 by telling you about some of the very touching gifts I have received as of late.

My awesome cousin Patrick and his beautiful wife to be, Karon, decided that they really do not want any wedding gifts when they get married on February 18, 2006. Instead they had invitations printed that asked for donations to the United Mitochondrial Disease Foundation in lieu of any presents. I knew they were planning to do this but nothing could have prepared me for opening the invitation and seeing their card about this. They want to do this in memory of Sammy and in hope for Zachary.

Brittany, who has not drawn a picture in years, drew a picture of Sam for Christmas. I cannot believe how well she captured Sam.

Zachary made a ceramic pot in school art class. His creativity is astounding and I am the blessed recipient of this gorgeous pot.

Abby, my sneaky 12 year old, told me that she could not remember how to play the song she composed for Samuel's funeral. I begged her to try to remember and she feigned sitting down at the piano and trying to recall it. "I just can't" she said in defeat. Little did I know she made plans to have her music teacher's brother record it at the studio for my Christmas present.

Josie, Sam's dearest friend in the world, was very excited about her gift for me. She managed to keep it a secret until she brought it over. Isn't it beautiful?

2006

Friday, January 6, 2006 10:21 AM

Jan 3rd was 10 months since my little Sammy passed away. Too long. Hopefully I am meeting with the fire department next week to AMIABLY straighten out the erroneous records issue. I will be so relieved if we can just sit down, truly communicate and come to an agreement without having to spend the time and money on an appeal. Please pray or keep your fingers crossed about this. I just want the last few hours of Sam's life to be recorded as accurately as possible. In some ways it is ironic that I care how his death is reported since most days I still cannot really grasp that Sam is not here and he is not coming back. I keep thinking that maybe he will.

Sunday, January 8, 2006 9:34 PM

Zach came home but had a pretty tough day today.

He continued to do very poorly with the new IVIg, (Gamunex). It seems to have mainly affected his throat (swollen), which in turn has made it hard to breathe effectively without the help of oxygen. It also caused a terrible and sudden onset of being hot. Not just a little hot but feeling psychotically hot as in I can't even think or do anything I am so hot. We presume it also caused Gastrointestinal tract swelling as he is in a lot of GI pain and requiring a lot of pain medication.

Today Zachy slept just about all day. He looks so tired and could not wait to get back in bed after a 5-hour nap. But you know – he is so amazing that I would not be surprised if he woke up tomorrow and felt great. He always surprises me so that is what I am hoping for. When he went to bed he said he wished Sam was here because Sam would always curl up next to him when Zach was sick. So true – Sam hated when Zach did not feel well and wanted to stick right next to him. Every few minutes he'd say "Zach – you better now?"

On a lighter note the highlight of Zach's hospitalization was giving chocolate ants and Mexican spiced larvets to his doctor for Christmas. It's an annual tradition – one I am sure Peter dreads - but he is a good sport. Zach loves indulging in those "delicacies" with his doctor. They always try to get me to partake in that event with them and I always stand my ground and say no. This year Marisol, one of Z's primary nurses tried one. So I gave in to peer pressure and tried one of the Mexican ones too. Ick and more Ick. Marisol and I won't be doing that again.

The girls are fine. My sister was here at the end of the week with their Uncle Sean so that kept them busy. Brittany will go back to school next weekend. If I can just brag for a minute (of course I can – I'm a mom) she got a 3.8 her 1st semester (with a very tough course load) so obviously she did not skip classes like her mother did during her first semester.

Thursday, January 12, 2006 06:34 AM

It's about 6:30 am and Zach has been awake for 20 minutes. He's upstairs laughing and getting ready for school!!!! We'll see how that goes but what a change that he actually feels good enough to be awake and getting ready. Even if he does not stay all day this is the right kind of progress - right? Thank you for all your thoughts and prayers. A cloud hangs over the house when he is not well. (Of course since in Wisconsin we never seem to see the sun - the cloud is still there but I think you get the idea)

Tuesday, January 10, 2006 02:34 PM

Zach is still not well. Exhausted is the word that best describes him. He is not requiring quite as much oxygen so that is very good. However, his liver labs are on their way back up and his electrolytes are wacko. Needless to say, he has not made it to school. He is very hard on himself about this but we have reassured him 20 times that his teachers want him to feel better and will help him to make up whatever he misses.

This invokes memories of another little boy who was "just so tired (tiwed as sam would have said)" last March. Nothing in life, especially not life itself, should ever be taken for granted.

Sunday, January 15, 2006 10:58 PM

It's Sunday night and tomorrow Brittany will go back to college. The time with her at home has gone so fast! We celebrated her birthday today – early – as she will not be at home on her real birthday, (January 30th.) Hard to believe that she will be 19.

Abby was busy this weekend mixing all sorts of liquids into various bottles – part of a science experiment. She also spent time painting her car for school – a car that runs on CO_2. She painted it orange of course. Last week her leadership meetings started which she has been looking forward to. Today she signed up for a mission trip to Duluth, Minnesota of all places. I guess the city is somewhat in need of help from volunteers so in July she will go for five days.

Zachary did make it to school both Thursday and Friday. He was tired afterwards but stuck it out. On Friday he took those nasty spiced bugs to school and some of the kids ate them at lunch. Ugh! Thankfully they're all gone now. I must say that the girls were apparently much more courageous in trying the bugs, while all but one boy wanted nothing to do with it. Zach was zonked out most of Saturday but he did manage to have a friend over at night for some electronic fun. I suggested they play a board game but Zach and his friend looked at me like I was delusional. You know that 13 year old look.

Zach's labs got incredibly screwy towards the end of the week, reflecting kidney and heart issues. Saturday night they were somewhat improved after we changed his TPN. I don't have a clue why they got worse as he got better clinically. Sometimes I think God gave me children with this disease so that it would be driven into my head that I don't understand anything – me who needs to understand everything.

I did meet with the fire department last week. We had a nice conversation and I will be able to submit an amendment to Sam's record. I think this is an acceptable solution. Most of all, I was impressed, as I have been before, with the fire department. I am impressed that they are so open and non-defensive. It's clear that their main agenda is to do the right thing. As I understand it they have reviewed Zach's emergency plan and feel all of what we have in there is within their scope of practice. Most importantly, Zach will go to the hospital that is most appropriate if I ever call 911 again – which is not necessarily the closest hospital. I have been tormented by this issue and feel such a weight off my shoulders, having heard this.

From a more global perspective – there are still obstacles for other children and adults who may be better served in a specialty hospital, yet cannot be directly transported there according to the current plan on file with the state. I hope and think this will change …but not without a lot of time and effort on the part of many. I recently submitted a proposal to speak at a state conference on the topic of pre-planning for medical emergencies in children with special health care needs. It was accepted so I will do that in April. I only hope that the lessons learned from Sam's experiences with the emergency system will help change things for other children – even if it is just making parents more aware of what can be done proactively to prepare for an emergency.

I am reading Joan Didion's book: *The Year of Magical Thinking*. It is about her first year after her husband died. Sadly, after the book went to publication, her only daughter also died. Though it is about a spouse dying – it is a wonderful book and one of the very few "grief books" that makes sense to me. I can relate to so much of it.

I'll leave off with a poem I recently "discovered." It is called In Memoriam, written by Robert Louis Stevenson. It reminds me so much of Sam's life, how he lived in Spring and never Winter, taking "his fill of music, joy of thought and seeing," and never "ceased to smile."

In Memoriam
Yet, O stricken heart, remember, O remember
How of human days he lived the better part.
April came to bloom and never dim December
Breathed its killing chills upon the head or heart.

Doomed to know not Winter, only Spring, a being
Trod the flowery April blithely for a while,
Took his fill of music, joy of thought and seeing,
Came and stayed and went, nor ever ceased to smile.

Came and stayed and went, and now when all is finished,
You alone have crossed the melancholy stream,
Yours the pang, but his, O his, the undiminished
Undecaying gladness, undeparted dream.

All that life contains of torture, toil, and treason,
Shame, dishonour, death, to him were but a name.
Here, a boy, he dwelt through all the singing season
And ere the day of sorrow departed as he came.

Sunday, January 22, 2006 3:05 PM

It's been a pretty uneventful, albeit busy week. Brittany went back to school Monday. It's amazing how much emptier the house feels when she is gone.

We got a bit of snow Friday, which I am happy about. If it's going to be cold it may as well look pretty and snow is pretty. Abby has been sledding a few times this weekend. Zach wants no part of that. Instead he has had friends over and went to a pottery class on Saturday morning with his friend. Both kids were off Friday, which was nice. I actually managed to take the Christmas decorations down – finally.

Zach has been feeling okay although has had a few low-grade fevers. Cultures, drawn a few days ago, are still negative. Hopefully that is a reliable indicator that he is not brewing another line infection. He is on a new anti-fungal drug. This week I will take him to Madison for his endocrine doctor visit. Last time we were there was February. Last time I brought both boys. Last time I had no idea that two weeks later Sam would be gone. Last time I had no idea how quickly life can change.

The other day I saw a nurse who has been on a leave of absence for a year and had just learned about Sammy. It made me cry. Part of me wants to leave it, as is – some superstitious thinking that if I don't tell people that he is not here then maybe it is not real. Maybe he really is not gone. So sometimes in the elevator when I am asked by someone who has not heard (fortunately there are few), "how are the boys?" I say 'they are fine" because for a moment I can believe that life has not changed.

Well, you can see where this is going so I'll end it here.

Thursday, February 2, 2006 5:00 PM

Zach has been inpatient since the weekend. He is getting Flebogamma, which is a different type of immune globulin than he has had before. He is not feeling very well with it. Today and yesterday he has felt especially miserable with brief periods of feeling "good." I feel so bad for him. He often wants his oxygen on because he feels he is working harder to breathe. His lactic acid levels are high, which goes to show he is indeed metabolically compromised.

There is an interesting article in Pediatrics this week that Peter pointed out to me. Basically it says that some IVIg brands are better for autoimmune problems (which is why Zach uses it) than others. There's more to it than that but that is the basic idea. What is very interesting is that Zach's bone marrow seems to be working a little bit better with this new IVIg. It's not perfect but for the last 7 years he has not been able to make his own red cells and now it looks like he is making some. Potentially he may need fewer blood transfusions if that continued. I don't want to be too excited and my guess is he will still need blood but even so - needing less blood would be a very awesome thing. So I am hoping that as we continue to look at this, his marrow still looks like it is waking up. And of course I am hoping he will eventually tolerate this IVIg better because this is really hard - for him.

Happy 19th birthday to Brittany on this past Monday - Jan 30th.

Tomorrow is 11 months without Sam. I wonder where he is and if he can see us and if he misses me as much as I miss him and who holds him when he is cold and reads to him before bed at night and counts out his 7 French fries for dinner. I wonder if any of his friends will remember him in 2 years - if they even remember him now. They were so young. I wonder if he would have lived if we had given him this new IVIg? Would he have lived if I had put him in the car and taken him to children's instead of calling 911. I wonder if I will ever stop wondering.

I read of a mother who had a child and husband die. 27 years later she said that if she could do it all over again she would not change anything because it gave her wisdom. I wonder how anyone can say that. I'd rather be naive than a wise mother without her baby. I don't fault her for saying that - I just truly wonder - how can someone say that? It seems surreal.

I read about another mother who, as her child lay dying, said "God you can have him now - he was never mine to begin with" and I cannot even begin to relate. Sam may have been God's but he was mine too. I never thought about him as being on loan. He is a part of me. So I guess if God took Sam back he took some of me too. I cannot possibly imagine giving God permission to take my child. But I guess God does not need my permission - I found that out 11 months ago when I begged God not to take Sam. So then I wonder if I will ever understand any of this in my lifetime - why some children die and some do not. I never have done well with unanswered questions. But if an answer was ever given - I cannot imagine that it will make any sense.

Tuesday, February 7, 2006 8:49 PM

Zach was able to go to school today – Tuesday – and has not required oxygen aside from his typical night time O2. These are good signs. I have one more culture to draw. The first one is negative at 24 hours. I, of course, hope it stays that way. His labs looked fine last evening as well.

A few weeks ago Josie, (Sam's friend – well really she is a friend to all of us) came over after school for a few hours. We painted some wooden hearts to hang on Sam's Christmas tree at his grave. I suppose the more appropriate term is his Valentine tree. I put them on the tree Sunday – it was very cold but also quite peaceful at the cemetery. Even in the winter the grass over Sam is a completely different color and texture than anywhere else. This always makes me smile – he was never into being subtle.

Abby started a writing class at the library. She was not terribly thrilled with it last night as it is "not like when Aunt Maribeth teaches me writing." It is pretty wonderful to have an aunt who is a writer and a good teacher. At any rate, we talked about how boring the world would be if we only learned from one kind of teacher – different styles are good. She rolled her eyes at me – several times. She'll be 13 in May.

209

Maribeth, aka"Aunt Maribeth" - my sister – has put together another Writers at the Beach Conference with all proceeds to go to the United Mitochondrial Disease Foundation (UMDF). It's all really very impressive and I admire and am thankful for her energy and dedication in putting something like this together. I wonder sometimes why we try so hard to raise money or raise awareness for this disease....sometimes a cure feels so distant, treatment seems elusive...there are so many diseases and causes out there. Will people ever really understand this disease? Yet just Saturday I read several articles about different studies of the mitochondria – they are, after all, the culprit responsible for aging. Sammy was a little boy in an aging body. His spirit was so young and strong but his body was old and frail like a 90 year old. We live in a world where no one wants to grow old so I do think we will see greater understanding and treatment that is more specific than the band aids we use now. And when that happens it will be because of all the people who dedicated themselves to raising awareness and raising money. I just hope and pray it is during Zach and the girls' lives.

It is almost time for Patrick and Karon to get married. Patrick is my cousin. I've written this before but it deserves repeating. In lieu of wedding gifts they have asked for donations to UMDF in memory of Sam – in honor of Zach. Generous, hopeful, compassionate, inspiring...these are the words I think of when I think of Patrick and Karon.

> *I believe that imagination is stronger than knowledge*
> *That myth is more potent than history.*
> *I believe that dreams are more powerful than facts -*
> *That hope always triumphs over experience –*
> *And I believe that love is stronger than death.*
>   --Robert Fulghum

Sunday, February 12, 2006 10:24 PM

Zach continued to have a pretty good week. His potassium levels are a little high but hopefully we straightened that out by adjusting his TPN. We'll see what his labs show Monday. He is enjoying a jewelry making class in school. Last semester he took ceramics. I am so glad he has all these wonderful art classes to choose from. I went to a Catholic school and the idea of art class was "get your crayons out and draw a picture." I am amazed at the art program the kids have had since kindergarten. Of course who knows what will survive the school cuts this year. It's so sad that schools even have to make some of these choices.

The highlight of my weekend was going to the Florentine Opera to see *Carmen* with Abby, my brother Mike and his wife Elaine. We had dinner beforehand and went to a neat restaurant called Coasts afterwards. The opera was absolutely wonderful. Abby loved it – and I am so thankful that Mike and Elaine thought of it. Of course we always talk too much – and it always leads to politics. But that's ok because its like a religious tent service when we're together.... we all agree with each other. Hopefully no one was eavesdropping on us! (Sorry -couldn't resist.)

I'm reading a hilarious book right now – I needed to take a break from the two I had been reading at night: one about a spouse that dies (*The Year of Magical Thinking*) and one about a child that dies (*Only Spring*). So instead I am reading *Eats, Shoots and Leaves*, which is about grammar of all things and is FUNNY. If they taught grammar like this in school our kids wouldn't think it was such a bore.

Saturday we picked out some new furniture for Zach and Sam's room. It will be delivered this coming Saturday. The room has become a bit of a disaster (well ok, a huge disaster) and it was well overdue for an upgrade. He chose a pretty bright orange for the walls and I ordered some new comforters for the 2 beds. I plan on matting and framing some of his nicest artwork.

I'm glad he is keeping Sam's bed. But I did have to get in there and clean out Sam's dresser and his half of the closet. I'm sure some of you are surprised I have not done this yet, but I just could not bear to do it –I am not sure how I can bear it now but it has to be done. Every little shirt and pair of pants holds a story – some made me laugh or picture times we were together. On some I could actually still smell him. His tiny little Buzz light year underwear, his favorite dog sweater than he insisted on keeping in his dresser even when he grew out of it. And then there were the clothes that still had tags on them and that hurt the most – because they did not have any memories tied to them and they never will. In the end I filled 3 big bags with the clothes that

211

I will likely give away at some point. Then there was one big stack of clothes I will never give away. Pajamas that I held him in - that he wore when we said the heart poem each night or sang, "You are my sunshine." His Rocket Power shirt that originally had been Zach's. Sam had a devious grin the 1st day he wore it – "Zach" he taunted, "you grew out of this shirt and Mama says it is MINE now!" I stuffed the clothes I can never give away in the drawers under his bed and then filled his Barney and Blues Clue suitcase with some. I found his leg casts that he wore at night. I threw them in the trash. I took them out and stared at them. "You don't need these," I told myself and threw them back into the trash. But after an hour it bothered me so I took them back out. In the end I am not sure exactly what I did today except I moved some of Sam's stuff out of their room and put it in Brittany's room. It occurred to me more than once that I am probably certifiable right now. I did manage to throw out some pre-filled syringes of Amicar – but believe me, I had great angst about even that. I think I know he will never need it again…but what if he does? It's all so irrational. At least I recognize that. Perhaps that is progress.

Valentine's Day is weighing heavy on my mind. Sammy loved Valentine's Day once he went to school. On the center of our mantel is a big picture of Josie and Sam from Valentine's Day last year. He has a big smile on his face and she is pretty in pink. He is wearing the Mickey Mouse ears she gave him that day - with his name embroidered on them. He was so proud… "look what Josie got ME!" When he walked into the party that day the kids all clapped – "Sam's here!" 2 weeks later he died. Who knew? Whoever knows? I hope that even if someday his friends don't remember his name or his face they remember that there was a little boy that they loved and were good to…that there was a little boy that they made smile and brought joy to. I hope they never forget what a gift they gave to him. He was so proud that "my kids", (as he called them), loved him. I'm going to think about that on Tuesday. I'm going to try hard to remember that love IS stronger than death.

Tuesday, February 21, 2006 8:36 PM

Zach continues to have on and off again fevers and fatigue. He seems like he is coming down with something and then he seems to feel fine. I really don't know what that is all about but I am glad it does not seem to be anything in his blood.

The dentist is pretty sure he needs a tooth pulled. He wanted to do it Monday since Zach had already been pre-medicated with antibiotics but I did not think we should do it without making a plan with the hematologist. Zach – silly guy – wanted the tooth pulled!!!!

Today was the endocrinologist visit at UW Children's in Madison. Zach has a whole range of endocrine problems stemming from a pituitary gland that does not seem to function. He receives a variety of hormones and steroids to replace what his body no longer makes. It was a good visit in the sense that we had time to talk about quite a few things. However, he is concerned that Preliminary tests are showing that something is wrong with Zach's parathyroid gland (hyperparathyroidism). He ordered some new blood tests and if they come back indicative of this then he need scans of the gland and most likely surgery. Potentially this is what is causing the bone problems. (His bones are basically being reabsorbed). I really can't think about this because surgery and Zach are not compatible for a variety of reasons. Dr. A. also increased Zach's steroids to see if it may help him start feeling better/less tired. He was also concerned at the almost total lack of growth in 12 months on what is considered a huge growth hormone dose. He said a higher dose might help but it may also really hurt – no one knows. For now we're leaving it alone because he really is well above normal with his dose as it is. I guess all of this was not too exciting for Zach as he informed me that he had just spent "the most boring 5 hours of his life" with me today. I was also told the worst part of the 5 hours was listening to "your music" in the car.

One thing that touched me deeply was that both doctors – the dentist and the endocrinologist -talked about Sammy. They both said they missed him. The nurses at UW Children's said it felt wrong for us to be there without Sam. They said they felt like Sam was looking down on us.

Valentine's Day: I survived. Josie and her sisters and one of their friends came over after school. They brought us cookies and candy. Josie also brought all of her Valentine's Day cards for me to look at – one-by-one. You never know how much fun that is – looking at each card with your child – until it is no longer something you can do.

Lest I get morose on you – and lately I have been pretty sad - I have 2 pieces of writing to share with you. The authors are Zach and Abby and their personalities shine through these recent English assignments.

The World in Year 2016: Zachary Juhlmann

Hello. I am Zachary Ryan Juhlmann's thoughts. He's a fun, smart, exciting, joking, action-lover, almost fourteen year old, teenage boy. He doesn't like to play outside much but once in awhile in the summer he'll play baseball. And usually on the weekends he'll go around the coldasac (cul-de-sac) on his electric wheelchair. Zach also likes video games. He has a Nintendo DS, a Gameboy SP, and a Nintendo Gamecube. Other than video games, Zachary likes art, a good, addictive book, piano, and computer games. His favorite subject in school is World Geography, and Ceramics, and he has a lot of friends. His favorite superheroes are Batman, Spiderman, and the Human Torch from the Fantastic Four movie. He wants to be a professional surgeon. But I have a question. What will he be like in 10 years? Will he have the same personality, hobbies, interests, want to be a surgeon? I have a thought of what he might be like so read on.

In 2016 our country will be taken over by deadly, unstoppable machines controlled by China. They will also have made a Great Wall of China II to reinforce their defenses. It will be made of steel and covered in nails connected to wire. We then will be turned into slaves and forced to make more machines for them so that they will be able to dominate the world. If we don't work hard enough we will be thrown into a fire. SAY IT ISN'T SO!! After they take over the world they will revive the dinosaurs and use them to clear the Amazon Rainforest. China continues world domination by using the lumber from the forest to build empires and dominate the world!

I will be an almost 24 years old. I will be in college training to be a surgeon. I will go to Marquette University or University of Wisconsin. I will also be planning on how to become rich and buy Children's Hospital of Wisconsin. I won't have a house or be anywhere near being married. I will have a cool, shiny new sports car and over 100 friends. Every afternoon on Sunday, Monday, Tuesday, Wednesday, Thursday, and Friday afternoons I will volunteer at the hospital from 2:00-4:00. At night I will bake something for my family including salads, muffins, and dessert. For a pet I will have a collie dog named Sparky and a Beagle named Mario. For fun I will still be doing the same things like video games, scary story books, chess, computers, and art because I will still have the same personality, and attitude.

Laughter as a Value: Abby Juhlmann

Laughing is an action that helps people express happiness. It is fun and lets all mixed feelings come out in a simple sound. It is scientifically proven to improve health by strengthening the immune system. Besides the fact that it is healthy, I personally find it relaxing and very enjoyable. I know that other people agree with me. It keeps life bouncy and light, just the way I like it. It is said that people who laugh live longer. I am a strong believer in this quote, from seeing my little brother Sam live until almost eight despite his life threatening disease.

He laughed constantly every day, and I know that this had a lot to do with the reason he lived as long as he did. This was literally the best medicine he could ever receive. As an honor to my little Sammy, this is one of my values that I put towards the top of my ever so long list of values. Even if people don't have a strong example of positive laughing, they should still keep this as one of their values. When people need some spark the most, you can count on this value.

Wednesday, March 1, 2006 11:19 PM

I have pondered what March 3 is to me. The day my little boy died – that I know. Yet, his death is not something I only know on March 3. I know it so deeply and heartbreakingly – every single day. It's not a day I want to set aside for celebration. I believe in God and Heaven but I can't believe in celebrating the day Sam left. It's not a day I want to go on with my "normal life" either; as if nothing happened; as if my life did not change in a moment.

Do I count the years? Do I tell everyone it has been one year now since Sam died? Even now I dread knowing that some day I will have to say, "Now it is eight. He has been dead longer than he was alive."

215

Do I go to the store and buy balloons; let them go into the sky; "These are for my son. He died one year ago today."

Do I watch the DVD of his funeral? Read the sympathy cards? Light a candle? Stay in bed all day? Or do I do things he would have liked - eat some French fries, get a book out from the library, watch cartoons on TV all morning. What do you do on the day your child died? It is not his Birthday – it is his death day. There's no getting away from that fact. March 3rd is the day he died.

Lately at night I wake up and think about the last moments. This is what I wore the day he died, these are the books I read to him the last time we read, and this is what we planned to do on Saturday. I washed my hair the night he died; packed for his admission the next day; we had spaghetti and meatballs for dinner. I feel my fear, I feel the cold as we walked out the door, I remember how I had no idea he would die. I just thought he would go to Children's Hospital and the doctors would make him better – like they always did.

That was all before – before he died. Before I knew how something can hurt so bad that you cannot talk, cannot cry, and cannot imagine that life could ever have real meaning again. In the days and weeks and months afterwards the pain was so intense that I wished I would die. And the hope was so real. I hoped so illogically that if I could just think about it, get it right in my mind, go back to that night, put him in the car and get him to Children's Hospital then he would come back to me.

How could someone so precious, someone so beloved, slip through my fingers so fast? How could his life that I knew minute by minute be so completely out of my control? I am his mother – his Mama. How could I have been so helpless to stop his death? Surely, I could figure out a way for him to come home. When I write that it sounds so completely insane, I cannot even believe it was what I thought. But I did. I thought he would come home.

Now it is a year. The pain is still breath-taking. I wonder, after a child dies, does a mother ever truly feel happy again? Does her heart ever stop crying when she sees his bed, holds his stuffed puppies and remembers the sound of his voice? Does a mother ever stop missing her little boy's delight - "Mama – you're home!" when she walks in the door, as if she had been on some long journey and not simply gone

216

for an hour. Does there ever come a day when a mother feels whole, after her little boy dies?

Now it's been a year. The hope – has faded, though not gone completely. I still have days I think he might be waiting for me if I just keep dreaming and don't wake up completely. Mostly I know he is not going to be waiting for me in his bed in the morning though. Time does not ease the pain. Time begets resignation; the pain is not going away, Sam is not coming back.

The night Sam died, as I held him in my arms in that emergency room etched on my mind, a hole was ripped out of my heart. Still, I do believe that there is a piece of his heart inside of the jagged hole of mine, a piece he left with me. It's a pieced together heart. On good days I can feel the beat of his heart giving life to mine.

A friend whose little girl Micaela died from mito disease sent me this.

No words capture him
No quote suffices
No image is complete
Yet he was
Yet he is
Yet he will be
Forever.
-- Steve Marsh

Sam was...

Sam was a little boy full of life and spirit who taught me about living a real life. The night he was born I was very anemic and could not get adequate oxygen to him. He was born with his heart beating too slow; he was born blue and I feared he would die. Looking back – is it a coincidence that his life began the way it ended or was I given a glimpse of what would come? If so, I did not know. What I did know is that within a few minutes I went from hope for my unborn baby, to utter fear that he would not live and then to profound thankfulness when his heart started beating normally.

That experience was to be repeated over and over throughout his almost eight years. He would take me to the brink of death and back to the sunshine many times – always for different medical reasons, but the feelings were so similar. When that happens over and over you cannot help but realize what a miracle life is; what a miracle your little boy is.

Sam was happy, mischievous, ornery, content. Sam, it can be said, lacked the speed bump between his brain and his mouth – it could not help but make one laugh. "Cut it out" I told him one night. "I'm going to cut your skirt out!" he replied. In reading group, the minute the attention was off of him: "I'm HOT!" he'd say loudly. He never complained about his medical problems – he did not even know he had any. He was content with going to school, playing with his siblings, reading books in bed with me. Like Thoreau, Sam wished to " *live deliberately, to front only the essential facts of life, and see if I could not learn what it had to teach, and not, when I came to die, discover that I had not lived. I did not wish to live what was not life, living is so dear; nor did I wish to practice resignation, unless it was quite necessary. I wanted to live deep and suck out all the marrow of life, to live so sturdily and Spartan-like as to put to rout all that was not life, to cut a broad swath and shave close, to drive life into a corner, and reduce it to its lowest terms, and, if it proved to be mean, why then to get the whole and genuine meanness of it, and publish its meanness to the world; or if it were sublime, to know it by experience, and be able to give a true account of it in my next excursion.* "

Sam was my little boy.

Sam is...

Sam is what I think true love must be; he is great big bursts of laughter; he is real in a way that most of us never are. Sam is joy despite unfortunate circumstances; he is belief in dreams and hope for stars and sunshine. Sam is a once in a lifetime experience. Sam is never ending.

Sam is my little boy.

Sam will be...

Sam will always be in my heart, part of my heart, the sustenance of my heart. Sam will always be all that he ever was and is.

Sam will forever be my little boy.

And I am thankful that I will forever be his Mama.

Tuesday, March 7, 2006 11:33 AM

Zach is inpatient. Zach's line slipped out of place in the last few days. Our surgeon, Dr. A., says that he needs a new one placed because if not it will fall out and we'll have an emergency on our hands. Surgery is scheduled for Wednesday afternoon. They requested the anesthesiologist that knows my kids well and is very careful. I'm sick about this but the surgery is not an option. It has to be done.

Zach is not well. I can't even say what is exactly wrong. He can not sit up or walk a few steps without getting so exhausted he has to sleep for hours. He cannot focus his eyes, doesn't want to eat, has needed pain meds for his stomach every few hours. He has been on oxygen continually. He was like this last Monday but got better within 12-15 hours. This has been since yesterday morning. We just sent off a slew of labs. He looks awful. I just want the labs to show something is wrong that can be fixed, because if not it ends up being the same old reason for everything: "acute mitochondrial decompensation episode = disease progression." I am sick of those words.

Wednesday, March 8, 2006 09:35 PM

Dr. A got a new line in the right subclavien vein. He felt it best to move the site so it is now on the right side instead of the left. At the request of dermatology, he also biopsied one of the deep nodules that Zach has all over his arms and legs. I am told it takes 7-10 days for the results.

He perked up a bit yesterday and then said he felt even worse today. However, he is watching *Star Wars* right now. His nurse and I just found that his surgery site has started to bleed - just a little right now. I can't say I am surprised and only hope it does not turn into something unmanageable. He has a unit of blood ordered which he'll get any time now. Other than that we just have to wait and see. The labs did not show much except that his lactic acid is high which is a sign of mitochondrial stress.

Thank you so much for all your prayers and kind thoughts.

Thursday, March 9, 2006 09:35 PM

The bleeding got much worse. He has had Cryo and Factor 7a (novoseven). In some ways he is feeling better though he cannot seem to go for more than 30 minutes without oxygen. His chest x-ray did show fluid in the lungs and decreased lung volume, likely due to weakness. He had a positive blood culture but from the line we pulled out. We repeated the cultures to see if that was the source. if so, these new cultures should come back negative.

There was a water main break at the Milwaukee Medical Complex this morning. Let me tell you how fun it is to be in a hospital with no running water (only bottled), no use of bathrooms unless you go outside to porta potties and no showers.

I did slip out tonight to Abby's speech meet. She got 2nd place. YEAH ABBY!!!!! She did a beautiful job!

Saturday, March 11, 2006 10:50 PM

This will be very quick. Zach needed more Factor 7a for bleeding Friday and got another unit of blood. This morning he was not bleeding but tonight it re-started and we gave him more Factor. He has significant stomach pain and is being treated with a lot of pain meds for that. The pulmonary function tests on Friday were not good news. His function has dramatically deteriorated since December - I guess that explains all of his air hunger. The good news is he is at home. He can be on oxyegn, I can give pain meds and we can deal with his bleeding just as well at home as at the hospital, (not that we don't LOVE "the nurses"). More later but thank you for all of your emails, calls, messages and prayers. I think he'll be just fine - we just need to get him through this post op period with the bleeding. His spirits are great despite it all.

Tuesday, March 14, 2006 11:53 PM

Zach is doing better in many ways except for the bleeding. He is able to be off the oxygen more and more each day. Today he was off of it from 6:30 am until 3:30!!!! That's nine hours (I just want you to know I can still do basic math!). True, he is not really that active but hey – last week he didn't even get out of bed. Today he went to school for about 5 hours. I figure that if he is going to bleed we can't keep him home forever. I have to say he did bleed much more this afternoon than he has in days so I may have to re-think that but that's my decision for now. Of course, now that I have decided that, his hematologist has decided that Zach needs to come to infusion clinic for cryo infusions this week. So who knows how much school he'll actually get in after all?

Cryo is a part of plasma – the best part with a lot of clotting factors in it. It has certainly helped Zach in the past so I don't disagree with the hematologist for ordering it. His thought is that maybe, just maybe, we can prevent the severe bleeding that occurs 7-10 days post op when the body starts reabsorbing clots it has made. (A normal reaction for most of the human population – just not beneficial in a person with a bleeding disorder).

Today Zach had an eye doctor appointment to see if we could figure out why he has so much blurry and double vision. He had already been to the ophthalmologist at Children's so we know his eyes are "healthy" but obviously blurry/double vision is not too functional. So today we saw a developmental optometrist. Her best guess after a 90 minute, very thorough exam, is that his eye muscles are weak and fatigue easily. Makes sense as every other muscle in his body does the same thing. She thinks he is working way too hard to focus his eyes and make them work together. She prescribed glasses so we'll see what they do. They are "therapeutic glasses" and in some ways their function is like the splints he wears on his legs – they give his muscles a rest by picking up some of the slack for him.

His Parathyroid hormone came back high again…so now he needs some nuclear scans to look at this further. Don't ask because this is the part of nursing school I slept through. I believe the standard treatment is surgical….given he is still bleeding 7 days after a "minor surgery" (no such thing for my kids), I am not too anxious to know much more than I do now…which is that he needs to get a nuclear scan before we can make any decisions.

Brittany is in Naples, Florida this week for her spring break with my mom. I admit to a deep jealousy but I am happy for her. She'll be home Saturday for one day to show off her tan and then we'll get her back to Minneapolis on Sunday.

I can't recall if I said thank you to everyone who sent messages, cards, thoughts and prayers on the one year mark of Sammy going away. It was not a fun day but I did feel your love for him and that was a comfort to me. I save all of your kind words. The flowers that some of you brought over or sent are still alive! The balloons are not even deflated! The Donald Duck Snow and Music Globe is a treasure! The orange candy made me smile. The hand made blankets...they are so soft and warm and perfect! Thank you for the cards left at his grave. I love the bear and the angel box and spring flowers in our hospital room last week! I laughed at the orange balloon that "Kaf" taped to his memorial plaque at the hospital. I was impressed how long it lasted there without anyone removing it. Most of all thank you for remembering Sam, for being a part of his life in big and small ways. He was and is so beloved. I can never doubt that.

Sunday, March 19, 2006 11:10 PM

Zach is doing okay. He spent a few days going to infusion clinic last week. I don't know if the blood products actually helped or it was a coincidence but his bleeding did improve. However, today he started bleeding from the old site again!!! I don't even get that. This was the original spot he had bleeding problems with when inpatient but they treated it and it had stopped by the time we left. While we were still in the hospital the new site started up and that is the one that was problematic all week. Now the old site is bleeding and it looks red/blue/purple and swollen. I'll have to call the hematologist tomorrow and ask him what we should do. My guess is he'll invite us back to infusion clinic. How fun! Good thing we love his clinic nurses.

Zach has been busy drawing with charcoal. He had never done this before but seems to be having a lot of fun with it. He did a terrific Spider Man picture this weekend. I'll have to see if I can scan it one of these days.

I would like to say a special thank you to anyone who donates blood, plasma or platelets. I have said this before but it always bears repeating. It does not matter if you donate directly to us - for whatever you give and wherever you donate - it assures an adequate blood product supply for anyone who needs it.

Your donation truly is a gift of life. Those are not just words - they are words that reflect reality for many children and adults who are alive because someone took the time to give a part of themselves.

Zach needs red cells because he does not make enough on his own to sustain his life. Zach needs plasma because that is where his IV immune globulin comes from. The cryoprecipitate infusions that he gets when he bleeds are also made from plasma.

Most of you know that Sam was dependent on blood products (cryo, plasma, platelets and red cells) around the clock for the last few years of his life. There were people at the blood center that worked tirelessly to make sure he had what he needed. There were donors that I will never get to meet, who gave and gave and gave so that he could live. There was never a time when giving Sammy his blood products that I forgot where they came from. I was acutely aware that a piece of someone was infusing life into his body.

It is the same for Zach. He lives because people literally give a piece of their life to him. So for all of you who make sure the blood supply is adequate in our country -thank you. I hope you can see your generosity and kindness reflected in the joyful life of Zach and the many others to whom your blood, plasma and platelets go.

Monday, March 20, 2006 10:20 PM

Zach bled all night. He was none the worse for it in terms of how he felt so I sent him to school. He needs to be a kid. This is how I felt with Sam. If I had waited for Sammy to stop bleeding before sending him to school he never would have gone.

The hematologist wants Zach to get cryo all week again. He was infused this afternoon. He actually left the clinic bleeding and bled through a new dressing on the way home. The great thing is that after I changed that dressing he did not bleed through the new one by the time he went to bed. It may be coincidental but it does seem that the cryo really helped. Unfortunately, the benefit never seems to last more than 24 hours. Our plan is to give Factor 7a if he acutely bleeds between cryo infusions.

223

Thursday, March 23, 2006 10:04 PM

Zach is doing okay. He bled some today but only a small bit. It was his day off from infusion clinic. Tomorrow he will get another cryo infusion and a unit of blood (red cells). Then we will see how he does over the weekend without cryo. That will be the test.

Our hematologist is going to talk with the blood center to request that I be given permission to infuse blood products at home like I did for Sam. This would be a huge help if they approve it but the approval is not a foregone conclusion. We were in discussions for a long time to get approval for Sam and he needed blood products every day. All day. Zach's needs are not as out of this world extreme so they may not make an exception.

But I hope and pray that they do. It would allow Zach to attend school and be at home. I could infuse while he did whatever he wanted to do. I could not ask for better infusion clinic nurses - I just love them - but I am tired and it is not sustainable to keep this kind of schedule up.

Last night I was talking to the kids about how I read in my parenting magazine that at their age they should have 10 min of homework for every grade - therefore they should have 70 minutes of homework a night. Without a blink Zach looked at me, and said "Then I think you should stop reading those parenting magazines. They're a bad influence on you!"

From the *Morgan Butler Press* March 2006, Vol. 8 No. 7

BUTLER COMES THROUGH
At the Valentine's Day dance, Butler students raised $1500.00!! This money will be used to buy TVs and DVD/VHS players for Children's Hospital in the name of the Juhlmann family. During the food drive, on the 13th-19th, student council collected new or used movies. They will help out the children at the hospital. Way to go Butler!

Note from Anne:
Yes! WAY TO GO BUTLER! I am overwhelmed at the generosity of the middle school students and their families. I am proud that Zach and Abby are part of a school family made up of wonderful kids and

awesome teachers. What an amazing thing to do for Zach and all the kids at the hospital.

Friday, March 31, 2006 9:32 PM

This week will be an inpatient hospital week – starting Sunday. Zachary finally seems to have stopped bleeding from both old and new central line sites. I am so glad and of course he is too. He still has pressure dressings on both sites but I think after he gets a shower tomorrow we'll see how he does without it.

He has been doing well in school, enjoying the actual learning process more. He is so sensitive about being behind in school that he often gets so caught up in catching up and misses out on the actual learning. I hate that because learning should be fun, meaningful, life-long and not a chore. He seems to have a new perspective - something I have not seen in some time and I love it. I'm not sure but I think his big sister has something to do with it. She is so full of enthusiasm for what she is learning at U of Mn and I think even her brief time at home a few weeks ago inspired him. It's hard not to be enthusiastic about learning when with her. She is simply thriving in university studies.

Zach has had some fairly significant back pain this week. We're not sure what it is but if he still has it Monday his doctor wants him to have a CT or MRI scan. His kidney function had worsened when I checked labs last night and we wonder if he has a kidney infection. I'm actually hoping it is simply back strain from lugging around his back pack with all his IV pumps but his physical therapist was not so sure when she saw him Wednesday. We'll see.

His metabolic labs look awful and indicate worsening mitochondrial function. They have been trending that way for months but this last batch really upset me. I am trying not to think about it because when I do I feel sick to my stomach. I know the right thing to do is to enjoy every minute of life and not worry about tomorrow. Mostly I can do that but there are days it is hard to see the relentless attack of this disease on my child and my family. I try to close my eyes to it – if I don't see it then it is not there. But when I open my eyes – there it is. It's hard to run away from reality.

I miss Sam a lot. I supposed that goes without saying but it's been almost surprising to me how raw the pain has felt in the past month. I don't know why…I seem to be reliving much of what happened last March, as if it is brand new, only without the shelter of being in shock that I had a year ago. I hate how lonely the process of mourning is in America. My friend Lynne recently told me of a Buddhist tradition and I could not help but wish it was a western tradition, regardless of one's faith. When in Japan, Lynne and her husband kept finding these little shrines everywhere – not just in temple gardens but on street corners and under lamp posts and tucked into alleyways in suburban streets. They found out they are shrines to Jizo, the Buddhist deity who is charged with the responsibility of guiding the souls of still born babies and dead children to heaven. Each of the little stone figures, some so worn with age you can barely make out the human features, represents a lost child. And wherever they are placed, the community around them tends to them, dressing them up on feast days with special little clothes, leaving flowers and lighting incense sticks. Their culture had a way of making the heartbreak of grieving parents so visible, so much a part of every day life. Because after all it is a part of life and it always will be.

Lynne, my much beloved friend, mama of Allie and Angus who passed away before Sam, also told me that she read a biography of Emerson. Apparently, on his death bed his last words were "Oh, that beautiful boy". Forty years after he lost his beautiful boy, his last thoughts were of him. Emerson, of course, led a very productive life and yet his love for his son and his pain at losing him was always weaved into every moment he lived – always a part of who he was.

Abby has had a fever on and off all week. I kept her home on Wednesday. She felt fine and was miffed. She tells me that many kids are sick too and "their mothers don't keep them home just for a fever if they feel ok." Nice. The school rules say if a kid has a fever over 100 they should not be in school. That of course does not mean everyone follows the rule. I bet if they had an immune compromised kid they might understand the importance of it. Thursday she went to school and seemed to be better. Today she came home from track practice looking very pale. I took her temperature and it was 101. I hope she feels better tomorrow as she and I have tickets to see ANNIE in Milwaukee. I did not realize that I have never taken her. I took Brittany a few times but I guess Abby missed out. I'm really excited for Abby to see it!

And Brittany…well she is doing great. We'll be going to see her in a few weeks. Every trip I've planned to go out there has been cancelled due to Zach being sick so I really hope it all works out. She sent us some pictures to show that she is now a brunette. She was tired of being blond! Her big news is she is going to watch a surgeon perform colon surgery. Now I can understand wanting to watch surgery but personally I'm not too sure I'd be excited at colon surgery. But hey – I hope she loves it!

I Measure Every Grief I Meet--Emily Dickinson

I measure every grief I meet
With analytic eyes;
I wonder if it weighs like mine,
Or has an easier size.

I wonder if they bore it long,
Or did it just begin?
I could not tell the date of mine,
It feels so old a pain.

I wonder if it hurts to live,
And if they have to try,
And whether, could they choose between,
They would not rather die.

I wonder if when years have piled--
Some thousands--on the cause
Of early hurt, if such a lapse
Could give them any pause;

Or would they go on aching still
Through centuries above,
Enlightened to a larger pain
By contrast with the love.

Wednesday, April 5, 2006 9:32 PM

Well, the spinal films show compression fractures of Zach's back at L-2,L-3 and L-4. A follow up bone scan this afternoon showed that all three of those vertebrae were "very hot" meaning the fractures are new. I'll share more details as I know them.

Today on a kidney ultrasound they happened to notice that he has some new abnormal findings of his liver. He needs this evaluated with a CT scan tomorrow. There's not much to say until we know more. Right now the radiologist has several things we need to rule out. None of the options are good news but hoping it is not worst case scenario.

Sunday, April 9, 2006 12:27 AM

I am going to apologize in advance if this is confusing. Unfortunately, there are more questions than answers right now for Zachary.

I'll start with the simple. Zach asked his doctor if he could have a hearing test this week because "I feel like I say 'what?' all the time." His last hearing test was December 2005 – 4 months ago. This week's test showed significant changes – more pronounced in the high frequency area but in low frequency as well. High frequency, as Peter explained to Zach, is when people talk like Mickey Mouse. Fortunately, most of us don't talk like that so it's good that these type sounds are harder for him to hear than low frequency, where most of our speech lies. The bad news is he had a significant change in both and at this point they want to re-test him every 1-2 months (I'm opting for the every 2 month plan). There are a lot of mitochondria in the nerves of the ears – hearing loss happens with mitochondrial disease. (What exactly does NOT happen with mito disease?) As most know, Sam eventually needed hearing aids. His were purple and bright blue – his choice. He was quite sure they made him "stronger – like Superman."

Compression fractures: Some of you have asked how that happened. Think of an 80 year old woman and there is your answer – his bone density is very poor. He has osteopenia or osteoporosis depending on who writes the report. We knew this – he gets a very powerful infusion once a month called Pamidronate that is supposed

228

to help. The reason his density is poor? Therein is the mystery. There are osteoblasts and osteoclasts in one's body. Osteoblasts build bone and osteoclasts break bone down, releasing calcium into the blood. We need a balance between these 2 processes for good bone health. Zach, however, seems to be stuck in the osteoclastic mode – hence his bones are constantly reabsorbing and releasing Calcium into his blood. The Pamidronate should stop the osteoclasts from working "over time" but obviously it fell down on the job and now he has these fractures. Why does he have this problem? We don't have a clue – only theories that somehow his Calcium sensors are broken so his body thinks it needs calcium in the blood even though it clearly does not. I think we have the smartest primary doctor, endocrinologist and nephrologist in the world so not knowing is certainly not for lack of thinking about it. In the meantime we doubled his Pamidronate dose for his infusion this week and maybe it will help. Otherwise, he remains at quite high risk for additional fractures.

So we're left with these painful fractures. Zach actually felt ok in the hospital unless he was up walking but now that we're home he hurts. The orthopedic doctor prescribed a brace for him called a Boston Thoraco-Lumbo-Sacral Orthosis (TLSO); personally I think they ought to just call it a turtle shell.

He is supposed to wear it whenever awake. Perhaps it was the incredulous look on my face that prompted the ortho doctor to add "but I know reality does not always meet science – I'm just telling you that ideally he should wear it whenever awake." Right now it is a moot issue because it does not seem to fit appropriately and it hurts him a lot. They cut holes for all of his tubes and lines but it still hurts him. I need to have the orthotics people look at it. The orthopedic doc wants to see him every few weeks.

The liver: It's not good but the problem is I really don't know how bad it is yet. He has what are called liver hemangiomas. Hemangiomas are common vascular tumors that occur in as many as 2.5 % of babies. Most are benign, and 70-80 regress by age 7 years. Sounds ok except Zach was not born with them. We know he was not born with them because his liver is scanned annually – last time in October – and they have never been seen. The fact that he has at least 5 of them is not good. That they grew since October is not good for they are obviously on the fast track. His worsening bleeding problems, hemolytic anemia and heart failure are potentially related to this...or not. We don't know. I am told there is a chance one or more of them can burst, in which case he will hemorrhage faster than we can imagine. That terrifies me but I am trying not to think about it. It brings up the very real possibility that he'd get transported to the community hospital and we all know how well they listened to me with Sammy the night he died (they did not) and how long it took that ER to call Children's for help (15 minutes of me literally begging them). There is a procedure called embolization that might help. There are some chemotherapeutics that might help. Children's does have a Vascular Anomaly clinic and we have a wonderful hematologist so I'll start there.

I'm sick of crying and worrying. I have not slept for days. It's all too depressing to be sad. It's a beautiful day today -a perfect day for a walk which I am going to do right now. But before I go - here are some random things I have read lately to make us all smile:

Be Merry, Not Ancient -- *By Frank Bruni in the Sunday NYT 4/9/06*
From the critic's corner - questioning if it is better to cut our calories to 890/day (per recent JAMA article), eat healthy 100f the time, drink our limited 1.5 glass/day of red wine and live until 100 or is it better to live until 80, eat our steak, have a guilt free 2 glasses red wine once in a while and find joy wherever we can find it. (personally I am opting for McDonalds and cheesecake every now and then!)

"We can't really predict tomorrow. We can't guarantee its arrival with a specified number of calories or a given allotment of sleep, with milligrams of dark chocolate or ounces of fiber. But we can often determine the measure of joy we wring out of today"

April Special Days – I only included my favorites
April 3 is . . . . . National Tweed Day and Don't Go To Work Unless It's Fun Day
April 4 is . . . . . National Tell-A-Lie Day
April 7 is . . . . . National No Housework Day
April 9 is . . . . . National Name Yourself Day
April 12 is . . . . National Look Up At The Sky Day
April 13 is . . . . National Blame Somebody Else Day

April 16 is . . . . National Eggs Benedict Day
April 20 is . . . . National Zachary Juhlmann's 14th Birthday
April 23 is . . . . National Read Me Day and World Laboratory Animal Day
April 24 is . . . . National Pigs In A Blanket Day
April 30 is . . . . National Honesty Day (You only have to do this once a year!)

Thursday, April 20, 2006 9:53 AM

Zach is doing relatively well. We've been in Minneapolis which I'll tell you about later. It was fun though I think it did tire Zach out quite a bit. The Children's Hospital in Minneapolis was wonderful - they helped us out a lot the 5 days we were there. But enough about medical stuff...today is Zachary's birthday!!!!!!

HAPPY 14th BIRTHDAY ZACHARY RYAN JUHLMANN (aka Z-Man)

It does not seem possible that 14 years have come and gone. I suppose every parent says that; I know I say it every time one of my children has a birthday. Watching a baby grow into a child and now into a young adolescent is truly an amazing thing. I admit that I don't typically take the time to look back and really ponder that miracle but it is – isn't it? There are moments I remember from Zach's infancy that I smile about now – for even at 2 months and 8 months I can see who he is now. There have also been so many changes as he has learned and experienced and grown so that who he is now is so different than that baby born 14 years ago, than the preschooler building Lego towers endlessly, than the first grader learning to read, than the third grader creating magnificent art, than the fifth grader walking his little brother into school on the first day of class, than the seventh grader having friends over and spiking his hair. Still....Zachary is and always will be Zachary, with his unique personality and huge smile and laugh, woven through each year of his life. It's a gift to be his mom.
Before he was born I anticipated him with such delight.
Even then he did the unexpected.

231

At 30 weeks I went into preterm labor. I was put on medication to stop the labor and told to rest and hope that the baby would not be born for a month.

He was born 10 days after his due date!

He loved a good joke even as a baby.

I have fond memories of him "running" around our old house in his walker,

He'd open a cabinet and pull down dishtowels, then look back to smile at me and off he'd go to make some more noise.

Zach loved books. He was the only baby I know that would sit for 30 minutes reading with an adult. He also loved to chew on his board books and he insisted on sleeping with *Good Night Moon*.

One

Zach spent his first birthday in Children's Hospital. He had surgery and I thought he would be cured. It was a sad time in the months after that when I realized that now only did the surgery not cure him but whatever was wrong, was very wrong and getting worse.

Abby was born when Zach was 13 months old.

The first time he saw her I was in the hospital holding her.

He took one look, screamed and did not stop until Grandma took him home.

After that he was delighted with her – and was so patient and kind to her.

He was always a wonderful brother to his sisters and brother.

When Zach was one he learned now to talk by using sign language. His favorite signs were "more" and "eat"

He loved to eat – anything and everything – though he struggled to keep it down.

Two

Zachary turned two in Florida while visiting Gramps and Nana!

Two years old - going to doctors in Madison, in New York…searching for answers.

He was the most patient child I have ever seen…..he rarely complained as we waited hour upon hour in doctors' offices, labs, therapy appointments, surgeries.

He is still so patient. I, who am so impatient, marvel at this and admire it so!

Three

Three years old!

He cried hysterically the first day I took him to school. He did not like anything new. But once he got used to it, he loved it and thrived with Miss Sue and all the rest of the staff at Banting.

He was so proud when he ran in the Banting Bolt!

His resolve was always evident: "Zachary do it. Zachary do himself!"

Zach is four!

He confidently walked into school – this is old hat now.

At home he spent hours with his Legos and puzzles.

Cooking was a daily ritual – he loved to cook and create.

When we went to get the Christmas tree that year he refused to get out of the car. It was not snowing …he remembered that it had snowed the year before and had concluded that one could only get a tree when it snowed. Change was still so hard for him – even with the simplest things of life.

Sammy was born right before his fifth birthday. He was so proud to have his own little brother.

Five

His first party with friends. I still remember that anticipation – it could not be contained.

His disease - still nameless at this time – had been stable for two years.
But it slowly began to worsen this year – and still he never complained.

Six weeks in casts from his feet to his thighs and he only cried once.

I wonder how someone can be so brave and resilient.

Six

Zachary's sixth birthday was celebrated at the hospital.

Zachary was fine but Sammy was in for a month that spring. Every night Zach came to visit; to make his baby brother laugh.

He was happy when Sammy had "tubes" placed in his stomach and intestine. Of course, he did not understand the significance of it. He only knew that "Now someone is just like me."

Kindergarten...Mrs. F. had to "encourage" Zach not to go to art center every day.

For Christmas he wanted a vacuum cleaner "more than anything else in the whole wide world."

A few weeks before Christmas we were given his diagnosis.

Seven

Zachary's seventh birthday was smack in the middle of a five month inpatient stay in the hospital.

That was not about to quell Zach's infamous birthday spirit.

No longer able to eat, he carefully chose what drinks he would have for each meal. It was heartbreaking - he who loved to eat more than anyone – painstakingly planning out each meal. Yet it was inspiring to me, to everyone who came in contact with him.

Zach wanted to be a surgeon so Dr. A brought up his "surgery tools" and they looked at them one by one.

The hospital staff and our friends and family spoiled him with more presents that one can imagine.

At the end of the day Zach declared that he hoped to celebrate every birthday in the hospital for this was the best one ever! Making lemonade out of lemons – Zach could teach us all.

Seven...welcome to being hooked up to infusion and feeding pumps 24 hours a day.

Zach confidently stood in front of his first grade class and showed them Barney. "He's just like me," he explained to the kids. Barney had a central line, J tube, G tube, leg splints and even the same scars on his legs.

Seven...he had learned to adapt to change, he had made friends, he looked people in the eye, he had a great sense of humor. At his IEP the school staff and I decided to remove the label that had been there since he was three: autism. I was overcome with how far he had come. Whether or not he has or had autism is not the point. What is amazing is to remember how hard it was for him to do anything differently than his rules allowed, how impossible it had been for him to look at someone and yet he had somehow learned to adapt.

Eight

When Zachary was eight he spent hours playing with Sammy each day. He taught Sam all those important boy things to know like Power Rangers, Pokemon, Batman and Superman.

His art skills were amazing even then and he began to write simple stories. They were always quite dramatic.

He said he'd never be a teenager. Something had happened to Brittany when she turned 13 - he was sure of it!

Nine

On Zach's ninth summer we went home to Ocean City.

His delight with the ocean waves, the sand, the boardwalk and simply staying in a hotel is something that I will never forget. Every night he, Abby, Grandma and Aunt Maribeth would plan out what we would have for "happy hour."

He was in third grade and the kids were writing fairy tales. Specific instructions were given – no gore, blood or weapons. Zach decided to ignore that. The more dramatic he could make it the better. To this day he is still mad that he had to re-write some of those parts.

Ten

For Zachary's tenth birthday he had a double party with Abby. No wonder the teachers looked at me like I was nuts – but they sure had fun.

We went to Disney World for Sam's Make a Wish that year.

At the Give Kids the World where we stayed every Thursday is Christmas. Zach still talks about that! Holidays are the be all and end all to Zach.

I'll never forget his disgust at watching the Barney Live show that I made them all sit through for Sam. This was the kid that had once said "this is Barney and he is just like me."

Growing up; He was disgusted with the rules that dis-allowed him on certain rides due to height restrictions. He was brave and not scared of those rides and he took the height restrictions as a personal insult.

Eleven

Zach was really sure he could not ever be a teenager now. "It does something to your brain," he said.

In Ocean City he constructed elaborate sand cities and towers. When Sam saw Zach in school he would wave and yell "HI BEST BROTHER!" And Zach would smile this big huge smile. He was so proud to be that best brother.

Fifth grade stands out as one of Zach's favorite years because 'we did art projects all year long!"

He and Abby had a great big Halloween party that year. What I remember the most is how Zach put all of his energy into the menu – food with names like witches fingers, snot, grave yard mud and bugs….he still loved cooking and creating.

Twelve

Zachary turned twelve.

We did not travel that summer. "That's okay'" he told us. "We can have a vacation right at our own house!"

He made his wish and Make A Wish granted it - a game room! He began to invite friends over more and more…and I loved to hear them, remembering the child that had school IEP goals about eye contact and spontaneously talking to other kids.

At night he used to read Sam from his favorite book series: *Captain Underpants*. It was way beyond Sam's level but Sam quietly sat with him and listened – I think he was just glad to be with Zach.

Sam "died" and Zach lost not only his little brother but his best friend, soul mate, "someone just like me."

A few weeks after Sam went away Zach told me that Sam is not dead. "He's with me all the time, when I wake up at night I know he is lying in bed beside me, and when I play cards he is there too."

ThirTEEN

Thirteen – suddenly he thinks it is just fine to be a teenager. What's the big deal anyway?

He is still never going to get married…but if he does his wife must like Yugi-oh and must have a good sense of humor. She should also like dogs and be a good video game player.

The child that cried for days after he got a "different hair cut" at age six is now the boy that spiked his hair at age 13.

Graduation from elementary school and the beginning of Middle school.

He's more tired but at the same time he lights up the room.

His sense of humor, always wonderful, has taken on a life of its own.

and he has become quite the conversationalist!

And today April 20, 2006 Zachary is fourteen!

Growing up and becoming

And still ...he is Zachary.

What an awesome guy he is!

Zach's doing ok. Fairly tired, a lot of blurred vision and eye pain - but hanging in there. His hemoglobin has been dropping by a gram every few days. He'll absolutely need blood. He'll be admitted Sunday, which is probably a good thing. While inpatient he will follow up with the orthopedic doctor to see if his back is healing. We'll also work on figuring out what to do for his liver. He was going to start a new medication to help his bone health, recommended by his long time nephrologist and I was very hopeful it would help. That may not happen now.

And while I'm on the subject of health care I have a major gripe: I'm tired of made up drug shortages by pharmaceutical companies who magically have the drug when you say the word media. I feel like an investigative reporter and it is never ending. Rarely are we given answers as to why there is a shortage ...but they hold all the cards because they know people's lives depend on those drugs. How do these people sleep at night? If there truly was a shortage of some of these drugs that would be one thing but somehow they always have it for the right price.

Zach had a wonderful birthday. I can't say he felt great but he sure loved every minute of the day when he was awake. In typical Zach fashion he had made a list of what I was to make for each meal. Freshly baked sugar cookie for breakfast with a side of pineapple juice. Lunch was an ice-cream sundae. Snack was Root beer. Actually to be specific it was Sprecher's Root beer. Dinner was the liquid portion of chili - extremely spicy please. And the birthday cake was mint chocolate chip ice cream cake from Cold Stone Creamery. He got too cold to finish either of his ice cream treats…but he had what he wanted and that's all that matters.

When we went to Minneapolis we went to the Mall of America – of course. That place is nuts. I'm not much of a mall shopper but there were some really neat stores in there. One of them was the Lego Store with Lego creations that were literally 3 stories high. Amazing! Zach picked out two Batman Lego sets for his birthday. His mother would not let him touch them until his true birthday so he really enjoyed building with those all day on the 20th.

Later in the day Zach's Grandpa, Uncle Mike and Aunt Elaine came over and we had a little family party. The friend party will have to wait, as Zach wants to take the guys to Comedy Sportz, (The kids version). I need to prepare myself for Comedy Sportz with seventh grade boys.

Thank you for all the cards, messages, phone calls, gifts and visits on and around his birthday. It's pretty cool to turn 14 - thank you for celebrating that great event along with Zach!

Back to Minneapolis:
My daughter's hair is actually more auburn than brunette and pictures do not do her justice. She is just as beautiful with auburn hair as she was with blond.

We stayed in the city and walked a lot – A LOT! The weather was gorgeous except for Easter morning.

I dragged the family to the Mills Museum. I loved it – all the history was so interesting. Zach will tell you that he went to a "flour museum."

"And did you like it Zach?"

"I liked the free samples of croutons."

The truth is they all hated it.

Minneapolis has an outside sculpture garden. Zach: "Why does everyone make NAKED statues?"

St. Mary's Basilica is beautiful. The kids and I lit candles for Sammy there. There is something to be said for that age old tradition.

Brittany is tired but doing awesome in school and having lots of fun with her friends. She seems happy.

We got a membership to the science museum so that the kids and I can go back to the Bodyworks exhibit this summer. It is truly an amazing museum and we all learned a lot.

Children's Hospital in Minneapolis is beautiful. I had to do Zach's labs a few times because his kidneys started to act up right before we left. They were great and called our doctor right away with all results and then he was able to call me and make a plan.

Also - Zach's cardiac drip that cannot be stopped did not arrive, as it should have on Saturday. By the time I realized it was not coming it was too late to do anything and the next day was Easter. Our home care company was going to send a driver from Milwaukee to Minneapolis with the labetalol drips but I called the Children's Hospital on the off chance they might help. They do not provide infusions for outpatients…but after I told them what drip he was on and after they stopped asking me "He gets that as an outpatient? " and after I reassured them that yes we do give it to him outside of the ICU they were more than happy to provide it for him for all 3 days that were left. This may not seem like a big deal but trust me –most hospitals would not have done it.

So now we're home. The weather is still beautiful. I don't remember every having such a nice weather spring in Wisconsin

Missing Sam terribly.

Last night Zach said that it would be Sam's golden birthday (he would have been 9 on May 9th) and he and Abby were planning out his cake. I wanted to go hide,but I also want to respect what they need to do.

Cleaning out a drawer this weekend I found a wallet-sized card with his school picture. It was issued by *Smile Safe Kids* to be used in the event he was missing.

Sam Juhlmann
Bethesda Elementary School
Issue date: 8-2004
Grade - 01

It tells me what I should do if my child is missing.
1. Call local law enforcement
2. Show this picture to authorities
3. Call the National Center for Missing and Exploited Children.

239

How I wish I could take his card to the police...find him for me please. Or call 1-800-THE-LOST with hope and trust that they will help me find him.

On the back it has space for me to write his eye and hair color, height, weight and other distinguishing features. I never filled it in. It seemed so unnecessary. I used to joke that one thing I never had to worry about was someone taking Sam because A) they'd have to take all 12 of his IV pumps too, B) he would scream his head off if they tried and C) if they actually did take him they'd return him within hours due to his incessant talking. It was beyond my imagination to think he would ever really be missing. But he is and it's heartbreaking to know that dialing 1-800 is fruitless. He's not coming home.

So I filled it in tonight.

Hair: Shiny blond, uncombed
Eyes: huge, brown, longest lashes ever.
Distinguishing characteristic: his laughter – there is nothing else like it.

Saturday, May 6, 2006 10:25 AM

May 9th would have been Sammy's 9th birthday. Precious boy...

Zach came home from the hospital about 10 PM Friday night. Some good news from the admission is that his spine x-rays showed an older fracture we never knew about at T-11 but nothing worse in the past month. His blood levels seem to be responding both to a higher dose of a medication that prevents bone breakdown and to a newer medication. Perhaps he will build bone if this continues...time will tell.

His liver – well I guess I am more confused than ever at this point. What we thought was wrong is probably not what is actually wrong. The problem they suspect he has is not good either –and probably progressive. They believe it is related to the nodules he has covering his legs and arms. Apparently his biopsy of one of those nodules back in March was not normal even though it was reported that way. It may also explain his increasing need for transfusions, his bleeding, his clotting (yes he both bleeds and clots pathologically – it's complicated)...and if so it probably explains Sam's severe

240

bleeding/clotting. On Friday he has an appointment in the vascular anomaly clinic and they are trying to arrange a care conference that day with the pathologist, oncologist, hematologist, radiologist, dermatologist, surgeon, his primary doctor and me. I really hope this happens although I fear they will simply say there is nothing to do to make it better.

It is nurse's week and I'd like to share just a snapshot of the difference nurses have made in our lives. We are so fortunate in having two wonderful homecare nurses – *Ione and Chris* – who have stuck with us through so much. They allow him to have as normal of a life as possible. You are such an important part of Zach's life and I cannot imagine your absence.

In the hospital we have an awesome group of nurses st that do whatever they can to make his stays as safe and fun as possible. As care has become more complex there have been more and more instances of not being able to find nurses comfortable with his care – but through it all our *4th floor consistent nurses* have learned whatever they need to in order to give Zach not only excellent care but quality of life.

There are of course other nurses to be thanked and honored – our *infusion clinic nurses* who never once have complained about fitting Zach in on short notice, even when the clinic is full.

There is *our school district nurse* who has assured both Zach and Sam's safety at school for as long as I can remember. The *nurses at Home Care Medical* have worked hard to find just the right home care equipment and supplies so that Zach is as functional as possible no matter what his medical needs at home are.

And *Mary, Deb and Holly, Tera and Penny* – amazing special needs expert nurses who are my resources and my models.

There is a nurse at Children's who has done more than anyone can imagine in her senior administrative position to support quality of life for my boys.

We have countless former nurses - some have moved, taken new jobs, or work in places we no longer visit…but I remember them and I think I always will. Sometimes it is only the things a nurse did that I can recall – having forgotten the name and the face – but after all it is what they do that matters. Those things a mother never forgets. Thank you to every nurse – named and unnamed – who has so unselfishly given of themselves to us over the years, never asking for anything in return. You epitomize what it means to be a nurse.

I wish I could end with something cheerful but my heart is too heavy to do so. Last winter my sister was organizing the first ever Writer's At the Beach Conference to raise money for the UMDF. She created a poster titled *"The Faces of Mitochondrial Disease"* that had pictures of about 10 children with mito. Sam was on there. Leanna and Natalie were on there too. All three about the same age – vibrant, alive and beloved. Sam passed away on March 3rd – the day the conference began. On March 20 - 17 days after that conference Leanna passed away. Yesterday, (May 5th) was her birthday – she, like Sam would have been 9. They were born 4 days apart and died within 17 days of each other. Natalie…has fought so hard and with such courage. She is loved by so many – most of all her Mom, Dad, sister and brother. Her spirit, like Leanna and Sam's, has stayed strong but her body was too tired to fight anymore. She passed away this morning, May 6th. I know Leanna and Sam will welcome her but I wanted her to stay here with her mother and family. My heart is broken every time a child I know dies. One would be too many. Sam, Leanna, Natalie, Angus, Allie, Jack, Austin, Samya, Samantha Rose, Britt and too many others -you are so loved. I just wish you were here.

Sunday, May 7, 2006 7:25 PM

My children are taught piano by the most wonderful, compassionate, enthusiastic woman you can imagine – Miss Nancy (who is actually a Mrs.). Miss Nancy is a music therapist, who works primarily with children with special health care needs. Abby is an exception. Miss Nancy comes to our house every Thursday and lights up the house. She "gets" Abby and has encouraged Abby's need to be creative with her music. She "gets" Zach - his needs, his humor, his personality. She has nurtured them both.

Today was Zachary and Abby's semi-annual "music celebration." The music celebration is always a miracle – children and youth with every conceivable disability playing the piano, singing, sometimes dancing while they sing, playing the drums….it is a miracle. What struck me today was the confidence just pouring out from these kids. Kids who are definitely "not cool" by today's teen

242

standards, literally beaming as they performed with more poise than most kids have. These kids KNOW they are special and have so much to give to all of us, which is a tribute to their parents. Amazing parents who have raised amazing kids. And Miss Nancy the thread that ties us all together, helping us to remember that as long as we are still alive – life is precious and full of possibility.

Monday, May 8, 2006 11:24 PM

HAPPY BIRTHDAY SAMUEL PATRICK

Sam's Birthday is Tuesday May 9th. He would have been nine but I can only see him as seven years and 10 months old.

Sam's birthday is terribly hard without him and yet I am determined that it remain a special day, a day I want to mark, the day he was born to me.

I've been thinking about some of my favorite memories of Sam. There are so many wonderful times we shared, treasured in my heart as broken as it is.

When Sam was about 3 he wanted to be a bird more than anything. He would often look out the window and wistfully say, "When can I go live in my nest and fly?" and this was quickly followed by, "and you can come live in my nest too." One day we were playing in the backyard and he started running with his little legs, chasing a bird. I heard him call "Birdie, birdie wait for me….I am just a boy and I cannot fly but I want to be with you."

Sam at just 8 or 9 months old he had a naso-jejunal tube. This was a tube that went into his nose and down into his intestine and that was how he was fed at that time. The pump was in a backpack and the tubing was long enough that he could play and crawl all over the family room. One day he discovered that if the backpack fell down and the pump was not upright, it did not work. It would alarm and Mama would have to come and fix it. He would look at me, pull the tubing so the pump fell over and give me this little grin when it started to alarm. This went on for days until he got tired of it.

I remember his smile the first time he put his feet in the ocean. He was four. The kids, my sister and I had been driving for 2 days to get to the Jersey shore. We were hot and tired when we got there in the late afternoon. I'll never forget all four of them running into the ocean with their clothes on – so happy to be at the beach. I bought Sam an orange plastic boat that night. He had not changed much since he was 8 months old. His entertainment for the next 2 weeks was to send the boat into the ocean and watch Mama go get it.

At Disney World for his Make A Wish trip when he was four…his wish was to meet Donald Duck. We looked for DD for 2 days and when we saw him – it was magical. Donald gave Sam his blue Mardi Gras beads and Sam just looked at him with such a look of admiration and awe. It rained a lot during that trip and the kids finally consented to wearing those awful yellow, plastic Disney ponchos. Sam and Zach, rain literally dripping off their faces, with their yellow ponchos, hoods pulled up, huge smiles on their faces, sending a video email to Dr. Havens…"Hi Dr. Havens. It's raining in Disney World!"

Grabbing my hand on the way into kindergarten one day – "Mama, don't tell the kids I need to have a hearing test today. They'll worry about me too much." On other days, leaving kindergarten and first grade, after being hugged by a long line of his fan club, "Mama – they really like me. My kids like me a lot!" Many a day in first grade I was summoned to reading group to take Sam to the bathroom. Once out of the room he'd walk slowly and chat endlessly. In the bathroom he NEVER had to go. "Ooops!" he'd say with that mischievous smile, "I guess I did not really have to go."

From the time he was one, his best friends were his Children's Hospital friends. When little he did not talk but had signs for them. Jackie, PT will never get over it that his sign for her was cracker while his sign for his OT, Chris, was Jesus. He made these signs up – I refuse to take responsibility for that. When Peter started taking care of him, for years it was never "Doctor Havens" – just "Havens" - formality was never for Sam. And later when Katherine became his speech therapist he leaned over to us one day and said "You can call her Kaf – that's what I call her." Sometimes he would hold a grudge against them for taking a vacation – how dare they do that!

In the mornings at the hospital he rose early. I'd be getting dressed in the bathroom and hear him chirping away with his nurses with that New York accent he had. I never could figure out how a child born in Wisconsin sounded like he was from the Bronx. How annoyed he would be with them if they called his Phenobarbital by its nickname of phenobarb. Or if they took too long to give him his Valium he'd say with such exasperation, "Mama pushes it right in. You're going too slow!"

His antics with Mrs. Clements, his home bound teacher, were a riot, though we tried very hard not to laugh. At the dinner table if anyone talked he'd say, "Excuse me. Only one person at a time can talk and I am talking right now." When Zach stayed home from school, before long Sam would suddenly be "tired." "I'm tired. Can I go home?" I was a slow learner and it took me several instances to realize that once home he'd practically dance around the house, so happy to be back with Zach.

I remember and I miss…

The feel of his little hand in mine and his arms around me.
The sound of his breathing while he slept.
The smell of his tousled hair
His impulsiveness, his stubbornness
And every time he had a bath – "Mama, do you want to smell me? I smell so good!"

The December that he was six and in kindergarten I interviewed him one day. I can't remember why - I think I was going to make a book for him to give to everyone he loved. I never did that but I saved it and am so glad I did.

Favorite Book:

Blues Clues Hide and Seek and *Blues Cues Snack Party* and all the *Harold and the Purple Crayon* books. "Also it is funny when I made Dr. Havens read the *Christmas Postman*. My kids at school said "Sam Juhlmann, you have a very funny doctor."

Favorite Color:

Purple because Zach likes it. I like to copy Zachary.

245

Favorite Songs:

"You are my Sunshine" and "Spider Man" - but I don't know all the words.

Best Thing About You:

I play good jokes. Every night I steal Mama's napkin at dinner and do things with it like throw it down the basement stairs, put it in her water or put it in the family room.

Best Friends:

Jackie, Katherine, Chris, Dr. Havens, Dr. Greenbaum, Abby, Zach, Brittany, Mama, Daddy, Chicken Food (Sam's favorite stuffed dog), Josie, Jonathon, Joey, Jimmy and all my kids at Bethesda.

Favorite Part of School:

I love Kindergarten and wish I could go every day. My favorite part is playtime -especially blocks. When I was big cheese this week my big cheese (visitor) was Dr. Havens. I sat on his lap and he had to read my Postman book. He thinks it is too long but I think he is just silly.

What I Like:

My dogs, I have a lot of them and I like to get more every time I go to the hospital. Mama buys them for me. Daddy thinks I don't need any more but Mama still buys them for me. One time I counted them and I had 69 but that was a long time ago so I think I have a lot more now. I know all their names like Chicken Food, Plopper, Mischief, Whiffer Sniffer and Mercury.

Favorite holiday:

Christmas because I like to open presents.

Favorite room:

My bedroom because I like to sleep and Zachary sleeps in there with me. One time Abby had a sleep over with us and we threw things at her to wake her up.

Favorite game:

Junior Monopoly and Katherine's bear game

Favorite Movie:

Buzz Lightyear

Favorite Thing To Do On Weekends:

Playing on the computer, playing cars, playing with my dogs, going to the library and doing puzzles. And Mama buys me McDonalds French fries. On Sundays Mama and me snuggle when the kids go to church with Daddy.

Best vacation:

Ocean City, New Jersey because I like to go in the ocean, make a city in the sand with Mama and eat at Bob's Grill. One time a seagull stole my French fries.

What is the saddest thing that ever happened to you?

When Zachary fights with me. He's my best brother. And sometimes he says I can't be a baby but I tell him "I can too be Mama's baby!"

What scares you?

The dark when Zachary is not there with me. I can't sleep without my best brother. Thunder too.

<u>What annoys you?</u>

Zachary when he won't duel with me. And he says I am not a baby and I say "I can still be Mama's baby."

<u>What do you want to be when you grow up?</u>

The Red Lion Wild Force Power Ranger or Buzz Light Year or some other good guy. I could be an ambulance too you know.

<u>What Kind of car do you want when you grow up?</u>

A speedy one – I hope the police man gives me a ticket like Grandma.

<u>What is the most interesting thing you have learned this year?</u>

How to make a turkey in Kindergarten
How to color and do all kinds of projects
How to read the word *Boo, Yes, No*
My flowers grow better than Mama's

Monday, May 15, 2006 10:41 PM

Thank you to everyone who remembered Sam's birthday. His death on this earth cannot erase the importance of marking his life. I know there is conventional wisdom that after a year the mourning and remembering and memorializing should be over. Obviously that "wisdom" comes from people who have absolutely no idea what a hole is left in life when one's child dies. A year? I don't think so! An entire lifetime will not be enough to remember everything special about Sam; it won't be enough time to miss him, to cry, to laugh at the thought of him. A lifetime will not be enough to be inspired by his joy and life attitude, nor will it be enough to not feel the earth is more silent without him.

Mother's Day is hard. I feel like half of a mother these days. Mathematically speaking, since only Sam is gone, I should only feel a 25 percent loss. But it feels so much greater than that most days. I realize that I am so lucky to have three other children here with me and of course Sam is still my child too – he's just not physically here. I've done a lot of things in my SHORT life (I'm quite young remember); being a mother is the one that has made my life the happiest.

Brittany came home from college Friday night. Right before she came home her college parent newsletter arrived in my inbox. It said "your child will be on a different schedule when he/s he comes home. be patient." On Saturday Zach and I went to a wedding while Abby and Lou were at a soccer game. Zach and I came home and the house was quiet. Zach asked "Does your book say how long to let her sleep?" I said "No but since it is 4:15 PM she is waking up." On Sunday she slept until 2 PM. Today she got up at noon. I have a feeling that is as good as it will get!!! It's wonderful to have her at home!

Zach…has been very tired again. His back is really bothering him. I am afraid he has fractured it in additional places but if he has there is nothing different we can do. So we'll hold off on x-rays until his scheduled follow up pictures in two weeks. We did go to the clinic appointment Friday and met the oncologist. I liked him though who really wants an oncologist added to the team? The radiologist also came with the CT scans and she showed them to me, which was helpful since I had never seen the areas of concern. Zach's longtime surgeon was there too. The bottom line is that they do not know what is wrong with Zachary's liver. It could be something that is limited and will not get worse or affect him in significant ways or it could be a worst-case scenario. Obviously the first choice gets my vote. A liver biopsy would help us know more but the problem is that this could cause severe bleeding for Zach. His doctors do not want him to have it right now. Mostly I agree though I am scared and hate waiting for answers. They will follow him closely now and he will have scans again in the next few months. Right now his liver function is basically okay – it's just these "spots" that are of concern. I'm sorry this is vague. It's just not that clear.

Everyone is in high gear getting ready for the Walk/Run. We're hoping for a bright, beautiful, warm, sunny day. The Walk gives me hope that someday there will be answers for this awful disease. Though it is in Sam's memory and he is the inspiration – it is for

Zachary and so many children (and adults) that we are walking. Just in Southeastern Wisconsin there are dozens that I know of...which means there are many more than that. The more we can put this in front of people, the more aware our communities will be and with that awareness comes funding...research...treatments...and ultimately a cure.

Finally, I hope you'll forgive the soapbox I'm about to stand on. Blame my dad or brother- I get it from them!

This week is National Emergency Medical Services Week. I never appreciated the job that these first responders do until the night Sam died. I wish things had been different but what I am thankful for is the caring and compassion that they showed to Sam and me. I have questioned so much about that night but I have never doubted that the men who came to our home from the Waukesha Fire Dept wanted Sam to live; I have never doubted that they did all that they could for him.

Wednesday is National Emergency Medical Services for Children Day. Anyone who knows me, knows how close I hold this issue – children's emergency medical services - to my heart. We gravely under-fund the pediatric EMS system in the U.S. and without funds, there is very little pediatric training afforded to our first responders. They are heroes but even heroes need the tools to do their job. The latest CDC survey results have just been published...they are sobering. Children are not little adults physiologically but we have a system that treats them as if they were. We can and must do better for our children.

From the CDC's "Availability of Pediatric Services and Equipment in Emergency Departments: United States"

1. Children account for about 30 million visits a year to hospital emergency departments.
2. A significant number of children are treated at facilities that lack the recommended pediatric equipment and a fully-trained staff,
3. More than 80 percent of U.S. hospitals serve fewer than 10,000 pediatric patients per year. Many of these hospitals admit pediatric patients who should be transferred to a better prepared facility, have few of the recommended pediatric supplies on hand, and have limited or no access to a pediatric emergency physician.

4. More than 15 percent of hospitals without pediatric trauma service did not have written transfer agreements to send pediatric trauma patients to another hospital.

5. Fewer than six percent of the hospitals surveyed had on hand all the supplies in the full range of sizes.

6. Only 25 percent of hospitals had access to a physician board-certified in pediatric emergency medicine.

What Are We doing?

1. The Emergency Medical Services for Children Program (EMSC Program) is a national initiative designed to reduce child and youth disability and death due to severe illness and injury.

2. The EMSC program is the only federal program that focuses specifically on improving the quality of children's emergency care.

3. Since its establishment in 1984, the EMSC program has improved the availability of child-appropriate equipment in ambulances and emergency departments. It has initiated hundreds of programs to prevent injuries, and has provided thousands of hours of training to EMTs, paramedics and other emergency medical care providers.

4. The 2007 federal budget calls for ELIMINATION of all funds to the Emergency Medical Services for Children Program. Read the survey results again. If we value our children how can we afford to eliminate this vital program when there is still so much left to do to do?

What can be done?

1. Everyone can play a significant role in improving emergency medical services for children.

2. Health care providers can be trained in responding to pediatric emergencies and ensure that their offices or departments are equipped to handle a childhood illness or injury.

3. Parents can talk to their physicians about what constitutes a child health emergency, learn how to access emergency care in their community, and take CPR and first aid training.

4. Teachers can discuss injury prevention measures with their students and learn what to do in an emergency or disaster situation, such as a school fire.

5. Those of us who live in Waukesha can ask for a change in city policy so that children with life threatening emergencies or children with pre-existing complex needs can be transported DIRECTLY to Children's Hospital without having to go to the community hospital first. Crucial time is wasted and this affects outcomes. This is sadly Sam's story.

Have a great week and if you live close we hope to see you at the walk Friday!!!

Wednesday morning May 17, 2006

Zach was transported to Children's Hospital last night about midnight. He had low blood pressure, fixed and dilated pupils, falling heart rate, unable to see or walk and finally was unarousable by the time he was leaving Waukesha Memorial to go to Children's. His temp was only 34 C (= 93 F). He had a head CT and it is not a brain bleed. Blood cultures have been done and I hope he is septic - we can fix that. They have him on IV antibiotics to cover him until we know. They presume this is a mitochondrial decompensation as they cannot find any other cause. By 4 am he was arousable and could talk - slurred speech. His blood pressure still too low, pupils react but sluggish, and about an hour ago he became acutely weak again and fell asleep. His heart is overloaded but we had to cut the rate of one of his meds due to the low blood pressure. we'll be getting labs again in the afternoon. I'm exhausted and worried...it was like reliving March 3 all over again. Thankfully Zach has absolutely no breathing difficulty and his heart rate is steady and never dropped terribly low.

He is irritated that he was in an ambulance with full lights and sirens and cannot recall any of it

May 18, 2006 - 7:35 PM

H*O*M*E*

All last night his BPs were in the 60's/30's range and his renal sats were too high, (which means he was not extracting oxygen from his

252

blood), etc. About 10am he perked up and by the afternoon we decided to bring him home after his blood transfusion. His BPs are now back to baseline and he is back on his baseline cardiac drip. In the end ..."acute mitochondrial decompensation/stroke." I don't think we understand why it happenned, nor do we know why he got better. He just is and I am so thankful. There are definitely residual effects. I am still in shock and have not really processed any of it. I am sure I will now that we're home.

We did the x-rays and he does have additional fractures of his spine.

Thank you for all the thoughts, prayers, calls and emails... THANK YOU!

All Zach can think about is the walk tomorrow. He was so worried that he'd miss it. And now he won't!

Sunday, May 21, 2006 11:18 PM

Friday was a beautiful sunny day – following what seemed like several weeks of dark, gloomy weather. It was easy to believe, when I looked up to the sky, that Sam had something to do with it. Beautiful day, smiling children, orange everywhere, and wonderful community – we are so lucky. We don't have the final figures for the Walk/Run to Wipe Out Mito yet but I believe it will be in the neighborhood of $10,000 to $11,000. Pretty awesome! As it was last year, I was quite touched that the final number comes from a lot of donations – not simply a few. Aside from the money, I hope that today there are more people that know about mitochondrial disease than yesterday. Thank you Sam and Zach for being our inspiration! Thank you to everyone who sponsored us financially or with in-kind donations, who gave of their time and energy to make this happen, who came out to share the afternoon with us, who rooted for us from a distance. A very special thanks to Debbie – who took her sorrow over Sam's death and turned it into action so that as a community we can fight this disease with knowledge and research that will make a difference not only for Zach and the many others with mito but also for those afflicted with other diseases caused or complicated by diseased mitochondria.

Many of Sam's little friends were there.... I cannot believe how they have grown so tall. Yet still the special kids I knew so well. They always make me smile. I don't always realize how much I miss their chatter and sweet faces until I see them. As hard as it is to not see Sam in their midst – I am so thankful that I can still watch them grow up even if from a distance. They were such an important part of his life and gave him so much to live for.

I got an amazing, unexpected gift on Friday. In talking with the paramedic that cared so carefully and kindly for Sam the night he died, I learned that some practices/policies have changed. Children can and have been transported directly to Children's Hospital at the first responder's discretion. He said that I should know that something good had come out of Sam's experience. I thought I was going to cry when he told me this…it is just so amazing and wonderful. Not just kids like Zach who they know about but ANY child…if the situation warrants it. Most kids, of course, can be cared for just fine at the community hospital but sometimes the situation is such that they need to go directly to a pediatric emergency department. Having the knowledge that the paramedics and EMTs have this latitude - to make the best decisions they can for ALL children - has given me so much peace and some other emotion I can't quite name. I don't know what would have happened to Sammy had he gone to Children's. Quite possibly he had fallen off the cliff and nothing anyone could do could have saved him. But I have been plagued by the "what ifs" and "If Onlys"…What if he had been at Children's? If only he had been at Children's? I cannot bear the thought of another mother (or father) feeling that. Perhaps now they won't – at least not in the city of Waukesha. I don't know any details of what it took to make that happen but I am so deeply grateful today for this gift.

Zach is okay. Tired and sleeping more but okay. He is going to try to go to school Monday. Thursday afternoon he will be readmitted for his IVIg. That sure beats an emergency admission. He is wearing his brace like a trooper. I'm really proud of him for being so compliant with it and barely complaining. Zach did the 5K run Friday – in his wheelchair - with Uncle Mike and Mr. G on each side. I don't know why they were so tired at the end – Zach looked just fine!!! He was smiling ear to ear! He "toured" the ambulance on Friday since he is still irritated that he can't recall any of it. Personally, I have had my fill for life of the ambulance.

The girls are great. Brittany and her friends helped a lot again with the Walk/Run. So nice to have them all home from college. Abby seems crazy busy with track, soccer, piano ...it will be nice when life slows down a little though she'll probably be bored then.

From the Butler Middle School Newsletter - May 2006

Student Council would like to thank all students, staff and parents that helped make our fundraising efforts this year a success. Since the last newsletter, Butler raised enough money from the Valentine's Day Dance to donate 5 televisions, 5 DVD/VCR combos, and 2 personal DVD players to Children's Hospital in the name of the Juhlmann Family. We also collected 2 boxes of movies for the hospital. We also collected 4 barrels, 40 boxes, and 20 bags of food, as well as over $645.00 to donate to the Waukesha County Food Pantry.

ARE THESE KIDS AMAZING OR WHAT?!?! I AM SO BLOWN AWAY BY THEIR COMMITTMENT TO THE COMMUNITY, TO ZACH AND TO OTHER CHILDREN. I AM OVERWHELMED AND INSPIRED BY THEIR GENEROSITY. THEY MUST HAVE SOME PRETTY WONDERFUL TEACHERS AND PARENTS TOO!

Monday, May 29, 2006 9:54 PM

I love the part of the Mary Poppins movie when the adults and kids are all hanging from the chandelier and singing "I love to laugh." Every time I hear that song I smile because it reminds me of Sam. He'd laugh so hard every time he saw the movie. (I hear the song quite a bit because I'm such a dork that I downloaded it onto my iPod). However, hanging from the chandelier in real life is not such a blast.

Zach...has been on medication for a few years to lower his blood pressure. He's on a lot of medication but it has been a relatively stable problem. Two weeks ago, when he was admitted emergently, he had alarmingly low blood pressure. We stopped all the medication that is supposed to keep his blood pressure down – obviously he did not need it. He got better and we re-started all of his medications. Now he has swung the other way and has high blood pressure. It's unnerving this

255

swinging. It's called autonomic nervous system dysfunction and it causes all sorts of problems. I hate it because there is no rhyme or reason. There is never anything we can point to and say, "oh that's why." Sam had it too. I know now that a chandelier can swing only so far and it can happen only so many times before it comes crashing down.

Other than the blood pressure swings life is quiet. We've been hanging out on 4 west since Thursday. The hospital is quiet with the holiday weekend. Zach had been doing great with his IVIg - until this afternoon. Now he says he feels the worst ever. His back pain is almost non-existent. His kidneys are working great this week and except for today he has not been too tired. There's not much going on with us, so here are some random thoughts.

Hospital Food: Why can't they make food in this hospital cafeteria that we can actually eat? For five days there has been nothing edible except coffee, doughnuts and jello. Isn't it enough that parents are stuck here? Is it too much to ask to have the grill open on the weekend or to have a meal that is not fried chicken, salt fortified soup or something covered with so much cheese that I don't know what it is and my stomach hurts for 3 days after I eat it? The worst is when I see the same food, show up 3 days in a row but called something different. Day One: spaghetti and marinara sauce; Day Two: ziti and marinara sauce; Day Three: spaghetti soup (which looks like day one with water added).

LIFE: the board game. Zach and I played it yesterday. I have not played since I was a kid. What is wrong with a game called LIFE that has such a narrow definition of a successful life. First gripe: one is forced to drive a car through life- no strolling along, stopping to smell the flowers, not to mention that it implies an "addiction to oil." So there you are driving merrily along until you see something in the road. You come to a screeching halt. The sign says STOP – it's time to get married. There is no choice in the matter. (Zach made his wife drive and he put himself in the back seat - presumably to play Gameboy). Then drive a little more – STOP – buy a house. Tough if you want to live in NYC and rent an apartment for life. Not only do you have to buy the house but you get to make a unilateral decision about it. Zach chose the cheapest house. I told him I thought his wife

256

would like the Victorian mansion and he said "Well, she's not getting it." This is not the real world – at least I hope it isn't. Back in the car driving and you may land on the spot that says you have a baby. Yes, that's right –you have a baby whether you want a baby or not. (I ended the game childless, never having landed on a "you have a baby" spot). If you do have a baby you get to choose the sex. No unexpected blessings for you. The babies, by the way, look exactly alike. Presumably they're all healthy. The same could be said for the adults. And so you continue on through life hoping to steal someone else's salary and avoid paying taxes until you come to the end and can retire in the nursing home. Who wins? Well the person with the most money of course. Yes that is how we define a successful life in the game of LIFE. Pete Seeger's "Little Boxes, Little Boxes" *..and they're all made out of ticky tacky and they all look just the same* comes to mind. Can you tell this is really bothering me? I'm going to have to take this up with Milton Bradley.

Cemeteries: One tends to think of them as creepy places. The thing is - and I know this sounds a little crazed – I really like the cemetery where Sam is buried. It's quiet. It's peaceful. There is so much love to be felt there. I like looking at all the mementoes people leave by the graves. A lime Coke, a teddy bear or a butterfly and sometimes a favorite CD for a teenager. Cards and letters in zip-lock bags, balloons on birthdays, flowers, children's drawings. Sometimes there are other people there when I am. I like talking with them and hearing about who they have buried there. Last weekend I met a young woman who was digging a garden and crying. Her dad is buried next to Sammy. It is her first summer and she asked me if flowers grow. I told her about Sam's marigolds last summer – how tall and vibrant they were. She stopped crying and laughed and smiled. "Marigolds are my dad's favorite!" Such a simple thing but I understood her relief.

Death: What does it mean when we hear thousands of people die every day? It's hard to get yourself around those numbers and feel the impact. I think we're numb to that. But when it is a person you know and love -one death changes your life. It will never be the same. All these holes are left in yourself so that you don't even know who you are anymore or what your purpose in life should be. People look at you and see the you they knew. But when your child dies, you look at yourself and see a stranger. It's like an out of body experience sometimes (please don't call the psych line just yet). You look down at yourself and see this functional, smiling person who acts the way she used to act and you want to yell "Imposter" because you know that the you that lived when Sam lived, died when Sam died. I wonder how many years – if ever – it takes to feel like you are you again. So back to the thousands of people dying every day…I try now when I hear that to bring it down to one person…someone's mother died today, someone's baby, someone's little boy, someone's grandfather. Every life is precious.

Being scammed: I read in *The New Yorker* that many many people have been scammed by email. It's mind boggling that intelligent people who have a functional life can get scammed by email. You know the messages: "I am a widow of this or that deposed ruler in Nigeria and I need your help to get my money out of Nigeria. Please send me 40,000 and in the end you will have a million." I delete these and figured everyone else did the same. Apparently not. Apparently, millions of dollars have been scammed out of upstanding United States citizens. I don't get how smart people can be so dumb!

Madagascar – the country, not the movie: Zach has to do a power point presentation on this for school. He has to pretend he is a travel agent persuading us to go to Madagascar for our vacation. Here's your job – it requires google.com unless you're a social studies whiz. Leave Zach one reason to go to Madagascar in his guestbook and we'll see how many we can get. He'll think that is VERY COOL and if you sign your name he'll give you credit in his bibliography. He needs to find pictures too so if you see any good ones you can leave him the link too. Don't worry –it's not cheating. He will do his own research too.

Wednesday, May 31, 2006 3:54 PM

HAPPY 13th BIRTHDAY ABBY!!!! WE LOVE YOU!

Sunday, June 4, 2006 8:22 PM

This is the last week of school for Zach and Abby! Yahoo! I am really looking forward to ditching the school schedule with homework and bedtime in exchange for something a bit more unstructured. (There WILL still be a bedtime, however.

Wednesday was Abby's birthday. I now have three teenagers in the house – not counting me, of course. Boy would Sam have been mad to be the only one not a teenager.

Zach has been missing Sam A LOT lately. Last night he asked me if I ever miss Sam so much that my chest hurts. Yes and yes and yes. I forget sometimes how hard it must be to have your little brother die. I know how hard it is to have my little boy gone but it's just as hard to have your little brother suddenly not with you anymore.

Zach has a bit of pancreatitis. Although Sam struggled a lot with chronic pancreatitis – Zach has never had it. Sam's episodes were severe and eventually became life threatening for him until we discovered a "cocktail" of drugs that made a difference. No one thought it would but - and this is why we have the best doctor - the boys' doctor read the literature I found, carefully considered the risks versus the benefit and decided there was little risk and possibly a huge benefit even if it was not the standard of care in the U.S. After that Sam still had pancreatitis but it was always mild – I never feared for his life again with it. When we realized Friday that Zach's labs were showing beginning pancreatitis we started that "cocktail" right away. Right now nothing is better but his pain is very well controlled and most importantly it has not progressed. I hope we have stalled the process. Another reason to thank Sam – we never would have known how to intervene so fast had we not learned it the hard way from him.

That's about all for today. I have been freezing cold and exhausted most of the weekend. I diagnosed myself with African Sleeping Sickness although sadly, I have not been to Africa. Brittany, however, had a point when she asked if I have been taking my medicine. Who does she think she is? Me?

259

Thank you for looking up information on Madagascar and sending it to me. I made my travel guide be Craven the Hunter, from Spider Man (he is a villain). My mom thinks this is not very good. What a surprise! She thinks I should not give an innocent traveler Craven as a guide.

Madagascar has many , brightly colored animals like a tomato frog. It took 2,300 dollars just to get to Madagascar. I think that's a lot of money but I plan to be rich when I grow up. (But I won't go to Madagascar because people take your valuables there and I can't live without my valuables.)

I'm finally getting out of school this week and I plan to have fun this summer. If we don't go on vacation I will still be happy unlike my mother and sisters who seem to think a good vacation is a beach. Hopefully my back is going to heal because I want to go to Six Flags Great America. My mom said there are signs that say you can't go on the rides if your back has problems. I did not see those signs.

Thursday, June 8, 2006 11:00 PM

School is out!

It's hard to believe an entire school year has gone by again. I am very proud of Brittany doing so well her first college year and of Zach and Abby having a great first year at middle school. I am also feeling very sad that an entire school year has passed without Sam. All his friend were second graders. He never was and never will be. It's very bittersweet.

Zach continues to have abnormal pancreatic enzyme levels. Until today it did not seem to be affecting him. However, today he was fairly tired at school. He had a low-grade fever most of the day. We thought maybe he was just overheated from the brace but it was 101 tonight – so I don't think it is that. He just looked wiped out. He is also complaining of "left side" pain, which is where his pancreas is. I really hope this is a one-day event.

Next Thursday Zach, Brittany and I are going to Atlanta. Back in the fall I had committed to speaking at the United Mitochondrial Disease Foundation Symposium. Zach was much more stable at the time and it did not occur to me that leaving for a few days would be a problem. Well, life has changed. His doctor and I talked about it and we feel that Zach needs to go where I go…so Zach is off to Atlanta. I think it will be fine if I can just get the logistics taken care of with such short notice. Thanks to some friends in and out of Atlanta I think I have found the resources we need there and just need to start making the calls tomorrow. I'm also thankful that we have a doctor who knows him really well right there if we need him. Dr. "Gween – BOMB" (as Sam called him) took a director of nephrology position at Children's in Atlanta this winter, While, we have not quite forgiven him for leaving we sure are glad he will be there if anything happens. He knows the boys really well.

Now I just need to get started on my presentation.....I have given it in one form or another many times but given my audience is all parents and I am used to speaking to doctors and nurses I need to change it a bit. Oh well, I would not be me if I did anything too much ahead of time. My talks are 6/16 and 6/17 and then we'll come home 6/18. Wish we could stay longer and see the Atlanta sites and visit with my Atlanta and Tennessee friends but it just won't work this time.

Our dear "J" friends are moving tomorrow: Josie (Sam's dear friend) and her wonderful family. We went out for ice cream last night – the 3 girls, their mom, Brittany, Zach and me. Zach figured it was worth hanging out with the girls if he could get ice cream at Coldstone Creamery. Tonight the girls came over for a few hours. It's difficult and I'm not sure I really believe they're moving yet. I am happy for them as the move is because their Dad got a wonderful new coaching opportunity in Indiana. And the girls are excited which is as it should be. But I'll miss them. Josie was not only a wonderful, caring friend to Sammy – but she was a comfort to me this last year. Watching her grow and love 2nd grade and playing games with her or painting or whatever we chose to do has always been special for I do believe that a part of him will always stay with her. He sure liked her and as Mrs. Ferschinger, their Kindergarten teacher said, he had "great taste. Beautiful girl and wonderful family!"

Zach and Abby both were invited to awards night at Butler Monday.) They had an awesome school team this year, which built on the wonderful foundation that their Bethesda teachers gave them. A lot of friends from out of state tell me how lucky we are to have such a caring, invested school system….and we are. But it is the staff – the individual people – that make it that way!

Sunday, June 11, 2006 11:40 AM

Ok -so I can be a little spacey sometimes...THANK YOU to whoever planted the tree behind Sam's cross at the cemetery. I was out there this morning, planting Sam's flowers for a good hour, when I finally looked up and thought "that tree is new!" ....I don't even want to know how long it has been there. My excuse is I usually am lost in thought when there (In my 8th grade yearbook it says "if we were members of an American Indian tribe our names would be....and guess what is says for me - "Princess Dazed One"). By the way, I was also voted the most talkative and the one with the best sense of humor. (My kids find that hilarious - "you were funny Mom????").

Back to the tree - **it is Beautiful. Thank you!!!!**

Zach has a fever; Zach does not; Zach has a fever; Zach does not...you get the idea. I'll do labs again tonight and see if his pancreatitis is worse.

Monday, June 19, 2006 9:44 PM

We are back from Atlanta. It was a fast and furious four days. I am exhausted but so glad that we made the trip. Zach, Brittany and I flew out of Milwaukee on Thursday. The Atlanta airport has gotten worse – if at all possible. Coming from Milwaukee that place is a zoo and a lengthy one at that. The Mitochondrial Diseases Symposium was Friday and Saturday. Although I heard things I already knew it was still such a privilege to listen to the experts explain the complexities of the disease in various ways. In particular, Dr. Shoffner, the metabolic physician from Atlanta who diagnosed my children, is such a gifted teacher. I wrote down every analogy he gave! I also got to meet a metabolic doctor from Boston who has helped Peter and me via email from time to time. It was so nice to finally put a face to the name.

It seemed that one of the things stressed over the weekend was that there is not one but hundreds of mitochondrial diseases. Saying that someone has one is like saying that someone has cancer – it's really just a general term and we have a long way to go before we figure out all the differences in types of mitochondrial disease. I knew this but it was stressed over and over so that one could not help but really contemplate what that means…there will not be A cure or A treatment. There will have to be multiple treatments and not everyone will work for every patient. Someday we hope there will be cures (plural). It's a little overwhelming and makes one realize how far we have to go. On the other hand there was a 90 year old physician there that had done some work on mitochondria as a young physician – to him we have come a long way! The research is very basic still but the flip side of that is that there is so much excitement in the field. Things like Alzheimer's, Parkinson's, Cancer, Friedrich's Ataxia…they all have a mitochondrial defect as part of their process. This will bring attention to mitochondrial medicine and attention and money are what we need.

I also felt such strong reaffirmation that Zach, Sam and Brittany have been cared for by the best of the best! I'd listen to these mitochondrial experts and it was so clear how our doctors have been so careful and on track! I'd give anything to have Sam back but I do know this - he could not have gotten better care anywhere than he did here in Wisconsin. I've always known that but there is a tremendous comfort in having that so clearly affirmed as I did this weekend.

It was so great to visit with friends that I rarely get to see as well as to meet new ones and also to "meet" the ones I had only known online – some for many years. It would be impossible to name all the names but I hope you all know how privileged I feel to know all of you! My Dad, 2 youngest brothers and sister came so it was family time as well! Saturday night I had dinner with friends I met when Sam was a baby. They have been a huge source of support over the last 9 years. I had not seen them since Sammy's funeral; we laughed a lot more this time.

Zach did well with traveling – better than I expected. All of our home care items arrived via UPS this time and I never had to draw his blood or take him to a doctor (Though there were plenty of "mito experts" had we needed them.). My Dad took him to the new Atlanta Aquarium on Saturday and he got to see a whale shark. I'm a bit jealous.

None of us slept well while there so we are all pretty tired today. This week is busy, as Zach will be readmitted to Children's on Thursday or Friday for his usual 6-day stay to get his IVIg. There are some decisions we need to make. His iron levels are too high and he needs to be treated for this but potentially it involves placing a second central line (permanent IV line). He also needs follow up x-rays of his back. He has had a lot of back pain since yesterday. Discouraging. He also has had what we think may be neuropathic pain due to a pinched nerve. We need to figure this out. I hate when he hurts. His labs were stable but I could see in tonight's results that his heart is working harder than it should. He's also a little acidotic. I'm not surprised, as he has had more shortness of breath all day than he has in a few weeks. I'm sure the trip wore him out a little.

Monday, June 26, 2006 8:43 PM

Zach is still inpatient. We went to ortho clinic today. New x-rays show that he has a new fracture on his spine. This one is further up at T7. The orthopedic doctor will get the old films and compare. I am afraid that tomorrow he will tell me he found even more new ones. I am so discouraged. We have been treating this bone issue so aggressively. Aside from surgical stabilization I cannot imagine what it is going to take to stop this process.

Aside from that he is doing well. Anne, the art therapist brought us a beautiful wind chime today for Sammy's garden. It is just so Sam - the sound of it, the color, the look of it!

The girls are awesome. I'm looking forward to being home with them soon. Since the first of May there has not been a 2 week time period that I have been at home. After this hospitalization we will have nearly 3 weeks at home and I plan to enjoy every minute of it. I'm also thinking about a vacation in August...can't say where yet...but it will be fun if we do it.

Thursday, June 29, 2006 10:02 AM

Zach came home last night...more about him another day.

264

To anyone reading this that lives in the Southeastern Wisconsin area:

PLEASE DONATE BLOOD

There is a **CRITICAL** shortage of blood in our area.

There is only a one day supply rather than the five day supply the blood center tries to keep on hand.

ALL BLOOD TYPES ARE NEEDED

The Blood Center of Wisconsin supplies ALL blood and blood components in Southeastern Wisconsin. The Red Cross does not supply any blood in this area.

Therefore it is crucial to donate to the Blood Center of Wisconsin if you live in the Milwaukee area.

Just this past hospital stay Zach needed 2 units of red cells. He is one of many children and adults whose lives depend on donations from those who can afford to give this free but precious gift

Tuesday, July 4, 2006 11:01 PM

Thank you to anyone who donated blood in the last few days. Thank you to those who may donate blood in the coming weeks - not just here in Wisconsin but where ever you live. While cleaning files the other day I found this picture...I felt like I had come upon a treasure to find a picture I did not know I had. It is a picture of Sam, getting his cryo (part of plasma) and holding his bear named "cryo bear" - a gift from the courier who delivered his blood products 4x/day.

Weddings: The other night at dinner the girls were discussing their weddings (not that either are getting married anytime soon) and Zach declared that IF (how he stressed the word IF) he does get married he would have a Batman wedding. His wife to be will be dressed like Batwoman; he will be Batman of course and guess who will be marrying them? The Joker. Then they will go off to live in a black house.

July 4th: We skipped the 4th of the July parade this year. Zach's favorite part of it has always been diving for the candy that gets thrown into the street. He wisely concluded he should not do that with his back fractured. The girls did not want to go - so we didn't. I can't remember not going even though it is a typical small town parade and

265

there's not much to it. Sam loved the parade ...it's hard to stop doing the things he loved even though it is so hard to do them. I don't know if that makes sense.

We did go down to the Fox River to walk along the river. It is one of my favorite places to be – no matter the season. Then off to Main Street. Zach ordered an Italian soda that only he would order and actually drink – lime and cinnamon! I tried it and believe me – don't order it. Of course this is from the kid who was mixing orange soda with root beer Monday night. Not only that but the friends he had over were mixing it too and they all solemnly told me it was GREAT. I tried it. Another drink I don't recommend.

Friends: I am thankful there are boys who continue to come over and hang out with Zach. I know they like him - what's not to like? But still we all know that 8th grade boys would rather run around outside and play sports than hang inside. They're good kids and I hope that they'll still have time for him as the social scene changes in the next few years. It's tough enough being a teenager and navigating ALL of THAT – let alone being a teen hooked up to IV pumps 24 hours a day, chronically tired and in the hospital all the time.

Zach's health: The new fracture seems to have started the pain up again. Some days it is fine and other days he needs a lot of meds. The most painful part is the muscle spasms that go down to his legs at times. He needs a new brace because he gets a fever in the one that he has. Since any increase in temperature speeds up metabolism this is actually a really bad thing for him. I hope they come up with a solution for him soon. He needs the protection and stability of a brace, but he also cannot afford the effects of the one he currently has.

A few days ago he told me that he won't be going to Six Flags this summer...wow -did it hurt to hear him say that. It's not that I would have let him go there and I cringed inside every time he talked about it, knowing I'd have to tell him no. And yes, I do know it is a positive thing that he came to that conclusion himself. But to listen to your child verbalize out loud that he is giving up his dream (even something as seemingly insignificant as going to an amusement park) is heart wrenching. *Rip* goes the heart. He does not want much – he accepts his limitations – he is happy with his life – so why does he have to give up the one and only thing he wanted to do this summer? But honestly – it's my problem and my heartbreak. He seems accepting of it all. If only I could be more like him. If only I could be more like all my kids.

Otherwise we are on hold. That is okay because in the next few weeks there may be answers and I am afraid of those answers. He needs his hearing tested again – 10-db loss last month, 20-db a few months before….not a good pattern. He needs a repeat CT scan of his liver. If the "spots" have grown the oncologist says we have no choice but to biopsy, which makes all of us leery due to the bleeding. He will see the neurologist in 2 weeks. He has developed intention tremors of his hands and arms and I am frightened as to their significance.

<u>Super heroes</u>: Zach, Abby and I went to see *Superman*. We decided it was good but not as good as *Spiderman*. Super hero movies are hard things for me. How can I not think about my little boy who wanted to be a super hero? He was so sure they existed. I hope they do exist in heaven. I keep score in my head. How many super hero movies Sam did get to see versus how many he will never see. So far the ones he saw are winning. But that will change. It has been 16 months now since I held him. And yet even tonight when we were sitting down to dinner, do you know that I went to look for Sam. A few days ago I checked on Zach when he was asleep and went to Sam's bed. I forgot he was gone. The moment of truth is sickening. I am shocked that this still happens. I feel the pain of a broken heart and yet there must be some beating piece of it that still does not understand he is not here.

So we went to *Superman*, as I said and Superman's father says: *"I will never leave you – even in my death. The richness of my life shall be yours. All that I have learned, all that I feel, everything that I have, all this and more I bequeath you my son. You will carry me in you – all the days of your life. You will make my strength your own, and see my life through your own eyes, as your life will be seen through mine. The son becomes the father, and the father the son."*

I felt so sad thinking how normal it is for a parent to pass on their values, experiences, love, feelings to their children. I will never live on in Sam. And if truth were told – even had he lived many years - I am not sure there is anything that I could have taught him. Oh sure, I would have continued to teach him manners, how to read, add and subtract and what happens when you mix vinegar and baking soda. But the things that matter - he seemed to always know those. Being

267

real without the least pretense, loving enormously, and finding joy in every day.

It is Sam who has passed on the richness of his life to me. It is his strength and the desire to honor him that keeps me walking on the days that the pain is so sharp that I'd honestly prefer a twisted knife in my heart. It is Sam who taught me to see life through his eyes so that the world will never look the same. Everyone says I did a lot for Sam - I could not have done more for Sam. Maybe that is true, yet it all pales when held next to the enormous things he did for me.

It is the same with Brittany, Zachary and Abby. They have affected me, changed me, taught me. I get so terribly busy sometimes and don't allow myself to be affected or taught by them. But when I do take the time I am always somewhat startled at how different life can look through their eyes. Brittany came home yesterday, talking a mile a minute about an hour she had spent with one of the pediatric hematologists who had kindly showed her around her lab and explained some of the research she is doing. I thought to myself - when is the last time I was *that* excited about learning something or meeting someone? Yesterday Zach told me that the kids and Grandma have been making plans for MY birthday…he was so excited just at the thought of how they will surprise me. I wondered when is the last time I was *that* excited to do something for someone else? Abby got a letter from my brother - it could have been from a movie star. When is the last time I was *that* excited to hear from someone in my family?

In the end I suspect these words are more about what the child gives to the parent than what the parent gives to the child.

"The richness of my life shall be yours. All that I have learned, all that I feel, everything that I have, all this and more I bequeath you ….you will carry me in you –all the days of your life. You will make my strength your own, and see my life through your own eyes"

On a lighter note: I'm really irritated that Superman left again. I suppose Spiderman will not stick it out either in *Spiderman 3* next summer. Zach is disgusted with me – don't I get it that saving the world should come before love? However, I did watch *Memoirs of Geisha* with the girls last night and thankfully that had an ending I found to be happy.

The day after Sammy died, the first graders all made pictures for us; the teachers put them in a book for me. The book remains one of those things that makes me laugh and cry. It is truly one of the most comforting things I own. I will try to post a different one every week. They're so precious!

Monday, July 10, 2006 10:59 PM

Busy summer days! What happened to the lazy days of summer? Still it is nice to be freed from the schedule of getting kids out the door by 7 am for school. I had a hard time today getting Zach and Abby out by 7:30. (In the interest of being honest – they were ready at 7:30 but their mom was not.) This week Zach and Abby are going to HIP Career Camp (Health in Practice Career Camp) at Children's Health Education Center. They both really wanted to do this. So far it seems to be a really neat experience, despite the fact that it is all the way on the other side of Milwaukee and traffic is a nightmare at that time of the morning. The camp is for kids in 7th-8th grade who are interested in a health career. They get to meet with all sorts of different health care providers, watch an open heart surgery (by video), visit the blood center, visit Marquette, do lab experiments, team building exercises, mock interviews, lunch with professionals and all sorts of other fun interactive activities. Oh – and they get a tour of Children's Hospital of Wisconsin. Woo Hoo! Bet Zach could give that tour. So far Zach is very impressed with one of the high school counselors who can speak Japanese. Abby, likewise, is impressed with ALL of the high school counselors because "they are really into school but they are really nice and fun!" It is wonderful when there are older kids for them to look up to and learn from.

Last Friday I took Zach, Abby and friends miniature golfing and then for ice cream. It was an incredibly hot day and the course was NOT accessible in the least. Way too many stairs to climb and Zach's legs were tremoring a lot with the activity. The next day he slept late and took a very very long nap. But he really had fun despite the stairs. Other than that he continues to have intermittent back pain which radiates to his right hip and leg. It is better than it was a few weeks ago and I am trying to be hopeful that the fractures are over – there will be no more. We are still working on getting a brace that works –

lots of communication problems have prolonged this process. Next week he'll be in the hospital.

Saturday I took the kids to this really neat place called Dinners by Design From their website: *"Dinner by Design is today's fun, convenient, cost effective way of getting dinner on the table. In just 2 hours or less, you can make 12 entrées or more. We do this by creating monthly menu selections and preparing all the ingredients for you. We save days of shopping in grocery stores, debating and hunting for items, preparing, chopping, and cleaning up."* Now tell me – who can resist that advertisement? Not I! I like to cook but I really do not like thinking about what to cook and I rarely have the time to make anything I actually want to eat. Aside from that it is dangerous for me to be in a food store because I always come home with 2x more than anyone could ever eat. (For this reason my kids beg me to food shop). So last Monday I picked out 12 meals and scheduled a time to prepare our meals. The kids had a blast! Had I asked them to help me cook at home, I'd be lucky if they chopped a tomato without whining or chopping off a sibling's finger. But here…they were fighting over who got to do what. They made a great team and no one has complained about dinner in 3 nights. I especially enjoyed that it was something that Zach really loved to do. He has always helped cook whenever he can so he just had a great time with this. I think we're destined to become Dinner By Design Groupies.

I read something really thought provoking last week in the *NY Times*– from David Brooks - who I respect but normally don't see eye to eye with. His editorial was titled "On Human Bonding" and in the piece, he underscored the importance of human attachments. *"We in this policy world debate education, incarceration rates, poverty, productivity and competitiveness and we try to figure out which qualities individuals need to thrive in the new economy.* ***But often it's the space between individuals that <u>really</u> matters****, the nature of their attachments."* David Brooks then quoted Adam Smith: ***"the chief part of human happiness arises from the consciousness of being beloved."*** I have thought about that last statement for the better part of the last week and have drawn comfort from it. There is no doubt in my mind that Sam was happy. Zach is happy - I know this too. Sometimes I wonder, "how can they be so happy when life has thrown them so many curve balls?" They are happy because they know they are beloved by countless people. I cannot fix this disease. I don't understand all of its complexities. I feel so helpless to help them most of the time. But I can love my children. That's easy. I love them beyond all measure, beyond all words. And I can remind them that they are loved by a world full of people. *"the chief part of human happiness arises from the consciousness of being beloved."* Those are the words echoing in my heart these days.

Saturday, July 15, 2006 10:36 PM

This past week did not turn out to be Zach's best. Monday and Tuesday he went to the health career camp at Children's Health Education Center. Tuesday evening I took Abby, Zach and friends to Pirates of the Caribbean II, precluded by ice cream at Oscars. This was a mistake in that Zach was already pretty tired from being out all day. However, he insisted on going. He did and slept through most of the movie. Good thing we can always rent it in a few months! The other kids had fun but did not think it was as good as the 1st Pirates.

Wednesday Zach could barely wake up for camp. I think he would have stayed home but it was the day they were scheduled for the live video cast of an open heart surgery at Advocate Christ Hospital in Chicago. There was no way he was going to miss that! I have to say it was really neat. The surgery, of course, was fascinating. But what I loved was how interactive the entire experience was. The surgeon talked to the kids throughout the surgery and took all sorts of questions from them. How neat that here we are in Milwaukee and there they are in Chicago and yet technology allows that sort of visual and auditory communication.

As soon as the surgery was over Zach wanted to go home and pretty much slept the entire afternoon. Thursday he woke up and could not move. He had tremendous pain in his back and hamstrings and it took a lot of medication to get him mobile. He opted to go to physical therapy and not to camp. Therapy probably helped loosen things up a little but he has still required a lot of different medications to feel good since then. Mornings are the worst. Friday he was still exhausted and so ended up missing more camp than he attended this week.

It was pretty heart breaking for me. He, on the other hand, seemed to take it in stride as he always does. I look at him to make sure there are not any clues that he is hiding his feelings but I really don't see it. He just seems to always look on the bright side of things – which is an amazingly hard thing to do as often as he does it.

Today he is still tired and has a low grade fever. His stomach and intestines are working even worse than his typical so he is only able to take some clear liquids. Hopefully we can get him on some antibiotics next week and that will help. His blood counts dropped a lot from 2 nights ago – if it is real he is quickly destroying his red cells. I'm sure he'll need a few transfusions of red cells when inpatient next week.

When I was saying good night to him the other night I saw that his big toe was bloody. I asked him how that all happened and he had no idea that anything was wrong with his feet. It's a little concerning to me that his neuropathy may be getting worse. In the past few months there have been other deep scratches and scabs that he seems to know nothing about.

Abby did go to camp all week and it was definitely a wonderful experience for her. She chatted non-stop about it all week. I am so glad she enjoyed it. The ride was NOT enjoyable. I never knew people drove like they were from New Jersey in Wisconsin. When we moved here from Jersey I marveled at how courteous the drivers were – they actually pulled over to the side of the road for the ambulance. I couldn't figure out what they were doing the 1st time that happened. However, I don't typically go to the east side of Milwaukee at peak rush hour times. I seriously wonder about the brain function of people who perform life threatening maneuvers to get ahead by one or maybe two cars. I am not a meek driver by any means and I had a major headache every morning by 8:30 am. This Midwest, rush hour crowd definitely has the skills to drive through the Jersey circles. They might even be ready for Boston.

I thought I would made a little slide show of Sammy. I initially thought I'd make a few –it is so easy. But it was really just too hard. Each picture is a memory and those memories, in turn, jolt another memory....I miss him so much. I guess I sound like a broken record. Broken - at any rate.

I have realized that there is no safe memory. One would think that if I could think about BS memories (before Sam) that would work out alright. But they never do. I hear a song and I think "oh that was when

I was at Rutgers (college)...I was happy...I had no idea that I'd have a baby named Sam and that he would die when he was almost 8." I think about our summer trips with my dad - on a mission to see every national park in the U.S. – and then I think about how Sam never saw even one of our beautiful National Parks. And AS memories (after Sam) are not any better because one person is always missing from them and that absence ends up being the most vibrant part of the memory.

My friend told me that Sam's death would never be something to get over – it would be something that became a part of me as his birth and life. What I did not understand was that in becoming part of me, not only am I a different person, not only is my life different – but my memories, my history is reframed with Sam's life. That's not necessarily bad – it just is.

I'm sure I'll make other little slide shows eventually. Thanks to my wonderful friend, Kathy, who flew up from Tennessee the day before Sammy's funeral and scanned pictures for hours (and hours) – I have a lot of pictures scanned. When I look at the pictures I miss Sam so much sometimes that it feels physical. Yet, the pictures also evoke a feeling of thankfulness for the amount of things he did, people he loved, joy he felt.

Friday, July 21, 2006 4:00 PM.

Still inpatient. It feels like a very long week.

Zach's spine x-ray showed additional fractures and worsening of the pre-existing ones of his back. This, at any rate, is what the resident told me. I have not actually seen the official report because the film is apparently MIA. I really don't even know what to say – it feels like all we do is get x-rays that show more fractures. Maybe the new tactic should be no more x-rays.

There has not been any more progress on getting his new brace. The ortho is going to finally measure him today but he tells me that they still do not have insurance approval. Lost in some pile of bureaucracy.

His pain is non existent which seems like a miracle given how bad it was last week. Zach's PT and I think it is the IVIG. His doctor

273

rolls his eyes – he does not think IVIg does all of that. Whatever the reason – it is nice to see him without pain!

The liver CT scan: another frustration. The report was one page of words that gave zero information. There are no absolute measures so that we can actually compare it....just "multiple lesions" (but not how many or what their measurements are) and that they are in multiple lobes of the liver. The radiologist says they are hemangiomas (benign liver tumors). The oncologist had already explained to me that there are too many and they are throughout the liver to be hemangiomas. The "hemangioma expert" would not see Zach in the clinic because she said it would be unheard of for him to have hemangiomas at his age. Yet the radiologist insists they are hemangiomas. I don't have a clue who is right. I know they are all doing their best and that the issue is they really don't know. But I wonder if they ever consider what it feels like to be on the receiving end of this "information" (lack of actually). I feel like a ping pong ball bouncing around.

Today the oncologist told our doctor that he will review it with the radiologist and get back to our doctor. I know Zach's primary doctor will tell me what he knows as soon as he does but it does not seem that there is any sense of urgency from the other doctors that have to decide what this is. I wonder do they really not understand what it felt like when they took me in a room with a zillion residents and med students and said "he might have a malignancy?" Do they not understand what it feels like to wait months to get an answer? Do they know that it feels like they are holding a forget me not and instead of saying "he loves me, he loves me not" they are saying "malignant, hemangioma, birth defect, malignant, hemangioma…" and I am sick waiting to see which one it ends up being.

Yesterday I took Zach to a routine orthodontist consult for braces. I was thinking that we were doing a typical teenage appointment. How nice. Turns out that a medication Zach is on for his bones will prevent him from getting braces. In addition it places him at high risk for bone disease of the jaw if we have to pull his teeth. I guess I should not be surprised then that he has several teeth that do need to be pulled. The orthodontist (who is also an oral surgeon) said he is very uncomfortable with this situation and does NOT want to pull the teeth. He said he will give it 4 months in the hopes that they will fall out on their own. Unlikely, given the teeth are not even the slightest bit loose. If they don't fall out I am unsure what we will do because the teeth cannot stay in long term. But necrosis of his jaw is not a risk that is easy to swallow.

I am having a hard time with this news. Partly because Zach really wants braces and now he cannot have them. I also feel like an idiot mother. This is information I should have known about the drug (Pamidronate). I usually research every drug the kids start on. Sam was on the Pamidronate too. But this one I did not really look into beyond the basics. Why –I don't know. Maybe I would still have chosen to use it for the boys – their bones are so fragile and maybe there is not a better choice. There are always risks to every treatment and you just make the best decisions you can make. But I did not make a good decision this time because it was a completely uninformed choice. Sometimes, I want so much to just trust….and not question everything. Well I did this time and it was a stupid thing to do on my part. I don't know what we will do now. It's not as simple as just taking him off of it. His bones are fragile and continuing to fracture. Even if we did take him off today – it likely is a medicine that stays in his bones for years. I feel like I have poisoned him with my own hands. Yes, I know I am being hard on myself but that is how I feel right now.

His hearing test showed another 10 decibel loss in both ears. Still only high frequency which means hearing aids will not help. (Most speech is not high frequency). They are recommending a hearing test monthly and also answer technology FM system for school called Edulink. This is a small explanation of it:

the teacher carries a small, wireless microphone (the FM transmitter) on his/her lapel or as a headset, allowing them the freedom to walk and talk while teaching. The student receives the teacher's voice directly into an earpiece, a resilient, inconspicuous and contemporarily-designed device, which allows them to clearly process sound and information.

The technology behind EduLink increases the signal-to-noise ratio, which provides the student with a much clearer and distinct audible speech signal. The system helps by improving the quality of the listening environment, effectively reducing distracting background and ambient noise, and enhancing the processing of auditory information, which ultimately increases the child's ability to learn.

Supposedly we can borrow the system in September when he starts school to see if it helps.

Hopefully Zach will be discharged sometime Sat afternoon.

Sunday, July 23, 2006 - 9:19 PM

Quick update -we did come home Saturday night. Zach was exhausted today but is building Batman lego creations as I type. Abby left today for Duluth, MN - on a youth group mission trip. She is staying in a 3 story church that overlooks Lake Superior. I just got an email that they have arrived there safely. She'll be home Friday. I miss her already.

Saturday, July 29, 2006 10:53 PM

August in 2 days! Unbelievable.

I finally saw the spine x-ray report and it did indeed show progression of his osteoporosis and worsening of his compression fractures. I had hoped that the resident got it wrong and the report was going to show improvement.

Thursday, I found out that the brace makers' office staff, who were supposed to get insurance approval for the brace, did NOTHING for 12 days. After 12 days I asked about it (this was when he was in the hospital) and they made one call to the pediatrician for a referral (that our benefits manual says we do not need). After that call, they promptly dropped the ball again until I called Thursday (wondering if the brace was made yet). So basically we have been waiting for a brace for 3 weeks that had not even been submitted for insurance approval because someone in an office was on Siesta time. Perhaps this would not be a big deal if it was his leg braces but this is a brace for a back that is progressively worsening and painful.

I did my best to get things moving Thursday but it was like talking to people who spoke another language…I could go on and on with the issues, attitudes, etc. I even offered to pay myself - that very day - and worry about the insurance later and was told I could not do that. Hey – since when can't someone buy what they need in America? Anyway – there is a bright spot to this story. When I came home on Thursday I had a message from Pam, the nurse who works with our orthopedic doctor. Someone called her (probably to warn her that a mother lion was on the loose at Children's Hospital) and she spent close to an hour on the phone and got through to someone – somewhere. Friday morning the referral was approved! Now let's see how fast they make that brace. Anyway – back to Pam. I barely know her but this is the second time she has stepped in and straightened out an issue for me. Startled by kindness. It reminded me that most people do care and do want to do the right thing.

The orthodontist/oral surgeon called Friday. He said he researched things because he knows Zach really wants those braces (talking mouth braces now). I was very touched that he wants to make the braces happen for Zach. He could not find much about kids on the problematic class of drugs (bisphosphonates) but had clearly spent time thinking about things in light of the information he does have. He did confirm that whatever damage has been done (if any) to the jawbone cannot be reversed, even with stopping the medicine. However, Zach has only been on it since November, which is not terribly long. He wonders if we stop it perhaps his baby teeth will still fall out on their own and we could try the braces. He thinks the worst thing would be the teeth just would not move. This is not a simple issue so in the next month we will need to have the endocrinologist, nephrologist and orthopedic doctor weigh in. After that Peter, (Zach's primary doc) and I can figure out a plan. I don't want to risk Zach's bone health but it is not clear this medicine is helping and even if bone is being built – it is unclear what quality of bone is being laid down. It's complicated but Zach has doctors that care an awful lot about him and I know we will do our best to make our best decisions.

Thursday Waukesha got 5-6 inches of rain in an hour. They say it is a once in a lifetime occurrence. I came home from work to find water in the basement. Fortunately, it was not in the finished portion where Zach has his Make A Wish game room. Our neighbors did not fare so well. Lou has been out of town but Brittany helped me a lot and our neighbor came over to make sure there was nothing horrifically wrong that needed immediate attention. I ended up

277

throwing out a lot of stuff that got wet. Thankfully, it was just stuff - and not irreplaceable things such as the things I have saved that the kids have drawn or written.

Abby came home from her mission trip to Duluth, Minnesota. She had a great time! She spent most of the time working in a homeless shelter, and was quite impacted by that. It strikes me how many times the very people we are supposedly helping, are in fact the ones helping us. Abby went to Duluth to help at a homeless shelter but you have to wonder – who benefited more? Abby or the homeless people she met? The same could be said about so many people in our lives and it brings a great sense of humility to me. I have been told a story about how one homeless, gentleman playing heart and soul on the piano asked the kids if anyone would play the other part with him. Abby jumped in of course. They played the piano together and apparently this made that man's day. Abby said "the only thing that is different between those people and us is money." I hope she always remembers that and allows that to guide her decisions in politics, God, friendships and life in general.

Zach got his new glasses today. They have prisms and some magnification. The hope is that his eyes will not have to work so hard and this will prevent some of the double vision, blurry vision and "things are jumping around" Afterwards we went to the book store and he got a few new books – *Star Wars* and another Andy Griffin book called *Just Disgusting*. He loves those Andy Griffin books. Not exactly high literature but I don't care as long as he reads. He spent a fair amount of time painting this afternoon, which was nice to see him do.

Yesterday Zach, Brittany and I went to *Click*. I really did not want to go and tried to talk those two into going without me. I thought a nap sounded really good. But they were having none of that. Maybe it was my low expectations but I have to say it is a great movie. I don't even like Adam Sandler all that much, and some may find the language offensive but it was still great. The message was nothing new -slow down and take time to enjoy the people in your life before you fast forward yourself through all the important moments that make a life worth living. Still…I was likely the only person crying at an Adam Sandler movie. As the critics say…."I laughed, I cried – fabulous!" For those of you who know Zach's laugh that can be heard

278

down the hospital or school hallways and out our front door ....he laughed and laughed and laughed. Always a great thing to hear.

Speaking of Zach's laughter.... A week or so ago while I was at work, his nurse found a dead baby mouse on the floor. Yes – a dead baby mouse just dead in the middle of the kitchen floor. She wisely left it there for Zach to deal with when he woke from his nap. Well he apparently decided it would be a great, funny thing to place the dead, baby mouse on my kitchen counter. I am told he washed his hands after placing that dead mouse on my counter. Abby saw it first and called me into the kitchen. I thought it was fake but no -it was a real, dead, baby mouse. I hate mice. I hate dead mice. I hate dead mice on my kitchen counter. We made Brittany dispose of it and then I scrubbed that counter for a LONG, LONG time.

Well, Monday (7/31) is my birthday. The kids love when it is my birthday because that means I do nothing except spend time with them and eat. Tomorrow, we are actually going to my Mom and Frank's for dinner, since I have to work Monday. Zach is going to go over early and help her cook. I don't think I will ever feel too old to ask my mom to make me a special birthday dinner and I am lucky she still wants to do it for me. Zach is more excited than I am since we said we'd play some board games and he LOVES playing games with a big group of people. It never ceases to amaze me how the littlest things are all that he really wants out of life.

P.S. Anyone watch that new reality show Thursday "Who wants to be a superhero?" on the Sci Fi channel. I don't ever watch TV except an occasional news program but I promised Zach's I'd watch it with him. Now I can't wait to see who is going to be eliminated next week. It's fun watching with Zach because he knows a lot about superheroes and is a good critic.

Friday, August 4, 2006 11:25 PM

Zach has been doing so well the past few weeks – less pain, more energy, having lots of fun. If not for the backpack attached to him with all his IV pumps I might easily forget that he has mitochondrial disease. Yes, I know you may think that is a stretch – could I really forget he has a mitochondrial disease? Yes – I could and do

279

sometimes. Of course, I still give him a zillion meds, take his blood pressure and listen to his heart countless times/day, draw his blood, talk to his doctor, try to count how many new bruises on his legs when he is not looking. But....those are just things I do like washing the dishes or cleaning the house and I forget why I am doing them. They are chores I get out of the way so that we can have fun and do all the things we want to do. Look how normal we are –we go to the movies, out for ice cream, play board games and cards, have friends over, tell jokes, go shopping, plan vacations.

Sometimes my heart is unsure. Like one of Sam's favorite books called *"A Fish out of Water"* my heart says *"But something may happen – you never know what." "But he looks too good for something to happen. He's really not that affected by this disease,"* argues my brain. And my heart believes that because it is always easier to believe what we want reality to be than to believe what we wish it were not.

And then something does happen. Today it is nothing terribly acute – he is just really tired. He can't get out of bed. It's not a big deal and he'll be fine tomorrow or the next day – I know that. But it is alcohol on a never healed wound because this little thing – being tired – reminds me that he has a mitochondrial disease. And inside his body, without anyone seeing or knowing, there are mitochondria dying prematurely.

This illness is a game no one understands how to win. There ARE winners; I remind myself of that all the time. Many kids with mitochondrial disease grow up to be adults and live to a normal life expectancy. They have a chronic illness – yes. But with careful attention, and even sometimes without careful attention, they do okay. Our idea of mitochondrial disease is so skewed – especially those of us who work in a hospital – because all we see are the worst cases. And when it is bad – it can be very bad. The problem is that it is not easy to predict who will win and who will lose. Why does it leave some kids relatively well, some with complex but stable problems and devastate and kill others?

Yesterday, a beautiful 2-year-old girl from Waukesha died – from mitochondrial disease. It made me angrier that I can explain. So unbelievably angry at this disease that takes such sweet children. All day yesterday I thought about the different children I know who have died from this disease and it all just seemed so unfair. Then, while Zach slept I sat out side and read this: *"Hope is about choosing to believe this one thing, that love is bigger than anything that anyone can throw at us"* (Anne Lamott) I thought of Sam and how sure he was that good guys would always get the bad guys. We even have a poster hanging on the pantry door that was made when he was still alive – it has a picture of Sam saying what was one of his favorite things to shout out at us **"Evil never wins!"**

The hour before Sam died his heart slowed. His brother and sisters surrounded him before the paramedics came and he went off in the ambulance. *"Sam – we'll get French fries tomorrow"* his sisters said…and his heart would speed up. *"And we'll play Yugio on Friday night"* shouted Zach and Sammy's slowing heart would beat faster again. That is love that is more powerful than anything life can throw at us. I thought about this all day and I realized that saying there are winners and losers is not quite right. Yes, some kids live *with* Mito and some kids die *from* Mito. But if death is the definition of losing then we all will lose so that can't be it. Sam did not lose. He is a winner because he gave us love and we loved him and that was far bigger and mightier than this crappy disease. And if Sam were writing this he would end this paragraph with a big "So there!" and "I won fair and SQUARE!"

Hospital Sunday through Friday again. Good news is the brace should be on Zach by Monday(Not sure Zach thinks this is good news).

Friday, August 11, 2006 1 PM

Zach did not turn around as I expected. He has been exhausted all week and having difficulty walking short distances. His oxygen needs are quite increased for him. Last night he was up a good portion of the night with GI pain, severe diarrhea, chills, etc. He does not look well. This morning he was acidotic and when we did labs again at noon they were worse. We've decided to keep him inpatient overnight so that we can see what direction his acidosis will go. We have drawn blood cultures. He was already on a few antibiotics and an antifungal - all IV. We have added 2 more antibiotics and a 2nd antifungal in the hope that we can prevent the blood infection that historically has followed these symptoms in him. I am so thankful that his doctor elected to proceed this way rather than wait for what we know will happen (because it has been his course at least a dozen times in the last 5 years). He got a unit of blood Monday and is getting another today. He is not tolerating his j-tube meds - they cause a lot of pain so we have stopped all but the ones to prevent seizures. Fortunately most of his meds are IV already. Poor kiddo. My heart breaks when I see him this way.

The rehab and physiology doctor came by this morning with our PT and someone from National seating. We are working to find something that he can use for school because we do not feel he can tolerate sitting in the school chairs. They had a lot of ideas so we'll see what they can come up with. The brace did get made but it is not what we had asked for. Frustrating to say the least. I am willing to give what they did make a try - that's all I can do.

Sunday, August 13, 2006 10:54 PM

We are home. Zach's doctor was supportive of keeping him in the hospital or sending him home. Whatever I was comfortable with he said he would support. I felt he might do better at home or at least just be happy to be with his family. I'm not sure there was a right decision to make about this. He is happy to be at home and for that reason I am glad we came home. Yet I worry about being the only one assessing him. I know another child in his situation would still be inpatient. I also know kids thrive at home and I am blessed to have a doctor for my boys that trusts me to care for them at home. It's true that since Sam died I am more frightened than I used to be that I am going to miss something or things will spiral down too fast for me to get help. But I have to try to swallow that and give Zach what so many people helped me to give to Sam - a life at home and in his community.

Anyway – it was a beautiful weekend and it IS nice to feel air and see sunshine, to walk around in bare feet and not be so cold from the air conditioning in the hospital. Before the boys had Peter caring for them, we used to live in the hospital for months at a time - for a few years it was 50-75 percent of the year. I don't know how I ever did that. I cannot even tolerate a week without going stir crazy these days.

282

Zach will be on this very aggressive course of intravenous antibiotics and antifungals until Friday – then back to just the Bactrim and Fluconazole. I was a little overwhelmed when I first wrote it out and saw how many infusions I was going to have to give in 24 hours but then I thought about Sam…he had all of that plus the blood products at home. I just needed to remind myself of that.

My biggest concern right now is that his heart rate is abnormally low at rest and increases too much if he sits or stands. The very low resting heart rate is far scarier than the fast heart rate so we decreased his beta blocker infusion even though we don't think that is the primary problem. (If it was he would never be able to have the very high heart rate when he stands up.) Decreasing the beta blocker did bring his resting heart rate up and decrease the variability. Now he is not going from 60 to 120 when he stands up, though he still jumps a good 30 beats and it is not transient. Quite honestly I don't follow him around taking his pulse every time he moves so for all I know he always has this extreme variability. But I do know that the low resting heart rate is not Zach's normal. I hope that as he sleeps tonight he does not brady back down. He has monitors on (though I am always wary of trusting machines too much.)

Zach's amylase and lipase have increased every day since Thursday; he has pancreatitis. There is nothing specific to do but watch and wait and hope it does not progress to the life threatening pancreatitis that Sam used to get. On a better note - he did seem to have a bit more zing today. He held his head up all day, walked a bit steadier and certainly seemed mentally connected. His electrolytes were quite good this evening when I drew his blood. He watched Star Wars tonight and actually read a lot today.

This week Brit and Zach will see their endocrinologist in Madison. I'm anxious to hear his thoughts on the medicine that is supposed to help build Zach's bones (but leaves him at risk for osteonecrosis of the jaw). The oral surgeon/orthodontist called Friday but I did not get to talk with him. I assume it is about this issue so hopefully we'll come to some resolution soon. I don't think there is going to be a perfect answer.

Update on the brace saga: Our PT, Jackie, called the company that has the material to make the soft brace (which the orthologist was supposed to make but did not). When the person she talked with from

283

that company heard Zach's story he told our PT to have me call him because he wants to make the brace for Zach *pro bono*. Wow! Jackie did not call expecting that – she was just trying to figure out where communication fell apart. But the man said that Zach clearly needs the brace and he really wants to help Zach.

We're supposed to take a vacation but this is really up in the air…which is a problem. With Zach things really have to be planned out ahead of time. I don't feel comfortable at the moment traveling. So we'll see. The pancreatic enzymes have to stop climbing. The home care company needs time to get things in place and I need to make calls to the various hospitals where we're going so a decision has to be made by mid-week.

I went to the cemetery tonight and found that one of Sam's wind chimes is gone. He had an old one from last year and that is still there. But the beautiful one from my friend Anne that she had so carefully picked out for Sammy is gone. I have not been there for a week because we were in the hospital. It was there a week ago. Last year there were several robberies at the cemetery. I don't know what to think but will call the caretaker tomorrow. I'm sick about it. Sam has this weird grass growing again….and I am glad. I was sad when it looked like his grass was blending in earlier this summer. I know that sounds crazy but ….Sam always stood out and for whatever reason I find it comforting that the place where his beautiful body was buried stands out too. I miss him so much; it just never stops hurting.

Thank you for all of your kind messages, thoughts and prayers for Zach -I know that so many of you care so much about him and I know it absolutely makes a difference in his life. Thank you also for remembering Sam - for just saying his name.

Friday, August 18, 2006 9:41 AM

Going away on vacation has been a hard decision but after a lot of thought – and of course getting his doctor's opinion - we're going.

Life has absolutely no guarantees. Even thinking about something as simple as an amusement park that is 90 minutes from our house I am reminded of how important it is not to think there will always be another day. Last summer we did not go…and I never imagined that

Zach would be in a situation, as he is now with his spinal fractures, that we would not be able to go this summer.

I have spent a lot of time planning out a "perfect" vacation to Ontario, Canada. The only problem was that I never considered that crossing a country border would be different than crossing a state border. A true DUH moment. We need a physician licensed in Ontario even to get oxygen or draw labs. God forbid we needed a Labetalol drip! Also, due to the recent terrorist issues, it was going to be a big problem getting back into the U.S. with Zach's multiple liquid medications. I can only imagine how long we'd be tied up in customs with the needles, narcotics, etc. I'm sure going to Canada would be ok if we had a few weeks to talk to customs and make connections at the Children's Hospital in Toronto but by the time I realized that we needed Canadian docs, not to mention that it sounded like the Pope himself would have to bless us coming back into the country – I simply did not have the days left to do that work.

So I looked at a map of the U.S. (I decided a trip to Paris was probably out too), and I began to think about how wonderful it would be to go to the Smoky Mountains in Tennessee. It's beautiful there. I found a cabin that is laid out in a way that will work for Zach - and it has a mountain view. The word cabin is used a bit loosely here – what "cabin" has an air hockey and pool table, swimming pool and 5 TVs and DVD players (who needs 5 TVs?). Zach may never leave the cabin but personally I am hoping to walk a lot and see the sights – there is so much to do! I did check Zach's blood counts last night as I wanted to make sure they were high enough for him to do ok in that elevation. They are and we have oxygen for when he needs it.

I am now going to spend the day packing, packing, packing and running errands. My sweet daughter, Abby, straightened up the house for hours yesterday(everyone knows I have this issue wherein I am completely unable to pack if the house is a mess).

Sunday, August 27, 2006 2:30 PM

Thanks for all the well wishes. We got home Saturday night. I promise to update about the trip along with pictures but for now just wanted to say we're home. Brittany is leaving to start her sophomore year in Minneapolis early Wednesday so I may not update until after that. Zach and Abby start school Friday. The absence of my little boy starting what would be his 3rd grade year is weighing heavily on me. He so loved school.

Wednesday, August 30, 2006 11:38 PM

Still no vacation pictures ….sorry. I have them all downloaded – now it is a matter of uploading them to this site. Zach actually dictated a journal entry about our vacation for everyone to read so as soon as I have time I'll put it all on here. He had quite a good time telling me what to write. I just need to find more time in the day to do these things…anyone have some time to spare that I can borrow?

This has not been Zach's best week. He has been having significant blood pressure issues since mid week when we were in Tennessee. His autonomic function (which controls all the things we do not think about like blood pressure, heart rate, temperature, size of our pupils in response to light, sweating, etc.) is getting worse. He is like a chandelier – one day he needs a lot of medication to keep his blood pressure down and the next day his blood pressure is too low and he cannot even hold his head up. It's frightening and none of it seems easily controllable.

The sun certainly seems to shine brighter when he comes out of those spells and feels better. Today he actually had a much better day. He called his doctor to let him know he was doing better - I can't recall exactly what he said but part of it was "I am not tired today and I feel every good adjective that you could ever think of today!"

For the last 48 hours he has had a Holter monitor on which continually assesses his heart rate and rhythm. I will send it to the cardiologist tomorrow and by mid next week we should hear if his heart rate is getting too low (our concern) or if he is having any abnormal rhythm.

His labs are screwy. Mainly he is struggling with high calcium levels and acidosis. The high calcium is not good because if there is that much floating in the blood that means it is coming out of the bones.

I'm sick to say that his central line stitches came out and the line has moved a fair amount. The question for our surgeon now is whether he will be able to keep this one in with new stitches or will he need it pulled and a new line placed. The thought of the bleeding that will follow this very minor surgery just makes me sick so I hope and hope and hope that Dr. Aiken will think we can get some more time out of this line. He will look at it next week when Zach is inpatient.

Brittany went back to school today. I will miss her so much. She, however, could not wait to get back to school and that is exactly how it should be. This year she is in an apartment - very close to campus – with 3 friends. How fun is that? I hope she has a great year.

Abby and Zach start 8th grade on Friday. This year Zach is going back to just the 3 shortened days. He gave a gallant effort at 4 days last year and it was just too much for him. By the end of the year he missed more than he went. Right now we're working on lining up his homebound teachers for hospital and also a few hours on the 2 days he stays home.

Abby has been savoring every last moment of summer....night games practically every night with friends, ceramics, swimming, shopping at the mall. You name it – she is doing it. I love her energy (and covet it too!)

And what about this little issue about Pluto not being a planet anymore. I am not happy at all. Just because Pluto is small does not mean it should get kicked out of planet status. That seems pretty discriminatory and elitist to me. One scientist said he felt it deserved an honorary place even if it did not meet the new and very arbitrary guidelines. I vote for that too!

Tuesday, September 5, 2006 7:32 PM

Dr. Aiken came to see us today and he looked at Zach's line and reviewed his chest x-ray. The line has moved significantly and is barely under his collar bone at this time. It cannot be stitched or saved. I am just sick - he has only had it since March. Surgery will be either Thursday or Friday depending on when a cardiac anesthesiologist is available.

I hope we can get a commitment from the blood center to give the blood products at home since there is no doubt in my mind that he will bleed significantly. I don't want him to miss school because he has to sit in the infusion clinic when I am perfectly capable of giving the products at home (and did for 2 years to Sam). He deserves to go to school whenever he feels well enough to be there.

287

He's gotten 2 transfusions of blood this week and we will give 1-2 more before he goes home to try to get his counts up.

Zach is trying to teach me how to play Yu-Gi-Oh which I think one needs an advanced degree to figure out. My brain just does not "get" summoning monsters and playing "in battle mode." Tonight our friend Adam, a volunteer here, visited and taught Zach and me a new card game called Egyptian Rats (or something like that). I need to go because I promised Zach I would watch all 6 episodes of *Star Wars* and we're only 3/4 of the way through #1. It's actually pretty good - who knew I'd actually like *Star Wars*.

Sunday was 18 months since Sammy passed away...it was a very hard day as was Saturday. It was not something I anticipated. Why would 18 months be any harder than 16 months? Still, it hit me very hard to realize my little boy has been gone for 18 whole months. It does not seem it could have been that long. It still seems impossible that he is never coming home.

Thursday, September 7, 2006 9:32 PM

Zach had the new line placed today. The surgery itself went fine and Dr. Aiken was able to place it in the same spot. Our hematologist has been very proactive with this surgery. We actually started giving Zach cryo before the surgery and will give it every 12 hours for 2 days. We also can give Factor 7a at the first sign of bleeding. We've never treated Zach proactively before so I am very hopeful this may make a big difference.

Unfortunately Zach has not recovered so well from the anesthesia. He went into it requiring more oxygen than usual because his heart is not working as well as it should and he is struggling now. He's getting another unit of blood now and we'll see how the night goes. Thanks for the calls and kind words.

Tuesday, September 12, 2006 9 PM

All in all Zach is feeling better. His pancreatic enzymes are still quite high but he really seems to be over the pain part of this. I really feel it is because of what we learned from Sam about increasing Selenium at the very first sign of acute pancreatitis. I just wish more doctors would read the studies out of England and try it -I will always believe it is what saved Sam a death many times over from pancreatitis. Sam's episodes were truly horrific and life threatening until we learned to use Selenium. Thank you Sammy for taking care of Zach even now. You will always be one another's best brother.

Not so good news is Zach bled from the CVL site again. We have increased his cryo infusions to every 12 hrs. Thank God for couriers who deliver blood products to the house!

That's it. It's just me and the kids all week so we're dining on Oreo cookies, French fries, chips, raspberry lemonade and any other junk we can find.

Sunday, September 10, 2006 10:25 AM

We're home.

Zach is not well but home is a good place to be (Though Zach and I do love our CHW family.) He just wants to sleep and that is probably good. I think he needs to sleep and conserve his energy so his body can heal.

The pancreatitis is very bad this time. Sadly, there really is no primary therapy for pancreatitis. It's a horrible, painful disease that comes on with no warning and goes away when it wants to; one just hopes it does not permanently damage the pancreas. Most kids are in the hospital for the duration of it but in Zach's situation I can do at home what they would do at the hospital (IV pain meds and IV nutrition). Thankful for that!

Breathing: he is worked very hard to breathe – especially when he sleeps – and it has had his nurses and I a little unnerved because it is new for him. He does have monitors at home. We added a 2nd diuretic (makes you get rid of fluid) to his schedule of drugs to try to unload his heart and help him breathe easier. It's called Diurel so between that and the Lasix Zach is drying out (which is good). His chest x-ray did not look worse Sat. and his heart seemed to be "happier." I hate adding the Diurel. Sam was on it. But again...thankful we still have meds to pull out from the hat that help.

He ended up needing 4 red cell transfusions this week. He is destroying his red cells very fast this week but maybe as he feels better it will slow down. At home he will get daily cryo (a part of plasma – it helps a person to clot). We also came home with a few doses of Factor 7a for emergencies and I can give red cells as needed. We would not have been able to come home if the home use had not been approved so this is wonderful. It's extra work for the staff in our blood bank and we're lucky they are willing to do this for us.

It's odd how something can be both comforting and haunting. Setting up delivery times yesterday with someone who I used to talk to almost every day at blood bank, signing the papers today when the cryo arrived, seeing the same paperwork with the temperature stamp that they had made for Sam… The words *full circle* do not even begin to describe this.

I used to say that Sam was following in Zach's footsteps and I remember the heartbreak when that first happened. At some point Sam sped past…and now in the last few years Zach has been following in Sam's footsteps. The speed lately takes my breath away. Of course I know they are each their own person and there are marked differences but in the middle of the night when I wake up and see the similarities shining through the dark it blinds me to those differences and I only see the parallels. Maybe that's why I dread night time these days. Life becomes clearer when the sun shines.

I did watch *Star Wars* I, II and III…and guess what? I really do like them. Zach tells me IV, V and VI are even better. As for Yu-Gi-Oh, I think I need some remedial training. I still don't get it. One day I saw Zach changing cards in my deck and I said "what are you doing? Stacking your deck against me?" Well no – do you know what he said he was doing? He was putting more "good cards" in my deck. He wants to make sure I win one of these days so I'll keep playing with him. He felt too awful to play later in the week but I assured him I will keep playing.

Sunday, September 17, 2006 10:21 PM

Zach is doing well – a little bleeding but mainly the cryo seems to be helping. His lipase was higher than ever on Thursday (pancreatic enzyme) and then a little better today (but still pretty bad). It's astonishing that he does not have pain. I've given up on trying to understand. In fact he made it to school 2 days this week. THANK

YOU Blood Center of Wisconsin, Zach's primary doc, his hematologist and the courier. Zach would be confined to the hospital on this cryo schedule if it were not for them making this work for Zach

School is great – Zach loves all his new teachers. He is in a different "house" than Abby this year so we have a bit of "my house is better than yours" going on. Homebound services started – he has a new teacher for home this year named Donna and they spend time together on both Wednesday and Friday. Friday they worked 3 hours – they looked at the clock and could not believe 3 hours had gone by!

Yesterday Zach and I went into Waukesha (big trip I know!) so that we could check out the Joke Shop. We met the owner there who knows all sorts of magic tricks. He showed us a few of them and even I was impressed. What a nice guy! He told Zach that he can come by anytime and he will help Zach with his own magic tricks.

Here are some random thoughts:

The Dept of Homeland Security advises that children with special health care needs have everything they need to stay at school for 72 hours in the event of a "lock down" due to bio-terrorism. So I wrote Secretary Chertoff inviting him to my home so that he can personally see what Zach needs for 72 hours. The people making these recommendations obviously don't realize what some of these kids in our schools need for 72 hours of care. I'll let you know if he comes!!

On a lighter note:

I can no longer sleep 3 hours one night and then 2.5 hours the next night. I am not in college anymore. I need to repeat this many times. And... Caramel Oreo cookies are delicious. Try them! Especially good with ice cream.

Wednesday, September 27, 2006 7:33 AM

In the week leading up to last Tuesday, Zach had some of his best day in months. He felt great, was able to walk without using the wheelchair and was not particularly tired. Some of his friends at school were helping carry his backpack when he went up the stairs at school but the fact he was taking the stairs was amazing. And then...he went to school Tuesday with a left leg that mildly bothered him and came home unable to walk without significant pain. Since then bearing weight takes a great deal of effort on that leg. Finally we

291

did an x-ray yesterday (Monday) because after a week of barely using the leg it is not any better. The x-ray did not show any fractures – good news, especially considering how fragile his bones are.

Still…he still cannot bear weight. We assume he strained one or more muscles in his upper left leg and I guess only time and rest will heal that. It is just so terribly frustrating. He was doing so great and now he is back in a wheelchair and worse – having to depend on adults to even walk 3 feet. He does not complain but he does talk a lot about what a good day he had last Monday before this happened and I am sure he is frustrated too.

He is a few weeks out from his IVIg now and it shows – his blood counts are dropping. The good news is he did not have to go in today for blood because he got it at home!!! I was holding my breath on that one until I could see the blood in my house. What a difference it makes to not have to miss school for infusion clinic.

We are so lucky to live near a blood center, where Zach is not just a patient or a number. He is a person to them. Yes, they may take a bit of time to approve these things but I understand that (admittedly with impatience), given the regulations and policies that fill our society these days. The bottom line is they have consistently done what is best for both Sam and Zach. I don't believe that would be the case just anywhere. I read yesterday that congress has allocated less and less money to hemophilia/bleeding disorder care centers in the past 20-years, in part because people no longer get what a difference good hematology care can make in keeping a child with hemophilia or other bleeding problems at home. Some of these centers are in danger of closing. Well let me go to Capitol Hill and I'll tell them exactly what a difference it makes – with pictures.

Zach's CHW volunteer friend sent him a flyer for the Milwaukee Scholastic Chess Federation tournament, which will be at Miller Park this weekend. I talked with the guy that runs it last night and he said it would be fine if Zach got tired and could not stay all day. So I think if Zach feels good enough I will take him. This man said that their mission is not to make better chess players, but to make chess freely available to schools and children/youth. If Zach can only come for one game, he said that is fine – he'll still get a medal!

A little bit of Abby news – she has been asked to play the piano for an hour at the Fox River Development dedication luncheon. This will be a big Waukesha event in our little city. That is next weekend. She is pretty excited and I am very proud of her.

I guess I ought to give you Brittany news too. She called a week ago to say she cooked dinner! Yes that is news. Other than that she has all her first exams this week so she is busy. I think she has become a Starbucks groupie.

I wish I had some Sam news to give you. This has been a hard September without him. I hear his chirpy little voice all the time and can just imagine the antics he'd be pulling in third grade. His best friend Josie called me last night – she moved to Indiana this summer. She is very excited because she got a part in their big Nutcracker production in the city they moved to. How exciting is that when you are eight years old!

Last week one of Zach's former teachers wrote me and said she was glad she had a small part in his life...but the truth is that his teachers, nurses, health care providers, friends, family – all of you– have had a big part in his life. He is definitely an amazing, resilient kid, in no small part because of the support and faith that everyone has had in him. You've all given him what he needs so that he can continue to be who he is meant to be. Whether that is helping support his care at home, thinking positive thoughts or saying prayers for him, teaching him, caring for him in the hospital, being his friend, providing therapy, sharing a joke with him – it all adds up and marks Zach's life in immeasurable ways. He knows he matters to a lot of people and that knowledge is truly the "wind beneath his wings." Thank you!

With every child's brain is a mind teeming with ideas and dreams and abilities unrealized. The greatest thing we can do as parents, teachers, physicians, friends is to nourish that potential – both intellectual and humanitarian so that each mind can fulfill its promise to the benefit of mankind--Ben Carson

Sunday, October 1, 2006 8:42 PM

Zach's still struggling to get through the day – very tired. He has a history test tomorrow that he has been trying to study for and a few language assignments he did not know he had until Abby told him.

293

He's pretty worried about it all but I told him all he can do is the best he can do. Then it is out of his control. He can't do better than his best and his best is pretty amazing.

Plus you know what tomorrow is – it is pajama day at Butler Middle School. How can a day of staying in your PJs be anything other than wonderful? I wonder why Children's Hospital never lets us show our spirit by wearing our PJs to work. I'll have to suggest it.

OOPs almost forgot – he is walking somewhat better too. Still not at baseline but nowhere near the struggle to walk that he had most of the week.

AND – he got a new non-power wheelchair on Wednesday to use mainly for school but also to sit in at the hospital. The amazing thing is that it was free. Yes it was! Here's the story – about a year before Sammy passed away our rehab doctor wrote a prescription for a wheelchair for Sam. The state kicked back the prior authorization because they had questions. Here is an example of the questions: "Please justify why he cannot use a stroller." He was 7 at the time! What 7 year old uses a stroller? And on and on – we'd answer, they'd ask for more information until finally one day they approved it. That was the middle of January 2005. He died 6 weeks later. It was the kind of thing that no one will ever forget, including his rehab doctor. So when we needed something more supportive for Zach to use in school he said he was not going through insurance and Medicaid again – he asked for a favor and he got one. It's a great wheelchair and the cushions are made of this gel that helps Zach sit straight as if he had a brace on.

I have Zach's big annual school meeting on Tuesday (IEP) and hopefully art class Tuesday afternoon (thanks to Zach's school OT Ellen who found the classes).

Sunday, October 8, 2006 5:01 PM

It is a hospital week for Zachary. He was actually looking forward to coming as he said he just wants to rest. He has been fairly tired although he looked better as the week went on. On Tuesday he got blood (at home!) and perhaps that helped some. On Thursday he stayed at school all day and even attended the first science club meeting of the year. Thursday was a great day! Yesterday he went shopping for another Lego Star Wars set and a new game for his Nintendo. He should be all set for the hospital (After he does his school work and reading, of course!)

As I mentioned last week, his annual school IEP meeting was scheduled for last Tuesday. It is impossible to have anything but hope after meeting and talking with the many people that are involved in his education. We may not always agree on the details but we all have the same goal – that each day for Zach be filled with learning, meaning and joy. It reminded me that awesome things can happen when people work together – things that none of us could ever accomplish on our own--one of many lessons I've learned from my children.

Abby played the piano beautifully –with great pizzazz at the Fox Riverwalk Celebration on Saturday. I'd say she played for about an hour – without any music whatsoever. I cannot imagine having that kind of courage at the age of 13 – I know I did not. She did an amazing job and I am very proud of her.

Tuesday, October 10, 2006 5:01 PM

Zach has had a lot of abdominal pain for the last few days. I am not sure what that is about but he has not wanted to eat a thing (and as many of you know - that is just not Zach). Even water seems to bother him though he has been drinking a lot because his airway is a little swollen and he just is very very dry. I got him a stash of hard candies from the gift shop so hopefully that will help and then he won't need to drink. (He does not really "need" to eat or drink since anything he has drains right out of the tubes in his stomach. He gets all of his calories from "TPN").

His left leg that was so bad got completely better last week and now - as of this morning - he can barely walk on his right leg. Don't ask - I don't have a clue what that is about.

Thursday, October 12, 2006 7:40 PM

The PT brought up a walker for Zach and he had a lot less pain walking with it. So we have ordered one for home. It's not something I anticipate he will need full time but it will help to keep him on his feet and mobile when he has these days where the pain is so bad. The more we can keep him walking the better his muscles will stay and also it helps with his bone density.

Zach did go to Teen group yesterday and made a bat box. He has to finish decorating it but it is quite cool. He also made a wood CD rack a few days ago and last night he sketched a bit. I'm glad he has his art – he sure loves it!

Sunday, October 22, 2006 8:12 PM

Thank you very much for your notes of encouragement in the guest book and by email. I keep telling Zach he has a fan club. Karen, a friend I work with, asked me how big the Bat Mobile picture is. Welllllll - really big! I think it will be perfect for our living room wall. It will match Sam's Justice League figures that I have on my windowsills and the Buzz Light Year night light that sweet Kyle just mailed to me (to remind me that Sam lights my path). I could start quite a decorating trend don't you think?

Zach continues to hang in there with amazing optimism and spirit. His back pain has gotten significantly worse in the past 7-10 days and he has required more and more medication. I see how this changes what he can do and wants to do but don't ever hear him complain.

I am quite concerned about the pain and hope in some ways that we can find something wrong/something different than what we already know to be the cause. Of course, I should qualify that - that something would have to be fixable. His orthopedic doctor ordered a series of spine x-rays which he completed Wednesday morning. I am trusting there will be results on Monday.

Thursday evening was school conferences for both Zach and Abby. Both are doing well. It was nice to meet the teachers I had not yet met and to talk with them. Talking with the teachers gives one a great sense of optimism about public school education, even in this era of cuts. These are definitely hard times for schools but these teachers obviously care about the kids!!!

Zach did find the time to make some brownies today. He got a bit too tired to eat them but they'll still be around tomorrow (I think!). He and Abby have their fall holiday Wednesday through Sunday. They are looking forward to it. Zach hopes to catch up on some movies, go to Cold Stone Creamery and Best Buy…what could be better than that? Tuesday afternoon through Wednesday 2 of the teachers are giving up their own time to take Abby and some other kids to a "leadership camp." She can't wait. I owe her a shopping trip since we never did back to school shopping so we plan to do that Thursday.

Brittany helped out with Habitat for Humanity on Saturday - fixing up a house! As in using tools. I don't think I have ever seen her pick up a hammer!! She has also been busy planning out some activities for children in the hospital who have cancer. She and some others in her group will be helping the kids decorate the children's hospital in Minneapolis this year. Sounds like fun.

Monday, October 16, 2006 9:49 PM

Zach did get to school today. He got a little Dilaudid there due to pain. Dilaudid is an IV narcotic. Apparently he became quite animated and chatty. I don't think the teachers were expecting that…they thought he would be groggy. Nope. I'm always worried the family secrets are going to come out when Zach has had his pain meds…he is quite the talker with Dilaudid. Too bad we're actually too boring to have any family secrets!

Today Zach brought home this awesome picture he made in drawing class. It is the Bat Mobile (who is surprised?) and really just amazing!!!

This morning I was getting ready to go to the hospital and had CNN on. They had a story about a little boy with a type of Mitochondrial disease called Leigh's disease. He had been the guest of honor at the Saints game and was able to meet a bunch of the players. He looked like he was Sam's age…he had blond hair and he was so thrilled to be at the game. Of course all I could think about was Sam. I got in the car and forgot that I had George Winston's *Velveteen Rabbit* CD in the CD player. It was something Sammy and I used to listen to together a lot. I cried the whole way to work. When I got to work I realized I forgot my hairbrush and my lip-gloss and I had big puffy eyes…what a way to start the day.

I thought about the Velveteen Rabbit who asked the Skin Horse "What is Real?" The Skin Horse told the Rabbit "Real is what happens when a child loves you. It takes a long time and by the time you are Real, most of your hair has been loved off, you get loose in the joints

297

and very shabby." The Velveteen Rabbit asked if being Real hurts. And the Skin horse said, "Yes - sometimes it does." The Velveteen Rabbit wanted to be Real more than anything. So he loved the little boy to whom he belonged and he was loved back....it hurt....but in the end he was Real. He probably had puffy eyes and forgot his hairbrush and lip-gloss too because he was so busy loving the boy – but he was Real!

Skin Horse was right – it does hurt to become Real. I don't pretend to understand for one minute why Sam is not here, why Zach is sick, why the girls have had to live a life so different than other girls their age....I don't know if I will ever understand all of that. But I do know that as much as it hurts to start a day off like today, to walk through the day with a heart that feels so heavy, to see Sam everywhere I go, to hear him in all that I do and know I cannot touch him ...as much as it hurts to see Zach in pain, to hear the worry in Brittany's voice when she calls to check on Zach, to read the beautiful poems and hear the songs Abby writes for Sam...as much as that all hurts I would not trade one moment of being Sam's mom (or Zach's or Brittany's or Abby's). I would have planned it all differently if I was in charge but I'm not...I only know that I miss Sam so deeply because he loved me – and because I love him. That was and is a gift.

If Sam was here he'd say that he loved me 900 cc--and believe me -this was A LOT in his eyes. Having lived a life where we measured everything that went in and out of him he assumed love was measured in cubic centimeters/milliliters. I was lucky to be loved 900 cc!

Wednesday, October 25, 2006 10:12 PM

I wish I had better news .I have not talked with the orthopedic doc but from the x-ray report there is severe osteopenia (loss of bone density) and most of his thoracic and lumbar spine is compressed. It sounded like one vertebrae in particular (T7) is much more compressed than it was in July (when he last had an x-ray) but I also know that the reports are dependent on the radiologist reading them. What I really need is for the doctors to line the films up from the summer until now and see if things are the same or worse in the actual pictures. Either way, his pain is significant and it's taking more medicine to make him feel okay. It's heart breaking.

There is a glimmer of hope but it is wrapped up in different bad news. His pancreatitis is very bad right now. On Monday his Lipase was 1300 and tonight it is 2900 (normal is 30-300). I'm sure you wonder why I think that is a glimmer of hope. Well, I am hoping that the increase in pain since yesterday is actually due to his pancreatitis. And once that subsides then maybe he will feel better. Of course we need to get him through this first.

His kidneys are worse tonight as well. His creatinine is as high as I have ever seen it and that means his kidneys are not clearing things as well as they should. I had to hold his TPN (his IV nutrition) because his potassium and calcium are way too high. Instead he is getting IV fluids with extra bicarbonate because his blood pH is too low. His hemoglobin is dropping and his doctor wants him to get blood tomorrow.

Right now the plan is to repeat his labs at 6 am and 6 Pm tomorrow. He really cannot afford for his kidneys to get much worse. Otherwise we probably cannot avoid admission(Though believe me I will try to talk our way out of it).

Figures that this is his Fall holiday too. He really wanted to have a few friends over but I am not sure if that will happen now. I hope so – I really hope so.

Thursday, October 26, 2006 8:57 PM

Twenty-four hours later and much better news! We stopped his TPN for the last 24 hours so he did not get any calcium. By this morning his calcium level was still fairly high but not as alarming. His potassium had come down enough to need some in his fluids. His kidney function was still poor but better without the terribly high calcium levels. Most amazing of all was that he was a new kid – more energetic, mentally with-it, and so much less pain. I found out that hypercalcemia causes mental slowness, a very sleepy kid and a lot of bone pain. When I talked with his doctor this morning we were both so relieved as things have been trending the wrong way all week and they looked very bad last night.

The awesome blood bank staff had his red cells ready for me to pick up by 10 am. I had a unit in him by 2:00 PM. His wonderful homecare pharmacist got his Pamidronate (helps decrease calcium) ready and to our house in the early afternoon. That will run over 2 days. The lab staff at Children's has just been awesome, (as they always are), with running his labs fast and faxing us the results so we can adjust what we are doing. The courier has been a life saver. Zach's doctor is willing to guide me at home with all of this – no one else I know would do that. He is only home because of all the wonderful people in our lives that do these things for us. It would not work without even one of them and it is times like this when the enormity of what they do overwhelms me.

Now the next 24 hours is the test. I just started the TPN back up with the calcium in it – same amount as always. Hopefully we got his calcium down low enough that even if it rises it won't rise too high to affect his kidneys. And meanwhile the Pamidronate ought to kick in a little bit by then…we need to get some of that calcium to stop hanging out in his blood and get into his bones where it belongs.

I should add that he picked last night to have terribly low blood pressures too. I cannot wait to sleep tonight!!!!!

I had promised Abby a shopping trip with lunch today and was just feeling like the worst mother ever to cancel. It was the only day of their fall vacation that I had a nurse to stay with Zach. But I am the only one that can infuse his blood at home per the arrangement we have with the blood center and he needed the blood. I felt so torn between both of their very legitimate needs - hers to spend time with her mom and his medical needs. His health has to come first but that does not make it an easy decision. So, I was feeling lousy about all of this until about mid-way through the transfusion Chris had the great idea of going to Q-doba to get Zach some guacamole (his favorite) and she offered to pick up lunch for Abby and me too. Abby loves Q-doba so that was a treat. And the blood was done at 2:05; we were out the door at 2:10; to the mall at 2:30 and back home for piano lessons by 4:45. Abby managed to find more than enough at the mall in those 2 hours. In fact I think it was a good thing we only had two hours!!!!

Zach did have a friend over for a short while this afternoon.

Simple things, brief moments but they are what makes a life.

Friday, October 27, 2006 8:47 PM

After 24 hours of TPN with calcium in it:

Kidneys: not at baseline but it's all relative and they look good to me.

Ionized calcium: Although it is "normal" it is barely in the range. It jumped up quite a bit so this is not perfect. If it jumps the same amount by tomorrow night we're right back where we started.

Pamidronate: still infusing. I sure hope it does the job it is supposed to do. We'll see.

Zach's orthopedic doctor called today. He will see Zach in clinic next Friday afternoon. Zach's PT will be able to go with us which is a huge help to me. Until then he wants Z to wear the old brace (since the new one is not made yet). He said there is definite worsening - "quite severe." There is a loss of height in many vertebrae meaning they are compressed almost flat. This can cause compression of nerves. He would like Zach to have a spinal MRI to check for nerve compression as the cause of his on and off inability to walk. He said we really need to get this calcium issue under control. I could not agree more!!!!!!!!

Gotta go…there are eight 13 yr old girls in my basement (and one brave boy – not Zach – he said no way is he going down there.

Tuesday, October 31, 2006 8:28 AM

I don't even know what to say about Zach's kidneys and back pain anymore. The word roller coaster comes to mind but Lesley (another "mito mom") has a better analogy. She said that she felt she had been stuck in a blender. Can you imagine it? At first you're just being gently stirred and then suddenly you're getting liquefied and then for good measure someone pushes chop…grind…its a little hard to go back to frappe after all of that!

Anyway Zach's creatinine (measure of kidney function)was almost at baseline and now it is on its way back up. Back to daily labs for now. His calcium? It's high – though mildly. Back pain? Not good especially with the brace. Zach is sure the brace does NOT help but I told him that discussion is for him and Dr. L (ortho) to have. That conversation would be after the one where Zach asks Dr. L if he can go to an amusement park with his broken back.

Now I have to interrupt this message to bring you this thought: why do we, who have children with kids with mitochondrial disease, refer to ourselves as "mito moms?" I hate it. We need to come up with a better name like Super hero moms or Awesome kid moms.

Back to my message – (as a Democrat I really need to practice controlling my message better than this!) This past weekend Zach and I went to Best Buy as promised. He sat in the wheelchair and dictated his purely electronic/video game Christmas list to me. He agreed to go to Barnes and Noble afterwards (probably to make me feel better that I have not completely failed as a mother) and he listed just about every Star Wars book in the store. This morning I found Abby's Christmas list in the med room (yes, we actually have a med room in our house). Now understand that she has always been my non-materialistic child. Her typical reply to "what do you want?' in years gone by has been "I don't know. Just get me anything like crafts or books." One year she made the specific request of "a blue ribbon for my hair." So imagine my surprise to find a 30-item list consisting of various hair irons (curling, spiraling, straightening), French manicures, make up, iPod, amplifier...do you get the idea? She, at least, had the good sense to put books and crafts on that list. Otherwise her mother really would have lost it.

Today is Halloween. Zach dressed up as Batman for school - but unfortunately the school does not allow masks or hats (sad but necessary in today's world). It's hard to be Batman without a mask but Zach rigged something up. However, he is looking forward to coming home and handing out candy with the mask. Abby is actually going to trick or treat which is good. I told her to go as fast as she can, hit as many houses as possible and make sure to choose Reese PB candy if there is a choice. Then give all the Reeses to me.

Last year Zach was in the hospital on Halloween, which was just fine with me. I miss my very cute little Scooby Doo, Red Power Ranger, Buzz Light Year, Barney clad Sam and this is a hard day now. Sam was only home two or so Halloweens in his life but he always had fun trick or treating in the hospital even if it was the middle of November when he finally felt good enough to do so. The nurses and residents always made sure it was Halloween for him on whatever day he felt good.

So that is about all. On Sunday I am giving a short "talk" at the Children's Hospital memorial for families who have had a child pass away at Children's (or in some cases – the child passed away in a community hospital like Sam but they were one of "ours" and just did not make it to CHW). I feel a little inadequate to be doing this. It has only been 19 months since Sam died ...not long enough to know anything and yet long enough that I feel I have lived three lives. I have no idea what I am going to say. The general idea is to offer hope – maybe just hope that it is possible to still walk forward even if you are slouched, limping and in pain?

Oh and **Vote Nov.7th** even if you vote for someone I don't like.

Saturday, November 4, 2006 2:55 PM

Zach's labs have been much better the last 2 nights. Maybe, we are finally going to see some stability! I actually took the night off on Friday and did not draw his blood. Let's hope this is a trend.

The ortho appointment was a bit sad. The doctor does not think anything can reverse the damage done. He does hope we can prevent further damage by using the brace and aggressively treating the Hypercalcemia. He said that just looking at the films makes him think of how much pain Zach is in. I agree. He showed them to me and they're pretty impressive (though not in a good way). There is a procedure done in adults, wherein they put "cement" into the vertebrae. He plans to talk with some adult doctors but it does not sound like it has ever been done on a kid. In addition, there is the ever-present risk of bleeding. In the meantime it sounds like Zach can get his new brace next week.

Last weekend was the first time in 2 weeks that I had been to Sam's grave as I had been sick and before that we were in the hospital. Whoever picked out the dead flowers –thank you! I was absolutely dreading that task – and I was so thankful to see that it had been done. The dead flowers bother me. Thank you, as well, for the wonderful, bright orange pumpkins. It meant a lot to me that someone took the time to do that.

303

Friday, November 10, 2006 9:09 AM

Not much new. It's been a beautiful week (in both weather and politics) but once again I have been sick. This is getting old fast. It gives me perspective as to how draining it is to feel sick so often.

Fortunately - or not, (depending on your party affiliation), I felt good enough to vote. Abby came with me as she has before. She loves to vote. Thank God one of my kids enjoys politics. She really gets into it. Of course, Sam did, in his own way, too–he was quite insistent that he was the "boss of the country" – "not 'Gowge Bush."

Wednesday, November 15, 2006 5:09 PM

Zach's MRI looked okay. Of course it showed all of severe fractures we already know about but there is not any nerve compression-- at least not any that we can see. This is wonderful news I think! His ortho is still working on figuring out if injecting the cement into his vertebrae (to "puff" them back up) is an option.

We have him hooked up to a PCA pump now. This stands for Patient Controlled Anesthesia. Basically Zach can push a button and his pain meds go directly into his central line without delay. There is a lock out obviously so he cannot overdose himself but it allows him to get relief more quickly. More pumps and more lines.

He is bleeding a little from his stomach. We have increased one of his meds to try to turn his stomach acid into an alkaline solution. Unfortunately, I'm not convinced this the problem. His surgeon just came by and he thinks Zach may need to have his Gastrostomy redone. It is prolapsed - which I realize means little to most of you. Let's just say that Sam did too and it was one of the biggest sources of bleeding for Sam. Right now the problem is minor. It's hard to know whether to intervene before it gets out of control at the risk of doing major surgery.

So far this week Zach has painted several ceramic items - a vase, an R2D2 bank, and a pumpkin. Ann, the art therapist will take these to get "fired" to make them very shiny. Yesterday, Zach's friend Adam, who is a volunteer, helped him make a fire breathing dragon out of wood. Now he needs to paint it. It looks very cool!

304

All the residents and nurses are quite impressed with how wonderful he looks compared to last admission in early October. During that admission he was in so much pain and having trouble sitting and walking and his spirits were so poor. But now he is looking very good, quite animated and social and entertaining everyone. It's nice for all of us to see!

He did do some school work today with the hospital teacher which was nice. Zach had been stuck on his 8th grade math and he asked me for help. No problem - I promptly found the hospital teacher, who happens to be familiar with the math curriculum that our school district uses.

Tonight is Teen Advisory Council so I have to go make sure he is getting ready for that. Then I can watch *Bewitched* while he is gone!

Friday, November 17, 2006 10:30 AM

Zach's ortho stopped by again yesterday. He talked to the adult ortho people - they won't do the kyphoplasty (cement into the vertebrae). I am really sad....that procedure takes away pain in all the adults that have it and I just wanted to take away his pain. One of our former doctors that moved away has told me about a bone expert at Kansas City Children's. I am going to contact them and see if they feel they could offer any other ideas. I think Zach has just the nicest ortho doctor ever - and he is very knowledgeable, compassionate, responsive. In no way is this a reflection on him but as he would say himself - he is not the expert on preventing the problem - he is the expert in helping us deal with the results. Maybe the people in Kansas City will have some ideas for making his bones stronger.

Sunday, November 19, 2006 9:03 PM

"I loved being introduced as Sam's brother." This was what Zach said after the Memorial Service a few weeks ago. He said that he missed being known as Sam's brother. *"I loved hearing people say his name and showing his picture to everyone at the service."*

This deeply touched me. Other children want nothing more than to *not* be known as "his sister" or "her brother." I always abhorred the teachers at Our Lady of Good Counsel talking about my older siblings.

305

But being Sam's "best brother" was Zach's pride and joy. He was and is and always will be the best big brother that Sam could ever have.

Zach is out of the hospital. He is getting used to his new brace, which is a good thing. It should help prevent worsening of his spine.

The kids only have 2 days of school this week. We are all looking forward to my family coming for Thanksgiving. They'll be coming from all over: Brittany from Minneapolis, Aunt Maribeth from Delaware and Uncle David and Anna from New York. The locals will also show up (Grandma, Grandpa and Uncle Mike and Aunt Elaine).

Life has been too busy. I am leaving work early on Wednesday and plan to leave all work behind at the hospital, take a deep breath, and enjoy cooking with my kids and welcoming my daughter home from college!

Happy Thanksgiving!

Tuesday, November 21, 2006 08:36 AM

I am at home – should be working while Zach is at school with his nurse. But my heart is so very heavy. Just two days ago I said Happy Thanksgiving and did not plan on writing any more before the holiday. But I am compelled to add to that message~

My cousins woke up and found that their beautiful 18-month old daughter had passed away in her sleep. There was no warning – there rarely is. Even as "sick" as Sam was, there was no warning that he would die on March 3, 2005. It was a day like any other day…. no better and no worse. *Just a day.*

I detest preachy words and I am sorry if this sounds that way. I am saying this as much to myself as to anyone who reads this for we all need to be reminded again and again: Be thankful for your family – whoever your family may be – biological or not. Hold fast to those you love. Tonight they may not be here, or tomorrow you may not.

I cannot even begin to imagine how my cousin felt…wake up and find their daughter has died. Their cherished, little girl. And yet I can imagine because I never really believed Sam would die – and certainly not that day. Sick or not a mother (or father or grandparent, aunt, uncle) is never prepared for a child to die. Knowing it could happen is not the same as expecting it to happen or being prepared for it to happen. It does not make it any easier or harder. It is all horrific.

306

There are many things I am thankful for but I will share this one: the night before Sam died, I was tired and he was not. He wanted me to read to him before bed. I considered trying to talk him out of it. One book, two book, three books…I think I read him about ten. I "woke up" reading to him and we laughed - especially at his book "Liar Liar Pants on Fire," which he had just received from book club. There are nights I told him I could only read 2 books– but that night I read many more. I am so thankful for that time with my little boy – just lying in bed and reading. Who knew it would be the last time I read a book to that precious child.

Slow down. Everyone we know – including ourselves – will die some day. So make sure you live and help those you love to live fully before that happens.

I wish I knew the author of this. If someone does - please tell me:

If I knew it would be the last time
that I'd see you fall asleep,
I would tuck you in more tightly
and pray the Lord, your soul to keep.

If I knew it would be the last time
I'd hear your voice lifted up in praise,
I would videotape each action and word,
so I could play them back day after day.
If I knew it would be the last time
I would be there to share your day,
Well-I'm sure you'll have so many more,
so I can let just this one slip away.

For surely there's always tomorrow
to make up for an oversight,
and we always get a second chance
to make everything just right.

But just in case I might be wrong,
and today is all I get,
I'd like to say how much I love you
and I hope we never forget...

Tuesday, November 28, 2006 8:45 AM

Zach is doing okay. He remains in a lot of pain without frequent dosing of pain medicine. There are times it does not seem to help as much as it should without completely drugging him. Hard to see. I am trying so hard to remain hopeful that this too shall pass – that in time the pain will diminish.

His blood work has been screwy and we're trying to sort through that and determine what it really means. As always – medically he does not fit into a nice neat box and we only learn the right thing to do by trial and error.

Thanksgiving was fun and busy. We all love Anna, who came with my "little" brother. Uncle Sean was with us in spirit and he sent beautiful flowers and orange balloons in honor of Sam, which brightened our house. We got to do some shopping in downtown Waukesha, which really is much more exciting than words can describe (Not really – but we like it).

Zach got to play chess with his aunt and uncles and Abby was able to play piano with David – **who has his CD coming out on Wednesday.** His song in memory of Sam will be available on iTunes (as will the entire CD).

I believe that the highlight of Zach's weekend was going to see *Santa Clause 3*. I admit to laughing during the movie even if it would not have been my choice.

It was wonderful to see Brittany. She looks good but is so tired. Only a few more weeks and she can come home for a rest, which I think she needs. Her big news is that she has been offered a research position with the head of the biochemistry department at U of MN – and it is quite possible that he will devise research pertaining to mitochondrial function.

I'd like to thank all of you for your compassionate messages of empathy and sorrow regarding Lilly. Although my heart rends for her parents and I can so easily imagine some of their feelings, my feelings are absolutely sub to that of her parents and big sister.

I have a tremendously big family as my Dad was the oldest of 11 children. I *think* there are 48 first cousins (many of whom have spouses) and 47 second cousins. (A family historian can feel free to correct me.) But therein is the problem - I *think* that is how many cousins I have but do not know for certain. Every one of us matters – none of our lives are insignificant and yet as time goes by we seem to connect less and less with the people we should be closest to. Perhaps this happens to all big families – but does it have to?

Sunday, December 3, 2006 9:07 PM

It has been 21 months since Sam passed away. A lifetime and a minute. Friday night I could not sleep and about 2 am I watched one video with Sam. I have not watched any videos of him since he died. I am not sure why exactly. I look at his pictures all the time and I desperately wish to hear his voice. Yet I could never watch the videos. This was one that Zach took – on Sam's second to last Christmas, when he was six. I heard his voice - it was sweeter and more precious than I have even remembered. But I could not watch any more.

Christmas shopping on Saturday - I find myself in the super hero aisle when I am supposed to be looking at girls' clothes. I have a feeling that Brittany and Abby want the clothes – not Buzz Light Year. I did manage to get a lot done despite my melancholy.

Zach's pain is worse? Or is he just more tolerant of his pain meds and we need to increase the dose? I am not sure but will see how tomorrow goes and then talk with his doctor if it is still not going well. Medically all else is fairly okay. He has an appt with the oral surgeon on Friday – just a 4 month check up to watch for osteonecrosis of the jaw - secondary to one of the drugs he is on.

Friday was a snow day!!!!! When we found out Abby, Zach and I went right back to bed!

Yesterday he had a friend over and they had a good time "gaming" (with Nintendo), playing chess and painting wood CD racks (courtesy of Children's Hospital Art Therapy!). It was so great for him to have some time with a friend. He needs to do this more…it really seemed to lift his spirits.

The kids are ALL working on papers. Brittany is researching the treatment of women in China (horrific still despite some progress); Abby is working on a debate about stem cells. She was told what position to research and since it is not the position she or I believe in, it has been interesting to say the least. Zach has done a final draft of his short, mystery story and I have been given instructions to provide editorial review by tomorrow. (So I better get going because it is 9 PM and …this is horrible…I have NOT opened the *New York Times* yet!!)

Farewell by Anne Bronte

Farewell to Thee! But not farewell
To all my fondest thoughts of Thee;
Within my heart they still shall dwell
And they shall cheer and comfort me.

Life seems more sweet that Thou didst live
And men more true Thou wert one;
Nothing is lost that Thou didst give,
Nothing destroyed that Thou hast done.

December 10, 2006— National Children's Memorial Day

Annual Worldwide Candle Lighting.

Everyone, in every time zone around the world, is invited to light a candle in honor of all children who have died, that their light may always shine.

As candles go out in one time zone, they will be lit in the next, creating a wave of light that will encircle the globe. Please join others in this 24-hour memorial by lighting a candle, wherever you are, at 7 PM on December 10 in memory of Sam and other children who have passed away.

For we are all born mortal
Like Stars and Candlelight
And all that really matters
Is what we do before we fall asleep each night
    --Transiberian Orchestra

Saturday, December 9, 2006 4:06 PM

This week has flown by. Zach made it to school all 3 days and even went back for science club on Thursday afternoon. It is nice to see him have that kind of energy. Pain is still an issue – and we've increased the doses of his pain meds a bit, which seems to have helped. Until today that is – when he just had to get something up way too high in the cabinet and in typical 14 yr old fashion did not want to ask for help. He stretched – and OUCH! Not sure what he did but he is hurting more. Hopefully, this is a temporary problem.

Abby, Zach and Grandma have been the chocolate pretzel making factory this week. On Friday they even got Grandpa enlisted. Then there was a little spat. The girls apparently thought the boys were putting too many sprinkles on the chocolate pretzels. The sprinkles are "only for decoration – not taste," they told Zach and Grandpa. Judging from the amount of sprinkles I don't think they listened.

Zach went to see the oral surgeon Friday. Everything looks great in terms of monitoring for infection and osteonecrosis. The baby teeth, however, have not moved, despite the fact there are no roots left. The adult teeth, just beginning to peek through when he started the Pamidronate, are frozen in place. But as long as he is not having problems we will not pull anything...so they could be like this for years or forever. Who knows but the risk of osteonecrosis after surgery would be higher than it currently is. All is well that we leave alone is our motto. He'll remain on an every 3 month check alternating between his dentist and the oral surgeon.

Zach entertained all of us during the visit with descriptions of what he wants for Christmas. He actually tried to convince me that one of the video game systems would be in my best interest much more than his because I could hook my iPod up to it. Imagine – I never knew how much I could benefit from a video game system.

His labs are ...well his labs. Kidneys not happy because the calcium is rising again. Things have been so steady with his calcium in the past month so I really hope we're not about to hop back on that roller coaster.

Sunday morning Zach will be admitted until Friday night (and hopefully not any longer) for his IVIg. I expect he'll be busy making Christmas cards and presents and decorations. He packed a bunch of Star Wars books, games and movies. Somewhere in that he will need to work on school work!

311

Friday, December 22, 2006 9:22 AM

Some people have asked me if this is a hard time of year. The answer is yes. "But isn't it easier than last year?" No – not really. In some ways it is harder because people assume that only the first is hard. I am sure I thought that too before Sam passed away, so I have to forgive it. But it simply is not true. I find myself split between playing Christmas music and enjoying sending cards, choosing gifts, decorating the house versus playing Sam's favorite songs, crying and most of all remembering my beautiful little boy.

Thank you to all the people who have gone out of their way to remember Sam - to remember that maybe it is not a black and white thing - it's more of a schizophrenic ride between joy and sorrow. Some of you have sent beautiful gifts in remembrance of Sam – remembering that he DID live and he IS still my child. Some have emailed me, some have written little notes on their cards about Sam or called or given me a hug at work or any number of things and I can only say – thank you. You could not know how much your remembrance means to me; your sensitivity and kindness is overwhelming - and there have been many of you!

A song about Mary has resonated with me this season. I have heard the song "Mary Did You know?" a zillion times in my life but on Wednesday, at a Christmas show with Abby and my mom, I **heard** it. The song asks Mary if she knew her baby would perform miracles. Did she know he was God? Did she know that her baby was the amazing I Am? In my head I also heard the unsung questions that are not in the song – "Mary did you know that your son would suffer? Weep? Die? Mary did you know that after he died you would miss him so much even if he did go to Heaven, even if he was God? Mary how did you feel when people said "But aren't you glad God chose him for this purpose? Aren't you glad he is spending his birthday in heaven?"' I can imagine her answer was "YES – I am happy he is in heaven with God. I am glad he is so special that he is God. But guess what guys – I still miss him and wish I could touch him and hold him and hear him tell stories and laugh!"

Did you know? It made me think of all that I did not know when Sam was born. I did not know he was going to have a mitochondrial disease. I did not know he would never ride a bike, read *Charlotte's*

Web, rely on other people's blood and platelets and plasma to get through even a single day. I did not know that I would not have enough hands to count the teachers, health care providers and others in our community that he would need to stay alive. I did not know he would die when he was not yet 8 years old. I did not know what it would feel like when he did die. Sorrow.

Did you know? I did not know that despite his mitochondria dysfunction that robbed his body of energy that he would have more zest to wake up and greet the new day than anyone I have ever known. I did not know that he would think getting a library card was the most amazing thing in the world and that even if he could barely read a few words, he would love to be read to. I did not know how generous the people in our community were – sometimes the same donors giving their platelets every 4 days because he had to have such special typed platelets. I did not understand, despite being a nurse, how giving and generous the health care community is and the capacity for love that teachers have. I did not know that despite 7 yrs and 10 months not being enough time, it would be enough for him to love and be loved by hundreds of people. I did not know that after he died, in the midst of my sorrow, I would get a call like the one I got last night from a father of one of Sam's first grade friends – to tell me that even though his son was a wonderful friend to Sam (and he was!), that it was reciprocal and Sam had deeply impacted his son and been a good friend too. I did not know that if I had a choice to re-live each day, knowing all that would happen – I would jump at the chance, for it would mean stepping into Sam's sunlight again. JOY.

I am sorry I have not updated on Zach. He began to perk up on Tuesday afternoon and went to school Wednesday and Thursday. By the time he came home he was hyped up (what kid isn't at Christmas?), unable to sleep yet desperately needing to sleep and back to somewhat labored breathing. Last night's labs really showed a huge change. His kidneys are not reacting very nicely to his heart not working very well –it was just too much too soon in the last 2 days. School is done now, so while the excitement of the holidays will continue to abound, he can rest in between the great "events." I'll do labs again tonight and hope they trend back in a better direction.

Brittany arrived home Thursday night, very happy to be done with exams. We are so glad to have her back home with us! A package was waiting for her from the Hailey Vincent Foundation. Zachary had received a package from this amazing foundation on Tuesday--The Haley Vincent Foundation. The boxes were filled with all sorts of little gifts for them in memory of a beautiful girl named Haley. What a wonderful surprise!

Abby is wrapping up her last day of school today. She has been so busy between school, some parties, her music recital, school dance…you name it, she is doing it. She made these wonderful peanut-butter/chocolate cookies with my mom last week. I could eat the whole tray of them – easily!

On this Christmas we remember our special children that have passed away…Ally & Gus. Leanna & Samya. Jack, Lilly, Natalie, Britt, Andrew, Eli, Morgan R., Madison, Morgan M, Austin, Laurangel, Haley, Mamie Rose, Heather, Michaela, Amber & Travis, Gabby, Samantha Rose (Sam's first friend), and so many others

Monday, December 25, 2006 11:22 PM

I don't even have words to describe some people. I went to the cemetery today. It has only been 2 days since I was there last and someone stole this cement sleigh that I had with some of Sam's dogs. They left the dogs – just took the sleigh. I walked around and it did not look like anyone else has things missing but who knows…I cannot imagine that whoever did this only took our sleigh. I was so mad – I went to the Retzer Nature Center and stomped up and down the trails about 3 times. I got some interesting looks. The others on the trails were probably thinking "crazy lady!" Well at least I got my exercise in for the day. I called the police when I came home and the sheriff said he was absolutely disgusted. Of course there is so little they can do but he said they will definitely patrol more at night there. He just kept saying how sorry he is that people stoop this low. Him and me both!

Christmas update: Actually I don't have an update but a question. A beautiful Donald Duck snow globe arrived at our house. We were good and did not open it until today. However, there was not anything with it to indicate who sent it. I am hoping that whoever sent it is someone who reads caring bridge. Please email us or call us if you are the one(s) who sent it. It is precious and we want to make sure we tell you that personally! Sam loved Donald!

Friday, December 29, 2006 9:08 PM

Medically things are pretty status quo. Zach has been a champ about wearing the rotten, back brace 23 hours/day. Try sleeping in a turtle shell –I guarantee most of us adults would not last an hour in bed before we gave up and took it off. Unfortunately, I cannot say the brace is helping the pain, though the pain is not worse. Progress? Maybe. However, his spine x-rays from 2 weeks ago show another collapse of yet another vertebrae since late October. We're changing some of his medications around – mainly adding more Vitamin D and increasing the Pamidronate infusion dose. In theory both should keep calcium in his bones where it belongs.

His kidneys look better because his heart is happier because he lost some of the fluid weight he was carrying around last week. You see how this goes. He's just so incredibly fluid sensitive and I think we need to be more careful when he is in the hospital next time. He gets too much fluid there and within a few days his chest x-ray is worse and he needs a lot of oxygen. So when he goes next time we have a plan that I think will help. Thank God for doctors, like Zach's, who pay close attention to this stuff and are so careful.

A few weeks ago he started a new IV medication – Kepra – for his myoclonic jerking. Last week we increased the dose and things seemed pretty good – no tremors or jerks. But in the last few days Zach says he is having many involuntary tremors and movements. We may have to change some stuff yet in order to find the right dose and combination of drugs.

Wednesday was a fantastic day. First off Zach made a new friend, thanks to his wonderful, homebound teacher - Donna. Donna has another homebound student and as she got to know Zach this year she thought the boys would really get along. Although Alex has different medical problems than Zach, he certainly understands realities like central lines, transfusions and hospitalizations. More importantly he play chess, likes to play video games and build with Legos. Donna and her son (also wonderful) brought Alex over so the 2 boys could meet. They had a great time! We also got to have Josie for a few hours

315

– all the way from Indiana. Wow has she grown tall! (For those who do not know of her, she was Sam's dear friend and now ours). It is hard to imagine Sam ever being that tall – he is frozen in my mind, as he was when he died. I could still hold him on my lap and pick him up and carry him.

On Thursday Zach went to a birthday party. This may seem like a mundane thing to write on here. "Wow – Anne," you are thinking, "he went to a birthday party....can't wait for what happens next!" But the thing is that when a kid has a chronic illness or disability, a mother never takes these things for granted. I don't know what happens between kindergarten and middle school but it seems that for children with disabilities and chronic illnesses, their good friends in early elementary school turn into acquaintances – nice in school, forget you when home. It is a rare thing to be invited to a party or to get a call asking, "Hey want to hang out tonight?" So a birthday party is a great thing. Mundane...yes. But that is what makes it so exceptional, for so often it is the simplest things that kids like Zach miss out on. It is not because anyone is intentionally mean but because they forget that at heart we are all simply human beings. We have the capacity to be friends and we want to have friends. I'm not surprised Zach was invited, though, for the birthday boy has been a true and unwavering friend to Zach.

I should also mention that Abby was willing to learn how to give him an IV medication so that he could go to the party without a nurse/parent. (I'm sure you can imagine the effect I would have had on a basement of middle schoolers if I went to the party). We knew he would need pain medicine and she was just great about learning how to do it. Zach would be fine doing this for himself – he is smart and more careful about being sterile than most health care providers – but with his myoclonus and tremors his hands are not reliable. So Abby helped Zach and they made a great team.

Another child died from mitochondrial cytopathy today. His name is Kyle. Kyle recently turned 8 years old. I met Kyle on what would have been Sam's 8th birthday. He and his mom and some other friends came to help plant a tree in memory of Sam at our school. Several months ago, while shopping with his mom, Kyle insisted on buying a Buzz Light Year night light for me. She told him she was not sure I would want that but he insisted and his reason was so wise, yet so simple: He told his mom he just knew that I would see the light coming from the Buzz Light Year night light and think of Sam and know that his light was always with me.

I Could ... If They Would

If they would find a cure when I'm a kid...
I could ride a bike and sail on rollerblades, and
I could go on really long nature hikes.
If they would find a cure when I am a teenager...
I could earn my license and drive a car, and
I could dance every dance at my senior prom.
If they would find a cure when I'm a young adult...
I could travel around the world and teach peace, and
I could marry and have children of my own.
If they would find a cure when I'm grown old...
I could visit exotic places and appreciate culture, and
I could proudly share pictures of my grandchildren.
If they could find a cure when I'm alive...
I could live every day without pain and machines, and
I could celebrate the biggest thank you of life ever.
If they would find a cure when I'm buried into Heaven,
I could still celebrate with my brothers and sister there, and
I could still be happy knowing that I was part of the effort.
　　--Matthew Joseph Thaddeus Stepanek (- Mattie had mito)
From *Journey Through Heartsongs*, Hyperion, 2002

2007

Friday, January 5, 2007 8:02 PM

Last weekend, while cleaning, I found a movie I did not know we had. It was of Sammy's Make A Wish trip to Disney. He was so tiny and so darn cute…I could still understand every word he said. Today, I had a wonderful surprise. The music teacher at Bethesda called to say that they were pouring cement at that moment for the plaque that goes with Sam's tree. His 1st grade teacher, Mrs. Brooks, had purchased this plaque a while ago. She retired in June but I hope she gets to see it soon.

Oh – I almost forgot the highlight of Zach's week. Making a catapult for mini marshmallows. He claims his teacher told him to aim for Abby!

Monday, January 8, 2007 11:02 AM

Things are not going well. Saturday and Sunday were fine although he seemed more tired to me yesterday.

This morning he "woke up, showing similar signs and symptoms to what happened in May when he was brought in by ambulance – although he is still responsive. He said his head just did not feel right – "It's so tired and heavy." Then he tried to sit and he could not. He insisted he could stand to get to the bathroom but even with the nurse and me holding on to him that was not a good idea. He could not even hold his head up. When Peter asked him to open his eyes, he could not do it. He was trying so hard but just could not make them do what he wanted them to do. We did manage to get them open to look and his pupils are dilated with a very sluggish response to light. This is very abnormal. The pupils of the eye should get smaller when exposed to light. It typically is a terrible neurological sign indicating a brain bleed or worse. In fact the first 3 or 4 times Sam did it they whipped him into CT scan thinking "this is it. He's bleeding in his brain." but he never was. Finally we came to the conclusion that for Zach (and Sam) it is a sign of an acute decrease in an already compromised ability to make energy (ATP) – aka mitochondrial crisis. Zach can tell us our phone number and he told Peter that Boba Fet is the name of the Star Wars books he is reading so that was good. But he said he just needs to sleep and that was it. He was out. He woke up a bit ago and again insisted he could get out of bed, but he cannot. The desire is there – his body just has this acute and profound weakness.

Our plan is nothing fancy – it is to aggressively minimize the demands on his body and hope that when he comes out of it, he has not lost too much ground. We're giving him a blood transfusion, even though his counts are relatively fine as we hope that will help get more oxygen to his cells. We are keeping the percentage of oxygen in his blood high with supplemental oxygen. We are doubling some of the medications that boost mitochondrial function. Other than that, there is nothing to be done but wait and for us that is so incredibly frustrating. I just want to do something but I am reminded by his doctor that sometimes doing nothing is doing something and it is the best thing to do. I know he is right.

Yesterday, we did play Star Wars Monopoly, which Hope, one of his nurses, loaned to him. That was fun but we'll just have to see who wins. The game is not over yet and I am still competitive enough that I hope I win! His school PT, Nicki and OT, Ellen, gave him Star Wars chess for Christmas. I personally feel that was a conspiracy. I am so busy trying to remember that Darth Vader is the queen and Yoda is a king, etc. etc. that I cannot concentrate on my strategy. Of course, Zach points out that I would lose even if we played with a regular chess set, which I told him is completely beside the point.

Tuesday, January 9, 2007 09:24 AM

Neurologically he is worse. At times he is oriented but at other times he thinks things are happening or people are in the room that are not. It's frightening but he certainly knows who we all are - just seems confused as to the specifics. Labs are a bit worse. He has pancreatitis now. His breathing sounds bad but he is on the same oxygen requirement, so that is positive I think. He is bleeding some. I'm worried terribly but at times I've had to laugh. Such as yesterday when he could not hold his head up but he asked several times if I would please stop reading and help him with his homework. When I explained that he might be too tired and it would be okay if he did not do it he said, "Well I'll just dictate to you. Ok? Let's do my homework NOW." Thanks for your concern and care. Really--thank YOU

320

Wednesday, January 10, 2007 8:54 PM

I am happy to report that Zach is doing better mentally today. Not quite himself, tired and still somewhat off topic...but oh my, what a difference 24 hours can make!!! This morning his pupils were reactive to light. Now this afternoon they were once again pretty non-reactive but I am hoping that is because it is the end of the day and he is exhausted.

His labs are remarkably better - both this morning and this evening. I could hear the change in his breathing during the night. It seemed as if I could literally "hear" the fluid coming off his heart and the labs definitely prove that. All I can say is I am so thankful for the doctor he has. It would have been a rare doctor that would have known to cut fluids rather than give more...because his labs just looked more and more like he was dehydrated. But he cut them a bit more on Tuesday and today you could just see how much that helped. He would have been in the ICU if we had done anything differently.

So there you go....He is doing better! Time will tell if there are long-term effects but for now I am so relieved. The rest we can work on. Thank you for caring about Zachary and us.

There is a quote about how there is no such thing as a "self made man." We are each made up of all of those who have touched our lives. Thank you for the strength and comfort you give to all of us. We are so very lucky to know all of you!

I forget how close to fear I live until something like this happens and it brings back that last hour with Sam...It's so scary. And yet, something happens when your child goes to the brink and comes back - you realize anew what a miracle each and every day they have is and how fortunate and blessed you are to have that child.

Friday, January 12, 2007 7:53 PM

Thoughts from the front:
Zach is **HOME**.
Zach beat me at Star Wars Monopoly...I know you were all voting for him so I figure you'd like to know this.

321

Now that he is fully awake, oriented and alert he no longer seems worried about getting that homework done. In fact, he has not asked me one thing about it.

Grandpa got his hands on an old chair life/stair lift, tore it out of one building and found someone to install it on the steps leading to our lower level, AKA Zach's Make A Wish Game Room. Zach has had far too many days he cannot get down those stairs. Now he can whiz down on the chair lift. Yeah for Grandpa!

Zach has some terrific nurses on 4-west at Children's of Wisconsin. In addition to taking great care of him they act as my alarm clock (some come with a snooze feature), bring food, make me laugh, tell me what is good on the menu (usually that would be nothing), do double time as guards of Zach's door so residents don't wake him up in the morning, understand my need to know every solitary thing and most important to me –love Zach and Sam. Zach would be in the ICU at any other children's hospital because of the care he requires. But he never is because his nurses are committed to doing whatever it takes to keep him out of the ICU environment, which would kill his spirit (and mine – I hate that place). Even when his blood pressure was 60/25-30 in May and he came in by lights and siren ambulance they wanted to keep him in the intermediate ICU.

The feature stories are rarely about nurses like ours. They always feature groundbreaking treatments or surgeries and high tech, state of the art ICUs. The fundraisers are never for patient care units like 4-west that don't even have some of the most basic equipment (such as a bladder scanner). Yet *this* is what **compassionate care** looks like: Loving and caring for a child and his/her family through chronic illnesses. Watching and waiting and hoping with families because there is nothing high tech left to do. So to our 4 west nurses –you are all awesome!

Boring medical stuff for those interested: (feel free to skip this) A few people have asked me in the last few days why he always gets sick when he goes into the hospital. There are a few reasons. Following is my very simple explanation

The problem:
Zach has an immune system that does not work well (immune deficiency). When it does try to fight things off it does not know when to stop so it ends up attacking his own body (autoimmune disease).

The treatment
Suppress ("wipe out" as Zach would say) his immune system with a very large amount of other people's donated immune – globulins (IVIg is short for intravenous immune globulins. Immune globulins are "good guys" that fight off germs).

Why does he get sick from IVIg?
In the beginning of the infusion the IVIg "turns his immune system on" – enough so that it "attacks" his body and he does not feel very well. Finally, towards the end of the admission, his immune system is suppressed and the new one takes over. Then he is good to go (as far as immune issues) for about 3-4 weeks until the IVIg wears off.

Can't you prevent this from happening?
He gets a lot of medicine every 6 hours in an attempt to decrease his reaction but nothing seems to completely help. Sometimes I think about it like chemo (not to compare what Zach goes through to the hell kids on chemo go through - it is not that bad)…but in order to get better he has to feel really bad first.

Second reason for getting "sick" with IVIg
He gets extra fluid in the hospital. This makes his heart work harder and if it cannot compensate all sorts of other things happen (breathing problems, kidneys not filtering the way they should, etc.) We're trying to perfect a plan for this. We did better this time. He came home on 2 liters of oxygen rather than the 4 he has been coming home on. He is down to 1 liter now.

What happened this past week?
What happened was not the normal "sick" that he gets each month that I explained above. In retrospect he was "off" and his labs were trending badly a few days before he was admitted. I should have seen this coming. At any rate, *this week* he had what some doctors refer to

as a "mito crash", some a "stroke like episode," and some a severe "mito decompensation." Whatever it is called – it is an acute loss of energy to his cells. Our brains use more energy than any other organ in the body and when the "energy barometer" dropped - Zach's brain got "sick." Sometimes it is other organs like his pancreas. For Sam it most often manifested as life threatening pancreatitis or a worsening of his bleeding problem – out of nowhere he'd bleed profusely for days. This sudden and profound drop in the energy supply is what happened to Zach in May and mitochondrial disease - not cardiac arrest - is noted as the cause of death on Sammy's death certificate.

Can you prevent it?
We're trying but the problem is no one knows what causes it. No one has a definite answer about what to do. There's often not much warning it is going to happen. No one knows why Zach got better in May and again this week. No one knows why Sam survived these episodes many times and no one knows why he did not on March 3, 2005. Their doctor and I have learned a lot over the years and I think we are doing the very best things that can be done but we often feel like we're out on a tree limb swaying in the breeze (and it is night time and the breeze is really a hurricane).

So there you go. It is scary and I'd lie if I said I don't worry - but I am thankful that today Zach is doing well.

Friday, January 19, 2007 9:26 AM

Things are okay. Zach is definitely doing better. He seemed to turn the corner in terms of energy and muscle strength on Wednesday and on Thursday was finally able to go back to school for a good part of the day. His labs did not look as good as they had Thursday night – I guess this is because he was at school and his heart had to work harder. Well, I suppose I could keep him home forever and his heart would not work so hard - but life has to be lived.

Monday starts a new semester and with that he gets two new classes that he is so excited about. One is "Foods and People." I think they learn about different cultures and cook…don't quote me on that but I do know it involves cooking, which he just loves. The 2nd new class is ceramics and he has been looking forward to that all year. For those in his art fan club, I'll try to scan pictures of it when he brings things home.

Finally he is starting a new math curriculum – which is actually the old math curriculum. It reminds me of that old song called "New Math." Well I think the new math of 1960 has become old math. He has struggled with the new (or is it new-new) math program our district has chosen – as have many kids. It's a great, hands-on, interactive, real life math curriculum but with him not there every day and the teachers all being unfamiliar this first year with it….it has been sucking way too much time from every other subject. So back to old math – which if you are over 50 may be new math to you. Did you follow that?

I wish I knew how to get a movie on here as he just brought home his group project from drawing class. It is a Claymation movie that his group of three made called, "The Bad Day." Basically, a guy slips on a banana peel, falls down, gets attacked by a dog, falls on a bridge, which breaks apart, which sends the guy careening down to land on a railroad track…along comes the train which smashes the poor clay guy and the dogs come and drag him off the track. Want to venture a guess as to who in the group had the idea for a good part of that story? It's really very funny.

Big plans for the weekend include taking down the Christmas tree. My kids inform me that the wise men have come and gone so I cannot keep using that as an excuse to keep it up. I just hate taking it down and putting it on the curb to be taken away – it feels a little harsh to be so nice to a tree and decorate it and then shove it out the door into the cold, frosty air. The kids' Uncle Sean is flying in from SC this weekend (hope he has a winter coat) and my brother, his wife and Grandpa Frank will be coming over…so a busy weekend but a nice weekend.

Wednesday, January 24, 2007 9:04 PM

On Monday Zach took a little trip to the hospital to see his doctor. His doctor checked him over and they discussed the pain thoroughly. They agreed that Zach was feeling a bit better than he had late last week, even though the pain still has its very acute moments.

It is terribly hard to see him in pain. If we medicate him enough to take it away he is tired. If we don't he is hurting. It's a problem. I need to start talking to the doctors and see if there are other things we can try. I'm trying to maintain hope that we'll find something.

It reminds me of a time in Sam's life when he had terrible migraines. Migraine is not even a good word for what these episodes were but it is all we have to describe them. They were just awful and would last up to a week sometimes. He was little – the first one was when he was only about 13 months old and he was so despondent. A few of them were bad enough that he had small strokes. We tried different medications and they did not help. I remember holding him and feeling so helpless and heartbroken because there was nothing that I could do to help. Finally, we were blessed with both the doctor we have now and an anesthesiologist who worked together to find medications and doses that would help. I can remember one Easter in the hospital when he had had a headache for a week…and then that Easter Sunday he woke up, played and smiled. He did not scream or hang his head and cry. It was like the roof had been lifted off the hospital and suddenly it was flooded with sunshine and hope. His doctors, the nurses, the people that clean rooms or deliver food or stock supplies who had all felt as helpless as I did smiled that day. After that we finally knew how to help him and with time he actually did not have as many…none were ever as devastating as the ones he had during his first few years. So I try to think of that and how desperate so many of us felt; how much we wondered if we could ever take away his pain. It was the one time during Sam's life that I seriously questioned what his quality of life really was. Before that and after that I never questioned it…his laughter, which even as a baby was in his eyes, was always the answer. I just hope that we will find something for Zach's pain and with time this will all be a distant dream.

Tomorrow Z is staying after school if he is up to it. He is helping his language arts teacher coordinate a coin war in the middle school. All of the money raised will go towards purchasing a laptop computer for the IICU at Children's – the floor Zach is admitted to. Last year the kids raised enough money to buy a bunch of DVD players for the floor. The laptop will be wonderful because 32 kids on the floor are sharing 2 computers. Many of these kids are there long term and this will be so nice for them to stay in touch with friends, do school work or even just play some computer games. Zach's teacher has gotten many of the kids in her various language classes involved. She really wanted to do this with Zach after she read one of his journal entries about how proud he was that the school had raised money. It is such a neat opportunity for him to be part of something at school. That, in and of itself, is enough for me.

It's been a busy week...so much so that I never did get that tree down last weekend and most of the house decorations are still up. Those that are down only made it as far as the library table – not even to boxes yet. My goal is this weekend – really!

Friday, January 26, 2007 4:15 PM

*** HOPE ***

I called the University of Wisconsin Children's Hospital and talked briefly with a nurse who talked briefly with a physician. They want to see Zach and said that it is reasonable to at least talk about doing the kyphoplasty!!!!!!!!!!!!!!!!!! That is already more than I got out of the adult orthopedic docs here.

Kyphoplasty is a procedure of injecting a substance into the vertebrae to increase the height back to normal levels. In adults, kyphoplasty has dramatically reduced pain. They have never done it on an adolescent but they have a lot of experience doing it for elderly people with osteoporosis and compression fractures – exactly what he has. We will actually see an adult orthopedic physician since peds has never done the procedure. UWCH is about 75 minutes from our house. It's a good place –that is where Zach's endocrinologist practices. I really like our current pediatric ortho and have no intention of transferring care but he, like all pediatric orthos, does not do the kyphoplasty and the adult docs he talked with would not even see Zach.

I am also working on an application to Shriners. There is a Shriners Hospital in Chicago but I plan to ask them if St. Louis is a better option for Zach. From what I can tell St. Louis Shriners specializes in metabolic bone disease.

Things are not great.

Zach has gotten progressively more "tired" since the weekend. It's not really a normal tired as much as his brain is tired. Since yesterday his pupils have been mostly fixed and dilated and he really cannot walk. At first it was just unsteadiness but now it is weakness as well. He looks drugged but he has actually had far fewer pain meds than usual. He cannot stay awake but it is more of a somnolence than a fatigue. His oxygen needs are higher but his other vital signs are fine. His creatinine is not good – his kidneys are really doing a poor job clearing anything – and yet it is not horrific. At times I think he is getting better. This morning I was so encouraged but from the time I came home from work today my heart has been in my throat.

I have talked with his doctor who is very supportive of him staying home OR going to the hospital -either one is fine he says. If we admit him there is really nothing else they can do that I am not doing. And the thing is that for a few hours there or a few here he seems as if he is improving. He went to therapy today and talked my ear off in the car about middle school relationships. He did well for the first hour his teacher was here and ate the homemade guacamole she made him. When I asked him what is 5+ 12 he looked at me with eyes mostly closed and said, "What do you think I am? An idiot?" He does not have a clue why I would ask him such a stupid question. And for all I know he may even go to school tomorrow. But none of that changes what is. I think the reality is that this is not an acute problem. It is not a cold or a flu he needs to get over. It is a sign of a child who has become very compromised. This "tired brain" stuff is happening more and more….this time it seems to have been exacerbated by standing for 20 minutes in cooking class. 20 minutes. It takes so little to stress his body out and that is a reality I can barely think about. One mistake, one bad choice….they are not so easy to rally from anymore.

It is hard to believe the changes in the last 2 years. Where did that child go that I had to advocate for because his had "hidden disabilities?" I don't have to fight for anything anymore except for people to not give up.

I spent a long time talking with him in his bed. I reminded him of his art class project -a ceramic Darth Vader that he is so excited about.

I told him I will take him to school just for art class Friday – it is not a day he normally attends. I reminded him of the Lego set he wants to buy. He is so excited about it and he talked me into paying 50% for it. He made me shake hands on the deal. We talked about the coin wars at school and how fun that is and what a great friend he has in Clark. I wanted him to think about all the neat things going on in his life and all the people that love him. I want to tie him to Earth – with me.

I hate everything about this disease. And I just wish it were me that had to go through all of this and not him. Why do I get to have the "mild form" and he has this? He is so good and so brave and he trusts that his doctor and I will always take care of him and make him better. I hate that I am his mother and I cannot make him better.

He's scheduled for admission Sunday…or sooner.

Brittany turned 20 yesterday!!! 20!!! It seems impossible. She said it is a little depressing to be that old. I'm sure you all feel as much pity for her as I do...poor thing - she is so old! But seriously, she is such an amazing girl and I am so lucky to be her mom.

Saturday, February 3, 2007 7:02 PM

Today it has been 1 year and 11 months since Sammy passed away. I don't think I miss him any less. Sometimes I think it is even more. I hope he knows how much I love him.

Zach

I don't know where to start. Thank you for all of your concern and prayers for Zachary. He is doing better but as I said before, it does not necessarily change reality. However, it would be a slap to all of my children to ever lose hope in life. My friend Janet once reminded me that a war is made up of many battles. I think I can now say that another battle has been fought and won and for that I am thankful.

The night I last wrote was probably the worst night I have ever had at home with Zach. Believe me, it has all been uphill since Wed. night. He was choking and gasping for breath multiple times during the night. I did not fall asleep until 5 am. The next day I talked with his doctor about ordering a suction machine. I hated the feeling that I had no way to suction. I think he was just so weak that he could not swallow his own saliva. He's been doing a bit of choking on water too, but not as bad as Sam did.

329

We've always had huge tanks of oxygen but he has needed a facemask this week to keep his sats up and that requires a higher liter per minute flow of oxygen. Thursday night it ran out in the middle of the night. Yes, we have back ups but that was enough drama for me. So now we have a compressor, which uses the air in the house and works off the electricity. Anyone want to pay the bill for me? Oh well – I'm happy to pay for the assurance that we will not run out of oxygen when we need it. We still have the huge tank and many small ones in case of a loss of electricity or he needs to oxygen at school.

Thursday he went to bed unable to walk independently and neurologically still not right. I was pretty close to asking for him to be admitted on Friday. Friday he woke up and could walk…just like that. His pupils were reactive too. His breathing is still not quite right. We'll have to figure that out because I am having a lot of trouble keeping his oxygen levels satisfactory at night and he still requires the full mask rather than the nasal cannula. His vision remains blurred for reading so I read a good amount of time to him Friday and Saturday. In fact I like his book, *Touching Spirit Bear*, so much that I read ahead.

He did not make it to school on Thursday or Friday but hopefully he will be all set for that when he comes out of the hospital. He absolutely did NOT forget that we had shook hands on the Lego set deal. It's too cold for him to leave the house and he is still not breathing well so I went out to find it today. It is sold out (It is some Star Wars ship) but we'll keep looking. I also got him the Star Wars Soundtracks from the library so we can upload them and a few books on tape that I knew he would like. So he is all set for the hospital now.

I also got some books on NYC from the library today. I hesitate to say much except that airline tickets have been purchased, a hotel suite smack in the middle of all the noise of Times Square has been reserved and Broadway tickets for 2 shows have been procured. I am trying to be very low key about this - even though this city girl is so so excited about the thought of going back east. I have such fond memories of going there with my Dad when I was a kid or with friends when I was in college. Actually our 8th grade class trip was to NYC too. The last time I was there was for a doctor appointment for Zach and Abby when they were 1 and 2…so needless to say we did not do much. That was the first time I heard the words mitochondrial disease and the first time he had a biopsy. Zach gets sick so fast and actually going to the city is far from guaranteed. But I also feel that if we can – we have to take the opportunity to do this. We may never get the chance again for any number of reasons.

$2214.95

That is how much the 7th and 8th graders from Butler Middle School raised in their coin wars. The money will be used to purchase laptop computers for the patient care unit that Zach goes to at Children's. Zach missed the last few days of the wars but he is so excited and proud! I am so proud to be part of this wonderful school district too. Thank you to everyone who participated.

Hope…how important it is. One of my colleagues and I had to teach our bimonthly workshop to the junior medical students this week. One part of this particular workshop is an interactive exercise. They have to pretend that they are the family and imagine as best they can the emotions, questions, challenges, frustrations, etc that families feel and experience. Well for the first time in many years one of our med student pretend families got in a fight. Usually they just have little discussions (and often they want to sue the doctors which I find hilarious but sad too.) Anyway, the fight was about hope. They drew the whole class into it and it was an amazing discussion although some of them were down right angry. I am happy to say that those for hope far outnumbered those who did not find it essential. These are tomorrow's physicians and my HOPE is that they remain this passionate about the strength that comes from hope and continue to realize the power of their words. As physicians they have the power to take away or to give hope with words.

Thank you for continuing to hope with me.

Tuesday, February 6, 2007 1:04 PM

Zach is still struggling a lot. WE are going to start him on a non-invasive ventilator system called Bi Pap with the hope that if he uses this at night he will not have to work so hard to breathe and therefore he might feel better during the day. He is working just too hard. We are also going to cut his protein some tonight and then some tomorrow if no improvement. Sometimes with organic acid problems like Zach has, protein can be a problem and cause acidosis which leads to the extreme somnolence he has right now. He literally cannot keep his eyes open even when awake. He sleeps almost all the time. We are going to start IV antibiotics while we wait for blood cultures to come back. Doubt there is an infection but in this setting it is better to be safe. Finally we are going to try stopping a med (Keppra) that we started in December. It can cause extreme weakness and somnolence. They doubt the med is the culprit but I want to try stopping it - I'd never forgive myself if the problem was as simple as a med side effect. His J tube had to be replaced today because it was clogged....he has had some intestinal bleeding but with factor 7a it has stopped pretty easily. He needs prayers.

FOR SAM...

From the Feb. 4, 2007 editions of the *Milwaukee Journal Sentinel*

<u>Family's tragedy spawns plan for action</u>
<u>Club launches database to identify unique residents</u>
By JACQUELINE SEIBEL

Anne Juhlmann did what any mother would do when her child needed medical help. She called 911.

The Waukesha woman expected that the paramedics who showed up at her door would know of the medical equipment that her son, Sam, needed and would know that her son should be transported to Children's Hospital of Wisconsin in Wauwatosa.

Neither proved to be true and Sam, 7, died that day, losing his battle with mitochondrial disease.

Juhlmann didn't blame the people who tried to save her son, but in the belief that policies needed to be improved, she set out to make sure things would be different if there were an emergency for her other son, 14, who also has special needs.

She met with the Waukesha Fire Department after Sam's death to develop a plan and to ask the department to change its policy to only transfer patients to Waukesha Memorial Hospital.

"The Fire Department was so open to looking at the situation, to learn from it," Juhlmann said.

Waukesha Fire Deputy Chief Jesse Alba remembers Sam's case vividly. He knew the family before Sam's death.

"I'm a friend of the Juhlmanns, and I felt terrible about their loss and it was my organization that treated Sam," Alba said.

Although the paramedics who took care of Sam that day almost two years ago followed department policies, the department wanted to learn from the situation, he said. The department has since changed its policy. Now if the child is stable and if the department can spare one of its ambulances for the longer trip, they can take that child directly to the Wauwatosa hospital.

Juhlmann and Alba aren't stopping there. They both sit on a committee that includes the Oconomowoc Junior Woman's Club that is establishing a database identifying children with unique needs in the event of an emergency or disaster. The database is intended to equip medical care workers entering an emergency situation with knowledge of children's needs, said Kia LaBracke, the club's co-chairman.

The committee is in its infant stages but hopes to first identify all children with advanced technological needs, such as feeding tubes, or an IV, starting with those released from Children's Hospital, LaBracke said.

LaBracke said starting the database with a small population helps the committee narrow its focus and complete the project instead of trying to take on all children and adults.

Part of the mission of the Oconomowoc Junior Woman's Club is to better the lives of children. Due to the perseverance of the club in the last two years, every ambulance in Waukesha County is equipped with a pediatric bag - a first responder's kit to handle emergencies involving children, Alba said.

Earning honors

The club received a 2006 National Heroes Award from the Emergency Medical Services for Children Program and also last year took home a second-place award in Community Improvement from the General Federation of Women's Clubs.

Headed by LaBracke and co-chairwoman Elizabeth Davy, the club raised and donated more than $65,000, including a $24,000 grant, to purchase the pediatric bags within two years for Waukesha County.

Davy is now heading an effort to spread the pediatric bag project across Wisconsin.

LaBracke leads the special-needs database project, something she learned about when she traveled to Maryland last year to accept the club's national award. At the conference, she met Children's Hospital emergency room physician Halim Hennes, who had wanted to start a database for some time.

Hennes called the project a "global, comprehensive approach."

"You want to make sure it's safe, has the information that is relevant to the people who come to help, that the parents are on board, and the local EMS departments are on board," Hennes said. He has been lobbying the state for funding for the database, which he said also must ensure privacy. While the club committee is waiting to hear if they will receive state funds, they are encouraging all parents of children with unique needs to check the protocols of their local EMS department, introduce themselves to the department and outline their needs.

One of the roadblocks to this project is convincing parents that an emergency can happen, Juhlmann said. Parents of children with special needs are well versed in their child's care and sometimes don't think that something could go wrong.

"Everyone needs to know in the end that nothing better could have been done. When you have a plan in place you are ensuring that," Juhlmann said.

Thursday, February 8, 2007 7:04 AM

We did the BiPap Tues night...once they got it running correctly the difference it made was extraordinary. Anyone who has watched how hard he works to breathe lately would be astounded. I actually had to look at him hard to make sure he was still breathing because he was not retracting or chin tugging or making any noise....amazing. Wednesday he decided to go for some more excitement and for a good hour had the tripple alarms going and quite a few people in the room. Not sure what that was because his chest x-ray was unchanged (not perfect but not worse) and he had a good night with the bipap again. Tonight he has a sleep study to officially evaluate him for bipap (can you tell we're doing things a bit backwards?). The good news is they can do it as a remote study and he can stay on the floor and not go to the sleep lab. No one was comfortable with him leaving the floor at this moment in time. He's far from doing well but he is absolutely holding steady and for now I could not ask for more (ok - well I could but steady is better than worse.)

Monday, February 12, 2007 6:54 AM

We came home Friday night. Zach did ok Sat. and had an absolutely wonderful day on Sunday. Unfortunately, no matter how good he felt (and he really looked and felt great) his heart had other ideas....it was beating very steady and strong but very S*L*O*W* - too slow after a while for my or his doctor's comfort. Sunday about midnight we went back to the hospital and he was in a room with "his nurse" caring for him by 4 am.

Cardiology was not impressed with his EKG abnormality on Friday. They had better be impressed today. We expect he will be coming home from this admission with a pacemaker. Why his heart is so slow I don't know - all I know is I want them to fix it.

I do want to say that Abby made Zach a pie this weekend - French silk no less - with a big Z on it. It made his night.

Tuesday, February 13, 2007 5:57 PM

Wednesday (tomorrow) I am meeting with Zach's doctor, his primary cardiologist, and the electrophysiologist (don't know him). Our cardiologist says it is his recommendation that we put the pacemaker in and of course this is what Zach's doctor and I feel is right. Sam did this many times (low heart rate) and was always fine which is why I did not bring him to the hospital the night he died. When I realized it was not going to be like the other 100 times he had dropped his rates it was too late. And now here we are with Zach. He is perfectly fine despite his heart rate of 44 for many many hours on Sunday and into Monday. In fact his heart was swinging so much from one extreme to another that we put him back on his beta blocker IV drip last night. But we have to learn from what happened to Sam. As one of the docs said, to not put the pacer in, knowing where this is going given Sam's history, is like playing Russian roulette. Yes, the surgery is going to be a huge bleeding issue but at this point this is the right thing to do. It is a bigger risk to not do the surgery. Not sure when the surgery will be...I hope soon but will let you know when I have more information.

The pulmonary doctor increased the settings on the bipap and he slept so soundly last night. If he does not breathe it will breathe for him and it will give his muscles a rest at night. I think it has the potential to really help him feel better though we'll see with time.

Wednesday, February 14, 2007 10:44 PM

Zachary will have the pacemaker inserted Thursday afternoon - no definite time yet. This will be an internal pacemaker, meaning the wires will be placed inside the heart. This will actually allow us to avoid opening him up completely to place an external pacemaker. There will still be an incision but due to his bleeding issues this is the best option for Zach ... he will still bleed of course. Our hematologist wrote orders for all the blood products which we will start before surgery and continue afterwards.

Today we tested for clots in his major veins leading to the heart. Fortunately these have opened up from the clots he had a few years ago so we can avoid going in through the neck. I met with the CV Surgery team and they explained everything to Zach - even let him sign his own consent form. (I did co-sign). There will be 3 cardiologists in the room and one of the cardiac anesthesiologists. Anesthesia worries me but all the cardiac ones know Zach and Sam.

Zach says he's not anxious about surgery but he's scared about the pain. We tried to reassure him that while he will feel pain, we will never let him stay in pain and will always give him whatever pain meds he needs.

I am worried but this is what he needs and I have seldom felt so sure about a decision...

On a lighter note who watches the Grease reality show? Is Max cute or what? He has to win! I never watch TV except an occasional Keith Oberlman show but Abby got me hooked on this show. We love Max and Laura.

336

Thursday, February 15, 2007 10:58 PM

Zach got out of surgery about 8 PM (I think - I've lost track of time). He is in the ICU. He is okay but he had one of his episodes during the surgery. His CVP shot up - this stands for central venous pressure and when it is high it means the heart is not functioning as well as it should. It went up very fast and his blood pressure dropped and he needed more ventilation. As I said he is okay although his CVP is still high for him. We are increasing his cardiac drip and hope to get him out of the ICU soon and back to his nurses on 4 west. The cardiologist and anesthesiologist just did not think tonight was the night to do that. He was very sad to not be back in "his room" tonight on 4-west and I have to say I am sad too but hopefully this will be short. His pain is controlled at the moment but gotta run back now. I have not eaten since this morning aside from Mountain Dew so I'm thinking I better grab something to eat too.

Thanks for all the cards - WOW! He loved them.

Friday, February 16, 2007 11 PM

He is bleeding. When a pacemaker is placed the CV surgeon creates a "pocket" under the collar bone and this is where the pacemaker goes. Then 2 wires are tunneled through the skin into the heart. Unfortunately this leaves places open to bleeding and you cannot see the bleeding until the swelling and bruising starts. Well it started and does not look too promising right now. He is getting platelets, cryoprecipitate (something like plasma) every 12 hours and Factor 7a every 3 hours. We tried to put a pressure dressing over the site but it is a hard area to do that and there is a lot of fluid (presumably blood) underneath the skin. It has become very painful for him.

He did great with starting Milrinone (cardiac drip).

Thank you once again for all the cards - I read them all to him today and he really likes them. Thank you to everyone who visited. I am sorry I did not answer the phone tonight - just crazy busy with 2 nurses and me (also a nurse) trying to get him settled and all his meds and blood products in to him.

Melissa, one of his nurses, was at Toys R Us today and found the Lego ship that he wanted. I thought he was going to hyperventilate

337

when he saw it. He was so excited. Thank you to all the people that offered to shop for him and get the ship.

Saturday, February 17, 2007 6:18 PM

Yes- he is on HIS floor with HIS nurses. Thankfully, on day shift in PICU he did have Sam's primary nurse so that was good....but other than that I can only say that the Intermediate ICU is the safest place for Zach given how well they understand his needs and issues and how ingrained it is in them to work WITH parents as a team. We love our nurses.

Still giving cryo every 12 hours and Factor 7a every 3 hrs. He got another dose of platelets (from a single donor again - thank God for those donors!). His hemoglobin dropped dramatically so he's getting red cells now.

Pain is a problem - meds help but he needs a lot.

Even so our doctor was willing to let us go home tomorrow since I can do everything they are doing here at home. I know I'l be exhausted but even so - home is always good.

However....we had to clear it with CV (cardiovascular) surgery) and they do not like the look of things. They are going to see what te surgery site looks like in the morning but they say they may need to open him back up and drain the blood out. They are concerned that if it pools there too long he will be infected. My question was what will prevent it from bleeding again...it is a hard issue because an infection could mean the pacemaker has to be removed but bleeding is huge for him and he has not even hit the time when he normally has a very hard time (7-10 days post op);

I'm not going to worry about it until or if we have to. I hope they come in tomorrow and think it looks good enough to let us watch it at home. However, I also appreciate that they want to be so careful and proactive.

Zach has had the benefit of having 2 nurses for most of the day - Hope and Marisol - which is good as he is really BUSY. Hope brought Spider Man monopoly in and Zach got to play a game with Abby and his Aunt Maribeth who is here for a quick visit.

Yesterday his friend Alex visited...Alex is a great kid and having been in the hospital a lot himself, certainly understands more than most kids could what this is all like for Zach.

I am off to check out the great cuisine in the CHW cafeteria now.

Sunday, February 18, 2007 11 AM

Not going home today...they want to take it one day at a time. We're starting another antibiotic as he still has a fever and the surgical site is something we just cannot mess around with. The CV surgeon says we don't need to go in at this point...as long as we can prevent more bleeding and infection.

Tuesday, February 20, 2007 4:21 PM

Zach is still in the hospital. The bleeding has continued but not for lack of effort on the part of our hematology group and primary doctor. They are doing everything they can to help stop it. As always, I feel so blessed to have the doctors we have. No one understands why the boys bleed so much but the doctors have always been very responsive even in the absence of answers.

Basically the site over and all around the pacemaker is swollen and discolored. No one wants to put a drain in due to infection risk. The pain gets worse each day rather than better and that is the most concerning to us. We increased his lock out rate on the dilaudid (a narcotic) today and will do so again if it does not help. This morning he could not lift his arm due to the pain....but with the extra pain meds he can move it. He had a CT scan this morning but the pacemaker interferes with the pictures and no one could see much of anything. They have decided he will have serial ultrasounds each day but I'm not sure why. They don't show a focal bleed but rather that he is bleeding diffusely all through the tissue. Since there is nothing to measure or quantify it will be hard to tell what has changed.

Home????? That's a good question. I was asked what I want to do and I said I want to go home – always…but certainly only if it is safe. Peter said he was not comfortable with discharge yet. He would like to see that he stops waking up each day worse than the day before. He always discharges Zach as soon as possible – well before any other physician would. So if he wants to keep Zach then I can only agree with that – knowing he would never do it unnecessarily. So my hope is that double dose factor 7a every 3 hours starting at 9 PM tonight will keep things at bay and we will be home soon.

His spirits are okay. He is tired but as always rarely complains. I could never be as brave as him.

He is working hard on algebra each day and reading his book for school. The rest we will have to catch up on later.

Grease Reality Show – they are picking the next Danny and Sandy to star on Broadway. Sunday nights: 7 PM central on NBC. Check out Max . He has my vote!

Thursday, February 22, 2007 10:27 PM

Still here in the hospital but discharge should be Friday. Zach's primary doctor is leaving town. Our hematologist is leaving town. I don't do hospital visits without them unless it is an emergency.

He still looks terribly swollen and there is blood that has collected throughout his left chest and upper arm. It is painful. There are hours we think it looks better and then a few hours later we think it looks worse. It also depends who is looking - seems everyone has a different opinion. However, I cannot complain at all about the care Zach has received. The doctors have been so careful with him and really not taking any chances at all. The nurses truly have a grueling schedule and somehow they have managed to stay on schedule and get everything into him that he needs. The blood center sent for more Factor 7a today so we should be all set to get through the next week. I think it is safe to say he has stressed the inventory but the blood center is so good about getting him what he needs and will have it all ready for discharge tomorrow.

In the hospital he has had IV lines in his arm which gives us an extra place to give his blood products. I won't have that at home which limits me to two places to infuse things and not enough hours. We had wondered about a second temporary central line to give him more access but it would have to be in his groin and I think that is asking for more trouble. His chest veins are taken up by the current central line and the pacemaker wires.

I'm a little overwhelmed thinking about what he will need when he comes home - there won't be more than 4 hours of sleep with the schedule he needs to be safe. We've also added the Factor 7a which will be every 4 hours, antimicrobials (too many times/day to count), cryo 2x/day and platelets daily...plus all his usual stuff. It 's not even worth counting all of his meds and drips when one word will suffice - A LOT. Keep thinking about Sam for my reality check.

AND ...it is just one week because unfortunately he will be readmitted on March 3rd (which again - unfortunately - happens to be 2 years to the day that Sammy passed away). Maybe it is a good thing that I have been so tired that it has not really sunk in yet. Or maybe it is simply that I realized last year that March 3rd is not necessarily any worse than any other day. Some days I miss Sam so much that it is like it happened yesterday and some days having that beautiful little boy in my life feels like a dream that I have woken up from and just cannot get back to... mostly I cannot bear to think that time continues to march on day after day taking me further from the time when he was with me. We change and he does not and I hate that.

Lately Zach has been prefacing his memories of Sam with "when Sam's body was alive." I really like that. It acknowledges that Sam as we knew him physically is not here anymore but Sam, the vivacious, mischievous almost 8 yr old little boy is still alive - the essence of Sam is living. Leave it to Zach to come up with a way to express what I have always wanted to communicate when talking about my Sam.

Thank you for all of the cards, presents and food....We are lucky to know so many wonderful people. Thank you also to all the people I work with who have been so good about picking up for me where ever or whenever they can these past 3 weeks.

Friday, February 23, 2007 10:02 PM

Zach woke up with a very swollen and hard left chest. The cardio vascular surgeon was summoned (I always know something is worrisome when the PA's call him to come up...and he comes quickly). He thinks Zach is bleeding under the pacemaker and this is pushing it up...REALLY pushing it up. Unfortunately this changed our schedule and now I get 3 hours of sleep instead of 4. But we got home about 6 PM and that's what matters. I'll watch him carefully and check his blood counts every day. I'm tired but I'm glad we're home.

Wednesday, February 28, 2007 7:19 AM

Sorry no update. I can't even describe how busy this house is right now with all of Zach's meds. The Sunday New York Times is still as it arrived on Sunday - untouched. It is my favorite part of Sunday so you know things are busy if I have not looked at it. However, I do admit to taking an hour to watch the Grease reality show with Abby on Sunday. Every time Zach talked we told him to be quiet…he left the room disgusted with us both.

From a bleeding perspective Zach was holding steady. Just a slight worsening (very subtle) on Monday but mainly no better - no worse. I was told he should start improving but that definitely is not the case. At any rate we held platelets last night -which I was completely comfortable with. As it turns out I don't think that was the thing to do. He woke up with a dramatically different looking chest. The pacemaker is pushed up even higher and there is more bruising. He does not have a fever but he is still on a zillion different antimicrobials.

The only thing we changed was taking away the platelets. I think it is a safe bet that the covering hematologist will reorder those today. He is still getting the Factor 7a every 4 hours. The incision still looks fine but I just don't think this is going in the right direction and it is fairly concerning to me. Thursday is 2 weeks since surgery so this is a pretty late problem. 7-10 days out is typically the time things get bad and by 2 weeks they begin to resolve. However, I do recall one of Sam's worst post-surgery bleeds was 2 weeks after surgery so maybe this is just a Zach-Sam thing.

Now from a non-bleeding perspective Zach is doing fantastic. His overall energy level has been phenomenal except for one day (Monday). I have to believe that some of that can be attributed to the bi-level ventilation he gets at night. He no longer has to work so hard to breathe all night –it forces air in and even breathes for him if his respiratory rate is too low. Tuesday he went to school and I sent him again today. Yes, he is bleeding but it is internal so not a danger to anyone else and he feels fine…I can't imagine making him stay home.

342

I'm sure some will think I am nuts to send him but sitting at home is not going to make him any better.

He did start building his Lego ship…with over 1000 pieces he has a LONG way to go. He is working on Darth Vader's head in ceramics class. In cooking he should be making muffins today. Normally he does not attend school on Wed because he has therapy. However, as I told his PT and OT –muffins won and they lost! But you know we love you Jackie and Chris!

Saturday, March 3, 2007 0:51 AM

Zachary is okay. We tried to reduce his Factor 7a and he re-bled. We increased the dose again tonight. It is after midnight - later this morning he will go into the hospital. I hope they can make the bleeding stop.

Today
It is March 3
It is shortly before 1 AM - the time when Sam left.
Two years since I held my Sam
I thought it would not be any worse than any other day
But I was wrong…all day I have re-traced my steps to this time and this date two years ago. There is nothing to describe these memories and the loss I feel each and every day. Back in November I gave a talk at the Children's Hospital Memorial Service. I will post it here. Still, there is so much unspoken and unsaid, so much that I will never be able to express about my little boy, the love he gave, the impact he had on me and the love I feel for him. If only that had been enough. I've made a new montage of Sam (end of book)--this time I had the courage to add his whole life and not just his first four years. He is such a beautiful, little boy.

Thank you to everyone who remembers Sam. Thank you for sharing your memories with me. I can never explain how much it means to me to hear people still say his name and to know that there are people that remember he was here. He was here and his life is precious.

Children's Hospital of Wisconsin Memorial Service

November 2006 --*by Anne Juhlmann*

I am Sam's mom.

Sam is the youngest of my four children and on March 3, 2005, when he was 7 years, 10 months and 21 days old, he died.

Sam is my tousled, blond haired, brown eyed little boy who loved super heroes, going to school, McDonald's french fries, being read to, dogs and playing with his siblings. He had this great big belly laugh and even now I can still hear and see it - and I smile.

I am Sam's mom.

I know that if anyone can understand how important it is for me to always be able to say these things it is the families of children who have passed away.

Like every parent who has lost a child, I felt that a piece of my heart was torn out on the night he died and at his funeral I felt that it was buried with him. That was 20 months ago and I still feel like a piece of my heart is gone.

So when I was asked to give a message of hope, I agreed but immediately felt inadequate. I don't have a prescription to take away your pain – let alone mine. What can I possibly say that will help? This past week someone answered that. He said, "You tell them that you cry every day and they will understand because they probably do too. But you are going forward -day by day. That is the hope."

In Longfellow's poem, "A Psalm of Life," he reminds us of the importance of leaving visible traces of our journey, even when it is filled with tears, so that perhaps another human being, feeling despair, may come upon our footprints -and perhaps take heart again. So here are my footprints. Thank you for your footprints. For all we can do is share our stories of learning to live through these unspeakable losses, to live in them and with them.

In the first days, weeks and months after Sam died the pain was physical, sharp, constant and like nothing I had ever felt. It was impossible to imagine that I would ever survive. Indeed, I was not sure I wanted to survive. The only thing that got me through that time period was to find a thread to hold me to Earth. For me it was my surviving children. I tried to focus on one task at a time. Wake up. Eat.

Take a shower. With each accomplished task I had faith that I might wake up, eat, and take a shower tomorrow.

If that is where you are now, keep holding fast to the thread that holds you to this Earth. Continue to wake up. Eat. Take a shower. And in time the thread holding you may feel more like a length of yarn and perhaps someday a strong cord.

For a long time I spent hour upon hour contemplating Sam's death. I searched for answers about why he had died, what was the cause, what did I do wrong, what was the meaning of his death? There was no shortage, of course, of people who offered explanations to me. They have probably offered them to you too.

Their words are meant to be helpful – but they are presumptuous. The words hurt and more than that, they are baffling. How can anyone be so certain that a child's death has some greater meaning to be found? To me, Sam's death felt senseless and no matter what my beliefs about where he had gone, where he is now, it is hard to feel that he should be anywhere but with me. There is nothing – no answer, no intellectual argument or belief and no explanation that can make this loss feel anything but total.

One day a friend of mine, a mother whose only two children have passed away, sent me something written by a Romanian Holocaust survivor. Paul Celan, wrote: "Rise up against multiple meanings. Trust the trail of tears and learn to live." It is folly to look for answers. All we can do as parents whose children have died is feel the grief and somehow learn to live with it. Perhaps that sounds hopeless but those words actually gave me hope…it made more sense to me that I should learn to live with my tears than to imagine that I would find an answer that would explain Sam's death.

And so I stopped trying to find meaning in Sam's death. That was hard… in putting some of the anger and the endless questions aside I felt as if I were betraying Sam. But a larger part of me wanted to honor my child's life and I knew that I could not do that if I was consumed by his death. So I took courage from other parents whose child had passed away – I stumbled forward and tried to learn how to live anew.

I thought that I could perhaps find a prescription for grief or better yet, a detour around the "trail of tears." I sunk all of my energy into collecting and trying to process every bit of information that I could

345

find on mourning and grief. To paraphrase a poem written by Emily Dickinson:

"I measured every grief I met
With analytic eyes
I wondered if it weighed like mine
'Or had an easier size..."

So when I read that some parents cleaned out their child's room a few months after their child's death, with analytic eyes, I wondered why 9 months later I still could not take Sam's clothes from his closet? When parents shared that they found comfort in giving their child's cherished items away I felt selfish for I could not bear to give even one of Sam's 152 stuffed dogs away to another child. And when I read the online journal of a mother that was still unable to go to the food store 6 months after her daughter died, I measured my grief against hers and wondered if I had loved my son less because I could shop.

Eventually I learned that our grief can only be our own. There is not a proven method, neither a detour nor a set of rules to follow, no universal timeline for anguish. The only thing that matters is that we do mourn, that we do shed our tears so that they do not drown us from the inside out.

Our hurt and pain as parents who have lost our child will be commensurate with the love we feel for them – it will never be bigger – and the story and meaning of our child's life will always be more powerful than the single event of their death.

On his death bed, the poet Ralph Waldo Emerson was heard to say "oh my beautiful boy." The beautiful boy Emerson lamented was his son who has passed away 40 years prior. In that one phrase - "oh my beautiful boy" – it is obvious that both his love for his son and his pain at losing him were intricately woven into every moment he lived, part of who he was until the very day he died. Like Emerson, it will take an entire lifetime to cry, to mourn and to miss our children– but also, an entire life to remember and be inspired by their lives.

In The Way the Crow flies, Ann Marie MacDonald tells us how important it is to nourish our memories.

"Tell the story.

Gather the events.
Repeat them.
Pattern is a matter of upkeep,
otherwise the weave relaxes the thread...
Repeat or the story will fall
Repeat -
and cradle the pieces carefully."

How do we cradle our child's memory? There is not one answer. I can only tell you what feels right for me and ask you to be true to what feels right for you.

Sometimes writing helps. I write down every memory I have of Sam. Part of this is to permanently record that my child did live. He was here. Part of it is that I know time fades memories and I am so afraid of forgetting. Sometimes all I can do is write down single words that remind me of him.

I have learned that it is vitally important to say our child's name and to talk about our child. At first, I desperately wanted to talk about Sam, but at the same time it hurt unbearably, for it seemed to underscore that he was not here anymore. But with time the telling has gotten easier and I feel I have grown from telling and that others have grown in listening. No matter how long or short your child lived - he has a story. Tell it so that we may listen and we all may grow.

Remember your child in ways that are meaningful to you - even if it is different than what others do. At the cemetery children who were buried after Sam have beautiful headstones while Sam's grave remains without one. It has not felt right for me to order his headstone just as it did not feel right to other parents to leave their child's grave without one. But a handmade, wooden cross is there, with a memorial garden filled with the things and colors that he loved. I tend to it with great care. This has been my way to tell the world – this child was loved – his life meant something. You will have your own ways.

Treasure the things that remind you of your child. In my house Super Hero action figures adorn some of my windowsills. I don't care anymore if someone thinks that is strange. Superman and Buzz Light Year are my treasures. I listen to music that my son liked and I hang his coat in the closet. I no longer think Sam is coming home but it reminds me of his joy, getting ready for school. You have and you will always have your own treasures that remind you of your child.

Continue to value the people that were a part of your child's life. Remind them of how they impacted your child and how in turn your child's life impacted another. This is how our children endure. On Sam's birthday we planted a tree at his school to bear witness to the fact that he had been there, the first graders had loved him and he had loved them back.

Trees, mementoes, shared stories, memories of our child's laughter or what it felt like to touch them - these are but a few of the many ways that our children remain alive. Not in a way that any of us would choose but alive all the same. Even though there will not be any new memories there will always be stories to tell, there will always be things that remind ourselves and others that our children were here and we are forever changed because of that. And when I tell my child's story and you tell your child's story, they become our shared stories. In this way our children not only touch our own lives but they touch everyone who hears their story.

Last week my older son's teacher, who never met Sam, said to Zach and me, "I just love that whenever you talk about Sam you wind up laughing." Then she laughed. Her words gave me hope and should give you hope that our children's lives can still have impact even though they have been cut short. The gift of their lives can still be shared and their presence still felt – even by those who never met our child

Yes, you and I would have planned it all differently if we were in charge, but, we were not. I only know that we miss our children so totally because our children loved us – and because we loved them – profoundly and entirely. Absolutely. That love was and is a gift. It has made us real and it will always be more powerful than death

In the beginning I said that I still feel as if a piece of my heart has been ripped out and it still hurts. This is true, but I know now that my heart piece is not in the grave. It went with Sam and in its place is a piece of his heart. Our children live on in our hearts and in the hearts of all those they touched. Every life that has been touched by our precious child in turn touches other lives. This is how our children endure.

Tuesday, March 6, 2007 12 AM

Zach is still inpatient. He was wheezing so bad this evening and said his throat hurt and he just was working so hard to breathe. We tried a breathing treatment and while it did not change things remarkably it seemed to help a little. They're going to try that every 4 hours to see if it helps while he has so much fluid in his body. If not they have a different medicine they can have him breathe in that might help.

We did get to play a game of Cheater today (a card game) and he won. Unfortunately we both fell asleep and missed seeing our friend Adam. Zach was sad about that.

Thank you to everyone who took the time to remember Sam. Hearing about how he is thought of or how his life impacted another is so meaningful to me and I store all of that in my heart. Saturday was hard but his nurses, who are Zach's nurses, were so wonderful about remembering him. Sam's Uncle Sean tells me that there was an orange moon on Saturday night. I have a view of the flight for life landing pad from my window so I missed the moon but loved hearing about it Thank You Sean! I have no doubt Sam colored the moon that night as he has colored and brightened every day of my life since before he was born. His Uncle David, who is a musician in NYC, played "You are my Sunshine" - Sam's favorite bedtime song - to his audience on Saturday night.

Saturday, March 10, 2007 10:24 AM

Zach and I are home from the hospital.

Even better news: when his pacemaker was interrogated on Thursday, the nurse told me the battery usually lasts 5-10 years. I had originally heard 3-5 years and focused on the 3 years, thinking we can NOT go through this again in 3 years. I know that seems far, far away but thinking of what Zach went through to get this pacemaker three years seemed round the corner and it scared me. But now I know it should be a much longer time before we have to replace it.

Zach ended up gaining 6 kg which, for all you non-metric system people, is 13.2 pounds. Even my pants would be tight with an extra 13 pounds so imagine that on a 34 kg kiddo. It's hard to move, breathe

349

or talk. It is all due to fluid overload. I think I've explained this before but if a heart does not pump fluid (blood) very well then even 300 ml extra a day is going to stress the heart out. He was getting at least a liter of fluid extra each day when on the blood products and antibiotics and after awhile his heart got tired. The kidneys are stupid enough to think they need to hang on to more fluid than they should when this happens. Everything swells, including his airway, so it is hard to breathe. Hence the breathing treatments every 4 hours, extra diuretics and doubling of his newest cardiac drip.

Now home he is starting to do better and his weight is coming down. I can see his eyes and his arms are thin again! Yesterday he still needed breathing treatments every 4 hours but I doubt he will today – I bet we can just do them as needed, rather than scheduled.

Zach made a comment to Brittany that he was sick because his heart is wimpy. I told him he has one of the strongest hearts I have ever met. All my kids do. Heart failure certainly has multiple meanings: Although physically, Zach has heart failure, in all ways that count he does not have failure of the heart – not in the least.

Brittany is home for spring break. You may recall that a few months ago I alluded to the fact that I had made plans for a grand NYC vacation. We were scheduled to leave for NYC on Sunday for a week. But then the last 5-6 weeks happened, none of which I could have predicted – and finally on Thursday it was clear to me that it was very unsafe to go anywhere. Zach really needs the resources we have here: a courier that is available 24 hrs/day, a lab staff that will run his labs stat and fax the results to me quickly, a home care company that will get us whatever we need, a blood bank that will let us infuse blood products at home....he's just not at a place where we can get away without the people/organizations that make it so possible for Zach to be at home. We're all sad but the people with the best attitudes are the 3 kids. Brittany just wanted to come home and see her sister and brother. Abby says it is okay. And Zach said we can have vacation at home. That comment reminded me of when we could no longer travel to the beach in the summer with Sam. Sam said, "Mama, I thought of how we can get to the beach for vacation – we'll just close our eyes and imagine we are there."

I hope there will be another time when we can travel - Zach certainly has his periods of stability and it is a matter of picking the right time frame to plan a vacation and hoping nothing happens. Too bad vacations require so much planning because it would be a lot better if we could just pick up and leave without taking the oxygen, refrigerator, monitors and other equipment and meds. If we could take the lab, home care company and blood bank - even better and if his doctor and nurses came we'd be all set. Maybe I should just buy one of those huge campers and load everyone and everything in it– but somehow driving that in NYC does not seem to be a good idea. At any rate, I doubt we can get the money back from the Broadway tickets and the airplane tickets but more and more I realize how meaningless money really is when compared to a life.

So big plans for the weekend include hanging Zach out to dry some more, unpacking from too many hospitalizations (I have yet to unpack from the one back in early February), watching Max win on *Grease*), returning my very overdue books to the library…want me to go on and on? Zach continues to work on his Lego ship…pictures will be forthcoming. In addition he had to make up a recipe for a sandwich for cooking class with a SECRET ingredient (I think he may have told all the nurses his secret though). He was taking orders for the sandwich at the hospital. He is very hopeful that he will be back at school with his ceramic Darth Vader on Monday. Last night he spent a lot of time sketching dragons. He did a very nice job until he fell asleep with the pencil in his hand. That was before he had a huge bowl of Choc chip cookie dough frozen custard which Grandpa Frank brought over. Grandpa told the kids that it was just fine to have frozen custard for dinner so we did. Sure beats cooking!

Sunday, March 11, 2007 1:11 AM

I've been sleeping on Sam's bed to be close…good grief there are a lot of dogs on that bed! Worried for my oldest son and missing my littlest.

Monday, March 12, 2007 8:47 PM

Kidney function was a bit better Sun PM and then a bit worse today now that he is on all day TPN…but not as bad as Saturday. I think his kidneys need a break. He is breathing better and hopes to go

351

to school tomorrow. He still has some of the fluid weight gain but I think if we get him a hair cut, that alone will take off a few pounds :-) Brittany is home and that is wonderful! And Max is still in the running for *Grease* on Broadway. Now what could be better than that? Oh I know - the sandwiches that Zach had to make a recipe for in school - the ones that I promised, in a weak moment, to serve for dinner one night this week. Picture this: double decker sesame bread with peanut butter, jelly, jalapeño peppers, turkey, cheddar cheese, pepperoni and a secret ingredient. Anyone want to come to dinner this week? We'll have some extra spots at the table because everyone else has suddenly developed plans.

Friday, March 16, 2007 10:15 PM

I read Zach all the comments about his sandwich and he smiled…your collective reaction is exactly the reaction I think he was hoping for. As for dinner, I have been working on him all week and think I am getting close to making an agreement with him: 2 different sandwiches – with the understanding that PB & J do not go on the same piece of bread as meat and cheese.

Zach only went to school one day this week. He really misses working on his Darth Vader project but simply has not felt well enough to go to school. I used to value academic success so much. What a stupid and arrogant prejudice on my part. Now, I simply want him to be at school for social reasons. I want him to finish Darth Vader, I want him to cook something in class, I want him to see Clark and Michael at lunch and I want him to joke with his teachers…I really don't care about the rest. Oh yes – learning is important – but the reality is I have learned more from Zach than I ever learned in school.

This has been a tremendously sad few weeks. After a while, it is hard to know what – if anything – to write. I feel as if the ups and downs that go with chronic illness have been transformed in the last 2 months into an out of control train ride that is heading towards the edge of the promontory. I look ahead and fear we are about to be plunged off into the ocean. And then there will be moments – Tuesday morning, Wed morning…. when things seem to be improving and I think that maybe this time we will round the corner. How do you "update" anyone when life is like that – "he's good," "he's not good," "he's a bit better," "he's a lot worse"…I am forever trying to emotionally catch up with where he is -- how can I expect anyone else to keep up? When he gets worse, it takes me a while to "get it" and then when he improves, I'm still reeling from when he was worse, trying to find my hope and my perspective.

This is nothing new or unique – every family with a child with chronic illness feels this. What is new is that the times when we just slowly clip along on an even track before and after the hills have all but disappeared. So let me just say that it is very hard to see my child slip away piece-by-piece, day-by-day, week after week. I tremendously resent how I lost Sam – without a chance to even catch my breath or hold his hand. He just slipped away when I blinked one night and I feel cheated that there was never a good bye. But this is not any better. It's not news that my heart is broken - but lately I wonder that there could be anything left to hurt or break. When is a heart so broken that it stops beating?

He has been sleeping lot, cannot walk or even stand-alone and I have not heard him laugh in a few days. He has periods of disorientation – he fell last night trying to get out of bed in the middle of the night (climbed right over the bed rail). Tonight he is very hypothermic even with heated blankets, his kidneys remain compromised and his lungs don't sound good. Yet, when I ask, he can do the math to tell me it is one month and 4 days until his 15th birthday (April 20th). He did a little schoolwork today with Donna, (in between naps) and he discussed the latest Star Wars news from his magazine with me. The respiratory therapist came over to bring some equipment for Brittany, shook Zach's hand and called Z a celebrity – quick as fire, Zach shot back "Well maybe my celebritiness will wear off on you!" That is MY Zachary.

I have enjoyed having Brittany home, though I know this is hard for her. We have watched a few movies together (I NEVER sit down and watch movies) and yesterday I let Abby take time from school and the 3 of us went shopping. I admit a reluctance to leave the house unless it is for work (and even then it is hard, despite liking the work I do). Chris, Zach's home nurse, practically pushed me out the door (Nicely) and I think it was good she did. So much for home cooking – poor girl has had take out all week. Both girls have been helping Zach with homework and other things. I am so thankful for my girls.

I don't deserve to have 4 wonderful children but I do and I am thankful.

Happy Saint Patrick's Day – which is also my grandmother's birthday – one of my most favorite people in all the world. Happy birthday to Katie K. – seven years old tomorrow! Happy Samuel Patrick's Day as well –I hope you all celebrate the holiday Sam assumed was made for him.

Please keep my dear friend Kathy's 7-month old, infant daughter, Anna, in your hearts. Anna had neuro-surgery today to clear out an infection in her brain. Anna was born with many medical problems and that she would have one more, completely unrelated thing, crop up seems beyond unfair to me. I have known Kathy since our boys – Alex and Sam – were babies. I only get to see her once every few years but she has always been there when I need her. So her littlest, Anna, is heavy on my heart tonight.

Please keep a friend in your heart with 2 young boys and a husband who is terminally ill. They are a loving, family – desperately hurting. The courage and hope they have had in the last few years is rare and beautiful.

Kiss your kids, hug them close and memorize their faces…don't ever take the gifts that come with our children for granted.

P.S. I have been slowly reading a book, written by Anderson Cooper (CNN)called *Dispatches from the Edge: A Memoir of War, Disasters, and Survival*. It is beautiful and poignant - it gets my highest recommendation.

Wednesday, March 21, 2007 10:43 PM

First off – I am a little overwhelmed with all of the guest book entries. When I read a few days' worth of entries this morning it truly was a "stunned by kindness" moment. I don't know what to say except thank you. That my children are loved and cared for – even by those who have never met us is truly a gift. That Sammy's life continues to touch others and make a difference touches my heart beyond anything words can describe. Saturday was by far the saddest, bleakest day I have had since the day Sam died. I don't want to even remember it much less share the specifics – it was just a devastating day. But then the sun began to peek out a bit from the clouds on Sunday. I have no doubt it is because a world of people love and care for Zach and keep him close in thought, prayer and heart. Thank you.

And now on to a day in the life:

Remember the disorientation and subsequent fall out of bed the other night? Can someone tell me why I did not immediately wonder if he had a bleed in his knee when he could not walk? He is a bleeder, after all. But my attention was focused on his bones and I was just relieved he did not appear to have broken a bone. I figured him not walking was related to his neurological status. He did not complain of pain until Tuesday. Then again he did not do much weight bearing until Tuesday morning. Zach saw the hematologist today and he has a knee bleed. He is back on daily cryo and platelets - we will take it a few days at a time. Hopefully he will be able to walk again without pain soon. The cryo and platelets should help. Our blood bank friends got everything ready likity split so I already have both products in him for the night.

It gets better – Dr. S (the hematologist) ordered an x-ray of Zach's knee just to make sure it was not a fracture. We really did not think it was but better to be safe than sorry. Another doc friend looked at the x-ray for me right after it was taken and said, "well it's not broken but has he always had the bright white streak across the knee?" I said in my most intelligent voice, "Um – I don't know." I did go on to explain in the same intelligent tone that we don't ever x-ray his knees and to ask what I think is an intelligent question: "am I supposed to care that he has a white streak on his knee?" Apparently so since the radiologists and this doctor have only seen it with lead poisoning. Are you kidding? Has he been ingesting paint from 1962 when I'm not looking? Only Zach.

As it turns out I sent in a lead level tonight and the awesome lab staff ran it pretty quickly and he does not have a high lead level. So what does this mean? I don't know but I would bet it is some other heavy metal that he is toxic on. Such as aluminum....he's had high levels for over a year. They bounce around from a minor elevation to what seems like a moderately high elevation but what do I know - toxicology has not thought the levels are high enough to warrant attention. So we'll need to look into that. After thinking about it, he

355

had a knee bleed in Jan 2005 so they would have x-rayed then. Let's hope it was the same knee so we can compare the films.

Kidneys are still giving him trouble. Once his doc is back in town next week we are going to have to look at this closely. There is a pattern to it all that I can see - I just do not understand what it means. They work at night and do not work every other day between the hours of 8 am and 10 PM. Nothing gets through those kidneys during that time period. I am dead serious and I am also convinced it has to mean something to someone. It is a huge issue because he cannot get rid of drugs that need to be excreted. They build up and his neurological state deteriorates.

Zach went to school for 2 classes and lunch today. I don't think he was too awake but perhaps it was a start and tomorrow will be better. That is my hope and prayer. I have included his recipes below. Honestly, they ended up quite good. He made them and I took pictures but poor kiddo has absolutely no memory of making them. To all of us nay-sayers (me included) I want you to know that when I shopped for his ingredients I saw things like "Jalapeno jelly" and when trying to figure out some spices for the wraps we saw a recipe for "peanut butter, pepperoni and jalapeno pizza." Apparently there are others with Zach's taste buds in this world.

...And MAX is in the finals of the *Grease* reality show. Max always wears orange - how can I not like someone who loves orange? Even Zach paid attention this week when Max told the audience that as a child he had a stroke and had to re-learn to eat, smile, sing, talk, etc. Abby is already bugging me to buy tickets to see Max on Broadway this summer – assuming he wins.

Ok - here they are. I honestly liked the PB and pineapple one.

Spicy peanut butter and pineapple sandwich

Ingredients
Tortillas
Spicy Peanut butter
  --Chili sauce
  --ginger
  --cayenne pepper
  --garlic

356

--creamy peanut\butter
Crushed pineapples
Butter
secret ingredient

1. Mix the spicy peanut butter ingredients. Put just a dash of the spices if you do not like things spicy.
2. Spread spicy peanut butter spread down the middle of the tortilla
3. Drain the pineapples really well
4. Spread crushed pineapples on top of peanut butter
5. Roll the tortilla up. *Z-master suggestion* – roll all the ends in so that the ingredients do not come out.
6. Melt butter and secret ingredient in the frying pan
7. Add Tortillas and lightly brown
8. Serve with pineapple juice as a drink

Spicy Meatball Sandwiches

Ingredients
6 inch sub rolls
Italian meatballs from freezer section of store
2 jars Ragu Marinara sauce
1-2 tbsp Hot red pepper
1 tbsp Garlic
"secret ingredient"
shredded mozzarella cheese

1. Meatballs
a. Put marinara sauce in crock pot
b. Add red pepper and garlic
c. Add meatballs
d. Cook for a few hours
2. Split rolls in half
3. Put meatballs in rolls. *Z-master suggestion* – cut meatballs in half so they don't roll out of the rolls.
4. Put secret ingredient on top of meatballs
5. Put shredded cheese on top of meatballs

6. Wrap each sandwich in tin foil and put in over for 10 minutes at 350 degrees until cheese melts.

Serve with Habanera Doritos. Add more hot pepper if you like it spicy or some jalapeno peppers.
Z-master suggestion: serve with lots of water.

Monday, March 26, 2007 11:33 PM

We had a much better weekend than last weekend. Zach was able to enjoy building with his Legos, reading and even doing a bit of school work, (which he enjoyed with Donna – not his mother!). A week ago things felt so dismal. But once again Zach rallied. And I am ever so thankful. It would be impossible for me to express the place we were in a week ago and where we are now and all the feelings in between. All I know if life is a miracle and a gift.

The weekend brought beautiful warm weather to Wisconsin. Warm and sunny. We had the windows open all day today, though it feels chilly now. I changed the things at Sammy's grave - reindeer and snowmen will get washed and bunnies and dogs sitting in a big orange boat have replaced them. It's a little "loud" with flowers and wind chimes and of course Buzz Light Year with his side kick Curious George guarding it all. But it is Sam. I miss him and miss him…

I am so very proud of Zach right now. I started talking with him about pain medicine last week. I suppose it could be viewed as a sad conversation because we discussed that maybe the pain control goal has to be different. Maybe it cannot be that he will have no pain but rather pain that he can live with. But truly – the conversations we have had are positive and empowering for Zach. We have talked about the fact that it is so important that he not be in pain and his doctors and I support him using whatever amount of pain medicine he needs to be able to participate in life and enjoy what he does. However, that may be a different amount than what is needed to completely get rid of pain. The problem with the goal of completely getting rid of pain is that it does not let him participate in life any more than having pain does if it takes so much medicine that he cannot do what he wants to do. We talked about how pain has begun to take over his life and really – who does pain think he/she is that it can tell Zach Juhlmann how to live his life? So here we are a week later and he is using 50% of what he used last week, despite the fact that his back is still broken and his knee is still hurt. It's a learning process for me just as much as for him and I am trying to be careful not to ever communicate that he should bear the unbearable. But wow – what a great job he is doing! I don't know that many could accomplish what he has in one week.

Kidney function is still bizarre. It's terrible and then adequate. Bizarre. That's what everyone says so at least we all agree. It has become clearer to me in talking with his doctor that the kidneys are really okay in and of themselves. There is not irreversible damage yet. They don't function secondary to a very poorly functioning heart. Ok, so that is not the best news but really – we have known that for some time.

His knee still hurts a lot and he has just had terrible pain walking even a few steps. He has been getting cryo every day. I did not give it tonight and need to call the hematologist tomorrow.

April Fools' Day is fast approaching. Zach is very excited for the big day! He will be admitted that day so Abby thinks she is free and clear. She forgets that he will still be home until about 9 am. That is plenty of time to play a few pranks on his little sister. He wants to make a list of things to do to the nurses.

Zucchini bread – that's what they're cooking in Foods and People tomorrow. I hope Zach and Abby bring some home for me!

AND – in case you have not heard – MAX and Laura won and will star on Broadway in the show *Grease*!

Saturday, March 31, 2007 9:37 PM

Zach has lost quite a few pounds -which is actually wonderful news. His weight had been the lowest since before Christmas until his mom had the brilliant idea today to give ½ dose of one of his diuretics. (I thought he was dry – I was wrong!) . Oh well, he is still much less bloated than a few weeks ago which makes it easier for his heart. And I will just leave well enough alone from now on. We plan to cut his fluids even more when he is admitted to the hospital Sunday in an attempt to hopefully prevent the inflammation/fluid retention that comes with the IVIg. I hope this plan works. The pictures above are from last weekend - he is working on the infamous Lego ship he had

359

to have. I did not realize how puffy he looked in those sandwich-making pictures from Samuel Patrick's Day until I looked at them again this week. I still do love those pictures, however, because they show how he was putting every ounce of effort into making those sandwiches.

He/we had some surprise visitors this week. My sister (Aunt Maribeth) was here for a few days. I have been pretty sick so on Thursday they made spicy chili (the spices did not exactly do it for my sore throat) and zucchini bread. The bread has been great! I could eat 5 loaves of it so I hope he makes it for me again. My Dad (Gramps) visited for a few hours on Saturday. Frank (Grandpa) brought over more frozen custard on Tuesday.

This week the pacemaker has been put to work. I am not sure why his heart rate dropped for a few nights but I am relieved it seems to work well. It does not let his heart beat any less than 60 beats/minute. When he is in the hospital we will "interrogate" the pacemaker to see the information. Doesn't that make you laugh – who ever came up with the phrase "interrogating the pacemaker?"

Tomorrow Zach goes into the hospital. He has a lot of schoolwork to do and I am really excited, (he is not!), because he is learning about the body systems, vitamins, types of nutrients and the first 6 presidents. This is my kind of stuff so he is going to get lots done!

I have not been well all week and still feel pretty awful so this will be the extent of the update. I do want to paste in some words from Elizabeth Edwards from her *60 Minutes* interview. No matter where one is on the political spectrum – these are words we can all learn from. What an amazing woman!

03/25/07 Elizabeth Edwards on the return of her cancer:
You know, you really have two choices here. I mean, either you push forward with the things that you were doing yesterday or you start dying. That seems to be your only two choices. If I had given up everything that my life was about – first of all, I'd let cancer win before it needed to. You know, maybe eventually it will win. But I'd let it win before I needed to.

And I'd just basically start dying. I don't want to do that. I want to live. And I want to do the work that I want next year to look like last year and... and the year after that and the year after that. And the only way to do that is to say I'm going to keep on with my life.

360

Thursday, April 5, 2007 12:23 PM

Zach has had a quieter admission than the past few. I forgot what that could be like. I am not feeling good yet and I seem to have passed this on to Zach now. What a great mom! Hopefully, his will not linger or be as bad given he has just gotten IVIg. I think we'll go home Friday night.

He did have a kidney ultrasound. It had definitely changed since a year ago. The read says that he has "resistance" in the renal arteries. "What does this mean?" you ask...it means he has "medical renal disease." Medical renal disease is code for "something is wrong with his kidneys and it is not structural. Don't you just love medical language? They have all these fancy terms for saying "something is wrong but we don't know what."

I talked with the toxicologist. What a nice guy and I really like that he is not interested in testing Zach for every known possibility under the sun. The "lead lines" are not lead lines of course, given he has an undetectable lead level. Basically, there are only a few metals that have been known to do that. We could test for them but unless he has been under attack from terrorists, it is unlikely he has an accumulation of these metals. I don't think we've been under attack so we agreed to forego that evaluation. Potentially it is from his Pamidronate (the drug used to help keep calcium in his bones). The question is whether or not this is pathological (something is wrong and we need to do something) or just an incidental finding that means nothing. We think it means nothing. The Tox did say Zach has the most impressive x-rays he has ever seen - a medical student could pick out the "lines" where his growth plates are. Part of this, sadly, is due to the fact that Zach's bones have such a dull, washed out look from losing calcium that the bright white looks that much brighter in contrast. Healthy bones are white - not washed out and transparent looking like his are.

He is walking a bit better with the walker. It is such hard work but every day he gets a little stronger and more balanced. We are going to need to make a lot of modifications soon in our house. This has become clear to me. I think the carpet needs to come out of some rooms so the walker moves more easily. We need ramps, he needs railings in the bathroom and most of all I think we are pretty close to needing to build a first floor bedroom and bathroom. I am little and when I am alone it is getting almost impossible for me to help him get upstairs. Not sure where the money will come for all of this. But it is close to not being a choice so we need to work on this.

Easter should be quiet. We thought Brit could come home but it will not work out for her. My brother and his wife will come for dinner but other than that it is just us. That's ok – quiet is good sometimes.

Zach and I were laughing about Sam this morning. When he was little we told him that shut up was a bad word (which it is). Well, after that, if he was really mad at the kids he'd say, "you are a shut up!" I always tried not to laugh - I know I should have been the mature parent. But it was hysterical because he thought he was giving the worst insult to them. Fortunately he never said it to anyone outside our family. Then if I told him he needed to go into time out he'd say "GREAT - because I LOVE time out!" I am quite sure it was this defiant spirit that kept him alive for so long. It never bothered me... it was something I always loved about him. His reactions were always so real. I like to think that even if he learned some social niceties as he got older than he would have kept the realness - it is one of the most endearing things about him and part of what made him Sam.

Friday, April 6, 2007 10:23 PM

Zach and I had a wonderful surprise visit today from Kyle's family – all the way from Ohio. Kyle is a little boy who is all about living life to the fullest. He had a Mito disease and passed away in December. Before he passed away he used to make his mom buy Buzz Light year items for me so that I would know Sam is with me. (This is a child that is a year younger than Sam). Today we were laughing about Kyle's strong will. Several years before he passed away he had a horrible infection and was left with double amputations of his legs and he also lost his thumbs. But you know - the kid loved his Nintendo gadgets - Gameboy and Gamecube. He taught himself how to play those without his thumbs. That is what so many of these children are like. They have such a strong desire to live and enjoy life and like Elizabeth Edwards said of her cancer - they are not about to let Mito win before it needs to. If we could all live life like these children the world would be a much better place!

362

Anyway - we're home. Looking forward to dying some Easter eggs tomorrow - lots of orange ones for my Sam.

Wednesday, April 11, 2007 11:21 PM

Zach is doing great. He is doing amazing in every way – except he still has the *(*&%^ virus his mom gave him! And she still has it too – the never ending virus that just keeps going. He's required breathing treatments every 3-4 hours when awake. Fortunately the BiPAP machine that helps him breathe at night allows me a break from giving those treatments at 3 am.

I want to share one story tonight. I was sitting in our library room on Tuesday and I heard a sound that was vaguely familiar. I realized it was the wheels of a rolling backpack. For a split second I thought "here comes my Sam," because Sam always came crashing into rooms like a whirlwind with all 12 of his IV pumps crammed into his big blue backpack on wheels. But of course, that split second ended and I knew it could not be Sam. Before I could feel the devastation of that realization – which still has the capacity to shock me - I turned around and saw that the sound was Zach.

Zach! Zach and his IV pumps in his rolling backpack! Zach who has not walked independently in I don't know how long. He was not teetering off balance. He was not disoriented and unaware that he should not be doing that. He was just walking as if he does it every day. In fact when I looked at him in awe he looked at me with a teenager expression of "What in the world is your problem?" Since then he has been walking all over the house. He gets his own snack. He gets up when he wants a book or a game. And I am not in the least concerned about it because he is steady and perfectly fine.

I don't think most of the world can appreciate that the sound of backpack wheels has the capacity to bring me to tears. The sound of those wheels makes me believe in miracles. The sound of those wheels brings me hope. Such a simple thing but I never thought I would hear that sound again unless it was me pulling the backpack for him.

I share this story for all of you who love Zach and have hurt so much at seeing how hard things have been for him since Christmas. If I could put a movie on here I would. I'd send it to his 4th floor nurses who know how it took 3 people last week to help him walk (and he had a walker too!). I'd send it to his doctors – especially Peter - who never stops trying to make a difference for Zach. I'd send it to his home care company, to his PT and OT and everyone else who participates in his care at the hospital, to school, to our family, to our friends, to the world...

I understand it may not last and tomorrow may bring something different. I understand that he will surely have days he cannot walk or needs help to even stand. But I will always treasure the sound that those backpack wheels made yesterday, today and hopefully will make many more days in his life

Monday, April 16, 2007 10:57 PM

Things are good...busy but good. Friday is Zach's 15th birthday and he is really excited. We have family coming for the big event and Zach has lots of other little things planned. Birthdays are such wonderful celebrations.

Like most of America, we are so saddened by the murders in Virginia. I cannot help but immediately relate to the parents and my heart hurts thinking about so many who woke up with their children here on Earth...and now life has changed permanently. I remember that instant of knowing that Sam left. Sam was only 7 and not yet in college...but the feelings are the same. It is not a feeling that anyone should know. I think about my own daughter at her university ...some, if not all, of those shot were just kids like her. Children died today and their parents' lives will never be the same. It makes everything else seem trivial doesn't it?

And yet I am chastened by my own lukewarm response to the initial report of one student dying. It came through as a CNN bulletin and I deleted the email and continued to work at my desk. It was only when the numbers were 10 and then 20 and then the horrifying 33 that I paid attention. The fact remains that initially one person died....a person who was someone's child, someone's friend, someone's student. One is not any better than thirty three. Every life is precious and not quantifiable. Although, I know people die every second of every day and we cannot possibly mourn them all, I wish there was a way we could pay proper tribute to the mark that each life has made and left. Perhaps the only way is to continue to value life, knowing

364

that those who died today would give anything if they could have one more day; their families wish for even one more hour.

This brings me back to Zach. He is doing well. He made banana bread in school today. He stayed for ALL of his class periods for the first time in many months. He read a book tonight and did not fall asleep. He walked up three stairs and back down again. He designed a car on lego.com. I have been hearing his backpack wheels all weekend. And... he will be fifteen on Friday. I do not take any of that for granted.

April 20, 2007, 0:49 AM

HAPPY 15TH BIRTHDAY ZACHARY

Your birthday is such a special day to me because it is the first day I got to hold you and see you. I remember the day you were born so clearly. You were such a beautiful baby boy and I could not believe how lucky I was to have you. I remember how proud Brittany was to finally be a big sister –she loves you so much. I cannot imagine what our family would have been like without you. I cannot imagine the person I would be if I had not had you to learn from. Thank you for being you. I love you more than you can imagine.

P.S. I think that every breeze we feel tomorrow will be Sam practicing to blow out your candles. He never could let any of us have a birthday without being right in there and pretending it was his too. I know he will be with you every second of the day tomorrow – celebrating his best brother and the time and love you have always given to him.

Z is for your infamous self-introduction, "I am ZACHARY Ryan Juhlmann the one and only" and truly, you are the one and only. Z is also for your ZESTFULLNESS.

A - I am AMAZED with your ARTISTIC ABILITY. Your AWESOME ATTITUDE is ASTONISHING. I ADMIRE it endlessly and truly feel AWE when I think of ALL you have ACHIEVED.

C is for your CURIOSITY about so much that I have ceased to question. I enjoy the COMIC relief you bring to each day with your wonderful sense of humor. You are COURTEOUS and CONSIDERATE of others. Your COURAGE gives me courage.

H is for your HAPPINESS that shines through even during the hardest times. You never lose HOPE. Your HONESTY is refreshing. you are always so quick to offer your HELP. Having you as my son is an HONOR and one of my greatest gifts.

A is for your ANTICIPATION of APRIL FOOL'S DAY, and your APPRECIATION of the simplest things in life.

R is for REAL– you never pretend to be someone or something other than your RARE and REMARKABLE self.

Y is for YOU - wonderful, kind, funny, talented, courageous, hopeful, best brother and ever so unique. You are truly Zachary Ryan Juhlmann, the one and only, and I love YOU immensely!

Monday, April 23, 2007 10:30 PM

Thank you for all of the wonderful wishes, visits, phone calls, gifts, cards and specially made food for Zachary's birthday. He had a wonderful day. Donna came by in the morning and they played educational games in place of formal school. She also brought homemade guacamole, homemade Oreo cookies (to die for) and ice cream.

Next came Miss Nancy (music teacher) and the beautiful Miss Nina and baby Jenna with a Coldstone creamery concoction that Zach ordered. Given he ordered it I can pretty much guarantee that no one will be eating it (mint choc chip with graham crackers, Oreo cookies, cookie dough, strawberries, caramel and maybe something else but not sure).

Adam and Elizabeth stopped by and caught up on all the Spiderman III news (I'm still trying to get over this storyline of Spiderman going bad…. Can't he just kiss the girl, get married and forget about superhero stuff?)

Finally, at night we had our family party with multiple family members (who else would be at a family party) Interspersed through

366

the day were deliveries, phone calls and all the wonderful email and guest book messages.

Thank you to each and every person who celebrated Zach's birthday - here or in your heart.

Friday, April 27, 2007 1:00 PM

Zach remains relatively well (I think parents of kids with chronic illness and disability could come up with their own theory of relativity – though Einstein might not approve).

He had a reaction to his blood transfusion this week. I give him an adult unit split into three small pediatric units over three days. All three units are from the same donor. At any rate, he had one pediatric unit Monday – no problems. Tuesday he had the second unit – no problems. Wednesday he had a very small amount of blood and very quickly he said "I feel funny." I stopped the blood immediately because nurses learn early on in their career that when patients say they feel funny it is wise to pay attention. He described that his jaw felt "very tight" and "like it fell asleep" and "difficulty breathing." Ok - that's enough description for me – I ran down and got his meds. His temp went up one degree within 10 minutes from pre- blood temp. I medicated him with IV steroids and benadryl and within 5 minutes life was good again.

His doctor and I agreed that it might be considered pretty stupid to give the blood at that point. The odd thing to me is that he was perfectly fine with part one and part two from the * same donor.* His doctor said that he probably was getting increasingly sensitized those nights to some antigen in the blood and then finally Wednesday he reacted within minutes. It ended up not being a big deal in terms of his health and safety but it may mean he needs blood more exactly matched to him. The blood bank is doing some testing on the donor blood and Zach's blood and urine. Blood is always matched according to blood type and Rh factor …but there are additional and specific ways blood can be matched for kids who get a lot of transfusions and build up antibodies to donor blood. I worry about donor issues as this was huge for Sam with his platelets…but then again Sam ALWAYS had his platelets because the donors were so dedicated to giving. People who we never met, and yet they did this.

367

In the last two weeks he has attended school 6 days – 100% of his scheduled days. It may be a record for 2007. We have decided to meet before school ends to discuss additional goals for him. That way, things will be in place for September. These would be very functional, real world goals looking at some of the skills we ALL need to work on in becoming better adults. For example: how do we communicate better, consider other perspectives, engage other people in conversations, listen instead of thinking about what we want to say, stay on topic etc. I happen to think that some of the presidential candidates in both the Republican and Democratic parties ought to work on the same things. The debate last night on MSNBC was good but so funny too – talk about not listening to the question and answering with something completely unrelated! Maybe Zach can give them some tips by the time we enter the peak season in 2008. On a side note…it is so fun to have the debates beginning.

Zach tells me he has finished the ceramic Darth Vader. It is apparently so big that it had to be "baked" in pieces. I wondered if he was entertaining adding it to my family room décor but he tells me it will go in his bedroom. Too bad!

I am pretty overwhelmed with quite a few work projects and presentations and on top of that there is a huge health insurance problem for Zach – once again. I should not say more than that until we know all of the facts – and finding the facts is a bit like investigative journalism at the moment. And maybe that is exactly what needs to happen – true investigative journalism. Suffice it to say that this is consuming time and energy and causing sleepless nights.

Sam's birthday is coming up - May 9th

Tuesday, May 1, 2007 2:20 PM

By the time we got to the hospital on Sunday, Zach was very unsteady and weak with walking. His labs were goofy and he had blurry vision and was seeing "little flashing lights." The only thing I was glad about was that all of this started before he had a drop of IVIg. That makes it clearer that the IVIg, while perhaps making him feel worse, is not the cause of this. Monday he could not walk and we started him back on antibiotics by 5 PM. Today he is still quite weak, has the fixed and dilated pupils and cannot stay awake. I hope that once he has had the antibiotics for 24-48 hours he will show signs of improvement like he typically does. It is always so hard to see him like this - heart breaking really. I also wish the inpatient staff could see him at his best so that they know he is not like this day in, day out. I tell them but that is not the same as seeing it.

Due to his blurry vision I have been reading his book for language arts with him: The Watsons go to Birmingham. Though I am sorry he cannot see right now, it has been fun reading it together. Previously he found the book boring but with us reading together he laughs and enjoys it. That is so nice to see.

Friday, May 4, 2007 10:39 PM

We're home. Zach is ok. He remains on IV antibiotics and will for another 10 days. It took a full 48 hours for the antibiotics to help but now he can walk and hold his head up and carry on a conversation. His pupils are not fixed and dilated and he can read and watch TV again. I wish I understood why he so completely neurologically decompensates and why he responds to the antibiotics. But I am glad he does. Long-term I am not sure what this means.

We are trying a new thing with him – thickening all of his fluids, making them all very very cold and having him only drink with a straw. He has been choking on liquids more and more and probably aspirating some into his lungs considering the chronic changes on his chest x-rays. It is just not safe. Today, Katherine, Sam's speech therapist, worked with Zach to make a smoothie of apple juice, raspberry yogurt and a banana. It ended up working well and he really liked it. I think this will be ok –Zach loves to "cook" and we can probably find all kinds of smoothie recipes for him to make himself. Hopefully, none will involve red pepper or jalapeno peppers. If you have any favorite smoothie recipes let us know. I am going to start a little recipe book for Zach so he can plan out his menu each week and shop for the ingredients.

I am so relieved to have a weekend without any major projects due for work. The last few weekends have been so busy. Of course those were the two beautiful weekends we had. I think it is supposed to rain this weekend…but it's ok.

In a perfect world I'd be in Toronto right now with Mary and John for the Pediatric Academic Society meeting where our poster is being presented about the resident training. Unfortunately it is going to take a lawyer to get me a passport. My name is apparently not Anne Juhlmann according to the government. It is still Anne Fischer. The problem is that all of my ID, my bank accounts and even my name at work are Anne Juhlmann. Yet the federal government says my maiden name is still my legal name. Initially they basically accused me of stealing my own social security number and identity. I got some pretty nasty letters from the IRS about this. This first came up a few years ago and once, I talked with them we agreed I could just use my maiden name on tax returns and it would be ok. It never occurred to me it would prevent me from leaving the country. The scary part is that places I have worked, banks, credit card lenders, etc have never picked up my name not matching my social security. It took the IRS 15 years to catch on too. So much for our homeland security! Really, I find it quite funny. Next, I'll be deported back to New Jersey!

That's all. Sam's birthday is soon. I wish so much he was here to celebrate. He would have been ten. I am not sure what I will do Wednesday – if it is sunny maybe I can plant his orange marigolds that he so loves. I don't want to lose sight of what a special day it is…. but not having him here is just so very hard.

Wednesday, May 9, 2007 1:06 AM

A very long letter I will never send….but wish I could.

Dear Doctor ER,
I understand that when my little boy came to you on March 3 what was most noticeable to you was his fixed, dilated pupils, his limp body, 2 double central lines, a G and J tube coming out from his tiny stomach, 11 infusion pumps and his diagnosis of mitochondrial disease. I understand that it was a crisis situation, his heart was not beating on its own, he was no longer breathing and those details mattered.

After he died you said, "I am sorry." You shook my hand and you walked away without another word. I wondered then and I wonder now – do you know who died in your hospital that night? Do you know that a beautiful, little boy's life on earth ended or did you simply think that his death was inevitable?

I wish that you could have known, would have let me tell you after he died, the truth about those particulars: that they were simply the peripheral details of his life. The truth is that when Sam died he was 7 years old, 9 months and 21 days but except for the last 77 minutes of his life he was never dying, despite his technology and medical care dependence. In spite of the prognosis that his disease implied, few have lived life as vibrantly as Sam did.

I wish that you had sat down and asked me to tell you about Sam. But you just walked away and never came back during all those hours that I sat holding my lifeless son in a strange hospital - where no one knew him. When Sam's doctor got there he sat down and said to the nurses and chaplain, "Let me tell you about Sam." He began with "He has these two front teeth that are starting to come through and ..." He told them about Sam - the child, not the diagnosis.

So Doctor ER– let ME tell you about Sam, who would have been ten years old today – May 9th. When he was born he was my only baby that would lay in my arms like a baby – calm, quiet, snuggled close to me. I thought that finally I had a calm child. That lasted about two days. After that he had to be held upright with his back to me – looking out to the world, taking it all in.

When he was little he wanted to be a bird, then an ambulance, then a super hero fighting evil....I think he just wanted to fly, be speedy and be free. I hope that is what he is doing now.

He did not learn how to talk until he was three. Before that he communicated with sign language, a few single words and lots of facial expressions. He truly had no difficulty making it clear what he wanted. But then he literally woke up one day and started talking - not single words, not even sentences. He talked in paragraphs and never stopped from that day forward. He loved to talk. He had lots of favorite things to say like "nice try French fry" or "TOOL!" (cool), "Evil never wins," "never give up!" and "You're a liar liar, pants on fire."

He liked dolls –much to his brother Zach's chagrin. He had 2 favorites named "Baby Abby" and "Baby Sammy." I distinctly remember driving to the hospital one night in the rain when he was about 3. Sam was terrified of thunder for all of his life but instead of saying this to me that night, he was crying "My babies don't like thunder! My babies don't like this at all!"

He suffered through horrific migraines from the time he was a baby. The worst ones lasted a week and a few ended with strokes. He had to relearn to sit about 5 times before he was 2 years old. One stroke left him unable to crawl as he had done before, so he figured out how to commando crawl all over the house, dragging his left side along. His resilience was nothing short of amazing.

There were countless times that it seemed he would not live much longer. And then he would pop up out of his bed as if nothing had ever happened....When he was five he coded and went to the ICU. The fellow woke me up at 2 am to tell me that he would need to be intubated if things got any worse. Intubation for Sam, with his bleeding issues, would have been a death sentence. Later that day his own doctor came to see him. He said "I love you Sam" and all of a sudden Sam opened his eyes and said, "I love you too. Where's Zach's green Game Boy?" and then with a horrified yell "and WHO put this Foley (urine catheter) in my penis!" They transferred him out of the ICU the next day. His doctor once said that no one who knew Sam could be an atheist. How true. The cat with nine lives has nothing on Sam!

The night before he went to early childhood his teacher called me to talk about her ideas to make him feel more comfortable as he was only going one day a week. She was concerned that he would be scared. He walked into the classroom, sat down and proceeded to monopolize circle time, talking incessantly. The only thing he wanted to do at early childhood was have recess like Zach and Abby. There was not any recess so the PT had to disguise PT as "recess." Otherwise, I fear he would have been a drop out at the age of 5.

He took a lot of pride in his "sense of humor." His idea of a joke was to take my napkin every night and throw it down the basement stairs. Then he would turn the lights off during dinner. Not exactly a comedy routine anyone would find funny but it was his complete and utter certainty that he was hilarious that made Zach and me laugh right along with him each night. His favorite joke was "why was Tiger looking in the toilet?" Answer: "He was looking for pooh!" I think I heard that joke 500 times...and he laughed like it was new every time.

Cleaning the couch one day I found dried up cream cheese all over it. I asked the kids, "Who did this?" He raised his hand, full of pride: "I did!" I asked him why. He looked at me like I was an idiot and said "because YOU forgot to give me a napkin!"

Going to the library on Saturdays was one of his favorite activities. When he was about four he checked out a book called "Princess and the Potty." For whatever reason, he loved this book and probably holds the record for most renewals of any one book. I'll never forget the look in his eyes when he got his very own library card. He was beyond proud. It was one of his most treasured possessions. I buried him with the card in the pocket of his little jeans.

He thought that one of the dumbest stories he ever read was "Barney goes to the doctor." Barney tells the reader not to be afraid because "doctors are our friends." Sam could not believe how stupid that was – he could not even begin to imagine being scared of doctors because he loved all of his so much. When he was in kindergarten he had a turn to be "Big Cheese" for the week. Most kids brought their parents as their special visitors but he brought Dr. "Hanens" (Havens but those V's were so hard to say). He was so proud that the kids thought his doctor was funny. This is status when you are in kindergarten apparently

He loved French fries. He did not just like them – he loved them. When we came back from a 2-week stay at the ocean one year I asked him what his favorite part of the trip was. He did not even think before saying "Bob's Grill – I like their 'fwench fwies.'" The ocean did not come close to competing with French fries.

His first and only pet was a hamster that he named Pancakes Waffles Toast Syrup Juhlmann. He adored that $7 creature. He wanted a dog more than anything but settled for a collection of stuffed dogs. His first one was named "Rabbit Food", After that came "Duck Food" and then his all-time favorite "Chicken Food." His sister, Abby, painstakingly made little sleeping bags for so many of those dogs. He loved to play Peter and the Wolf with his dogs. We did that many Sunday mornings.

When he was four he asked Abby, to get him the moon and stars. She made him these little cling on stars and a moon for his window. They are still there. He told everyone, "My sister got me the moon and the stars!"…and she did. He was so proud when Brittany took him for

373

a ride in her car the day she got it. How cool is that to ride in a car - just you and your big sister? He shared a room with his best brother, Zach. He would absolutely not go to sleep if Zach was not in the room. It could be hours later when Zach came up and Sam would be sitting up, eyes half closed. "Sam, why are you awake?" I asked. "Mama, I can't sweep (sleep) without my best brother!!"

I have a lot of memories of our trip to Florida for his Make A Wish trip. One of my favorites is sitting at dinner at the Gingerbread House every night. There was a player piano and Sam would entertain everyone around him by dancing to the music. He loved to be in the spot light.

He had no idea that it was odd to have tubes and central lines coming out of one's body. He probably could not remember not having them. But oh my – then came the casts on his legs. They were on the night we were to go to Open House for first grade and he was adamant that he was not going. He was simply mortified that people would think he was so different because he had casts....never mind that he was connected to 11 or 12 IV pumps –it was the casts that bothered him.

He could not add and subtract to save his life in school but funny thing – if I said "Sam if you have 10 dogs and Zach takes 3 how many will you have left?" he would say "SEVEN!" In the weeks before he died he was finally learning to read a little. He was so excited when he recognized a word.

When we found out he needed hearing aids, the audiologist said I had to let him choose and choose he did. He is possibly the only child to ever pick out blue and purple hearing aids. He got in a habit of hiding them for a while. The kids and I would be looking all over the house and then after an hour he'd say so innocently, "Maybe they're under the couch cushions?" Of course that was exactly where they were.

When he was all of four I told him one day that he was fastidious. He said "Oh no Mama – you are the prettiest – not me!" After that he told everyone that he was fastidious and his mama was the prettiest. When I was out and then returned home he always made me feel like the most wonderful person in the world. "MAMA – you're home!" he'd say – even if I had been gone for a mere 20 minutes.

He was a child of firsts. The first child to have the heart IV drips he had outside of the ICU –at home and in school. The first child to get blood products around the clock while he attended sock hops and went on field trips. There was nothing that stopped him from living the life that he wanted to live.

He may have been the first child with his degree of medical problems that his school friends knew, but if they thought it was odd, they really never showed it. They lined up to give him hugs good-bye when he left school. When he arrived they stopped whatever they were doing and one by one announced, "Sam Juhlmann is here! Hi Sam Juhlmann!" They were not simply nice to him –they were his friends. There was a sign up list at school because otherwise the kids would fight about who got to go to therapy with him or stay in for recess. He was looking so forward to going to his first birthday party – but he never got to go. On the morning of March 2nd he woke up tired, but happy and talkative. I did not know it would be the last day I'd hear him talk or say I love you. 18 hours later his physical body was dead.

In the days between his death and his funeral the children at his school made beautiful pictures and wrote notes. The kids that knew him from kindergarten and the ones he had met in first grade showed a wisdom in their pictures that many adults never gain. The kids showed that they could see beyond the superficial details of Sam's life, straight through to the person he was and is. In their pictures he does not have a wheelchair or casts on his legs or hearing aids in his ears. He is simply playing and happy.

That is who Sam is, Doctor ER. He would have been ten today. Instead he did not live to be eight. And yet he impacted this world more than most people do in a lifetime. Today marks the day he was born and all those who were lucky enough to know him – even if from a distance – were touched by his life. I only hope that in some small way his life touched yours so that if another child comes to your ER and dies someday you take the time to sit down and say "tell me about your child." I'm sure you have heard that life is not in the plot –it is in the details. Sam's life was full of magnificent, joyful details and I could never be more thankful than I am that he was born and drew me into the details of his life for almost 8 years.

Tuesday, May 15, 2007 10:35 PM

I am thankful that Zach is alive. This is always true but I am especially focused on it right now. Saturday was a wonderful day until about 6 PM. I gave Zach three IV medications – meds he has received for years. Within about 60 seconds my lively son was gray and glassy eyed. He said he was so tired, his head was killing him, could not breathe and he was burning up. His blood pressure dropped alarmingly, he gagged uncontrollably and he began to paralyze – first his eyes and facial muscles and then his limbs got very weak. Solumedrol (an IV steroid) did nothing. Epinephrine knocked him out of the paralysis and some of the symptoms but he persisted in a shock like state with profoundly low blood pressures, ice-cold extremities and poor blood flow to his kidneys until 4:30 the next morning. It happened so fast. It was just Abby and me. That poor girl has seen way too much in her lifetime.

Later, all I could think was that if it had been night and I had given those meds (which I do at midnight) I would not have seen this happen. We do not know what caused this. It is not the meds themselves. The possibilities are endless. Perhaps an impurity, a false ingredient, a wrong label…. it is terrifying to think of how fast he went down and we do not even know why. It is frightening to realize how little we can control in life. I am so careful with all that I do. I gave him his medicines that are supposed to help and instead infused poison into him…. and I cannot even tell you what went wrong in that process. I am reporting the lot numbers to the FDA but unless this is a wide spread problem we will likely never know. Life can change so fast. Just in case I needed that reminder, I got it on Saturday. Since then he has been okay. Tired and labs a little whacked out. I am not surprised as this was quite a profound stress to his body. We changed his IV antibiotics today.

Zach cracked me up on Wednesday when he called his homebound teacher to cancel "because I need to make a cake." He did go on to explain (thankfully) that the cake was for his brother. Otherwise, I can just imagine how that would go over…canceling school to make a cake.

On Friday his favorite pediatric resident came over to our house. They played a few games of Yu-Gi-Oh. A doctor that knows how to play Yu-Gi-Oh is quite impressive to Zach! Actually I find it quite impressive too. Having tried to learn that game I personally feel medical school would be a breeze next to remembering the rules of the game.

Thank you for all of the wonderful birthday wishes and shared memories of Sam. It's been a very hard time. I cannot say why…after all this is not the first birthday without Sam. But it was by far the hardest. I guess it once again shows that there is no rhyme or reason to grief – it just is. But let me tell you some of the happier moments – the ones that made me smile or cry. Inevitably, they made me feel that Sam's presence remains strong.

A few weeks ago I got a letter from the mother of a favorite friend of Sam's. She included a picture of her son standing by Sam's tree in front of their school. This little boy apparently stops by the tree each morning to say good morning to Sam and a little prayer. His mom says it does not matter if it is raining, snowing, sunny…. he stops each day. Two years later he remembers Sam. I cried of course. I do just thinking of it. But those were happy tears.

On Friday a package came from Josie, another one of Sam's favorite friends, with a necklace that I know she just knew I would love. Mother's day was in two days and Sam's birthday had just passed.

On Mother's Day it was sunny and so the kids and I decided to take a walk. "Oh wow," you say. "You guys are just wild over there in Waukesha." Well the thing is that Brittany is home for 2 weeks – she got back about midnight on Saturday. (Or would that be Sunday?) And Zach felt good enough to get in his power wheelchair. The battery was dying which served to keep him from speeding away. We walked up past Bethesda and there was Sam's tree…. decorated with orange ribbons everywhere. I don't know who took the time to do that but it made us smile. Thank you to our tree decorator(s).

Before Sam's birthday I went shopping. I had to -how do you just stop shopping for your little boy's birthday? Zach and I gathered all the presents up and took them over to kindergarten on Sam's birthday. Sam's first grade teacher retired so the kindergarteners get it all! We stopped by the new automatic doors that Bethesda installed…there is a plaque that his OT bought that says the doors are in memory of Sam. Walking in is like walking home.

There were orange flowers and cards and emails…. I have been so thrown by the depth of the sadness lately. Yet the breadth of his impact on others equally startles me. My friend sent me this quote from D. H. Lawrence on his birthday. It is so Sam I just laughed and laughed when I read it - even through the tears. I can just picture him stomping his feet and saying "You cannot have it!"

"Nobody can have the soul of me. My mother has had it, and nobody can have it again. Nobody can come into my very self again, and breathe me like an atmosphere."

Friday, May 18, 2007 8:35 AM

Zach's blood work was awful last night. It's the kidney function again with a creatinine that is going up by the day. I am sure it is his heart that is causing the kidney issues but either way it is not looking good. He is acidotic and his calcium levels are too high. Zach is particularly sensitive to a high Calcium for some reason - gets very tired and S-L-O-W in thought and in how he moves and talks. I found out yesterday that he has been falling asleep in school all week...which makes me really wonder what is going on. So I will draw some blood cultures. His counts have dropped so he needs blood today. I hope that helps. We also have temporarily increased his diuretic. One good sign is that after not getting calcium all night he is talking at a normal speed - that ought to mean his levels are coming down. We'll see.

Sunday, May 20, 2007 9:11 PM

Zach's labs did temporarily improve and then got bad again. He seems to be struggling more than usual with keeping his calcium levels normal -they are too high. He got blood but looks like he will need more tomorrow.

We got some avocadoes today so that Zach and I can make some guacamole. I've actually never made it so we'll try Katherine's (Kaf according to Sam) recipe. Hopefully we won't mess it up.

Yesterday was beautiful - lots of sun. Zach sat outside for a while in the sun with his socks off. He is not a big outdoor fan but it was too gorgeous out there to let him hibernate. He brought his Spiderman book outside so he ended up enjoying it. I tried to clean up our back garden but ended up sitting in the sun reading a magazine.

Today Zach's friend Adam and his girlfriend (Adam's not Zach's) took Zach, Brittany and me to see *Spider Man III*. It was good. More importantly it is so neat for Zach to get invited out to do something and for that person to be Adam. We met Adam when he was volunteering at Children's. In the past 2 years (I think it's been 2 years) they have gotten to be great buddies. I think Adam is the big brother Zach would choose if he were given the opportunity.

I was remembering this morning about the time I walked into the boys' room and there Sam was...singing Spider Man. You may not be able to appreciate this if you do not know that in general Sam did not like singing. He allowed me to sing to him and he did not mind listening to songs at school but he really did not like to be the singer with a very few exceptions. He participated in his kindergarten mother's day concert, semi participated in the Christmas sing along in the gym and eagerly awaited Christmas Eve each year when he and Zach would leave a message for his doctor by singing, "We Wish You a Merry Christmas." So there he was one morning belting out Spider Man and he knew almost all of the words. I have no idea when he learned it but it was priceless.

Tuesday, May 22, 2007 11:23 AM

Two journal entries in 2 days...it's a world record maybe! I have Zach's high school transition meeting in a few hours....I'm a little unsure about the best thing to do for him to maximize his energy and maximize his socialization and maximize his education....too much maximizing and not enough time. Hopefully, we'll make a good plan today.

Last week there was an op-ed in the New York Times, written by Dr. Atul Gawande. He is a staff writer for the New Yorker and a surgeon at Harvard, I believe. Anyway, he is a guest columnist this month and I have been enjoying his perspective. The title of his piece was Doctors, Drugs and the Poor. It was about the price of some drugs (he highlighted anti-retrovirals used for HIV/AIDS) and the implications of those prices -especially with specialty drugs – on the poor. I was compelled to write to him with the following comments.

Dr. Gawande,

I appreciated your column in the NYT this week about the cost of pharmaceuticals and the obligation to get these drugs to those who need them at prices that are affordable. One class of drugs that particularly concerns me is the coagulation factor products for people with bleeding disorders or hemophilia. These are drugs that no one can go without if they want to stay alive. And my understanding is that in undeveloped nations, getting coag factors is rare and inequitable.

You used the word grotesque - I could not have found a better word. My oldest son is dependent on Novoseven (Factor 7a). Novonordisc makes it and without it he will bleed uncontrollably – perhaps lethally. His dose is $7500 - 15,000 when he is in the hospital (a little less when we are at home) and when he bleeds he needs it every 3-4 hours. This drug is the sole reason that the cost of his care has been driven up so high in the past few years that the HMO insuring him recently imposed a lifetime limit, which he will go through in 1-3 years. Once he loses that he'll be covered by our state Medicaid but as you know, the citizens will pay for that in taxes and higher hospital bills and even so the hospital will lose money.... meanwhile Novonordisc will continue to make a profit at the expense of everyone.

At one point our physicians and the home care provider appealed to Novonordisc for a discount based on quantity for my youngest son, because he needed so much more factor 7a than any other child in the U.S. They refused. When my little boy passed away in 2005 our insurance had spent millions of dollars on that drug alone for him. It sickens me. As a mother I am thankful my sons have this drug and of course, I would never refuse it for them on principal. And yet...as a mother, I also cannot help but think of other mothers in other counties, who watch their children bleed into joints and wounds, become crippled or go into shock and many times lose their very lives. I can barely see straight some days due to grief over losing my little son. But I also know without any doubt that he had excellent care – the best that was available – and this allowed him to have a joyous life. I cannot imagine what I would feel if I knew there was a medication available that could have helped him and because I did not have insurance or because I lived in the wrong country my child did not get the medication that could have saved him. Grotesque is absolutely the best word choice I have heard for this issue.

Wednesday, May 23, 2007 10:23 AM

Zach bled significantly last night. He is having a renal ultrasound today and then getting platelets and cryo and red cells as needed. I hate bleeding.

Thursday, May 24, 2007 07:23 AM

The ultrasound did not identify a specific problem. We did not expect it to but hoped it would. His counts started to drop last night as expected. I forgot about the time delay with bleeding rapidly. When a person loses a lot of blood fast the counts initially look ok because the blood is so concentrated in the body. Once a person stops bleeding (losing fluid) and they are no longer "dehydrated" then the counts start dropping.

All that to say that the bleeding did slow down and even stopped for a time yesterday so we did see that drop in his counts. I think the platelets and cryo helped. But last night and this morning he is bleeding again. I think this will be a weekend of giving many many blood products. It did not seem to bother him yesterday but today he looks pale and is pretty tired and weak.

Saturday, May 26, 2007 9:44 AM

Actually we are not dialing the blood products back just yet. The doctor does not feel it is safe to do so...and I really don't disagree. I think I mentioned that I hate bleeding...so if this better assures he does not re-bleed then that is fine with me.

It's Saturday and in a little while Brittany and I are off to birthday shop for someone in our house who will turn 14 on May 31. ABBY. Tonight we are having my brother and his wife over to celebrate a little early since her birthday falls in the middle of the week.

My mom and Frank won't be here for the first time ever as my Papa (the kids' great grandfather) has not been well. He fell a few weeks ago. (He is quite the independent soul – at the age of 88 he lives solo in Arizona,). He had a significant brain bleed and now is struggling with congestive heart failure and kidney insufficiency. It struck me that Zach and his great grandfather are grappling with the exact same health issues at the moment.

Yesterday Zach did homebound school with Donna for a few hours. Typical Friday. However, once school was done Donna ran to the food store and came back with…you guessed it…ingredients to make Guacamole. She had Zach chopping and mashing and they made a delicious Guac that ended up being my breakfast and lunch. They did a great job!

The school meeting was okay. I have to meet again with the high school team on Tuesday May 29. I may write more about it later…or not. Right now I need to not think about it. I have a birthday to celebrate, flowers to plant and a daughter to send back to Minneapolis.

Two more days and then Brittany leaves to begin her summer research job. This is hard. I know it is good, I know it is normal and I am really proud of all she has accomplished by sheer determination. But, I'm her mother and I will miss having her around - a lot. However, there is no doubt in my mind that she will shine.

And then there is my cousin, Emily. Emily had decided to run the Chicago Marathon in memory of Sam, in honor of Zach and to raise money for the United Mitochondrial Disease Foundation. She is writing a weekly blog for the online publication *Her Active Life*. This is one excerpt from the first week but given Emily is a beautiful writer, everything is worth taking time to read.

"My cousin has lost one son, Sam, to the disease, while her other little boy, Zach, continues to battle daily, bravely. I'm running the marathon for them, and for the United Mitochondrial Disease Foundation (UMDF), an organization that funds research for a cure and offers a support network for those affected by the disease.
Whenever I start to slow down during a run or contemplate turning back, I think of Sam and Zach. I have the option to stop running when my legs hurt, or to slow down when I'm breathless; they have never had that luxury. Sam's memory and Zach's determination encourage me to stay focused and to uncover my hidden strength."

Tuesday, May 29, 2007 10:34 PM

Tomorrow (Wednesday) Zach is going into the hospital. We're a bit off schedule because of the Memorial Day weekend. It was nice to have the three-day weekend. Zach got outside a little bit which is so good for him to do. He is really doing quite well. I have not given any platelets or cryoprecipitate since Sunday and so far so good. I'm rather impressed with how well and quickly he responded to the treatment, given the extent of his bleeding. And that's all I'm going to say about that lest I jinx anything.

A week or so ago he and I had a conversation about chronic illness and how hard it is to feel ill so often. He seemed to be feeling sad about it and so we talked about what we might change to make him feel better. Obviously, we cannot change that he has mito but there are things he does have control over and I wanted to hear what would make a difference for him. He said it would make a BIG difference to him if he could go food shopping with me one day to see what all the new things are at the store because he is getting tired of his limited repertoire of things to eat. Food shopping. That's all he wanted. The simplicity of it stopped me in my tracks.

Sunday, Zach, Abby Brittany and I went food shopping. Brit wanted to take stuff back to Minneapolis, Abby is having some friends over Friday night and Zach...well he just wanted to see what is new and improved. He did come home with a bag of cheese whiz (that stuff should be banned), frosted animal cookies, chive and onion cream cheese, several types of crackers and cereal, chocolate doughnuts, hot mustard and probably other things I cannot remember. I know that at the heart of this is that he continues to mourn the loss of eating (he can only eat extremely limited amounts of things that drain out from his stomach). It reminded me of what an enormous loss this is – I know he would give anything to eat again like he used to but it is rare that he feels sorry for himself about this dismal reality. Just as I have almost never heard him complain about other changes – no longer able to walk through a mall or run or jump or ride a bike or stay in school all day or participate in phys-ed or the class trip at the Fox River or any number of things that most kids and their families just take for granted. I don't know that I would handle such life altering changes as gracefully and positively as he does.

The school meeting went well today. This is going to be a learning process and I have to remind myself that it will take time. I get impatient because I don't want Zach to lose even one day while we figure things out. But I also have to remember that our school district has done a beautiful job with the kids – all four of them.

My principal concern is social issues. I want him to have more than "five hour friends" –kids who are nice to him in school but never call, never invite him anywhere even though he invites them to do things, never notice that he is gone. I know it does not have to be that way. I cannot believe we have a world without good kids – in fact I think there are many. It's simply an ignorance issue – I doubt they even know how their actions (or lack of actions) feel to those on the outside. We have got to figure out a way to include – really include – kids like Zach in school and society. Not just because it is good for him, but also because it is good for everyone.

Dr. Robert Hickey is the author of the preface to the Pediatric Advanced Life Support course book. I read the preface the day after Sam's funeral and it touched me deeply. Ever since that time I read it to the medical students when I teach them and to new CHW employees at their orientation. Dr. Hickey wrote this in answer to the question many of us who work in pediatric health care get, "How can you take care of children? Isn't it so depressing?"

*...They ask me, "How can you do what you do? You must see horrible things!"... Yet those of us who take care of children know better. We know that children are a rejuvenating wellspring of love and wonder, and caring for them nurtures us as well as them. We know that our work results in more laugher, more discovery, more sleepovers, more birthdays, more cupcakes, more dances, more graduations and eventually **more of us.** It is my belief that nowhere are the stakes higher or the rewards greater than in the care of children. It is our duty and our privilege to do our best. Those of us who have dedicated out lives to caring for children do so because we understand these things."*

How can you continue to teach kids who have so much trouble learning? How can you wake up each day knowing that even if you help one family, there are hundreds more that don't have what they need? How can you befriend a child who might die or one who cannot do what you can do? Why does this matter when you cannot fix it and make it better? It matters because although you do not have complete control - you can control whether or not you make a difference. And when you make a positive difference in the life of a child who has a disability or a chronic illness - the result is more. More of *the child* and more of *you* - and consequently more of *us*. Inevitably, with all of that "more" the question becomes, "How could you not?"

For everyone involved in Zach's life, for everyone who was involved in Sam's life, for those who have made it a priority to be an important presence in my girls' lives - THANK YOU. \

May 31, 1993: HAPPY 14th BIRTHDAY ABBY

My beautiful, intelligent, funny, compassionate, empathetic, creative, wonderful daughter. You are an amazing girl and I love you!

Saturday, June 2, 2007 10:46 PM

The hospital time is going pretty well. Zach's nurses, the residents, pharmacists and doctors are all so happy to see how good he looks. It's been a long winter/spring for all of us – no one enjoys it when he struggles. I'm always so glad when they can see him looking well. There's been too many months this year when that has not been the case.

We have elected not to try to get the IVIg done in 4 days anymore. His admissions have all been 6 days in the last year and every time we try to push things as if he will get out in 4 days, it only makes it all worse. So we're just giving the IVIg at a very slow rate, assuming he will be in all 6 days and we will not attempt to challenge him. His body seems to like this better. It's still not perfect as he was de-sating all last night. (This is when the oxygen levels in the blood are not adequate). Today he is working hard to breathe and this has worsened through the day. It's definitely not as bad as it can be and he is compensating okay for now. The worry is always that it takes so much energy to keep his oxygen levels up when he is like this. He uses a lot of muscles trying to breathe and after awhile he just gets tired and needs more help. I am hoping things at least stay stable. His oxygen requirements were high last night but better during the day. We'll see

385

what happens when he falls asleep tonight. Right now he is watching *Eragon*.

Zach spent hours and hours today writing a story on his computer. I'm not sure exactly what it is about – I know it has two brothers who are rivals but beyond that I'm not sure. He was unable to participate in the speeches that his language classmates are giving this week so the teachers asked that he write a story. I was not sure if he would take to it but obviously he did. He'll have to edit it with Donna or me in the next day or so but that is secondary in my opinion. It was just so neat to see him that involved in something, letting his imagination take over as he did. I think I'll have to get him to write more stories this summer if he continues to enjoy it.

Thanks for all of the happy birthday wishes for Abby. I'll make sure to show her when I go home. I was able to go home for her birthday evening which was nice. I'm mad I forgot to bring some ice cream cake back with me, however. Last night she had her 8th grade dance.

Brittany loved the first week of her new job. She said her research team has been so friendly and nice and very supportive and helpful as she learns new things. She said she is learning a tremendous amount. I miss her so much but I am also so happy for her. Hopefully the kids and I will get out to see her very soon.

Monday, June 4, 2007 9:52 PM

We're home from the hospital. Thanks Melissa for helping us get out the door so that Zach could be at his award ceremony. We sped home (don't tell), picked up Abby and had 15 minutes to spare.

The kids both got awards tonight. Abby got academic excellence (for 3.75 or better GPA), outstanding achievement in language arts and consumer science and the 8th grade Citizenship award. It made me cry when she got that last one.

Zachary also got an academic excellence award and an outstanding achievement in art award. His retired art teacher came to the ceremony tonight because he wanted to make sure Zach got the art award.

I am very proud of how hard they both work - they certainly deserve their awards.

Zach is doing really well except for one small problem that had better not become a big problem – He is bleeding AGAIN! I could not believe it. I had a feeling this was going to happen as he had many blood clots from his GI tract today in the hospital and he definitely has more bruising everywhere. None of that is a big deal. However, when we got home from the award ceremony he had a lot more bleeding. All I can say is it had better stop – he does not need to deal with this his last week of school.

In the past few days Zach had a few visitors to the hospital. Friday, Tanner, a friend from elementary school came to Zach's hospital room. They had fun catching up and making plans for the summer. They will be at the same high school in the fall. On Sunday, Alex, his friend that he met this winter stopped by with his mom. It was so nice for Zach to see both boys. Thanks to their parents for taking the time to bring them by for a visit!!!!

Zach was getting a little "girled" out in the hospital – especially on Sunday. We have some pretty cute girl patients right now and they spent the better part of the day in the hallway doing karaoke with the nurses. Every now and then they'd shout for Zachary to come on out and join in….you can imagine his eyes rolling at that. Girls! He wanted no part of that whatsoever. I think he kind of enjoyed their silliness though. It was nice to be on 4 west this weekend. The nurses did not skip a beat –singing and dancing with the kids and yet taking such good and careful care of them. There was a lot of joy despite all these children have to deal with, because the nurses made sure to remember that they were children and needed to be kids just as much as they needed medical care.

Ok – I have a load of things to unpack and I am just procrastinating now! (This should not be surprising to anyone who knows me).

Tuesday, June 5, 2007 12:32 PM

I'd like to write a bunch of expletives here but I am going to stick a sock in my mouth (or a speed bump in my brain may be more appropriate given this is in the written form). We are back to daily platelets and cryoprecipitate infusions for continued bleeding. We cannot use the wildly expensive Factor 7a that takes 2 minutes to give

387

because it may cause too much clotting Instead we can go with the volume overloaded, several hour infusions of good, old-fashioned blood products. I'm really not complaining about the time factor for me - I have plenty to do while they stuff infuses. I am, however, frustrated for Zach's sake. I do find it ironic that the kid never bled the 6 days he was in the hospital but we're not home more than 5 minutes from the ceremony last night and he re-bleeds.

Expletive, expletive, exclamation mark x 5!

Oh well – thank God for kind and wise doctors, blood banking experts, on call couriers, home infusion pumps, a mother's nursing license and most of all donors. If you've never donated blood or plasma or platelets please consider it – especially as we come upon summer when the need typically increases and the giving typically decreases. It truly is a gift of life –a gift characterized by different (read nicer) expletives: amazing, wonderful, unselfish, invaluable, magnificent – ended with exclamation mark x 10 !!!!!!!!!!

Wednesday, June 6, 2007 11:32 PM

Still bleeding today but ever since Zach got his 2nd dose of platelets and cryo tonight I think it slowed down. I hesitate to say that – so we'll see in the morning. For now – perhaps this is at least a reprieve???? In talking with his doctor today we wondered if he is getting to a place where he may need some sort of scheduled dose of platelets and cryo. We're not ready to say that yet - but if he shows the same pattern of getting better with platelets and cryo followed by re-bleeding within a week then we may need to think about that. I do worry that he is not healing from this particular bleed.

Anyway, bleeding is not the reason I am writing. Sam is.

Today, one of my favorite colleagues, Eileen and I taught our workshop for the junior medical students on caring for children with chronic illness. Eileen and I have been doing this together for quite a few years and we really enjoy teaching this particular workshop. We do a bunch of different things with them and they never quite know what to make of us initially. We definitely do not behave like their typical workshop leaders. The last 45 minutes of the workshop (it is about 2.5 hours long) I share my family story. I always tell it from the depths of my heart but because I have told it over and over again for many years, I worry that it sounds too perfect, too contrived....so I mix it up and use different stories and examples. To be honest I am never exactly sure what I am going to wind up saying.

Today, Sam was so heavy on my heart and at the last minute (I was running late as always), I printed off the Dear Doctor ER post in the caring bridge journal that I wrote on his birthday – May 9th. I was not exactly sure what I wanted to do with it or even if I would use it. Like I said, I never know exactly what is going to come out of my mouth. But as I was talking about the kids, telling their story and looking at the students, I just felt strongly that I should read parts of it as my conclusion. So I began...*Dear Doctor ER...*

I usually don't have notes but of course I don't know the letter by heart so I was looking down a lot. I was struck when I first looked up to see their eyes riveted on me – and yet not on me for they were seeing Sam. They laughed and laughed at some of the stories. And they cried. Honestly, I could barely finish because I have never seen medical students cry as much as they did today. It was hard to see and keep going.

I reminded them that I could easily tick off what helps families and what does not...but ultimately the most important thing they can do for a family is to say "tell me about your child" or "tell me about your husband, your grandpa, your baby..." Everyone they take care of is someone's child, husband, grandma, baby, aunt, brother....and if they remember that they will impact lives far more than if they memorize their text books. The knowledge will come and the wisdom will come but knowledge and wisdom are meaningless without the words, "Tell me about your child -not only the disease – but tell me about who he or she is."

Sam. Sometimes (many times) I feel like he is slipping through my fingers – even gone. I hope every night I will dream of him but I have not dreamt of him in a long time. I look at his clothes and hold his dogs and sometimes it seems like 100 years ago that he was here. I find myself wondering, "Was Sam here? Was I really his mother or was that someone else's life?" for it feels so coldly distant. It is only the constant heart ache that tells me it was not a dream. I am under water many days and even after all this time I still feel confused – as if I have lost my map of the world. I try so hard to remember every detail of his life but the truth is I am forgetting pieces each day. Peter asked me what antibiotic rotations Sam was on – I did not know and I had to look it up. I cried that I had forgotten – such a silly, stupid thing but I could not bear to think I had forgotten even one detail of his life.

So today I read *Dear Doctor ER*. In the beginning it reminds Doctor ER that the medical things were simply the peripheral details of Sam's life. They were not Sam. Perhaps I needed to be reminded of that myself. Forgetting what antibiotics he was on, forgetting what size his G tube was or how I ordered his platelets....those are simply unrecalled, peripheral details. Losing those details does not mean I am losing Sam – who he was, is and will always be.

Sam impacted lives today. Sam taught. Sam made a room full of stressed out medical students laugh. And Sam's life showed those same medical students that it is okay to cry. Sam's story reminds us that we can care, show our humanity and still be professionals. Thank you to everyone who encouraged me to share "Dear Doctor ER." I have not sent it to the real Doctor ER and I don't know if I ever will. But today I shared it with a future Doctor ER, Dr Internal Medicine, Dr. Pediatrician, Dr. Cardiologist and many other would-be Drs. I am glad I did. I may not dream of Sam tonight but I remember now that he is with me, wherever I go, speaking through me and continuing to make a difference.

Sunday, June 10, 2007 10:52 AM

AM: Zach has stopped bleeding. We have him off the daily platelets and cryoprecipitate again – we'll see how long he can go. He's doing rather well and for that I am thankful - beyond what words can express.

Things I am thinking about:

Our language, developed to deal only with things in the universe of our experience, is simply inadequate to talk about anything else that we might imagine --Donald E. Simanek

Time is also an arbitrary thing. What we consider a minute, hour or year has meaning only to those of us who live on this planet. To someone on another planet their year would be whatever they

determined it to be. Our clocks and time standards are based on a number we have picked and nothing more. We decided that a year was the time taken for the planet Earth to go around the sun once. We decided that the day was the time it takes Earth to rotate once on its axis. We decided that the hour was one 24th of the day and the minute was one 60th of an hour. These increments are wholly based on our own desire to describe time and build a standard with which we need to describe events and record history

Several years ago when my friend Lauren's son, Jack, was dying she told him that before he blinked his eyes he would see them again. He should not be afraid because they would be there when he turned his head to look. I always thought that was beautiful and I wanted to believe it…but sometimes at night I was afraid that maybe it was just a nice thing to believe. But I've been reading about time, matter and space lately, (as above, though I have lost my source) and what I read affirms what Lauren told her son.

******

Before there was Zach there was Callie. I have always avoided sharing her story because somehow I thought it was not my story to tell. I realize, now, that it is. Callie was the beautiful baby girl of a friend, who was found to be HIV at the age of 4 months old. At the same time her parents found out they, too, were HIV . Their world changed in a moment. Her mother, plagued by guilt, left one night and never came back. I did not understand that at the time - I do now, even though I don't think I would make that choice. I heard she passed away several years later. I have often wished I could have told her what a wonderful Mommy she was…the HIV did not change that.

Callie's father stayed. I first learned from him about parental resilience, fierce advocacy, endless love, ever present joy and thankfulness for each day even in the face of indescribable, insurmountable grief. On Christmas when Callie was just over a year old, I dressed her in the early morning while her father slept on a cot beside her hospital crib - one crib among four in the room where she lived most of her life. And I knew then that Zach was going to have an illness, though I did not know what. I remember the knowledge of that hitting me like a ton of bricks – I cannot explain it – I just knew.

Over the next few months I dismissed that moment and checked it off as a moment of pre-birth jitters -fear.

On Valentine's Day, when Callie was 16 months old, she died. I held her - lifeless; I felt Zach move and kick. I remember her father telling me that because she had touched my life, it would touch my baby's life...and she would live on in him. I could not understand him saying that at the time. Did that mean Zach's life would replace hers? That somehow Callie's death was okay because Zach was alive? I was in dis-belief that a parent would say that.

Now I understand. I understand that her father never meant that Zach's life could replace hers nor was he implying that Zach's birth could make her death okay. I understand now that he needed to believe that she lived on in me and ultimately in Zach, for this would mean that his little girl was not "dead." Callie's dad passed away years ago, but I hope he knew, *really knew*, that what he believed was more than a hope. It was a truth. I can say with certainty that Callie is still here - part of me, part of Zach, part of all my children and perhaps part of you.

PM: disregard above. He is bleeding again...bleeding enough that he needs platelets and cryo again.

Wednesday, June 13, 2007 10:52 AM

We're doing daily infusions of cryo and platelets for a week and then we will decide what to do. Maybe with a longer course the clot will stay.

Thursday, June 14, 2007 9:21 PM

No deep thoughts tonight. The deepest thing I've had on my mind is "what day is it?" I don't know what it is but by Tuesday evening I was surprised it was not Friday...it just felt like those 2 days had been a week's worth of things. Funny thing is I walked into work with a guy today that said pretty much the same thing to me and walked out with a woman who told me how very tired she is. Maybe it is the humidity and heat hitting everyone.

So let's see – the urinary tract bleeding stopped and then re-started this evening. Not much – but enough to remind me he has a bleeding disorder – as if I did not know. And, while cutting his fingernails he must have cut his finger because it has been bleeding all day. "No big deal," you say – just throw a Band-Aid on it. Well the problem is that in this house with oxygen, IV pumps, 5 zillion medications, monitors, every type of gauze and dressing imaginable…there are no Band-Aids!! Seriously. Not one to be found. Gee, it never occurred to me we might actually need something like a BAND-AID. Being the helpful Mom I am, I said "well just stick some gauze on it," as I was walking out the door. Too bad I did not have a camera as he had about 5 layers of gauze around it when I came home. Hey - you can never be too prepared for bleeding. The sad thing is it was pretty bloody. So now I have a real pressure dressing on it. Who would've though nail clippers were such a danger? He's still getting daily platelets and cryo – and I did think they were helping until tonight. We'll see. He's supposed to get them through Monday, at which time I will talk to his hematologist again. You can't imagine how our hematologist looks forward to my calls! (Not really)

Today I had the opportunity to talk with a metabolic doctor that I met briefly last year in Atlanta. He takes care of many kids with mitochondrial disease and has a heart of gold from what I can tell. People who know him well say that what I say about Zach's doctor, Peter, is what they would say about this metabolic doctor. For me that is the best endorsement I can hear. He practices in Boston and initially I thought I'd try to take Zach to see him. Then the last 9 months happened; obviously Zach was not going anywhere. Well, today we talked by phone at great length and he was just so incredibly helpful and so patient with my questions. It's not that he had some great cure for us…but he was able to look at what we do and offer ideas and explanations and ask more questions, which is exactly what Peter and I want. I feel as if I have a few things we can try and that I understand things a little better.

I also was happy to hear someone with his breadth of experience say over and over how impressed he is with the care Zach has received from Peter and "Zach's team." Of course, I know we have a wonderful group of people caring for Zach that have given so much of themselves to him…but it is especially nice to hear this from a pillar of the mitochondrial community. He also offered to continue to help us as we have questions or want to run ideas by him. And though he'd love to meet Zach he recognizes how difficult it is for Zach to travel to Boston so he is willing to do this from a distance. He was sincere - said he would really like to do this. It was a true "startled by kindness" moment. It's really quite remarkable and yet we have been blessed with that attitude many times over, from so many people that care for Zach.

Sometimes, it really strikes me how very lucky I am to have found the people we have caring for Zach and Sam. It's not that it was easy – the ones I liked seemed to move away and the ones that stayed were so often not right for the boys. But little by little I have found the right people. I know there are so many parents who are where we used to be…feeling like no one is listening or including you or looking at the big picture. All I can say is keep trying and working on those relationships. There will never be perfect, all knowing doctors but there will be perfect doctors for your child.

Tomorrow is finally Friday. I still have not planted flowers for Sam. I so hope to do that this weekend.

I'll leave you with a funny Sam story that I told at new employee orientation today.

One day Sam lost one of his approximately 152 stuffed dogs. Unfortunately, the dog he lost was "Chicken Food," who was definitely the favored dog. This was not good. This was in fact bad. We looked everywhere but Chicken Food could not be found. So Sam decided we needed to report this to the police. After all -Chicken Food was now a missing person/dog. Well, the closest thing to the police that we have at Children's Hospital is Security. So off to Security we went. I was pushing his stroller but I somehow felt like he was dragging me. "Hello" I said, when we got there. "We're here because - um – well – because – we'd like to report – well he'd like to report that his dog – I mean his stuffed dog – is missing." I was prepared for either laughter or "Lady -we're a little too busy here to be looking for stuffed dogs." Instead, the person working came over to Sam's stroller, knelt down and looked him in the eye, pen and paper in hand.

"What is your dog's name?" she asked

"Chicken Food – My FAVWIT (favorite)" - said with a lot of drama because this was Sam.

The guard did not crack a smile.

"I need a description"

"He's Bwown and little."

"Where was he last seen?"

"In my hoptipal woom (hospital room). I threw him at Zach."

After writing all of this down the Security guard said, "Sam, I want to assure you that we will do everything possible to locate Chicken Food."

Honestly – I half expected to hear them call a missing child code for Chicken Food next.

Fortunately Chicken Food was indeed located in short order– at a Hallmark store, courtesy of one of his nurses. It would not be the last time Chicken Food had to be reincarnated.

Sunday, June 17, 2007 9:21 AM

I'm glad the saga of Chicken Food Lost made so many people smile. I've always wondered where or how or why Sam came up with that name for his dog...but he never explained. I think he thought I was quite dense for even asking the question.

I want to thank so many of you for your kind messages - now just in the last week but always. I always feel badly that I cannot call each of you personally and say thank you and have a conversation with you. I hope you know (and if you don't I am telling you) how very much your support, concern, compassion, strength, ideas and shared stories mean to me. You embody all that community means to me. Thank you.

Tuesday, June 19, 2007 6:40 AM

Zach is doing well. However, due to the fact he has re-bled so many times now, we are continuing daily platelets and cryo until he has gone a week without bleeding.

I suppose the good news is that on Sunday evening he will be admitted for his week of IVIg. If he is going to re-bleed I hope it is while he is there. I think we're in a better position this admission as we have a urologist who Zach's doctor talked with and he plans to see Zach anyway next week.

Bone density scans came back and they're not good. He has lost bone density in the last 18 months – not what we wanted to see given all of the aggressive medical care he has received. I do wonder if part of the problem is that on top of his calcium metabolism problems, he had months and months of time this year where his weight bearing was extremely limited. When people do not get up and walk, they lose bone density. This is seen a lot with the elderly. Zach could not walk for most of the school year except for a little bit in the classroom. There were entire weeks he could not hold his head up this past winter and early spring.

I may be in denial but I am hopeful he can gain some of it back. The fact is that his activity level has been nothing short of amazing in the past month. He can walk around our cul-de-sac (which has a hill and all together is likely a block) and he can walk up and down the stairs a few times a day. It is hard to capture how remarkable this is – but it is just that! I did not think he'd ever walk up stairs or even down our driveway again. We have out theories about why he has so radically improved which I won't bore the masses with. I continually have this image in my mind of Zach on St Patrick's Day (Samuel Patrick's Day), unable to hold his head up, talk, disoriented, breathing only 4 times/minute, the girl's faces... It's just extraordinary and I think that is all we really need to know for today.

Zach had his friend Tanner over yesterday while I was at work. Zach is so lucky to have a home nurse, Chris, who is always willing to do whatever she can to make his life as "normal" as possible. Chris is here the 3 days I work. She takes Zach shopping, out for guacamole, to school, classes, etc. She never minds if he has a friend over...she just wants him to have these opportunities. I hear horror stories a lot about home nurses but not us – ever since our first, Linda, we have had great people caring for the kids when I am at work. A doctor asked me last week, "So what do you do for respite?" I said "Well, I go to work!" which is the truth. But isn't it wonderful that I can go to work and not worry that someone is going to deliver less than excellent care to my child?

Abby has been busy with friends, sleeping in (that does take time you know!), reading and watching cooking shows on T.V. For some reason she loves these shows but I have yet to see her make dinner. Hmmm. Brittany still loves her job. She is learning so many new things and it sounds like she has a really supportive team leader. We miss her a lot. I miss her loudness. When I went away to college my mom sent me a letter and wrote something about how much she missed my loud music and talking on the phone and friends. I remember thinking "Ok – whatever." (Sorry Mom but I was only 18). Now I totally understand how my mom could miss my noise. Hopefully the kids and I will go visit Brit in a few weeks if it works for her.

I'm working on vacation plans. As I said to a friend, "I'll believe it when I see it." However, I think it is really important that we plan as if we are going and grab the chance if it happens to work out. Travel books and me are not good. I read them endlessly and then I cannot make up my mind what to do. I think I was meant to be a world traveler. Every place I read about looks interesting – I want to go to them all. Sometimes, I think it is related to just wanting to run – kind of like how Sam wanted to be a bird and an ambulance…he wanted to go fast and fly. So location for vacation is to be determined but I am fairly sure it will be somewhere on the West Coast since the kids have never seen the Pacific. I suggested to the kids that we take Amtrak wherever we go but they think that may be my worst idea yet.

I have a pile of things to do. Actually there are many piles of things to do all over the house. You know it's bad when I have now made lists for the top of each pile to tell me what is in each pile since things go into piles and tend to get lost there forever. But I do have my priorities - for today it is to learn how to play Star Wars Risk.

Wednesday, June 20, 2007 6:40 AM

Should keep quiet when Zach is doing well. I knew before I sent his labs they would be off – the changes in him during the day were subtle but after 15 years I know when things are not right. He was a little more tired and a little more out of breath. Nothing much…but it got worse and he asked to lay down several times throughout the day. His creatinine came back very high (2.5 if you like numbers) – the highest it has been in months. This means his kidneys are not working well to clear things. It's secondary to his heart failure. We held some stuff out of his TPN last night and that should help but we have to try to add it back in later today. I wish I knew why his heart/kidneys so suddenly go from ok function/responsive to treatment to very poor

397

functioning and obviously not responding to his treatment. We have not changed anything except IV antibiotics. I doubt that is the cause.

Friday, June 21, 2007

He needs to see the oncologist again. Since last summer we have known that he has quite a few lesions on his liver – some sort of vascular tumor process, which is believed to be benign. We scan his liver every few months and the good news is on last scan in February. they had not grown. The problem is benign tumors/growths can release proteins and hormones and other substances and they can secrete them in very high amounts – and of course this can cause big problems. Zach has inexplicable high levels of quite a few things and now the question is – are the lesions secreting these? This has been a question in the back of our minds, especially because levels (mainly of different proteins the body makes) are getting higher every month and other levels are refractory to pretty aggressive drug treatment. I have to say that the word oncologist is scary when it is said in the same breath as your child. We don't think this is some horrible cancer…we truly don't. But if the lesions are producing this stuff, that is a big issue. I am not sure how to shut down the factory (lesions) except via demolition. Not so sure that is an option for a person with his degree of bleeding problems.

Thursday, June 21, 2007 8:52 PM

Things have not improved - in fact some of his labs are even worse. He failed his trial back on regular TPN - failed with flying colors. Usually his kidney function bounces around when it is secondary to a bad heart day but this time it is remaining bad. He fell asleep at the dinner table tonight and is moving and thinking slow again. His blood counts dropped so already he needs blood again. He just finished his 3-part unit on Monday night.

I cannot imagine how this could be related to the change in antibiotics. However, tomorrow we are switching them to a new combination anyway. It will be interesting to see if that makes any difference. It truly is the only thing we changed. He cannot go back on the antibiotics he was so good on for another week because then he

398

is at high risk for developing an infection resistant to antibiotics – or worse a yeast infection in the blood. So we'll try this new combo – they are 2 he has never used before.

On a few completely different subjects:

Our pediatric residents "graduate" on Sunday. Since Zach will be admitted I won't get to see them receive their certificates. It is hard to believe they are already done residency. This group is the hardest ever for me to see leave. Partly this is because they are the last residents to have cared for Sam. They were interns the year he passed away. That there will never be residents that know Sam again is very hard to swallow. Partly I am sad to see them graduate because they are generally awesome as a group. Many of them will stay on as fellows in various programs but some really wonderful ones are leaving town. Of course the biggest part of me is happy. This is a huge achievement for them. Yeah for our residents!

Thank you to whoever planted the beautiful orange marigolds all around Sam's tree at school. We trudge up that hill many times a week and we love to see them smiling out at us.

Zach is signed up to have a therapy dog with him during physical therapy. The dog came on Wednesday and he loved it! I think this will be wonderful for him. He is getting therapy 2x/week now that it is summer so we'll be making good friends with the dog. I'm not sure if they use the same one every time or he will meet different ones. We'll see. It does feel a little bittersweet...it is hard not to think about Sam and how much he would have loved this. I can just see his eyes.

Wednesday June 27, 2007

There's not much to say at the moment about what is going on with Zach. I met with the oncologist today. After talking with Zach's doctor he had done a pretty thorough review of all Zach's old scans – not just of his liver but of other parts of his body. He also talked with the first oncologist we saw last year. He feels we need to do some more scanning – starting with a head MRI and a bone scan. There are good reasons for wanting these scans and I completely agree that we need to do them. He has some other tests in mind but wants to talk with Peter first and also wants to do a lit search to see if there are specific cancerous problems that could cause the combination of

399

abnormal labs that Zach has. He, of course, wants a liver biopsy. We all do but it is such a risk. We agreed that he will talk with Zach's hematologist and get his opinion about whether the benefit of information would out weigh the risk of bleeding. I trust our hematologist and Peter so I know that they will present honest and unbiased information to me. And I did like this oncologist.

The oncologist said it is clear that the abnormal labs started shortly before we saw the lesions on Zach's liver. He feels the spleen lesions are cysts and likely not related. That was good news. He said he cannot assure me this is not malignant but it is a very good sign that the lesions have not gotten bigger. So I am going to focus on that. I am just glad that people are trying to figure this out because something is obviously not right. I really just want to know what. He cannot continue to lose bone density at the rate he is losing it and the oncologist agreed that we have to give our best effort at finding out what is the cause because maybe there is a potential to stop the process if we know what we are dealing with. That's really all I care about. Right now his body will not stop signalling his bones to release calcium. The hormone that controls this will not shut off despite multiple medications that are supposed to be able to turn it off.

Zach's doing ok. As usual he is retaining some fluid – about 5 pounds now since Sunday night. He is getting blood which does not help. His breathing is a bit labored but all in all he is happy and mentally quite fine. Today, his teacher Donna came to visit with some Q-doba guacamole and chips. He loved that!!!! (Thank you Donna!). He has also had visits from the hospital teacher to do real school work…yes in the summer. The hospital teacher is an awesome guy so Zach does not seem to mind and the math practice is really a good thing for Zach. He worked on a mosaic picture the last few days – it may take a long time to dry because there are a lot of pieces of this and that on it. But it is very cool looking!

I had a huge surprise this week. Peter called and said, "Hey you did not tell me you got an award from the residents." I said "ummm – no idea what you are talking about." Later I got an email from the director of our pediatric resident program telling me congratulations. Apparently the residents give teaching awards every year -one to a pediatrician and one to a non-pediatrician. They chose me for the non-pediatrician. They wanted to surprise me and present it at their graduation on Sunday. The only problem is I could not go due to Zach's admission. I am so touched and honored. There are amazing people that teach the residents that fall into the non-pediatrician category –radiologists, surgeons, psychiatrists, urologists, researchers, etc. To be chosen from that field is such a neat thing. I feel I learn just as much from them as they do from me. I love being a part of their resident education – and I am so incredibly touched by their award to me. I am also cognizant that without Sam and Zach I never would have cared about teaching the residents and we all would have missed out on so much learning from each other. It is amazing how wide the ripples extend from the impact of just one tossed stone (or in this case two-named Zach and Sam)

Thursday, June 28, 2007 10:45 PM

Small update -we cannot do a head MRI. We all forgot he has a pacemaker which is an absolute contraindication to any sort of MRI. This is not the best of news because a CT of the head is not as accurate as the MRI. However, they have a new CT machine which instead of taking pictures of every ½ inch thickness of the brain they take pictures that are just 1-2 millimeters thick. Supposedly the pictures are really quite good. So we'll have to try that.

The oncologist added on quite a few more tests. We will now CT neck, chest, abdomen and pelvis. The fancy new CT will be used on his abdomen because that is where they will see his liver. He is also having a tagged RED cell study. They will inject a contrast into him that binds to his red cells. A few hours later they do a nuclear medicine scan to see where the red cells congregate. If they are all hanging out at the liver that means whatever there is more vascular (has a lot of blood vessels and blood flow). They may do something called a PET scan – if this one shows anything "lit up" then this will be considered a suspicious area. The bone scan will be of his entire body to see if anything has eaten away at his bones to make them lose density. It cannot be done until Monday because it requires contrast and he is already getting contrast with the tagged red cell study.

And then there is the issue of the biopsy. The oncologist came to tell me what the hematologist said when he brought it up…I said I don't need to know because I can imagine verbatim what he said. The hematologist did come too and the fact is that a liver biopsy carries a risk not just of bleeding but life threatening bleeding. The agreement we all have is that there will need to be something that looks more than a little suspicious to proceed with the biopsy. We're all hoping we do not have to make that decision.

The oncologist looked at Zach's scans with three different radiologists today and it sounds like no one knows what he has. He did a thorough review of the literature, talked to many doctors, and in general has really worked hard to give this his best effort. I am thankful for that even though I am scared and I hate this. I think it will be benign but I hate that it is a question at all.

I'm sorry for the completely medical update. I hate doing that because it is not who Zach is. But I know so many want to know…and I also want to say thank you for all of your concern

Tuesday, July 3, 2007 9:00 PM

Bone scan results: lit up areas along his spine – especially in the thoracic region. I'm not surprised about that since we know he has fractures but I am surprised that the thoracic region is the brightest. It also lit up at 2 ribs. If I understood the Dr. correctly they appear broken but he does not have pain and they cannot say for sure that they are broken. Believe it or not I hope they are broken. Better to have broken ribs than bone cancer. A part of his pelvis where the leg (femur) fits into the hip also was quite lit up. This too is odd as he has not fallen and has no pain. I was hoping for a clean scan aside from the known vertebral fractures so this was really disappointing. Even if it is not metastasis it is more bad bone news. The scans will go along to tumor board and everyone can give their opinion. This is good because I would like more than one radiologist looking. Right now this really is not meaningful information to me because it could be any number of things. We'll see what the doctors say. I am beginning to think this is going to be very difficult if not impossible to sort out without biopsies from multiple places. Patience is not my virtue – I take after Sam or he after me.

Zach is in his game room now, enjoying his night, oblivious to the thunder and rain. He is not in pain and he is doing great. I'm going to try hard to emulate his positive attitude.

402

Tomorrow is July 4th. This is a picture I love of Sam at the Waukesha parade -the only point of going was solely to collect candy thrown in the streets.

Monday July 2, 2007 3:14 AM

This is so hard to write and even harder to believe this is real:

Fifteen months ago we found out that Zach has multiple lesions on his liver. The oncologist we saw at that time and the radiologists who read the CT scans said they were benign. A few weeks ago we began to question whether the lesions on Zach's liver were releasing a hormone that was causing Zach's bone problems. Even benign tumors can do that sort of thing.

We met with an oncologist this week –a different one than we saw 15 months ago - and he had a different perspective on things. He felt we should pretty much scan Zach head to toe just to make sure that the liver lesions did not represent a metastasis -a cancerous process. In other words he wanted to make sure that there was not some primary cancer somewhere in Zach's body that had spread to the liver. He (and we) did not expect that would be true but he felt it would be unwise to assume this was all a benign process.

On Friday, the scans showed a completely unexpected mass on Zach's thyroid gland in his neck. It is not simply a nodule. Oddly enough one cannot feel it but the radiologists measured it out and it is quite present. This means exactly what the oncologist was trying to rule out - the mass on the thyroid is likely malignant and it has metastasized to his liver. Because the liver lesions have not changed in size or number, it cannot be the opposite (that the liver lesions are the primary malignancy). There is a chance it may not be malignant and therefore the liver lesions are completely unrelated to the thyroid mass but the doctors don't seem to think that is very likely. I suppose the good news here is that it is slow growing and also thyroid cancer is not the worst. The bad news is that it is never good when cancer spreads, which this appears to have done. You have to wonder how something so horrible can just happen inside the body and you don't even know it, you have no idea your life is about to change.

Right now it is about 3 am on Monday (what a shock that I cannot sleep). Zach is scheduled for total body bone scans this morning. The

403

concern is that his back fractures are not that simple -that in fact something ate away at the bone. I cannot tell if the oncologist thinks this is likely or not. I do know Zach's back pain has really increased in the last 7-10 days.

It's not easy to know what to do. With any other kid they'd biopsy both the thyroid and the liver, classify it, stage it, treat it. Zach's bleeding issues are a huge complication. Our hematologist feels that the liver could cause life-threatening bleeding. The thyroid biopsy poses a bleeding risk as well, but not as bad.

The plan as I understand it right now, is for Zach's oncologist, hematologist and primary doc to present Zach's case to tumor board on Thursday. Tumor board is a weekly meeting of oncologists and hematologists. The residents tell me that the room is usually pretty packed with people so you have a lot of great knowledge and wisdom in one room. I think this will be good in terms of getting the best ideas and help. Zach's core team of doctors can sift through the ideas and weed out what does not make sense for Zach. Zach's pre- existing issues complicate all of this and the bone scan could change everything.

This is about the extent of what I know. Mostly this is because there are many unanswered questions for all of us and we will have to go muddle through this. I was also in too much shock to even know what questions to ask when the doctors told me. Zach's June resident was also there when they talked with me Friday. I am glad she was there because later I could not recall anything they said and she was able to sit with me and tell me the things I forgot. That has never happened to me before but I just did not hear after they told me what they found. I never in a million years thought I'd be sitting in that room on Friday having that conversation.

I do feel very thankful that the oncologist we are working with now is the one that was on call this week because we could have easily have had someone on service that did not take our concerns seriously. I like this oncologist for a few reasons: he talks with Zach, he is very respectful to me, Zach and our pre-existing relationships with Zach's hematologist and primary physician and he is obviously careful and thorough. He does not make assumptions like "someone with mito cannot possibly have cancer" and he has said, "I don't know" to me many times.

A natural question I have heard many times in the last few days is whether or not Zach is at the best place for treatment. That's one of the easiest questions to answer: I sense we have found an excellent oncologist by the luck of the draw (or the hand of God), Zach's hematologist has always been wonderful and of course we all know I don't think my boys could have ever had a better primary physician than Peter. If he needs surgery I trust our surgeon completely. His nurses take excellent care of him and the pharmacists work so hard to find the best options for him - I have great peace about who is caring for Zach and one of the few things I am certain about it is that he is in the best hands he could ever be in.

It's hard not to wonder how many fewer bone fractures Zach would have had (and how much less pain) if we had met this oncologist 15 months ago. But as easy as it would be for me to sink into anger about how this was handled initially, I can't afford that right now. That's not to say I don't have my moments – but it's not where I want to be. I just want to focus on finding the right thing to do for Zach right now.

I only hope there is a lesson learned by the people that need to learn it and that is this: just say, "I don't know" when you do not know. Don't tell a parent you know with certainty that everything is fine when, in fact, you do not know that at all. Zach's core team of doctors tell me "I don't know" all the time …that is one of their greatest gifts to me. It does not mean they don't care and don't want to know or that they will stop looking for answers. They are simply honest and if anything this makes me appreciate them even more.

This is longer than I intended so I'll end with a few things:

1) I brought Zach home Saturday night. There was no reason to stay. Today was a beautiful, sunny day and it was good to be home. I even went to my neighbor's house for an hour to sit outside with all of "my neighbor ladies."

2) Zach has had some bleeding from his intestine. Incidentally, when doing all the scans they could see the bleeding inside. He is getting daily platelets and cryo again but we'll reassess in a few days. He has needed quite a bit of blood but his counts are pretty good right now -finally.

3) I walked back into Zach's hospital room on Friday – I could barely see straight and then one of the residents came into the room.

If only I had a camera. How could I not smile? Aaron had just gotten off work from the ICU and instead of going home he came to play Nintendo with Zach. Earlier in the week, Zach's June resident, Ellen, brought Zach a spicy chili recipe because they both love hot and spicy food. Perhaps these seem like little things but these are the things that are so special about the residents we have at our hospital. By and large they all find a way to connect with children even in small ways.

4) I don't know what I would do without Zach's nurses who are just amazing people. They make me so proud to be a nurse because they truly embody all of those qualities that I aspired for when I first got out of nursing school. I am glad that we were in the hospital when I heard this news because I was with people that have been through so much with us -many heart breaking times - and even so continue choosing to care for Zach.

Friday, July 6, 2007 6:24 AM

I will write something later. The news from tumor board was not bad. It was not good. It just was opinions - some that made sense and some that did not. I promise my silence does not mean I heard anything horrible. I just need to figure out what I did hear before I can explain it to anyone else. More things to think about.

Saturday, July 7, 2007 10:18 AM

First the good news: Tuesday night about 10 pm I heard my daughter walk into the house with a friend. I assumed it was Abby but it was actually Brittany! She took off from work, got a ride home with a friend and is here until Sunday. I cannot think of a better surprise! Zach's face was so funny when he saw her.

Tumor Board:
I have not made any more sense of this but this is what I know. There were probably as many different opinions at Tumor board as people. Here are the opinions I heard about. I am sure there were others:

1) We cannot mess around and need to remove the thyroid mass as soon as possible. It will be bloody and hard to control but we'll get through it. It is his only hope for bone health.

2) Surgery is a horrible idea because the mass is right up against the carotid artery and internal jugular -the chance of him bleeding uncontrollably is enormous.

3) A fine needle biopsy is a huge risk because he WILL bleed and what do you do when someone bleeds into the neck and it puts pressure on the airway? (Answer: I have no clue)

4) Why don't we thread long "IV lines" into his inferior vena cava (in the groin) and his neck (internal jugular maybe?) and then we'll measure the levels of all those whacked out protein levels to see if they are really high as the blood comes out of the liver and the thyroid gland. If they are high this *suggests* that said proteins are being produced in mass quantities in those areas. Of course lines in those areas are not without risks. Apparently no one has done this on kids so they are talking with an adult oncologist to see if Zach is old enough to get helpful information worthy of the risk.

5) Let's collect more blood and urine. I have already drawn the blood tests. The urine tests are another story. Some of Zach's medications interfere with the tests they want. We already tried this with Sam and the lab could not run it so honestly, I don't get the point but I am doing it. For medical people they are looking for evidence of a pheochromocytoma, wondering if he has multiple endocrine neoplasia.

6) Let's wait and see if it gets any bigger (you can imagine how that opinion went over with me. Been there and done that with the liver lesions and look where that got us).

7) What if we wait 3 months and then we will be able to do some other contrast study to see if the liver lesions light up indicating they are in fact thyroid tissue? That will show metastasis definitely.

8) What if we just treat it and if the liver lesions go away then that proves they were thyroid tissue all along and therefore they represent metastasis?

9) Unanimous opinion: his bones look awful. Let me just say that bones should be bright white on scans. It's more than a little disheartening to hear them variously described as "cellophane" and "wax paper" and to hear that he absolutely cannot afford his bones to

get worse. This I know and it is perhaps the biggest threat to his quality of life.

10) The lesions on his ribs seen on bone scan are rib fractures. The abnormalities on the hip are fractures or possibly a bone bleed. Never mind that in the past 12 months he has had at least 30 x-rays of the chest, a chest CT, x-rays of his legs and a bone scan and not even one showed these things. Never mind that none of us can recall that he has ever had pain or even discomfort with breathing. I think it would be worthwhile to have a second radiologist look at the scans. I am not a radiologist and I guess Zach could be one of the only people ever to have rib fractures and never know it but I will not feel right about this interpretation until that happens. I admit I am allowing past experience to affect me on this - in college a friend had scans interpreted incorrectly and he ended up having metastasis to the bone.

I have no idea how to sort through any of this and decide what to do. I think we need a care conference. Unfortunately, it is summer and vacations are a plenty. Zach's primary doctor will only be in town a few more days in July. I did make it clear that I do not want to do anything invasive until everyone is back in town – which will not be until end of July. I have no idea if we will be able to take the vacation we have planned for August now…I will plan it but realistically it may not happen.

It seems like five years since they called me out of his room on Friday and talked with me. Having this hang over us is beyond awful. I am terribly frustrated by the lack of consensus but on the other hand I know that Zach's doctors are doing their best to decide the right thing to do. The bleeding issues are the problem here. The last thing anyone wants is to do something unnecessary that could lead to uncontrollable bleeding. On the other hand the last thing we want is to be so worried about bleeding that we do the wrong thing. There is not a tried and true formula to balance the two problems and both are risky stances to take.

Does anyone have some patience, wisdom and grace to share?

Wednesday, July 11, 2007 11:11 PM

Life has been busy and I think that is probably good. The girls, Zach and I went to see Fantastic Four on Sunday with one of Zach's hospital nurses and her husband. We had a good time. I love Johnny Storm. Afterwards we went back to our chaotic house. Brittany left, which was sad. My sister arrived which was not sad.

Maribeth is here for the week and the kids love all of the attention. I had to take Abby to the pediatrician Tuesday which was fine with Zach. He cooked lasagna with Maribeth. Today she was writing with Abby and a few friends. They do really neat things and the kids love it. Zach wanted to join in but after a few paragraphs of whatever he wrote, he fell asleep. Maybe tomorrow.

Last night my brother, Mike and his wife Elaine, Maribeth and I went to see Michael Moore's movie, *Sicko*. I thought it was about people who are not insured but it was actually about people who do have insurance and yet end up not getting the care they need. It was incredibly well done. Sure, there are parts where you know he is getting a little dramatic but the thing is that in the end it is chillingly real. Funny at times - but mostly sad. It was nothing that I don't know – I have learned the realities of insurance companies first hand. But it really makes me wonder how this happened in our country when every other civilized country manages to have universal health care AND citizens living longer and healthier lives than we do.

Zach is not doing great. He has a mild case of pancreatitis in terms of the lab values but a pretty significant increase in pain. His breathing takes more effort and his labs are a screwy mess again. I can barely remember the days when he used to actually have the same TPN 2 months in a row. He cannot even go 2 days without needing a change due to his kidneys and heart that function anywhere from ok to awful. He is getting blood and I hope that helps him feel better.

I have talked with his oncologist a few times this week. His oncologist has talked with many other physicians. His primary care physician has talked with his surgeon….lots of talking and this is good. I am just trying to take it one day at a time because that is all we really can do right now. When I look even a week ahead I get very overwhelmed with all the choices and risks. I am trying my best to block out anything that is not today.

The doctors who have known Zach the longest – as well as the oncologist - truly view keeping Zach from bleeding as a top priority and so they want to choose very carefully what they do in order to minimize bleeding. On this Friday or next Friday he will have a PET scan. The PET scanner is mobile and it is only at Children's on Fridays. It requires insurance approval and as of now we do not have that. It could potentially allow Zach to avoid a liver biopsy so why insurance would have any problem with it is beyond my understanding.

Tomorrow Josie is coming for a few hours! Josie - Sam's dear friend. She moved to Indiana but she is visiting in Lake Geneva. I can't wait to see her.

Thursday, July 12, 2007 10:11 PM

Dr. J, Zach's oncologist, called Humana today and he got the PET scan approved. Humana almost always does the right thing for Zach if we go through the local staff. The problem was the people seeking approval did not know that and went through corporate where they just don't know Zach. He will have the scan in the morning. The hope is that it will provide information to make us smarter about the problem than we are now

Sunday night July 15, 2007

Zach had the PET scan Friday morning. It was an interesting experience going into the mobile unit. Everyone was beyond kind to him. We really are lucky to have such caring people that work in radiology. Zach's oncologist, Dr. J., called Friday night with the preliminary results. He said it did not look as if the scan had provided any more useful information. In other words, we did not get any smarter. I thought when he said it looked negative that it was a good sign. He said it is neither good news nor bad news – it is simply no news.

The oncologist said that the endocrinologist's first response was "take it out." They plan to talk more this week so we'll see. It does seem that all of the doctors who know Zach seem to be coming to "take it out." I don't feel I know enough to feel anything about that except fear. I think the bigger question is what to do about the liver and are they connected? I don't know but the more I read, I do think the thyroid mass could be at least partially responsible for bone destruction. Right now Zach's doctors are all coming and going due

410

to work and vacation schedules. It is impossible to make any decisions right now and I won't until I can talk with them all. I think I may call the surgeon this week, however, and at least find out what kind of surgery we are talking about. Of course, even if it is a minor surgery it will cause severe bleeding. That's the part I cannot think about.

Zach is pretty oblivious about this, save he is very tired of having tests done. He definitely has had his share in the last month and I don't blame him. The PET scan was particularly tough because we had to take away any glucose for a total of 8 hours....he was really feeling lousy with a low blood sugar by the time they were done with the test. The good news is I don't think he will have any tests for a few weeks. The kid has got to be radioactive or close to it by now!

Tonight he and Abby had a bunch of their friends over to watch some scary movie. He was not fazed. I doubt he would be scared of much in terms of movies. Tomorrow night he has another group of boys coming over to play video games. All in all he is doing quite well. He still has pancreatitis but it seems to be less painful than last week. He is breathing much better and after a few days of blood he is not so cold all of the time. After last week it is so nice to see him walking around and just hanging out with friends.

Abby and I went to Madison yesterday with my brother, and his wife. They had a wonderful art fair by the capitol, which we browsed for a while. Then we went to the theatre to see the musical, *Carousel*. I grew up hearing my mom play the songs on the piano but I never saw the show. The story is sad but very honest and above all very hopeful. We loved it. Afterwards we went for dinner at a great Mexican restaurant and then for ice cream. It really was a fun day. I did Zach's labs before we went so I did not have to rush back for that.

Carousel...In the play the characters talk about how someone is never really gone, never really dead, if someone remembers them. Sometimes I think that is just a cliché - because no matter how much I remember Sam, he is still not here. But most of the time I know he is in my heart - the lessons he taught, the love he gave, the joy he found, the gift of his very soul - deep in my heart

When we were kids, my mom often played the piano and taught us all these wonderful Broadway songs. One of our favorite songs was "You'll Never Walk Alone" from Carousel. I have not played the piano or really even thought about "You'll Never Walk Alone" for

411

many years – certainly not in the days since Sam passed away. So it caught me off guard, how this song I grew up with and played on the piano 1000 times, so beautifully describes the one thing that I have learned to treasure above almost anything - HOPE.

When you walk through a storm
Hold your head up high
And don't be afraid of the dark
At the end of the storm
There's a golden sky
And the sweet silver song of the lark
Walk on, through the wind
Walk on, through the rain
Though your dreams be tossed and blown
Walk on, walk on, with hope in your heart
And you'll never walk alone

Tuesday, July 17, 2007 9:49 PM

I talked with the endocrinologist today. It's pretty clear that some sort of open surgery is inevitable. He thinks it is the right thing to do and at this point so do all of the doctors. Zach's surgeon is out until the end of the week. I do know that given his schedule the earliest we can do anything is August 21st, unless someone feels it is so urgent that we need to do it sooner with a different surgeon. I don't think that is the case although I don't think anyone feels comfortable waiting too long without knowing. It's pretty hard to talk intelligently or make decisions when we have no idea what we are talking about.

I am buying the airplane tickets for vacation. I think it is really important that we go to San Diego - which is a destination the kids picked. I have already been told not to plan vacation for after the surgery given the bleeding. So we are going unless I hear differently. Brittany is able to take off work and come with us too.

The kids are all doing well. Brittany's boss took everyone in the lab out for ice cream today - spur of the moment. He seems like such a great guy and she continues to learn so much from everyone she works with. She just loves going to work every day and making

412

protein! She is also volunteering at the Ronald McDonald House, which she loves.

Abby survived a very close call today. Her iPod froze. This was a complete catastrophe in our house. I tried to help but to no avail. Fortunately, Best Buy knew what to do (Press 2 buttons simultaneously in case you want to know). I am not sure I would have survived if she had to get a new iPod and redo her play lists. So yeah for Best Buy (which may be Zach's all-time favorite store.)

Zach had fun with his friends last night. They're really nice kids, who he has known a long time. There were too many empty mountain dew cans that came up from the game room, however. He's working on a comic book – writing the story and making the pictures. I am sure it will be wonderful. I'm trying to talk him and Abby into having their friends over to cook again on Friday. Think how good this could work out – they have fun cooking and I get out of cooking. (Thank you Donna for making us dinner last week!)

One other exciting piece of news for us: I got a call today from a University of California – Irving late this afternoon. Well, let me back up. When I first found out the recent news, I emailed a scientist who I have heard speak at the scientific portion of mitochondrial disease conferences. He is a great speaker and a wonderful writer. He has written some things on the role of abnormal mitochondria in cancer and other diseases. I wanted to know if he thought that mitochondrial disease would alter the natural progression of cancer. He emailed back that no one knows enough to know yet (it was a very nice email but that was the gist of it.) However, they are interested in our family given the symptoms that are prevalent along the maternal line. They cannot guarantee anything but if they can identify things more specifically this would allow blood testing, rather than muscle biopsy testing for the girls and me. Because it is research, any testing they do will be free to us. I doubt this will give us information any time soon – and maybe not ever. But it is worth a try and if not helpful to us then maybe to someone else.

I want to thank many of you for the kind emails, messages in the guest book, phone calls and cards or for just asking how things are or saying "I care." I also know that there are people praying and caring everywhere. I am beyond lousy at returning email and phone calls - most of you know that. Please know how much your caring ways

413

matter to me. I especially appreciate your understanding that it is usually easiest for me to update here rather than telling people individually. It may seem so impersonal but know that I recognize and cherish the gift of caring and support that I receive from the circle of family and friends surrounding us. Thank you!

Monday, July 23, 2007 11:29 PM

Zach is doing relatively well. On the bright side…his kidney function looks awesome the last few days according to his labs. His calcium is, as always, an issue but the other things we look at are stable. In fact, I am so bored with his results that I am going to take a day off from drawing tomorrow. Woo Hoo! It truly is an occasion!

No news about all the other stuff and no plan. I don't do well without a plan so this is quite a challenge for me. I talked briefly with his surgeon today, who is happy to do whatever Zach needs, but he does not know the plan either. And by the time the oncologist and Peter come back next week the surgeon will be gone. And by the time the surgeon is back the hematologist will be gone. Moral of this story: don't get sick in the summer. Attending physicians go on vacation so the chance of getting them all in the same room is about zero and on July 1st new interns fresh out of medical school staff the units. My advice -plan your illnesses for the fall.

Saturday we dragged Zach down to the Carl Zach Cycling Classic and block party in downtown Waukesha. I have watched this race a few different years and I enjoy it. I am not so sure that Zach felt the same enjoyment but it was a beautiful day, we took a walk around the river and he got some ice cream. At night the plan was to watch JAWS, which he and Abby desperately wanted to see. Zach fell asleep during one of the attacks so maybe it was not so exciting after all? Abby liked it. On Sunday I decorated Sam's gravesite with quite a few orange pinwheels that my friend sent to me. His orange marigolds are prolific. When I left, they were all whipping furiously in the wind...a truly vibrant, joyful scene that so befits Sam.

We picked up some supplies at the craft store last week so hopefully there will be some interesting Zach and Abby creations in the near future. The current idea is to use things we would normally throw away in his projects. I'd like to say this is because we are

414

environmentally conscious but the truth is we just think a lot of the medical paraphernalia we throw away will make interesting creations.

Remembering Sam…

When Brittany was home a few weeks ago, the girls and I watched a lot of old home movies. There were not near enough of Sam -typical for a fourth child but sad all the same. The ones we do have were beautiful to watch but really quite painful as well. I just wanted to reach out and grab those children I saw in the movies. Four healthy looking, happy children – so loud and energetic and just beaming confidence in themselves and that all their dreams that would surely come true.

I kept thinking -*this was your life Anne. These children really were and still are yours.* And yet it almost seemed surreal to watch each new baby come home, toddlers bouncing off the walls and little girls and boys taunting each other…. And I examined our faces and saw no sign that we ever knew when those babies came home that one would die and there would be an empty chair at our table, an empty bed.

When those toddlers were energetically running in endless circles with each other I never knew that a quiet destruction of mitochondria was slowly and insidiously depleting that energy and that someday one of those toddlers would no longer be able to run.

When the kids teased each other and tried to push each other out of the camera's eye they never imagined mourning the death of one. They simply did not know a time would come when they'd sell their own dreams if it could buy them the chance to push their little brother back into the camera's eye, that they'd gladly let the light reflect on him and him alone if only he could come home.

I so treasure each of my four children but because I treasure each one so deeply, the loss rips through to my soul. It really was beautiful to see and hear Sam. His voice is so very familiar and yet hauntingly distant. It took me a few days to dig out and realize that as hard as it is to see him and not be able to touch, to hear him but not really, to know there will never be any more chances to capture him in still life or motion…it is still a gift that we have these records of him. He was here.

These lines are from an old and familiar poem, *"For The Fallen"* written by Lawrence Binyon for the soldiers of World War I. In many ways, it seems written for my little hero, Sam, as well.

Solemn the drums thrill; Death august and royal
Sings sorrow up into immortal spheres,
There is music in the midst of desolation
And a glory that shines upon our tears.

They shall grow not old, as we that are left grow old:
Age shall not weary them, nor the years contemn.
At the going down of the sun and in the morning
We will remember them.

But where our desires are and our hopes profound,
Felt as a well-spring that is hidden from sight,
To the innermost heart of their own land they are known
As the stars are known to the Night;

As the stars that shall be bright when we are dust,
Moving in marches upon the heavenly plain;
As the stars that are starry in the time of our darkness,
To the end, to the end, they remain.

Sam was here. We remember him. He is known to us, as the stars are known to the night. And in the darkness, to the end, he remains.

Sunday, July 29, 2007 11:11 AM

Well we have a plan
The plan is to make a plan.
That's progress.
Seriously, the oncologist called Friday night. He's been away. He asked if we could have a meeting this week with Zach's main physicians. (Zach will be inpatient all week – going in tomorrow.) He said what I knew he would say - we have to surgically take the mass on the thyroid out. That should give us more information about what it is and what else we need to do. There are simply not any non-

416

invasive options left. I am not sure if a biopsy of the liver will also be included. Although our surgeon is out of town now, the oncologist spoke to him before he went away. It sounds like they want to do this in a few weeks but beyond that I know little. The oncologist said that we need to talk about some things in depth. Yes, I'd agree with that. When I spoke with the surgeon this week he said he does not want to just remove the mass because it has pretty much overtaken the right side of his thyroid. So he wants to take that right side of the thyroid out.

I don't know about vacation…just cannot guess if we will go or not at the moment. Did I ever mention that I don't do well without a plan? It's true. But then I thought this morning about how many times a plan is made but never followed. I do plan to cook dinner every night…I just don't get around to it. And honestly, I have planned to clean the basement for the last 3 years - I'm just waiting for the perfect day. So I've decided plans are highly over rated. That's not to say I like not knowing what the plan is for Zach – just that plans are generally not accurate predictors of the future. My house is a great example of plans that do not come to fruition…I really did plan to exchange my tables, floors and counters for filing cabinets, photo albums and shelves.

This week I've been thinking about a conversation my friend Kathy and I had last year when we were in Atlanta. Kathy and I were talking about our little circle of friends - all with kids who have mitochondrial disease. We were remembering when we first got to know each other – about 10 years ago now - how as a group it seemed we had such faith that if we were only smart enough, discerning enough, well-read enough, advocating enough we could beat mito.

We had these highly scientific discussions, battled our insurance companies (and almost always won), took our kids to the best doctors, read the latest research and helped each other through crisis after crisis. We rarely dwelled on what our children could not do and instead dwelled on what the gaps were in our knowledge or our children's care and how we could fill those gaps. I think we had an unconscious belief that we could hold the disease at bay by sheer determination, knowledge and positive thinking. The only crack in that confidence was that our friend Lynne's little girl had passed away before we all met…but I think we reasoned that if only the doctors

417

had diagnosed Allie before she got so critically ill then surely we could have collectively read enough and talked to enough doctors to save her. It's hard to believe we were so arrogant and at the same time so naïve but we were.

Then Austin passed away, and Angus and Jack.... and we came face to face with the fact that we did not as a group have power over mitochondrial disease. The disease was bigger than us...and yet I still believed that with Sam and certainly Zach it was different. Even though both of Lynne's children had passed away I remember her writing after Sam died, "I really thought he would be different." After all – look how many times Sam had come back. The energetic bunny personified!

That sassy little boy passed away and it became cruelly apparent that I was not in control. After Sam died, I contemplated becoming fatalistic...but I don't think you can become that if it is not in you to start with. But even without being fatalistic I understood, maybe for the first time, that mitochondrial disease might be bigger than me. I still have hope. I still research a lot and know a lot and fight hard to make sure Zach gets only the best. But my resolve alone is not enough. If it was, then Sam would be here telling me that if I told him to cut it out one more time he would cut me out. I understand this -that determination alone does not win the war.

And yet... Zach is doing remarkably well right now. He's quick and funny, he is walking and doing little things so many take for granted like running errands, going to the library, having a snack at a coffee shop, painting for hours at the ceramics studio. He just yelled at me to get off the computer so he can email Mrs. Evans. He's just really doing quite awesome so that it's easy to believe we can conquer mitochondrial disease – or at least keep it on the defense. And you know, whatever leads to that belief – be it superciliousness, innocence, unrealism, idealism or overconfidence – I'm not convinced it is bad. I think that without it Angus and Jack and Sam and Austin would not have lived as long as they did...and I think that Zach and Kathy's Alex and the other kids in our little group would not have accomplished all that they have and lived the lives they continue to live.

I know God is in control but I'm not so sure he would chastise us for continuing to have times when we believe that we are stronger than mitochondrial disease. It absolutely IS arrogant – but that belief is also borne out of love and hope and conviction that our children's lives are a gift worth fighting for. It is a promise kept to "our children" of our little group - Angus and Allie, Austin and Jack and Sam - a promise that we will remember their courageous fights by always remembering that life is worth fighting for.

Wednesday, August 1, 2007 1:11 AM

Still working on a plan. We know he needs surgery - there are differing opinions about when that should happen. Maybe tomorrow we will choose the date. I'm not holding my breath. Am I frustrated? Yes. I think it's a guy thing (sorry guys). All these male doctors who think the meeting will magically get planned by the "meeting genie." And what do they need a meeting for anyway ? What else is there to discuss? We're going to do surgery. He's going to bleed and we'll going to do whatever we have to do to make it stop. They're amusing aren't they? And I'll give them points for their ability to summarize the situation in as few words as possible. However, we need a plan. Now they tell me they have a plan, which is, "Do surgery. Stop bleeding." So after finally catching on to their shorthand I said, "No meeting. No signed consent." That's about the point where they all back out of the door and say, "we'll talk tomorrow," which brings us back to that amazing meeting genie that coordinates meetings. It's a good thing I love them. They love Zach and I know they will always do the very best for him. I would never trade them. We're a good team.

Zach bled again from a shot. In and of itself the bleeding was not awful but it is a sign he is not at his best. Unfortunately, it has been 3 months since his last intestinal tube change so he needs to have that done today. Because of the fact he bleeds from the tube changes we gave him cryo and platelets and plan to give factor 7a, cryo and platelets for a few days afterwards. Hopefully that prevents significant bleeding.

Zach has been progressively itchy for a few months now. It goes away for a few days and then comes back. Benadryl does not help and he can't breathe from Vistaril. It does not seem to be an allergic problem. We wonder if it is his neuropathy acting up. (Basically the nerves send the wrong signals. In this case they are telling the brain "ITCHY" even when there is no reason to be itchy.) We increased his neuropathy medicine so hopefully it helps before he scratches his eye balls out.

Zach and the nurses surprised me yesterday by decorating the room while I was out for my birthday. We had singers, cake and presents. Zach, apparently, coordinated all of these plans with the nurses. Later Abby and Donna came by with lunch, guacamole (for Zach) and more cake. While they visited, there was more cake from the friends I work with (and more singing) and then chocolate from another friend. I fell asleep at an all-time record early time of 9:30-- probably passed out from my sugar high. This morning I have a headache - my hangover from the sugar I think. But there's still cake and it looks good...and someone has to eat it! And another present this morning! Now I understand something Zach said on his seventh birthday. It fell in the middle of a 5 month admission and everyone said, "We're sorry you're having your birthday in the hospital Zach." To that he replied, "I hope I have my birthday every year in the hospital. It was fun!"

When Peter told Zach what a great job he did making my birthday special, Zach said "well she always makes my birthday special so I wanted to do that for her." Pretty sweet. And Abby was wonderful to take time to visit (thanks Donna for bringing her) and Brittany apparently called and asked the nurses to make sure to sing...so I have awesome kids looking out for me. I missed my Sam a lot, though. He would have insisted on opening every present "because it's kind of my birthday too."

That's all for now.

From the Land of Limbo...

Saturday, August 4, 2007 10:12 PM

We are home. Zach has fever - mostly low grade but for whatever reason even a slight increase is spiking his heart rate up. The resident asked Peter if we should stay. Good thing he gave the right answer which is "NO - she never stays." I'll try to write more later. Just really tired tonight but wanted to at least let Zach's fan club know we are home.

I have to say I feel like I am running a marathon. I am just swimming in things to do, trying as hard as I can to take one mile at a time and accept that I can only run my best, and nothing more. But wow - do I have a lot to do! Yes, I know that every American thinks they have too much to do so why am I whining about how busy I am? Well because I do have a lot to do *to get ready to go on vacation Friday afternoon!* Yes, we are going unless things change and then I guess we will not go. But it looks promising. Hence, the marathon I am running at the moment so that we can get on that airplane.

To back up, I talked with Zach's oncologist, hematologist and of course his primary doctor last week. They said it would be okay to wait to do the surgery until the last week of September. This is important to me because those three and the surgeon will be in town and that matters a lot to me. If the mass in/on the thyroid grows before that time, we will have to go in earlier. But for now it seems stable. And we are setting a real date and time for the meeting. This is all good.

Pushing surgery back will allow Zach to go on vacation...something I think is important to do while we can. It is uncertain if or how life may change once we know what is going on with the lesions on the thyroid and liver. I do know the surgery will be terribly difficult for him, given his bleeding. Zach's doctors have been very compassionate and while they worry about him traveling they are doing all that they can to make it happen. The end of September date will also allow Zach to start high school with all the other kids. He says he does not care but I do and I think it matters.

There are a lot of systems we have in place at Children's of Wisconsin and without them Zach is simply not safe. That means we must have assurances before we leave that we can do in San Diego what we do here. Replicating Zach's care in another city is just a logistical nightmare and there are countless details to attend to.

Yet it is all working out thanks to multiple staff members at Rady Children's Hospital in San Diego. The kindness and willingness to help a child they have never met is fairly overwhelming. I have taken the kids to a fair number of places and by far, these people are the most accommodating I have ever worked with. What a great reminder

421

of all the goodness in the world, despite all the horrible things we hear on the news.

Our hematologist talked with their hematologist that cares for the kids with bleeding disorders and she is very willing to help us if he bleeds or needs a transfusion. I have not talked with her but our hematologist seems to feel very comfortable that we will be in good hands if something happens.

There is an IV pharmacy affiliated with the hospital and I cannot tell you how kind the pharmacist I talked with today was. I told him how much Zach wants to go to Legoland and that was all he needed to hear. They will support Zach's care in any way they can. Our local IV pharmacy ships us things every few days but it is not as if I can call them up and have a medication sent to CA in a few hours. It takes a day to get to us. So, the San Diego infusion pharmacy will be our back up in case we need something quickly.

The lab manager has been equally helpful. We explained how Zach often needs daily or even 2x daily labs, I draw them myself and the results are faxed directly to me. She said that is not something they are accustomed to but they will be happy to make it work in San Diego, just as it does in Milwaukee.

The final big thing to work out was oxygen on the airline. I can't believe it never occurred to me that Zach might need oxygen with the cabin pressure changes. Good thing his doctor has the wherewithal to think of it. Our homecare company is able to get a portable oxygen concentrator that can be taken on the airplane and also used "on land" in San Diego.

So now there is just all the packing... and making lists of what gets shipped and what gets carried on, what days this or that needs to be sent by the pharmacy and how many are needed. List and more lists. Plus all the usual packing that the rest of the world does. Thank God none of the medical stuff counts as carry on or baggage when we travel or we'd be well over our two bag/person limit.

How is Zach? Skinnier, that's for sure. It took him six days to gain 6 kg (13.2 pounds for you non metric people) and only two days to lose it. Obviously it was fluid. He looks a lot more like Zach now. I was thinking about how horrible he did this past admission – that weight gain was so over the top bad and he was struggling to breathe the last 2 days, etc. Well it's all about perspective because on the way home from the hospital Zach said, "you know, that was one of the best admissions I ever had! I felt great until today!" So that tells you how much my perspective is worth. What an awesome kid – he really takes it all in stride - a lesson to me many a day.

On Friday my children's uncles, age 13 and 15, came to visit. Matt, Alex and my dad have been here since Friday. They're leaving Wednesday morning. Zach and Abby have had a lot of fun with my little brothers. How cool is it to have uncles that play Nintendo, like Pokemon, skate board and play DDR (dance dance revolution for the non-informed)? The kids had a great time and it was nice to see my dad. I am just sorry that I am in the middle of my marathon at the moment.

Well I have to get to bed…I am drowning in work (as in my paid job), laundry, unpaid bills, incomplete forms that are due, a growing email inbox - and most of all I am drowning in *planning and packing for vacation*!

I can't wait to see, feel, hear and smell the ocean.

Monday, August 20, 2007 8:59 AM

We arrived home from sunny San Diego early Sunday evening. What a slap of reality to go from 10 continuous days (counting the 2 travel days) of perfect weather to gray skies and chilly rain in Wisconsin. I suppose it is good weather for unpacking and laundry.

The kids all look tan and healthy. Zach and Abby loved having Brittany with them for over a week. I think Lego Land was everyone's favorite aside from the ocean and the pool. We have lots of souvenirs and pictures, which I will upload in the next few weeks. Zach took many pictures too. Maybe I can talk Zach into writing about the vacation again. At least this year he cannot say anything about my driving since we flew out there.

Zach is doing ok. From a bleeding perspective things were and are not perfect. We made it through without a serious mishap but it was a little bit of playing with fire. He had a few doses of Factor 7a that held things off but there came a time when he clearly needed blood products. However, it was towards the end of the vacation and I did not take him in. Today he is getting platelets and cryo and I am sure he will need blood tomorrow. Was it the wisest thing to do - not taking him in for the infusions? No – not medically. And yet on the other hand when I saw him in the pool or walking along the bay or going to Lego Land…well, it is hard to think it was that bad of a decision. If he ended up in a severe bleeding crisis hind sight would be a little different right now - but he didn't. I don't think Zach's doctors would recommend this become our new practice, however.

That's all for now. Zach has an admission at the end of the week so there is no end to the amount of things that need to get done before that time. I'm not complaining …San Diego is absolutely beautiful and I am so glad we got this chance to go away before his surgery, which is now about a month away.

Monday, August 27, 2007 11:42 PM

Last week was hard for him Zach. Partly, I think that the excitement from the vacation caught up with him. The first time I did labs after vacation they were really awful. It makes me want to start sending his blood out to San Diego since that seems to be the place where we get good results. Kidding aside, I know exactly what the issue is and it is not something I can change. In San Diego he did not get any blood products. That means he got less fluid each day and less fluid is better for his heart and when his heart us doing better, then his kidneys do better. The day after he got home he was back to his platelets and cryoprecipitate and he has needed red cells just about every day since being home…all of that adds up and takes a toll on his heart and it shows.

Zach is in the hospital now. He did not come in at his best and struggled much more than he usually does right from the get go. He came in weighing 3 Kg more than usual and is now up 3 more and he is not quite through half the infusion. His breathing has been a problem from the beginning and he has needed much more oxygen than usual and some breathing treatments. He is tired too. He usually does not sleep so much. And then there is the bleeding which has required more blood products and a very enlarged abdomen -for reasons we don't understand completely. Even so his personality does shine through and he has his very chatty times. Sunday afternoon he felt well enough to play card games and Nintendo with one of our nurse's husband. He loves Tom and I think it is pretty incredible that

424

Tom takes time to come up and hang out with Zach. Zach had a great time.

His best day at home last week was Friday and that ended up being the best day to feel good. It happened to be the day of his friend's birthday party, which he had been looking forward to. I am so glad he was able to go. I think that neatest thing for me is something so little that it would be hard to appreciate how magnificent it really is. He went to the party with Abby and came home with Abby. The friend lives a block away so he rode in his wheelchair with Abby and one of their friends walking. He waved good bye to me and off they went. I could not count the amount of times Abby and Brittany have waved good bye and gone off to friends…but Zach never has a chance to say, "Bye, mom" and then independently go somewhere. Is it the safest thing to let him go somewhere with friends? No – of course not. The kid is on a bunch of cardiac drips, narcotics and has a central line with many other infusions. But sometimes the right thing medically has to be over shadowed by the right thing emotionally and socially. This was one of those times.

I did get a call about ½ way through the party that his foot was bleeding. Abby had done her best with her band aid treatment (unlike her mother she is actually prepared with band aids) but the foot bled through. I ran down there, put a pressure dressing on it and left. A few hours later he came home and said he had a wonderful time. It's a little thing but it is also huge and I am so glad he got a chance to do it.

A week from Tuesday school starts – HIGH school. Just a little overwhelming for me, though Zach and Abby seem to be taking it all in stride. I am worried how it will all work out for him – new teachers, new school, and new kids…none who know Zach. It will be a learning process for everyone. The beginning of any school year is always a bit hard in terms of coordinating everything Zach needs.

Brittany is doing well. She will work full time through this week and then switch to part-time once school starts. I think she has had a great summer working in the lab. She works with people who sound wonderful – a very cohesive team from what I can tell. She has a new apartment to move in to so she will be quite busy.

This has become one of my least favorite times of the year…it is hard to see all the school supplies and advertisements and to know that Sam is once again not going to school. It was such a privilege in his mind to be able to go and that makes it so very difficult to think about another year starting – another year for his friends but not for him. I used to think I would miss him less as time went by or hurt less when these things like first day of school popped up but that just is not the case.

Zach did manage to work on his robotic bat today. He thought I might help him but anyone who knows me knows that is a disaster. He did pretty well on his own so we'll see if the bat is up and running some time tomorrow.

Wednesday, August 29, 2007 5:32 PM

He's ok. Still bleeding from his GI tract which is highly unusual for him to do for so long. More platelets and cryo today; several days of blood before that. His weight finally stopped going up last night and actually went down this morning. Maybe this is due to the fact we increased one of his heart drips. Who knows...lately I feel like we don't know much. Every time I think I understand what is going on or can predict his response, I see something a little different. At any rate, he looks a bit worse again since this afternoon.

Yesterday he had an abdominal ultrasound to look at possible reasons for why his abdomen is so distended. Well he has a big liver but that is not news. His kidneys don't look perfect but that is not news either. So basically we did not learn anything we do not already know. This afternoon he had a KUB (abdominal x-ray) but I have not heard the results yet.

I have a care conference with the physicians tomorrow. I think they were all struck by lightning at the same time because within 2 minutes they all decided that they could come at the same time, on the same date. Who knows what happened.

Friday, August 31, 2007 10:23 PM

We are home. Zach is just utterly exhausted and still working hard to breathe. His blood pressure is still too high so we continue to turn his Labetalol drip up (Labetalol helps his heart work better and also decreases blood pressure). I do think this was the hardest admission on him in a long time. Not the worst physically -though that was certainly an issue – but emotionally. He was miserable, in pain, and I did a lousy job distracting him. I have a good dose of mother guilt about that right now.

I was preoccupied with work, fatigue, the surgery stuff and some shifts with nurses who were not terribly familiar with him. I'm not complaining as they were nurses who took great care of him and/or Sam in the past -they just had not staffed him in some time. Between the increasing complexity of his care and a new electronic medication record system that is going to drive people batty, staffing Zach takes some getting used to. For me the good news is we have three great nurses who reoriented to him and can step in if we need them to.

Like Zach, I am beyond exhausted. Yesterday afternoon I was so tired that as I was walking in the skywalk, Zach's orthopedic doctor walked right up to me and stood in my way so I could not walk before I even realized he was there. The sad thing is I believe this was the exact way we ran into each other last month. I had to work today and someone asked me how vacation was. In my mind I was thinking, "Vacation? Huh?" I answered promptly enough but it did feel like a slow motion response in my head. "Yes, Anne, there was a vacation even if you can barely recall it."

I'm placing some of the blame for my brain cloudiness on the hospital cafeteria, which seems to deteriorate by the month. Eating has become a challenge at the hospital. Thank goodness for muffins and coffee every morning. Note to Bill: NO I don't want you to eat cheese steaks for me – I want you to figure out how to fly them in on a daily basis when Zach is inpatient.

The care conference... happened. It was difficult. It is clear that they think this is cancerous – the question is only what kind. They seem to feel he has paraneoplastic syndrome, which I admit describes Zach fairly well. They are careful to say they might be wrong but the oncologist's answer, when asked point blank what he thought it was, did not escape my attention.

It was also difficult in that I went in there thinking we were going to discuss surgery and we left with more treatment questions. Partly that is due to my own questions, which as always were endless. I asked if we should remove his parathyroid glands in addition to his thyroid or if we should repeat the parathyroid test that was normal in April 2006. So that led to a long discussion of a different and more extensive surgery, but potentially a more appropriate one. That should teach me to not ask so many questions.

However, the prize for the question that blew the plans out of the water goes to his hematologist. There is now consideration of burning/killing/destroying the thyroid gland with radioactive medication. This was apparently struck down during the tumor board meeting but for a variety of reasons it was revisited yesterday. It has its own set of risks – mainly that there is a risk of internal bleeding and infection. We would not necessarily know he was bleeding until it was too far along. Aside from that, as far as I know, (and I admit to knowing little), it requires a pituitary gland that works. His does not. My fear with this is if the liver lesions are destroyed and he bleeds in his liver he will never stop.

When I expressed that I did not know what to plan for anymore, I was told to plan on surgery Sept 26. This morning we further discussed issues about surgery. But this afternoon the endocrinologist and oncologist again discussed other options. Needless to say I don't know my right from my left at the moment.

None of this is wrong. This is what makes Zach's doctors good doctors. It would be so easy to stick to their first decision without a second thought. The process they are asking me to be patient with is necessary but that does not make it easy. It took me the better part of the summer to get to a point of not wanting to cover my ears every time they mentioned surgery. Now I wish I had put some ear plugs in and covered that with ear muffs because yesterday we flew the Concorde back to limbo with the possibility of being sent off in a completely new direction soon. Probably surgery but potentially not. At this point I am afraid to mentally prepare for anything. Somehow, some way I need to just take this a day at a time and not feel so ungrounded. It's completely against my nature to do that but if I don't, I am going to make myself sick with playing out different scenarios in my head. Maybe I should take a crash course in knitting or something.

At the end of the care conference, which was close to 90 minutes, I was beyond overwhelmed. Crying in front of four men is the quickest way to clear the room so not wanting to be responsible for that I left the minute we were done. Despite giving up a good portion of the workday, Zach's hematologist and primary doctor both stopped by at different times later in the day. They both took time to re-explain things and talk with me so that I understood the different perspectives, worries and reasoning better. Today, the oncologist called our endocrinologist, who is on staff at a different children's hospital. The email I got at the end of the day says they feel he should have the tests I asked about. Depending on the information we get, they may help us more clearly decide what to do. Then again – I would not hold your breath.

I hate this decision seesaw. I hate not having the answer key. I hate changes in plans that I hated to begin with. I'm tired. They're probably tired. Everyone just wants to do the right thing and no one knows exactly what that is. I forget sometimes how lucky I am. Of course I always know I have great physicians for Zach (and Sam). They're amongst the most highly regarded physicians at our hospital. But it is their compassion, honesty, humility and our trusting, respectful relationships that I could never over estimate. So we'll muddle through this and do our best. It's what we have always done - together - and I have faith we will always do - together.

Friday, September 7, 2007 3:31 PM

I have had a bunch of email messages asking if Zach is better and if we're ok. I'm sorry...I forgot that the last thing I had written about him was that he was not doing so well.

He is doing fine really. The usual stuff but certainly nothing to make me even blink. I am behind on my entire day (I woke up behind...never a good sign) so I am going to leave it at that. I will get back on the computer later this weekend to tell you about high school. Right now I am trying to get my stuff done so I can go to our new neighbor's house. She is from Georgia and if TN is the land of guns and knives (per Zach after our trip there) I am quite sure that GA is the land of friendly, social people. She moved in and she is having the cul-de-sac ladies over for happy hour. Gotta love a new neighbor like that! I am a single mom this week so I'll probably have to end happy hour for myself after an hour.

High school. I realize every mother says this but...it seems like yesterday that Abby and Zach were my toddlers/preschoolers - each other's best friend. They did everything together. We did everything together.

It is hard to see your children grow up, only in that you realize the days with them at home, eating dinner with you, running errands or just talking about the most mundane of things will be fewer and fewer. But I am so proud of them and who they continue to be. They are both kind, curious about life, creative, compassionate and funny. I am sure they will both shine, each in their own way, in high school.

The first day was NOT a banner day at West High School. Zach was just plain old tired and Abby was not thrilled with how the day went. She spent a long time on the phone that evening with her big sister and that seemed to help a lot. The next day she came home and was happy. She likes her teachers and her classes for the most part. Zach had a better day his 2nd day too (he only went Tues and Thurs).

I think both felt a little lost in such a big school. They are used to going to a school like Cheers. No, not the bar part – but the part where everyone knows your name. In their case, everyone knew their name, their family, their history. Now they are at a place where most of their teachers don't know they have a little brother named Sam, that Abby is a writer and that Zach loves art. Abby's teachers may not know Zach exists and vice versa. No one really knows WHO they are. But they will in time.

Medically, Zach has been well. However, I made the mistake of thinking to myself several times this weekend that he has not needed platelets or cryo (extra special part of plasma) for bleeding in over a week. Don't you know that as we were reading about the scientific method this afternoon I noticed blood dripping down his arm, which was already bloody. He was bleeding from a shot site. I put a pressure dressing on it but it has not done the trick yet. I think the run of good kidney function is about to end too. He has been very somnolent today – he only gets this way when his kidneys are not clearing things well enough.

He's also had about four headaches in the past 10 days.... something I have not seen in about 3 years since we started him on a medication to prevent them. They seem pretty bad and the fact he is getting them while on a very strong narcotic for his back pain bothers me. Sam's headaches, at times, led to strokes, so that is why it worries me that he has had so many. His doctor and I will have to discuss this week.

I miss Sam a lot. The marigolds are thriving everywhere – in his home garden, at his grave and around his tree at his school. The fact they are not dead at school is amazing because the soil is so rocky there. I suppose it is a beautiful reminder of his resilience and determination to live no matter the circumstances of the day.

I was looking for old folders and binders for the kids to use last weekend before school started. It was inevitable that I would come upon Sammy's binders of papers. The simplest thing hurt. His attempt to draw circles around the right things on his worksheets, his name, not written too well, but definitely recognizable as Sam – hurt.

He colored in his patterns in scribbles because he never could be bothered with too much attention to detail when coloring. Why would he color the whole thing in when scribbling a few lines of color still showed he knew the pattern? He did his math in the only way he would do math – by adding French fries, subtracting stuffed dogs and measuring Pancakes the hamster – his head, body, water bottle and cage. He wrote (dictated) silly stories and accounts of his day. I would not trade the binders of papers for anything despite the bittersweet feelings. HIS work. His hand touched this and his brain thought up that. When I open the binders, it is as if Sam just stepped away yesterday. Worksheets and stories and colored pictures... his personality shines through even these. I can feel his pride - still. "Mama, I go to school like *the kids*!! (his siblings)

His friends are in 4th grade now. I really can't imagine that for Sam. I don't even try to. I have not read the below poem in a long time...it was in his funeral booklet. I know his brother and sisters still feel "we are seven." I'd like to believe that perhaps some of his friends still remember him. I hope as the new kindergarteners arrive at school, even without knowing him, they feel his spirit as they play around his tree.

We Are Seven (not all the verses)
By William Wordsworth

A simple Child,
That lightly draws its breath,
And feels its life in every limb,
What should it know of death?

I met a little cottage Girl:
She was eight years old, she said;
Her hair was thick with many a curl
That clustered round her head.

"Sisters and brothers, little Maid,
How many may you be?"
"How many? Seven in all," she said
And wondering looked at me.

"Two of us in the church-yard lie,
My sister and my brother;
And, in the church-yard cottage, I
Dwell near them with my mother."

"You run about, my little Maid,
Your limbs they are alive;
If two are in the church-yard laid,
Then ye are only five."

"Their graves are green, they may be seen,"
The little Maid replied,
"Twelve steps or more from my mother's door,
And they are side by side.

"My stockings there I often knit,
My kerchief there I hem;
And there upon the ground I sit,
And sing a song to them.

"And often after sunset, Sir,
When it is light and fair,
I take my little porringer,
And eat my supper there.

"How many are you, then," said I,
"If they two are in heaven?"
Quick was the little Maid's reply,
"O Master! we are seven."

"But they are dead; those two are dead!
Their spirits are in heaven!"
'Twas throwing words away; for still
The little Maid would have her will,
And said, "Nay, we are seven!"

Tuesday, September 11, 2007 10: 27

Today Zach and his 200 pound electric wheelchair got in a tangle. Unfortunately, the wheelchair won. I don't know exactly what happened, as I was not there. It seems like everyone remembers it differently or did not see it until afterwards. In a sense it probably does not matter what happened because it's the result we're left with. The chair moved forward. He was standing in front. The chair pinned him against a table (maybe -still not clear) and he went down. He immediately bled around his J tube (in his intestine). I knew it would get worse but at the time it was only that one source of bleeding.

I talked with his doctor and we decided to give platelets and cryo knowing it would be unlikely that he would escape without more bleeding. We also knew that most of it would be in muscles and tissue where it is hard to know exactly what is happening. We were and are worried about additional fractures given his terribly thin bones.

Since coming home he has been in pain. Mainly the pain is on the left side from his heart to mid abdomen. Bruising has started and I can feel the blood collection already forming inside. Once I was able to assess him myself I talked with his hematologist who had me give a dose of Factor 7a. He wants an update tomorrow though he said to plan on giving more platelets and cryo. I am really worried at this

433

point that he fractured a rib. If it is any worse in the morning we'll have to x-ray.

His knee has abrasions too – a bad sign in someone like him. My hope is that since we used the Factor 7a right away tonight and right after the platelets (which makes it even more special) that we helped stop some of it.

The whole thing is just heart breaking. I can take a fall if he is not bothered. I can deal with large amounts of blood because he really is not affected as long as we keep his counts up. Seeing him hurt tonight with the chest pain is like a knife in the heart. Even in his sleep he is grimacing when I touch that area. He so does not deserve this. He was doing so well going to school, walking, not bleeding, maintaining his strength, dealing with the pain he already has in his back. Earlier this morning he was so tired at his pulmonary appt and I asked him if he ought to stay home… but he said he wanted to try to go. This should not be the price paid for trying so very hard to go to school and learn.

I will say that the aid who was there had the good sense to immediately pick up Zach's backpack with all his pumps and tubing, which is **attached to Zach's central line inserted in a major vein.** Had he not done that it is likely the line would have ripped out, which would have required surgery. Thank God is all I can say.

Please pray for Zach, think of him, hope for him…whatever you believe helps is fine. He could use all of it.

Wednesday, September 12, 2007 10:01 PM

Zach is hanging in there. His chest pain is significant so that even if he moves his arms the pain worsens. His knees hurt -both of them. He must have hurt his right leg too. The pain wore on him through the day….it's always worse at the end of the day. But he soldiered through algebra with Donna later this afternoon. If it was me I would have taken any excuse to ditch algebra but he didn't.

The biggest worry is that blood will pool in his chest but in that case his doctors think we'd see increasing trouble breathing. I was so scared about his breathing last night. It was hard to sleep much – but he was stable and stayed that way today.

I think it is likely he fractured one or more rib. He'll get an x-ray Friday when he has all his other scheduled scans. We want to know but there is no reason to put him through a car ride unnecessarily because there is nothing to do for fractured ribs. The biggest problem is that people breathe more shallow breaths due to the pain and then they can get sick. He is not breathing as deeply for this reason and when I listen to his lungs the left one is quieter than the right. That's not perfect but he's compensating ok, so for now we can just watch and listen carefully for a change.

He got platelets and cryo again today. His hematologist wants them to infuse again tomorrow. He said we'll do daily until we both feel comfortable. There's too much history of bleeding from a minor bump or fall and this was not minor. His hemoglobin dropped. This makes it more clear that he is bleeding inside and needs some blood transfusions. Me - I need a camera installed inside of him so I can see what is going on.

When Zach woke up this morning I said "how do you feel?" He was in obvious pain--could not even get to a sitting position without help. He smiled and said "GREAT!" I said "Really? You don't look like you feel great." He said, "Well, it hurts but I am trying hard to feel great."

Thank you for your thoughts and prayers, empathy and concern for Zach. He/we are really lucky to have so many people who care. I'm scared because with bleeding there often seems to be a lull before the storm -at least for my boys. But I am hopeful that with wonderful doctors, unselfish blood donors and the hopes, thoughts and prayers of so many, the storm will blow by.

He has tests Friday that will not be fun and especially hard on him now with this situation. He has to be there at 8 am for a medicine and then they take pictures several times with the last at 2 PM. We hope this will help us know the right surgery. This accident definitely got the surgery off my mind. It seems so distant next to the immediate issue. I'll update again Thursday or Friday.

Friday, September 14, 2007 7:12 AM

Quick note: Zach's testing got cancelled today. The techs were trying so hard to figure out the right way to do it with Zach that everyone forgot the I-123, (needed to do the test), is not made on Fridays. Seriously - it's not made. They felt badly. I understand them

435

forgetting and am not mad. But I'd love to know what is so special about Friday that I-123 can't be made. So now they are rescheduled for Tuesday all day.

Had I known, I would have brought him for the chest x-ray Tuesday. We absolutely need to go do that since he is in more pain than is reasonable. He starts out ok in the am but by night his meds don't take the pain away.

Saturday, September 15, 2007 12:23 AM

How about some good news for a change? The chest x-ray looked better than any of us expected. No broken ribs or lung bruising. We were surprised to say the least. So why does he have such significant pain? The most likely reason is that he is bleeding into his tissue – which can be very deep and painful. His hemoglobin dropped so much that he clearly bled significantly. But even though the pain is bad, the fact he does not have broken ribs made me happy in that he ought to hopefully feel better soon. That was my thinking yesterday...

And today, I am happy to say that for the first time since Tuesday his pain has stopped escalating and in fact is far less at this point (about noon) than it was 24 hours ago. The sun is shining (for real) but even so -it seems extra bright and colorful today in our house. It is amazing how dreary and heavy everything feels when a child has pain that cannot be controlled adequately.

His back hurts a lot still. The fall likely made the compression fractures worse. It is it is hard to tell because it looks worse on every x-ray anyway.

Back to the good news: We should eat well tonight as Zach felt good enough to make some guacamole this morning. That requires lots of mashing with the arms so I know his chest is better if he can do it. He also helped make the Chili (using Brett Farve's Grandmother's recipe, which Ellen, one of the residents, gave to Zach).

We're still planning to give platelets, cryo and red cells through the weekend because if we pull back now he will likely re-bleed. We'll see what his counts are on Sunday and if not better we will have to assume he is still bleeding and continue treating.

Too bad he needs all the blood products because a friend just invited him out for a church youth group night. Despite the fact he cannot go (which is disappointing), I am thankful that he was asked. There are a few kids who remain good friends. They don't see him much and they are clearly interested in different things (girls and sports usually - neither of which Zach cares about). Yet they make an effort to continue being his friend and they include him.

Zach and Abby are calling some of our neighbor kids to come over so hopefully that works out for tonight. I'd like them to do some fun things before he gets admitted Thursday night(for IVIg and then surgery on 09/26). It's coming so fast and I have so much to do to get ready to leave. The problem being I have no idea if we'll be gone just 2 weeks or a much longer time. Either way the piles of bills and paperwork are huge. And I have to admit that the amount of clothes I have piled has reached a previously unheard of height. I have to laugh when I hear people talk about how their kids keep their rooms....in our house my kids have nothing on their mom.

One last thing: I truly appreciate those who emailed about donating blood. Yes, you're exactly right...whether you donate in Atlanta or New Jersey or anywhere else it helps. He may not get your blood but that is not the point. So many people need blood. In the end it is a gift to him and everyone.

The blood supply is only as good as the people who donate. Without donors we have an inadequate supply or worse no blood supply. And without that, kids like Zach would not survive. That may sound overly dramatic but it's really what it boils down to. It IS that dramatic. So thank you to anyone and everyone who has donated - whether today or last year – it makes a difference. I worried a lot when Sam first became so dependent that one day he would not have what he needed. But day after day the Blood Center supplied whatever was needed to keep him alive. And gradually I stopped worrying. It's hard to explain what a gift that is.

I know many of you cannot donate and I feel badly that you apologize to me about this. I can't donate blood either. But thank you, nonetheless, for telling Zach and Sammy's story to others. You never know who you may inspire to donate simply because you took the time to remove the abstract from this need and make it real. Two boys

437

- able to enjoy life - only because of the many, nameless donors and the staff at the Blood Center of Wisconsin. Thank you.

Saturday, September 22, 2007 2:37 PM

We're in the hospital for Zach's IVIg. So far he is actually doing quite well. He's been sleeping a fair amount but when he is awake he is great!

He's had a procession of friends. It seemed like everyone had to wait in line to get a turn with Zach. Donna came and worked with him on school stuff. His hospital teacher stopped by too and will work with him on Monday. Jackie did PT with him, Ann (without an E) brought him art supplies for the weekend, Kristin and Hope braved playing Game Cube with him, Grandma and Grandpa, Karen, Eileen and Meg stopped by. Brad tried to stop by but the room was a circus. It's nice to have so many people who care for him. He really loves to be here! That is sad if I think about it as a consequence of how much time he has spent here. But in general I just think it is great that if he has to be here so much, he feels so loved and at home with the staff.

We had to do an x-ray of his leg today. It was hurting him more and more in school yesterday and by last night he could not bear weight on it. Today he could walk a little but it hurt him still. The femur looked ok aside from some vague statement the radiologist made about metabolic changes…whatever that means. It's not broken – that much I know.

He had the all-day nuclear medicine testing on Tuesday. The results definitely have not added clarity. I had hoped they would serve as a neon sign telling us that surgery is the right thing or the wrong thing. No such luck. Thursday was a day of being a tennis ball - surgery was a good idea, a bad idea, a dangerous thing or maybe not so dangerous....you get the idea. I can't say that I feel good about any of it. I don't know what the right thing is anymore and no one else does either.

We could try ablation with radioactive medicine which would spare him surgery. Yet it has its own set of drawbacks, not the least of which is that if it fails then we are 9 months down the line. At the rate his bleeding issues are progressing - 9 months could take us past the window of opportunity for doing the surgery. 9 months and it could become metastatic.

We can do surgery - because after all we have no idea what we are dealing with and it is the standard approach in pediatrics - especially with a mass of this size and clinical signs of malignancy. There are many benefits to this approach....and yet he could go to the ICU and never come out. That is what I cannot bear to think about. Still...I have to. I have to think about all of it in order to make the best decision I can.

Did I ever mention I do not gamble? The oncologist said to me, "There is no wrong answer." I said, "Oh yes there is. We just don't get to know which one is wrong until after we choose something."

A friend sent an article about motherhood...by Anna Quindlen. Here is one excerpt:

Raising children is presented at first as a true-false test, then becomes multiple choice, until finally, far along, you realize that it is an endless essay. No one knows anything....Eventually you must learn to trust yourself.

That is true about being a mother but for me it rings more true about medicine. I used to think that by and large there would be one right thing to do – I just had to find the person who knew. I now realize that the answer is within one endless essay with pros and cons and contrasting opinions. The right answer could be the wrong answer depending on factors that we can and cannot control. All I can do is to collect as much information as possible. It's overwhelming sometimes because I could probably find an endless number of opinions. The information is ever changing. Things I believe to be true are often true only for a given situation or at a given time. I guess in the end it is a matter of doing the best I can and trusting that I did just that. I just wish it was as easy to do that as it is to write it. I wish there were assurances that if I do my best then I won't be haunted if my "best decision" turns out to be the wrong decision. But I know myself well enough to know I will be haunted...so I keep searching for that ever elusive "perfect answer" - which likely does not exist.

That's all except to say that a friend's beautiful little boy passed away a few days ago. His name is Connor and he has an amazing spirit and love of life. He was just about Sam's age. My heart has been so heavy for his Mom and Dad.

Tuesday, September 25, 2007 11:22 PM

So it is the night before Zach's surgery....Perhaps it is a good thing that I am beyond exhausted and sensory overloaded so that I have barely thought about what tomorrow may bring. So many people came by yesterday and today so that we can make the best plans possible for the surgery and post op period. We also have numerous friends at the hospital that have been part of the boys' lives over the years and many of them stopped by to say hello. Some others wanted to get up to see him today but I'm telling you – this is a popular guy. I'm going to have to start keeping an appointment book for him pretty soon.

Thankfully, Zach has been in rare form. He's keeping us all laughing. Very much a teenager but in a nice teenage sort of way. I wish I had written down some of the things he has said. Here are a few:

Just now he told Janet, "I'm going to challenge myself to stay awake during the surgery." Ok then, I better let the anesthesiologist know that.

He told his night nurse, Nichole, to stay away from his Androgel (Testosterone) because "It's a medicine just for men and you don't want to get a moustache do you?"

He told Mary that he LOVES her black, leather binder because "after all, you can never have enough binders Mary." He also told Mary, "Long time no see" and then corrected himself, "Well actually I have seen you but all you ever do is talk in the halls."

....Maybe you have to be there for some of them and without his dramatic expression it may lose something but I can tell you he has kept the nurses and me laughing a lot. This is good.

We have made what I think is a good plan with the ICU staff. We hope he does not go there but if he does I think they have done a lot to try to make it as safe and consistent with his current care as possible. There are good people who know me, know Zach and will try hard to make this work IF he goes there. The goal remains for him to go to the intermediate care unit, which is where he always gets admitted but making a plan is good – and perhaps a good luck charm as well. You know if we didn't he'd go there for sure.

440

I do feel Zach is going into the surgery as strong as he can be. He is finished his IVIG and he actually did fairly ok with it. The weekend was not so hot as he became progressively more tired until Sunday when he fell asleep and there was nothing anyone could do to wake him up. Believe me we tried but he was completely unarousable. It scared me to be quite honest. He had a gastrointestinal infection (we think) and they seem to always do something nasty to his brain. We started a 3rd antibiotic and after two doses he woke up Monday and was really doing quite well. I definitely would not have sent him into surgery like that.

He is one heck of a busy kid right now. We're going to have to get some more IV access tomorrow or they will never be able to get everything in him that he needs to get between the antimicrobials and blood products. So the plan is 1) remove the right thyroid which will be sent for biopsy, 2) repair his Gastrostomy site (essentially a hole where a tube goes into his stomach. He has had this since he was a year old) and 3) get more IV access.

Our hematologist is not messing around so he will be on an aggressive treatment plan and maybe this will be the difference between a smooth recovery and one that I cannot think about. We never have had such an aggressive plan before. And this time it will be followed because the right people will be involved in his care and they understand it is not an option to be on time with his blood products.

Zach is happy to be going to surgery. Seriously. He loves Dr. Aiken and he loves the "gas." He is the least anxious kid about surgery that I have ever met. It's just his mom who is a mess.

Well, it's late and I still have a few things to do and need to sleep. They'll come for him at 7 am and I will have to hand him to the anesthesiologist at 7:30 – always the hardest thing for me about any surgery. I am so thankful that Dr. T will be doing his anesthesia. This is the doc who did all of Sam's anesthesia and I trust him so much. If I have to hand Zach to someone at least it is this anesthesiologist and of course Zach's surgeon, who has cared for him since he was little. The first incision is likely to be at 8:30 am….from there we'll see how it goes.

Thank you for everything – the prayers, visits, positive thoughts, crossed fingers and toes, hugs, notes…and I cannot forget – the Darth

Vader Balloon! It is about 3 feet high and Zach loves it! I'm not so sure about waking up in the middle of the night and seeing Darth looking down at me but Zach told me to "get over it." Thank you so much to everyone

Wednesday, September 26, 2007 2:20 PM

Zach is still in surgery. It has taken much longer than expected. I am sure I will learn more in the next few days....second hand I have heard the mass was difficult to get out. His parathyroid glands did look bigger than they should have but for now they are still in and they have closed his neck.

Ultrasound came up and found that we can put a second central line in Zach - and it will be a permanent one like the one he has now. It has some very real risks in terms of clotting off the vein but we are between a rock and a hard place. He needs more IV access -not just now but 365 days a year. So the OR nurse called me just now and said they have just started to put the line in. Hopefully Dr. Aiken can get it in easily.

He has had some high fevers - it could be they warmed him up too much. We'll have to see as time goes on. The plan now is for him to go to recovery room and then they will decide if he should go to ICU or not. If he has to go I know it is the right place for him to be because his anesthesiologist and other physicians would never put him there unless they felt there was not another option.

I don't know if I will be able to update again until late tonight so I wanted to do it now while he is still in surgery. I anticipate they'll be done about 4 PM.

Thank you again for caring so much for Zachary and me. We are blessed to have such a wide circle of support. Zach was talkative and happy this morning. I know I sent him in to surgery as good as he could be.

11:38 PM

Zach finally got to the floor at 5:30. The anesthesiologist asked me if I was okay with him going to IICU and of course I said yes. He said he felt we could give it a try. It's been busy -for a while it took essentially 3 nurses to get him settled (me and 2 staff nurses.) But I think we have a good system now. It helps having more IV access.

He did not get the line we wanted - which would have come out of his chest. The surgeon tried for a long time but it just was not the day I guess. Interventional Radiology very kindly went to the operating room and got a different sort of central line in his upper arm (PICC Line). It's not perfect and we'll have to do something more permanent still. I'm not sure when.

Zach is in considerably more pain then we anticipated. I hope it feels better tomorrow but for now he has as much pain medicine as he needs. He still has a fever but not quite as high as I hear it got in OR.

His arm where the new line is has bled some more since early this evening. Unfortunately he has a large tissue bleed on his back....likely from lying on the operating room table for 8 hours. It's no one's fault...he just has such weak bones.

The problem with both of those things bleeding is that they indicate he is likely bleeding in his neck - which of course we cannot see and will not see until it is enough to cause breathing problems. He's on pretty high flow oxygen now but looks ok and sounds ok with his breathing.

The residents and critical care fellow have been watching him closely along with his nurses. He has labs every 6 hours for now so I hope we'll see if he starts to decompensate metabolically before it gets too out of hand. I'm glad that tonight a fellow is on in the ICU that I have known since he was a resident. I trust him.

Zach's oncologist will talk with pathology tomorrow. I guess we'll get trickles of information day by day on the biopsies. He did say we'll have to full body scan him again in 3 months. That's all I know about that for now.

Zach is what the hematologists call a "late bleeder." Sam was too. Most people think that if you make it through the first 12-24 hours without bleeding it will be ok. They are the opposite. They're always relatively stable the first day and then it all goes south on day 2 or 3.

Zach is the most courageous person I know. He has been through so much today and yet he tries to smile to people, he asks for things politely, and he has put up with a lot of post-surgery stuff that likely makes him feel uncomfortable.

I never like it when they take my kids away to OR but today was by far the hardest. It's hard to express exactly what was going on in my mind this morning when I said good bye to him this morning....in essence it boiled down to a question I could not have articulated: would it be the last time I ever heard his voice or the last time he said I love you. He was joking with his anesthesiologist and as I heard him laugh, and while I laughed too - I was trying to commit his words to memory in case it was the last time I would ever hear him tell a joke. I am beyond thankful that tonight I have heard his voice and held his warm, living, hand. He is asleep - breathing - heart beating. He's nowhere near being out of the woods yet but every day with him is a gift and today I was given another day.

Thursday, September 27, 2007 11:53 AM

Things aren't going as well. What a shock! No, not really, but still disappointing if that makes sense. I can be prepared for things to not go perfect but it still is hard when they don't.

He is definitely swelling around the neck incision site now. The incision is horizontal across a good portion of the front of his neck. Last night there was almost no swelling. However, this morning the swelling measures about 2.5 cm. If this was a leg or something else it would be considered small but any swelling in this case is of concern given where the surgery took place. The mass was on/in the right lobe of his thyroid and because the mass was so large it was actually easiest to remove the entire lobe than to try to get the mass off. The thyroid has 2 lobes. One is adjacent to the right side of the trachea and the other is adjacent to the left. So that might give a sense of why any swelling is a huge concern – just a little can have a big impact on his airway (trachea).

For now hematology has increased his platelet infusions to every 12 hrs and his cryo infusions also to every 12 hours. They'll keep his Factor 7a at every 3 hours and hope it does not cause a stroke. Factor 7a is used a lot in Iraq, actually, with the soldiers because it stops bleeding fast and gives them time to get to an operating room or get fresh blood products. However, the most common problem – and it definitely happens enough to be a true risk – is it causes so much

444

clotting that the person has a stroke. Having said that, Sam and Zach have both received more Factor 7a than has likely ever been used by anyone and neither have even had a suggestion that they are going to clot too much. So I am actually not worried about that risk…but it makes the hematologists worry tremendously when we use a lot - rightfully so.

Gotta go. My mom is here with my very very favorite soup – Mushroom Madeira

Thursday, September 27, 2007 5:40 PM

Not doing so hot here. The swelling and discoloring increased and it did so fairly fast. I looked at it about 1 PM and was struck by the change. I will say they acted very fast once I told them it had changed. They got an extra dose of factor 7a up and we have doubled his every 3 hour dose. We also got some platelets right away.

His breathing is still fairly ok but he has periods of time when he is really working too hard. So they now have a special type of tubing in his nose that can both give him oxygen and also measure his carbon dioxide levels. It's nowhere near perfect in terms of accuracy but we can watch trends and will know if it starts to climb too fast. For accuracy we will still send his blood gases fairly often.

He's resting now which is good. He has been so restless and unable to sleep for any period of time since he got out of surgery. He looks absolutely exhausted. His doctors and nurses are taking awesome care of him.

Friday, September 28, 2007 10:18 PM

Zach is okay. After he had such an acute change in the neck bleeding yesterday I was scared that it would only progress. But I think we arrested it. This morning it was slightly worse but had slowed considerably and quite honestly it looks the same to me this evening. This is one of those times when I feel that despite some of the horrendous bleeds the boys have had, we have at least learned along the way. There was no watch and wait this time, no hemming and hawing…the doctors just immediately made an even more aggressive plan. I cannot imagine how bad this could be without physicians who

445

are willing to treat Zach despite the fact that we really do not understand exactly why he bleeds.

This morning, our surgeon said that if the neck remains stable in terms of swelling, he will not need to put a drain in. I hope that remains true. Zach is showing that he cannot be off oxygen right now. The minute his oxygen falls off his sats go down too low. I am sure this is related to all of the swelling.

The hematoma/bleeding/edema of Zach's back really bothers me. It is very painful to him and it looks just awful – almost like he has a hunchback. It is not life threatening but I do wish it would get better.

This morning Zach's chest x-ray showed that the new line had "flipped" up into a different vein (jugular). The radiologist who read it said it was not a concern. When Zach's resident told me that it did not sit too well with me. It did not sit so well with Zach's doctors either when they were finally told about it (unfortunately none of us knew anything until about 3 PM). It was a clot waiting to happen because that meant what we put into his line (like platelets for example) were being sent upstream even though the regular flow of blood in that vein is downstream. Not a good situation. So finally about 6:00 PM Interventional Radiology was able to see Zach. Thankfully one of the senior radiologists was on call and he was able to get it back into the right place. He said it could stay that way for a day or 5 months. Well, we cannot x-ray every day so it only makes it more clear that we need to do something more permanent next week. We'll need to try to get a line into his chest again and hope it happens this time.

Zach's oncologist said that pathology is not able to say whether or not the mass is malignant yet. I guess it is a little confusing (why am I not surprised that once again something cannot be figured out easily)? It is very vascular (lots of blood) which is not consistent with what was seen on the scans or the fact that he did not have it a year ago. I have no idea why….it's all confusing to me and I was too tired to ask any questions. All I know is they'll keep working on it.

Today my grandmother came to visit us. My Uncle Tom and cousin Mimi brought her. There is a great comfort that I'm not sure I can describe having my grandmother hug me, tell me me she loves me and that I made a good decision. Maybe because she raised 11 children, maybe because I admire her so much, maybe because it makes me remember all the times I spent with her and my Gramps when I was younger....all I know is it was exactly what I needed even though I did not know I needed it. Of course it was great to see my uncle and cousin too. I just wish Zach had been awake to see them.

Mimi- my cousin – brought a cookbook for Zach. He was having fun looking through it with my mom tonight. They decided that almost everything looked good. My mom and Frank came and played cards with Zach until he had to go to radiology which was good for him. They brought me Chinese food which was good for me – especially because I forgot to eat again.

Hope to sleep soon. The nurses are doing an amazing job of keeping up with all that Zach needs. I asked them if they wanted to send him to ICU because he really is beyond busy. But for now they want to keep him!

One of Zach's primary nurses has her son in the ICU right now. Baby Grayson had complex heart surgery yesterday. So please think of them too. Melissa(Zach's nurse) is the one who found Zach the Lego set he wanted more than anything after his pacemaker surgery. She also found Chicken Food's identical twin for me to have (quite difficult since he had been discontinued). Chicken Food is Sam's favorite stuffed dog and so I buried him with Sammy. She is such a giving person and it' hard to think of all she's gone through with her own little guy.

Saturday, September 29, 2007 10:48 PM

OOOPs, forgot to say thank you for all of the great Email cards. The pictures they let you choose from are a little silly but Zach likes reading the messages. Then we hang them up.

Brittany borrowed a friend's parent's car and came home last night so that she could see Zach. Her friend's parents filled the car with gas and snacks....she had never even met them. I am continually amazed when someone has such unrestrained generosity and utter compassion. Zach was so happy to see her. They played some Nintendo and painted. She hung out with us most of the day. My brother, Mike, stopped by too. It was nice for all of us to see him.

I am not sure what is going on with Zach. Peter thought the discoloration around the swelling of the neck had spread slightly this morning and I agree. The on call surgeon came by and said that if Zach was any other kid she would take him back to OR and open the incision up and drain the blood. I guess she discussed this with Zach's primary surgeon who told her he was not so sure that was a good idea for Zach. I said I am okay with whatever they think is best. I really don't know.

This afternoon the swelling measured bigger than this morning which was very concerning to me. He just does not look right to me. His face has been getting more and more red/flushed today. And his face has swollen markedly from this morning. It does not seem like his typical swelling that occurs with his heart failure because he is breathing okay and his labs look good. I worry that something is going on inside of his neck to make his face swell so much. We'll see what the doctors say in the morning.

He has also had a lot of chest pain and it progressed through the day until it was quite acute at one point. The nurses were able to print his heart rhythm off of his monitor and it looked abnormal to all of us. The intern did an EKG...she had some trouble with it so I am not sure how good if was. She showed it to the cardiology fellow and I am told he or she said it was all artifacts. I don't know enough to know if that makes sense or not. I'd like to believe it but it seems odd that at the moment he had such severe chest pain he would show this abnormality that he has never shown before. (And he is constantly monitored for the one week he is inpatient each month so we do know his baseline). I'll have his own doctor look at it tomorrow. In the meantime we got another chest x ray to make sure the line did not flip again. It didn't. So the chest pain remains a mystery.

Marisol (his nurse), Brittany and I were talking about dating. Zach piped in that he did not think anyone should date until they get married. Hmmmm....that could be very interesting. He, of course, is not going to get married and therefore he won't date (since it is best to date after marriage).

Sunday, September 30, 2007 11:32 PM

It has been a long and unsettling day. Zach's chest pain just progressed and progressed. It seemed no amount of dilaudid really helped him (dilaudid is a strong narcotic). Zachary is an incredibly stoic kid…it is something that always makes an impression on any one who spends time with him – especially those who provide medical care to him. His surgeon said that sometimes he worries Zach is too stoic. So knowing that, perhaps it can help one appreciate that my son had tears coming out of his eyes at one point today. He does not cry when he is in pain. Not a few weeks ago when his left chest side hurt from the wheelchair accident, not through major abdominal surgeries or any other invasive, uncomfortable procedure. He said that on a scale of one to ten his pain was beyond a ten….again, something he would never say unless it really felt that way.

The on-call radiologist came in and did a chest CT scan. It did not show anything that told us what is causing the chest pain. However, they could not use the contrast because his body is saturated already with iodine from the thyroid testing. So that may limit what the radiologist can see. An MRI is out of the question because of his pacemaker. Obviously, our diagnostic testing choices are limited at this point.

Tomorrow he will have a "real" EKG (as opposed to the one the intern did). He continues to show this somewhat abnormal aspect to his heart rhythm. It coincides with his worst pain episodes. We also drew blood to look for heart muscle damage.

Back to the chest CT: His trachea and main bronchi (basically his airway through which he breathes) is partially collapsed. He had a chest CT done in late June to look for cancer and this was not seen t that time. It's concerning because he has been having more and more trouble keeping a good oxygen level in his blood tonight. His neck CT showed a "mass" which we assume to be a large collection of blood that is causing the ever increasing swelling.

Hematology does not want to change anything at this point which is fine with me. Clearly he continues to worsen so it would hardly be wise to start pulling back on any blood products.

His head continues to look very swollen and flushed. He is very very hot and sweating through pillow case after pillow case. Tomorrow we will do an ultrasound of his neck to see if any of the veins that bring blood back to his heart have narrowed since his ultrasound on Wednesday. If this was the case it would be a possible reason for the swelling of his face and neck.

There is no way that he can get a line placed under these circumstances. His chest pain is unreal and until we know why, I don't think anyone will want to put anything into his chest. So I don't think we'll be leaving here anytime soon.

The girls came by and played Yahtzee with Zach today. They had a lot of fun though I think laughing may have exacerbated his pain. Still…it was an incredible diversion and one he needed. He has such good sisters and I have such wonderful daughters. This is so hard on them. Brittany is worried and trying to go to school and work and volunteer. It gets to be too much sometimes. Abby is a new freshman and her mom is not home and I know she misses us a lot. It was hard to say good bye to both of them today. Brittany went off to Minneapolis and Abby just to Waukesha but it feels like they are worlds away. I miss them. I am also so proud of them for showing such strength and resolve even in the face of such a stressful family situation.

That's about all. I just hope someone can figure out why Zach has so much pain. It's awful to watch. And I'm still waiting to hear what pathology thinks about the mass removed. I may not want to hear when all is said and done.

Monday, October 1, 2007 11:29 PM

Today has been a long day. It is clear that the swelling is increasing and now includes his shoulders and upper chest. The mass that was his incision site is moving up. Between that and the swelling we had a long night and day trying to give him enough oxygen. It looks like tonight will be the same. It is scary as he will suddenly drop his oxygen levels and it is not so simple to get them back up. It takes a lot for me to get scared when we are inpatient but there are times I have been today. It is comforting to have nurses who take such good care of him and a senior resident on the floor that I really trust.

I had hoped to see his pulmonary doctor today but she was out. We need help because his current breathing machine (BiPAP) settings are not enough right now. He is on 8 liters of oxygen at night and struggling still. I don't like it.

We had a heart scare with him today and it makes me know without a doubt that we did the right thing putting in the pacemaker.

His pacer was firing on and off for what we thought was a low heart rate. As it turns out, his heart rate was not low but part of his heart was not conducting as it should. The cardiology fellow (who is also an ICU attending) explained a lot about Zach's pacer to me tonight. It practically has a "brain" and can sense many things aside from heart rate. This doctor was the fellow who cared for Sam many years ago when he coded and had to go to the ICU….he is so smart and I learned a lot. At any rate, we'll get the pacer interrogated in the morning to see what really happened. I wonder if his heart is just so stressed from the surgery.

In terms of bleeding treatment, our hematologist said it is not time to back down on anything yet and I agree as does Peter. I did not see the oncologist today so I am sure there is still no news from pathology. Kind of unsettling that they still cannot say it is not malignant.

Zach's pain is still quite present but he seems to finally have the right dose of pain meds to help when it gets bad. The problem is that if he uses enough to completely take the pain away he is too compromised with his breathing. This is yet another reason we really need the pulmonary team's help tomorrow.

He was able to do some school work today. He cracked me up when I heard him tell a nurse "I need to work on my personal finances now" (he is taking personal finance). He also tried reading some of his book for language but apparently he was too distracted to read much. When Brett (resident) stopped by he said "I can't read because I have one woman on my right talking (me) and one on my left (Hope) and I can't get a thing done!" I think he has had it with "women talking" as he also complained to Peter this morning that he was sleeping until "Mama and Melissa woke me up talking SO LOUD at midnight."

I did get the kid completely cleaned up today which I bet felt good to him. He took a short walk with Hope and me. Of course it was afterwards that his heart went wacko and I am a little afraid to take him walking again until we know what happened. Still---at the time it was nice to see him up and walking.

That's about all I can think of now. I cannot tell you how much your messages and cards mean to Zach and to me. Thank you so much for your prayers and positive thoughts and compassion….I don't think I could ever overestimate the strength that comes from knowing so many people care for us. It does not take away any of the heart break but it does being me comfort.

Tuesday, October 2, 2007 11:26 PM

Today....started off ok but has not ended that way. Zach was awake for a few hours this morning and even did some mild exercises with Jackie, his PT. The rest of the day he was in and out...mostly asleep.

The pacemaker interrogation showed that Zach's pacemaker was not sensing some of his ventricular beats and so began to pace. They changed some settings on it so that it will be able to detect those beats and not pace unnecessarily. We'll see if that helps. The interrogation also showed that he is using his pacemaker about 10 times as much as he did 2 months ago (though still a small percentage of the time). I'm glad he has it.

He gained 4 Kg (almost 9 pounds) in 24 hours. That was this morning and he looks worse tonight. It is hard to see this happen to him. His heart just cannot handle the extra fluid he is getting with all of the blood products. Yet he needs the blood products so it is a catch 22.

His heart is not doing well at all right now and that has caused an acute secondary kidney failure. He has done this many times in the past but never to this extent. It's really bad this time. His 5 Pm labs were awful so we had to stop his TPN because his potassium and calcium levels were too high. He is on fluids now and Sarah, his nurse, just drew labs again. Once we get the results we can decide if he can stay on the fluids we ordered earlier or if we need to change things again.

If he doesn't improve by the morning we will likely start a new diuretic. It's an IV drip and he may need to go to the ICU for it. It has never been used at this hospital before but the attached adult hospital has used it.

A little while ago I saw that he had started to bleed from his urinary tract again. His shoulders and chest continue to get more swollen but it is impossible to know if it is blood or swelling with fluid. For now the blood products remain where they have been.

452

His pulmonary doctor came by today. I really like her a lot. She changed some settings on his BiPAP machine and it has really helped. We can go up more if we need to but for now he is not dropping the oxygen levels in his blood every 10 minutes.

I wish I had better news to share. Maybe tomorrow?? I am very tired so going to try to sleep for a bit until the labs come back.

Thanks for thinking of Zach. I wish I could write about Non-medical things today but medical problems seemed to consume the day.

Wednesday, October 3, 2007, 5:53 PM

I am not sure if I will have time to update later. Zach is sleeping now as he has been most of the day. He is, at least, comfortable and free of pain when he is like this.

His urine output did increase for several hours early this morning but by 10 am slowed and he had virtually none again since about 9 am. We had been very hopeful this morning that he was turning the corner but that is not the case. The pharmacy had to call around to get the new drug – it is called Conivaptan. They will start it at 7 PM – he'll get a loading dose over an hour and then it will run for another 1-4 days slowly. It can only be given for a maximum of 4 days but we're hoping one day will be enough. We'll see. He will stay on his two other mega dosed diuretics as well.

I'm not sure anyone is too crazy about starting this and night time is an especially bad time to do it. Yet, no one is comfortable with him going another night without urine output. They have decided that since he is monitored so closely on the intermediate unit we can stay here and not go to ICU.

For the first time in a week we did hold a blood transfusion because he just cannot handle it right now. He is still getting platelets and cryo 2x/day and Factor 7a every 3 hours. It is hard now to tell if he is bleeding more as his swelling is everywhere - he does not look too much like Zach at the moment.

His abdomen remains quite distended. Apparently the radiologists say that his intestine is quite dilated – which has never happened with him before. Surgery is concerned and wants to test further to see what is going on. However, that requires a trip downstairs to the 1st floor -

453

more of a stress than he can handle right now. Peter and I will talk with the surgeons tomorrow and decide how best to approach this problem. This could turn into a bad problem with obstruction or perforation but at the moment it is way down on my priority list. Kidneys and heart take precedence.

A very old friend, Bridget, (I've known her a long time -not that she is very old) stopped by today to see Zach. I met her when Zach was 2 and Abby was 1. Zach and Abby had PT, OT and speech several days/week as did Bridget's daughter. We used to drag ourselves in many mornings – she was one of my first friends that I met that had a child with special health needs. We were pregnant together - me with Samuel and Bridget with Anthony. Today she brought a prayer blanket that she knit with Elizabeth and Maria – her 2 daughters. They learned how to knit and decided to knit for Zachary and me. As they knit, they said prayers for Zach and those are interwoven in the blanket. You cannot imagine how much this blanket means to me.

My cousin Emily stopped by today with a big box of sweet treats. I was just complaining to Zach's nurse that I needed a doughnut. It was ironic to have Em show up at that exact time. Please think of her as she is running a marathon in Chicago to raise money for the United Mitochondrial Disease Foundation in honor of Zach and Sam this weekend. I am so proud of her for trying. Emily – we love you so much and wish we could be there this weekend!

10:30 PM - I don't know what to say or do. The med started at 7:00 PM and so far he has had 3.5 cc of output (not even a teaspoon). He cannot continue like this. Please do whatever you feel is right - pray, hope, think positively, hold him in your heart. If this medication does not work I am not sure what there will be to do. He is such a good kid and he tries so hard to be positive and kind. It breaks my heart to see this happen to him.

Thursday, October 4, 2007 9:41 PM

I am sorry for those of you who hear it by this website.

Zach is in the ICU. He is intubated (has a breathing tube) and sedated and paralyzed (intentionally). Last night about midnight his oxygen levels dropped and his heart stopped. They told me at one point that they would only try to revive him one more time...They tried and his heart started beating again. He is on many drugs to help his heart. I was in the room during the code but not able to be near him.

Only time will tell what happens next. Zach will have to take the lead I think. For now they will leave him completely paralyzed and sedated so that his tired body can rest. He is not in pain and he looks peaceful. I love him so much and wish I could take all of this away from him.

I am thankful for the ICU fellows that were there last night. They did everything right for him. I am thankful for the staff nurses on 4 west - he could not have a better team. I am thankful that an anesthesiologist just happened to be on the floor so that Zach was able to be intubated within minutes. I am thankful that an attending ICU doctor was in house and able to come right away. I am thankful that his own doctor came in as soon as they called him. I am thankful that so many of his 4 west nurses came in from home at 1 am to be with me through such dark hours. I am thankful for Rachel and Patty - both Sammy's primary nurses who now work in ICU. Rachel came in at 2 am and worked till 5 pm and Patty came in at 5 pm and will work until Rachel comes back. His 4 west nurses are also staffing him so that he has people who love him and know him at all times. I am thankful for an entire hospital of people who love Zach and have stopped by to visit him today.

All I can do now is pray for Zachary and hope with all my heart and soul that he wakes up, breathes on his own and has his same wonderful smile, laughter and sense of humor.

I have been awake for 48 hours now and need to sleep. It is hard to update when he is in the ICU...I will try to do it when I can

Saturday, October 6, 2007 11:17 AM

Sorry for the delay. I guess I wanted to have a sense of which way things were going before I updated but nothing seems too clear to me at the moment. Well that's not true -it is clear that Zach is loved. Thank you for guestbook entries and thank you for visits and prayers and hopes.

Zach is still intentionally paralyzed. I have my moments i just want to tell them turn that off now and let's see what he can do. But mostly I know it is not time. His right lung worsens a little each day and he needs to rest so that the energy needed to repair that lung goes where it needs to go. He is on a continuous drip of a pain medicine. I can say without a doubt that he is comfortable. Even when we had to start another IV yesterday he never had a change in his vital signs. Sometimes I wonder what he is dreaming about. I hope he can hear me.

The ICU team has been able to wean him significantly from the continuous medications that keep his blood pressure up and his heart beating. From what I understand he was on huge amounts to start with so he still has a way to go to get off of them. But our goal today is to try to do that if possible.

Brittany flew home on Thursday. Thank you to everyone who helped coordinate that. She made some decorations for his room and Abby helped make them more colorful last night. The gift shop refilled his big Darth Vader balloon and it is looking down over him. a few of the residents said that Zach is the only kid who would take comfort in Darth Vader looking down on him.

The ICU team has been completely respectful of me and my role in Zach's life. They listen and they talk with me about changes. They have taught me a lot too as they explain things. Although his primary doctor cannot be his ICU doctor, they also respect him so much. He adds so much value because he is able to provide the big picture and give perspective. And he is a Zach expert so I think they are thankful for his role in Zach's care. I know I am. In the past some of the ICU admissions have not gone so well but this time I can say that so far I have not had that burden of having to beg to be a part of Zach's care.

The future is very unknown right now and will be until we try to wake him up a little. I am trying hard to take one moment at a time. I believe in Zachary and i believe that there were too many "right things" that happened when he arrested for it to be a coincidence. I am holding on to that hope and I continue to.

Thank you again for so much support. It is seemingly endless and it means the world to me

Sunday, October 7, 2007 6:23 PM

Yesterday we were able to wean Zach off the Epinephrine and Vasopressin drips. He did well weaning and in fact I felt he was showing clear signs that he needed to be off. His heart no longer needed that support. The doctor who ran the code stopped by yesterday and said she just is amazed and so glad that his heart is doing well enough to get off the drips.

We started him back on his Labetalol drip and one of his other medications that help his heart. These do different things for him than the ones that he has needed the last few days. He is on a much lower dose than he was before the arrest...we'll have to see how much he really needs as time goes by.

He was having trouble with some of the changes we made with the ventilator yesterday and by the time I went to bed they had some of the settings just a bit higher than they had been in the morning. But his blood gases looked very good through the night and today he has tolerated very tiny changes to his settings. The ICU doctor feels that it is important to go very slowly with him so that his lungs do not get more stressed. His right lung showed a small improvement this morning. It still looks pretty bad but at least there was not worsening.

To that end, it was the ICU doctor's recommendation that he remain paralyzed and sedated to allow his lungs to heal a bit more. Peter and I both feel that is a reasonable thing to do. Keeping him paralyzed is a day to day decision but he may likely stay in this state for a few more days. Tomorrow we get a new ICU doctor. I have liked the one working with him and she really seems to "get" him. It was hard to see her go off service.

Brittany has really decorated his room-- it is quite colorful with all his favorite characters. She also brought pictures of him for the walls so that everyone can see who he is and why they are doing what they are doing for him. His 4th floor nurses, residents, 1st year fellows and regular attending docs know who they are fighting for but I think it is important that those who never knew him before see pictures of how much life he has in him.

Thank you for everything you are all doing to help: prayers, food, Mountain Dew, notes in the guest book, visits, phone calls, hope and compassion. I tell Zach a lot that he has a huge fan club in this world.

None of the doctors can make any promises or predictions right now but the entire health care team is doing everything possible to make a difference for him. I know he could never get better care than he is getting now.

He remains comfortable and I know his best brother, Sam, is by his side.

Monday, October 8, 2007 11:29 PM

Today did not start off so great as about midnight Zach was having low oxygen saturation levels in his blood. Whatever they did, he was not really improving. His oxygen ended up at 70 There was a trauma going on so all of the fellows and attendings were tied up there. The resident ended up calling the nurse practitioner and she was great. Turns out he needed his "breathing tube" pulled back 1 cm as it was causing spasms. He also ended up needing breathing treatments every 2 hours.

I had a horrible feeling of dread throughout that incident. I wonder how long it will take to not feel sick to my stomach every time the slightest thing goes wrong. Although I would never want to be anywhere but in the room with Zach during that resuscitation, it leaves vivid memories that do not fade. I know this from Sam.

This afternoon we de-Veced Zach. That is to say we stopped his vecuronium which was the paralytic agent. This week's attending ICU doctor felt we had to try. Since he sat with me last Thursday and watched how bad Zach's myoclonic jerking was before we put him on the Vec I trusted him on this issue. I knew he would not let Zach go back into that state because it was awful to see. So we stopped it.

I was very nervous - actually beyond nervous. He started twitching his fingers and toes about 45 minutes after we stopped (this is normal) and then started having some myoclonic jerks (normal for Zach when he is weakened and stressed but they zap energy from him that needs to be used for other things like breathing and circulation). The doc started him on a Versed drip quickly before it could progress. He is on a relatively low dose and doing okay. I feel a little bit better but still worried about how it will go when we need to wean him off these drugs. However, that is a ways down the road and there are so many other things we need to do before that. For today this has been a great step. The biggest worry was whether or not his lungs would get worse without the Vec and for now they seem to be unchanged. A small step but a very important one.

I am not sure what the plan will be for tomorrow. We hope to stop his inhaled nitric oxide. He is having blood pressure issues and unfortunately there is not a consensus on what to do. He is bleeding some but not terribly. He's been getting red cells just about every day - sometimes multiple transfusions. I would guess that tomorrow they may try to wean the vent a little bit if his x-ray looks better. Today it remained unchanged - but at least not worse. I think we have finally dried him out and as so often happens in medicine we did too good of a job and he may be a little dry. I'm not entirely convinced he is and I think they cut his diuretics too much but we'll see what the labs show. Medicine is never an exact science.

Tomorrow we will have PT and OT start working with him to passively exercise him. He is still completely sedated and looks very peaceful and pain free. I think I will start reading *Star Wars* to him tomorrow. Thank you so much for all of the cards and gifts and visits. For those who stopped by today and could not see Zach I am sorry. With him coming off the Vec I needed to devote my attention to him.

Saturday, October 13, 2007 2:13 PM

I'm sorry that I have not updated. Every day seems like a year from the day before and his surgery seems like another lifetime.

We have been decreasing Zach's sedation steadily but everyone wants to do it very slowly so that he does not go into withdrawal. The Mon-Thurs ICU doctor said that if he goes into withdrawal we'll be going backwards and none of us want that. So....having said that, he is still quite sleepy and has not opened his eyes yet. He does move his eyes and blink responsively. The ICU doctor from Mon-Thurs said that Zach was responding "appropriately to mom" in report and I agree with that. It may not be dramatic but he clearly is much more responsive to the questions "Do you want to go to Best Buy?" and "Do you want a Nintendo Wii?" than he is to "Do you want to do homework?"

There was concern that he was not coughing. Coughing is a sign of the ability to protect his airway which is needed for extubation

459

(removal of breathing tube) to be successful long-term. A few hours after everyone raised the concern Zach coughed and his blood pressure went up in response to getting suctioned. He did it again later and also when the dentist came to look in his mouth. So I guess that concern has largely been put to rest.

He started "helping the vent" on Wednesday by using some of his accessory muscles when the ventilator gave him a breath. Friday he started to breathe over the vent (which was programmed at 8 breaths/minute) but it was sporadic. During the night he consistently was breathing over the vent. So that also answers an important question. Now that we know the answer, the doctors decided to turn the vent up to 10 breaths/minute so that it would give him a rest for the time being. However, he is still giving 1-4 extra breaths a minute so they may have to turn it up again.

He has had an extraordinary increase in bleeding from multiple sites in the past 1-2 days. I have lost count of the amount of blood transfusions he has had at this point. It seems blood is constantly getting infused. It seems like it has slowed in the past few hours but I hesitate to say that until he goes a few days. For now we can only replace blood as he loses it and continue with his cryo, platelets and Factor 7a.

One place he bled a lot from yesterday is his mouth. It looks like he likely had some trauma when intubated during the code (understandable given the situation) and now that he is 9 days out he is re-bleeding. It's his typical for him but a problem given this is where his ET (breathing) tube is. Yesterday his dentist came by and we were able to see the precise source of bleeding. This was great because it allowed us to put topical thrombin on it versus blindly trying to stop the bleeding. This morning when the on call dentist came by I was able to look with her and it is not even oozing. As bad as all of this bleeding is –there is a silver lining. Had he not bled so profusely from the mouth yesterday then we would not have known he had this area of trauma. This could have been a major catastrophe when they pull the ET tube out. Now we know and can be prepared by giving him extra treatment right before and after and having an anesthesiologist extubate him rather than a respiratory therapist. This will give him the best chance so oddly, I am very glad he bled from the mouth.

Other than all of this it is just a little of this and a little of that and a lot of waiting and hoping and praying. Every time there is a question posed to Zach, I feel my heart drop until he answers. He answers slowly sometimes but so far the answers have all been what we hope for.

Can his heart beat without help? YES
Can he respond to his mom? YES
Can his lungs recover? YES
Can he breathe on his own? YES
Can he protect his airway? YES

I just have to keep reminding myself that baby steps are good.

We have a new ICU doctor now but at least he will be on service for the next 7 days. All Zach's doctors said he is a great guy and they are right. He seems very good and approachable and willing to work with all of us as a team. We have had wonderful nursing care. I cannot express how appreciative I am to the 4 west nurses for their willingness to staff him – an unfamiliar environment for them. They have also picked up hours in order to make sure he always has someone that knows him working alongside the ICU nurse. He continues to require 2 nurses and we all appreciate how kind and informative the ICU nurses have been to all of us.

Well this has been long and I have to get back. I left him with the headphones on listening to his new Star Wars CD. Yesterday he listened to some of the movies. I asked him if he wanted me to read him *The New Yorker* and he ignored me. I asked if he wanted to listen to *Star Wars* and he blinked his eyes quite definitively.

Wednesday, October 10, 2007 10:36 AM

We did not do much yesterday in terms of changes. Zach's blood pressure has been chronically high so we have focused on keeping that down so that he does not bleed.

Today I think they are changing too many things at once. I guess it is either do one thing a day or do 10. No middle ground? His sedation drips have been decreased as have his vent settings and his nitric oxide has been turned off. I'm not sure how we'll tell what does what since everything was done within an hour time span. The hope is that he will wake up enough to breathe above his ventilator settings.

461

He is too sedated to do that now. Waking him up has to be balanced with not letting him get agitated so we'll have to see how he does and may have to go back up on sedation if he shows us he is not ready for this.

His kidney function is fairly bad and it is slowly getting worse. This is a major issue and today nephrology will come by so that we can have a new set of eyes look at the problem. I think we have exhausted all of our collective ideas and none seem to be helping.

I hope that the doctors maintain hope and dedication to Zach. I am so tired that I can easily admit I may be miss reading people and drawing conclusions erroneously...but this morning I just felt some impatience. To a certain degree I guess that is okay for it allows progress and probably makes people think harder. So it can be good. Still....Zach cannot be pushed too hard. It's not that they do not care about Zach. They do...I just need them to be patient and to remember how miraculous so many things already have been - the fact his heart is working, the fact he has done well coming off the paralytic and coming down on vent settings, the fact his lungs look a bit better, the fact that he did not bleed in his chest or get broken ribs from CPR. He has done so much and come so far in 6 days.

Monday, October 15, 2007 9:51 PM

Zach continues to do small things each day that encourage all of us. Saturday night we changed his narcotic (fentanyl) to a different one (Dilaudid) and he has done so much better. It seemed he was having an adverse reaction to the first one. I was glad to see it go. On the new one he has actually opened his eyes and done less tremoring. Also his muscle tone improved within about 6 hours of changing which is both interesting and good.

He is having trouble focusing his eyes on anything but today he seemed to open his eyes more and it seems he has improved his ability to control them. He still has a lot of work to do but there was definite improvement today. It is the same with any of his muscles. If he wants to move a leg or arm he will tremor uncontrollably. I can stop the tremors by putting my hand on his arm or leg so they are not seizures. I think it must be very frustrating for him. I have seen this a little in the past when he has been especially weak and I have a feeling this is for the same reason. It is hard to watch but even today I felt he calmed more easily and did not do it quite as much.

He has been listening to his *Star Wars* music and DVDs and I have been reading a little to him. He still sleeps a lot. We are trying to keep the lights off at night and the lights on during the day as he comes out of sedation so that he can get back to some semblance of nights and days.

He continues to breathe over the ventilator even though they turned it up to make things easier for him. At this point we may try to extubate him towards the end of the week. It's hard to say for sure. He has to stop bleeding in his nose as when the breathing tube is removed he will have to temporarily be on 24 hr/day BiPap (non-invasive ventilation with a nose mask) until he can oxygenate himself effectively without assistance. So far today has been a good day in terms of bleeding. He actually has not had a blood transfusion since this morning and believe me – that is a record for this ICU stay.

For now life continues to be very moment to moment. There are times I am so worried and other times I am not at all. It's heart breaking to see him so fragile and so in need of help for every little thing. But it is also very humbling to be the mother of such a courageous, resilient boy. I cannot imagine how he must feel now not being able to talk or move without assistance. I wonder if he is scared or confused. I hope he is not in pain -we don't think he is. I tell him all of the time how much he is loved and I hope he truly knows that in his heart.

Thursday, October 18, 2007 2:54 PM

Today Zach had what is called an "extubation readiness test." It started at 4 am and was scheduled to last 2 hours. I am pleased to report that he got an A++. Without getting too technical he was not on the ventilator he has been on but rather placed on C-pap. The C-pap requires him to breathe on his own. They watched his effort and the quality of his breaths and everything was very good. They ended up leaving him on it until afternoon. Right now they are giving him a rest and then he will go back on it later this afternoon. The ICU doctor said he could actually be extubated today. That would be great but because of the bleeding issues an anesthesiologist has to do it and the dentist needs to be there. So we have scheduled it for 8 am on Friday. It will be so nice to see him without that tube in his mouth and I bet he will feel much better. He'll have a full face mask with the BiPAP (what he uses at home for breathing help)but nothing invasive. How nice will that be?

He continues to open his eyes and in the last 24 hours he seems to be blinking more. I'm not entirely certain but he seems to have regained his very definitive blink that he used last week to answer yes to questions I asked. Last week before he could open his eyes he seemed to respond very appropriately with different types of blinks. He had stopped doing that – probably because he was trying so hard to open his eyes and that took all of his energy. Rachel one of his nurses thought she saw him move his leg a few times today. His pharmacist saw it too but I missed it. Hopefully he will do it more and more so that I can see it.

This has not been a perfect day for him. As he wakes up more he definitely feels more. He hates getting suctioned. He is going through some drug withdrawal and has his tremors back that I had not seen for a few days. We originally planned to cut again tonight but we're not going to do that now. I think he needs a break and given he has been breathing on his own for so many hours there is not quite the urgency we felt before.

Funny thing is that we are giving him calcium boluses and having a harder time keeping his levels up. All those years of the levels being too high and now we have to give extra. It's a nice problem to have!

Yesterday we took his arterial line out. He really did not need it anymore and the risk had become greater than the benefit of having it. I held pressure on it for over an hour (Usually only requires 5 minutes) and so far it has not bled. We also stitched in the central line that is in his arm. That has bled but we needed to do it. We also ditched a monitor that looked at the oxygen utilization in his kidney and brain. So all in all we are taking away and not adding. This is very good.

His Darth Vader balloon was looking very deflated and finally it sunk to the ground. His doctor told me that out of deference to Zach I should refill it so I took it to the gift shop to be refilled. Well Jim refilled it with helium and he plumped right up but he was still lying on the ground. It seems that somehow air had gotten into Darth and

464

since air is heavier than helium, he is destined to be hung from the curtain rod from now on.

So that's about all. The days go by fast and yet I have no idea what I do all day aside from talking to Zach and talking with the staff. Brittany decided to come home for the weekend. I think it will be good for Zach even though he is easily over stimulated at the moment. A few nights ago she called and when I put the phone to his ear he started blinking his eyes a mile a minute.

Thank you for all of the cards and also for the kind messages. I keep telling Zach how loved he is and how proud we all are of everything he has already done.

Friday, October 19, 2007 10:05 PM

The extubation was a catastrophe and Zach had to be reintubated. He is okay but we will not be able to try again for a few days.

He was ready from a breathing/lung health perspective but as always the bleeding got in the way. When the anesthesiologist pulled the ET (breathing) tube Zach did not take a breath. As it turns out there was a large clot sitting on his vocal cords and it was impossible for him to take a breath. His oxygen saturations dropped. They had some difficulty reintubating him because there was so much blood. His heart struggled and he needed compressions and emergency medications again. It was very brief with chest compressions no more than2 minutes – though it seemed like an eternity again. No one thinks there will be any negative effects on him beyond what he has already suffered from the first code when he was down much longer. He actually opened his eyes within 10-15 minutes of this and blinked to things that Peter said to him. His pupils remained responsive unlike last time, which was great to see.

His blood products and Factor 7a have all been dosed higher again. He has needed blood which is not surprising. During all of this his neck incision from the thyroid surgery opened a little but that is not a bad thing. It was all so swollen. His surgeon was planning to come back today and drain it down which will be best long-term I think.

His vent settings did not need to be changed and Peter said his lungs sound good. He is still doing a lot of breathing over the vent.

465

They left the rate at 5 breaths per minute so that he will continue to breathe more on his own. He was doing so well and we don't want him to go backwards with that. His heart is beating fine and has a normal rhythm. He did not need any further medications to assist him. I was afraid they were going to want to put an arterial line in again but no one mentioned it which is great.

The plan at this time is for the ENT doctor (ears, nose and throat) to do a bronchoscopy and laryngoscopy on Monday to see what is there. They'll have to remove the ET tube to look. If it looks clear we can extubate the next day. If not then we'll have to figure out what to do. They will only do this in the operating room and not at the bedside. There is a part of me that does not like that given the potential for things to go badly but then again the operating room is the safest place to do this. I will not let him go unless he can go with one of the anesthesiologists that knows him.

I have to say that I was completely unprepared for what happened. I anticipated he might bleed a little but this was beyond anything I imagined. The doctors were not anticipating this either. We're all so glad that we had the right people there. Typically kids are extubated by a nurse and respiratory therapist. He would not have survived that. He had one of our best anesthesiologists with him and also the attending ICU doctor, the dentists, a senior fellow and two wonderful nurses along with others. It was horrific for everyone involved. I am still in shock that I watched him do this all over again. I will never be able to express how thankful I am for the anesthesiologist who was there today and for the many others who helped.

That's about all. Right now his nose and mouth are packed to stop the bleeding and it seems to have stopped from his mouth and slowed from his nose. The plan is to do nothing and let him rest this weekend.

Monday, October 22, 2007 9:44 AM

Zach will go to the operating room this afternoon. He is an add on case so it is hard to say when he will go exactly. I hate the thought of him going but I know they have to look. Clearly we cannot extubate him if there are additional clots...and there probably are. The anesthesiologist who was with him Friday said he will go with him today. I am so glad. There are only 3 anesthesiologists I would trust to take him back at this point because it has become so complicated.

Not being able to talk, no one knows exactly what he is feeling or thinking. However, when I asked him if he was scared yesterday there were many many tears...that was enough for all of us to start him back on versed yesterday. Versed should decrease anxiety and also leave him without memories of anything that happens while he is getting it. We are also about to start an infusion of a sedation medication so that he does not have to feel anxious about going. Under normal circumstances he would be excited about going to the operating room. He loves it. But these have not been normal days and no one wants him to feel any more scared than he may already feel. I'm glad that the doctors involved in his care are so compassionate and are not discounting how he feels emotionally.

He got a new bed yesterday that can give him percussion (helps keep his lungs healthy). It also turns him. At first we programmed it to be a 20 degree turn over 9 minutes. Well that was almost a disaster. Marisol had to go running over to the other side of the bed because it flipped him over on his face. He did not seem to care but now he is programmed to make a 10 degree turn over 20 minutes and his position changes every 90 minutes. It seems to be less stressful for him. The ICU doctor also asked the nurses to do their best to keep lights down at night, be quiet and play music for him. It's not always possible but he wants them to pay particular attention to doing that as much as possible.

Saturday the ENT doctor looked in his nose and pharynx. He did not find a fresh source for the bleeding but there were a lot of old clots. They got cleaned out but he has bled a lot since. It's a never ending cycle. The plan is to give him more blood products and Factor 7a to see if it will finally stop.

Brittany went back to Minneapolis yesterday. I know it was hard for her and I am proud of her for going back and continuing to go to class and work and do all the things she needs to do. Abby was able to come see Zach for a little while on Saturday. She also helped pack up some of his favorite movies and sent some of her CDs that she thought he would like. He has 2 wonderful sisters!

Monday, October 22, 2007 10:08 PM

Zach did well - much better than I expected to be honest. I sent him off with Vasopresin (a medication that used a lot of during his first code). I was very worried that when they removed the ET tube the same horrible thing would happen. Thankfully it was uneventful. I can't express the relief I felt when I saw that he was okay - nothing bad had happened.

Zach came back to ICU with the troops (docs and fellows). The ENT doctor cleared out a lot (an understatement) of blood clots - throughout his airway. This is good because no one can breathe with the amount of blood clots he had. The best news was that Dr. R did not identify a specific source for the bleeding on his trachea or in his pharynx. The nose looked "raw" and that makes this the likely source of the bleeding. Although bleeding anywhere is bad, it will be easier to get at his nose then to make something stop in his lower airway.

Zach's hematologist prescribed a massive dose of Factor 7a. It was a hard decision to use it for me because it holds the risk that he'll clot so much that he has a stroke. AND we had just decreased his anti-clot medication. But at this point we had to take the risk. The big dose slowed the bleeding down tremendously and he has handled it ok. Then we started a Factor 7a drip at a very high dose. We'll do this for 24 hours and then take him back to the operating room and look again. So far I think things are going well.

Dr. B, the anesthesiologist/intensivist with him on Friday, went with him and was able to just use the sedation drips we already had running. He gave a slug of versed so that Zach won't remember anything. He said he will go with him again tomorrow. He also put in a few peripheral IVs for Zach so now we have more access. He just has so many things running so that even with the 2 double lumen central lines we don't have enough spots for it all. We started him on decadron which should reduce any further swelling of his airway. This is in anticipation of extubating him in the next few days. Of course it is all dependent on him not bleeding so much that he cannot breathe without being intubated. So if you want to know exactly what to pray for it is for Zach to stop bleeding.

As for his kidneys his creatinine is now down to 2.2 (bad but so much better than 4!) and his BUN is down to 139 from the all time high of 151. The BUN is pathetic (normal is 0 to 20) but at least it is going in the right direction again. And his pancreatitis seems to be resolving because his lipase is down to 1500 now. I hope these are all signs of his body healing.

On a lighter note, Zach got yet another new bed delivered while he was in OR. "Rachel squared" (he had his nurse team of Rachel and Rachel today) decided they did not like the bed he got yesterday because it turned him too much. So now he has a bed that can still turn him but it is completely nurse controlled and they can do smaller turns. Sadly it does not do percussion. That was kind of neat. It does not vibrate like the other one either -which is just fine. When I tried him out in the vibrate mode before we ditched that bed he looked like someone had put him into the spin cycle of the washing machine. Not exactly soothing. So we'll see how he likes this new bed.

Wednesday, October 24, 2007 9:46 PM

Brittany gave me *Saving Graces* by Elizabeth Edwards for my birthday. I have not been able to read the entire time we have been in the hospital. Acquired ADD at its worst I think. Finally, I had the attention span to read a chapter yesterday. Within the first few pages she writes, "One thing I have learned over the years: hope is precious, and there's no reason to give it up until you absolutely have to." That's always been how I feel. Hope is invaluable and I fight hard to hold on to it. I guess I have also learned that when it is lost there is little left to keep me walking forward.

Hope is something I have thought a lot about today. I am trying hard to keep it in my heart and I think I still have plenty. But hope does not mask reality and reality today has left me scared and sad and worried.

The day started off wonderfully because all of Zach's bandages were white. He did not seem to be bleeding anywhere. I felt so hopeful when they sedated him to look in his mouth. Maybe he could even get extubated on Thursday. About noon, Dr. B sedated Zach again at the bedside and then he and Dr. R looked in Zach's mouth. It was so hard to hear that they once again found significant clots in the back of his mouth/throat. Dr. R decided to pack his nose. I don't want to go into detail but it is not nice packing like some gauze stuffed in the nose.

469

It's completely intrusive and both doctors told me that adults say it is painful. So now my starting to wake up child is sound asleep courtesy of higher doses of narcotics. It's ok – he deserves to sleep through this. He opens his eyes a little and I just hope that he is not in pain….that we will know if he is. He does not deserve to be in any pain. On that we all agree.

I hope we're doing the right thing. I ask everyone and all have different opinions. I think this means there is not an obvious answer. Everyone is doing their best. The concern is that he is too weak to cough out clots if he is not intubated. That's why the clots need to be gone. But how do you do that? He bleeds and we try to stop it. If it stops it is because he makes a clot. If he clots then they clear it out. Then he bleeds and it goes on and on and on. I asked why we cannot just leave him intubated for a week. Let him make as many clots as he wants and then after a week we can clean them out. Presumably his tissue would be less fragile at that point. Sounds ok to me but Dr. B, his anesthesiologist, saw an erosion today on his tongue from the ET (breathing) tube. That is a huge concern. We moved the tube to the other side of his mouth but clearly he needs that tube out. And they worry that he may not heal so well if we leave the clots in since we cannot apply pressure. All true. All fair arguments.

I hate that I am the one allowing things to happen to him. There are a lot of things I do know about him and I have little uncertainty advocating for these things. But most of the time I don't know enough. I just wish I was smarter or more discerning or had more time to really think it all through. But the choices get presented and there I am and all I can do is look to the people I trust, listen to what they tell me, make a decision with them and hope with all my heart that it turns out ok. But always there is the fear that in the end I will consent to the wrong thing. And always there is the hope that this time we have chosen the right thing even if it is not immediately obvious.

We went into the hospital on Sept. 20th.and tonight is 3 weeks since he was admitted to the ICU. The day we drove to the hospital was so long ago. I look at this precious, beautiful boy (who will not be happy I referred to him this way when he is awake) and I just hope and hope and hope that he will stop bleeding and be okay. "There's no reason to give up hope unless you absolutely have to."

Today marks the beginning of the fall school holiday. Every year the kids have off for 3 days in October during the teacher's convention. I can hardly believe that time of year is already here. Donna, Zach's homebound teacher, spent the day with Abby today which was so wonderful for her. Tonight she is out to dinner with Grandma and Grandpa. My sister, brother and sister in law have both spent time with her and my Dad has been here too. I am sad to be missing time with her – her freshman year. I am thankful that friends and family surround her so that she is not alone. Thank you also to all the moms who drive when I cannot and those who look out for her while I am gone.

Saturday, October 27, 2007 7:25 AM

Thursday all the various doctors and I did a lot of talking. Although we could not get everyone together at the same time, Zach's primary doctor and I were able to get a few doctors together in the morning and then a few others together at night. I think that was helpful even though there were various opinions and as always no clear answers. We decided to remove the packing in his nose Friday morning. However, his nose has been bleeding quite a bit since then. It does not seem the packing helped.

Thursday night, before the packing was removed Dr. B sedated and paralyzed Zach temporarily again. This allowed Dr. R, the ENT, to look in Zach's mouth and we were able to look with him. There was no evidence of bleeding in his mouth. This was an important piece of information. The packing in his nose had blocked anything from going through the back of the nose to his mouth and throat. Had we seen any evidence of bleeding or clots it would have meant that his bleeding was not only coming from his nose but also from his trachea. So this was really very good news to determine once and for all what the source of bleeding is.

Unfortunately, this is not a little bloody nose. It is a life threatening bleed. The reason it is a big deal is that even if he clots, the clots will have to be coughed out eventually or they will drop down into his airway. He will be too weak to cough them out initially. How to stop it has precipitated many discussions and opinions and ideas....but still no successful treatment. Another thing we agreed

Thursday and again on Friday as a group was to take a minimalist approach with Zach for the next few days. No more sedating and scoping every day and definitely no suctioning or anything else invasive.

As it turns out, he will have to go to the operating room this morning (Saturday). In the past 4 days the staff has had a harder and harder time suctioning his ET tube. They were using smaller and smaller diameter suction catheters. Finally last night no one could pass a catheter and he was having a harder and harder time breathing. By 1 AM an ENT doctor, critical care doctor and anesthesiologist were here and determined that his tube has a kink in it. It has to be replaced. Although some people felt it could be replaced at the bedside last night I expressed how completely uncomfortable I am with that. The ENT doctor agreed with me that it would be a most unwise thing to do unless it was an emergency. They were able to maneuver things a few times to suction him but as of now they cannot pass it again. He sounds ok so hopefully the docs will get him in there before he starts having problems again.

I don't think it is useful to share specific details of this entire issue but the bottom line is this should not have been addressed on Friday at midnight. No one should have been dragged out of their bed to come in when it had been an issue that progressed all week. It makes me realize again how imperative it is to never leave the hospital. I had expressed my concern about this so many times and the answers I received were always that it was something he was doing. He was biting or he was agitated, even though the majority of time he was neither. In the end this is what we're left with and the most important thing is to safely change it out today in a controlled environment. It's unfortunate that it is a Saturday and it will be hard if not impossible to get an anesthesiologist that knows him. However, waiting until Monday is not a viable choice.

I think I am most thankful right now that I am a mother who has the choice whether to stay at the hospital or not. I have a flexible job and I do not wonder how I will pay for the heat this winter if I take a day off. I have always had people who help out with the other kids at home. So many parents do not have the luxury of being at the hospital full time with their child – often for socioeconomic reasons. So many parents do not have the understanding of the medical system that I do

472

as a nurse. I often think about how hyper vigilant I have to be and how confused I get. What must it be like for a mother who can only come one hour each day, or one who is here but does not speak or understand English or one who does speak English but does not speak "medical" or one who was raised to never question physicians? It is true that I am exhausted emotionally and physically but that is my choice and for that I am truly very thankful.

Saturday, October 27, 2007 9:45 PM

Dr. B, from anesthesia, came in this morning to go to the operating room with Zach. When he says that he will take good care of Zach in OR I never doubt that. I worry - of course - that despite the good care something bad will happen. But I always know Zach is with one of the best anesthesiologists we have. No matter what happens I know he will have the best care possible. It's hard to quantify the gift of that assurance.

Before Zach went to OR things were pretty dismal. There was a tremendous amount of concern about the ET tube. There was a lot of doubt that something as "simple" as a kink could be causing the inability to advance the suction catheter. There was a lot of uncertainty about what might happen in the OR. I felt heart sick when they took him away and stayed that way until they brought him back.

The on call ENT doctor said it ended up being "just a kink" and not a clot or worse. There was a small amount of swelling but they could still place the new tube easily. They once again confirmed that he is not bleeding in his trachea but scoping him set off his nose again and the right side is now packed.(with nice packing if that exists. It's better than the contraption he had last week!)

The sad news is that now he cannot go to the OR and get extubated Monday or Tuesday. It will likely be 1-2 more weeks we have to wait before we can try again. I am sad but I know this is what has to be done. I just worry that the longer this goes on the more potential he has for further complications. I have asked the doctors to let him be on C-PAP as much as possible during the day. This gets him away from dependency on the vent and makes him do the work of breathing. Otherwise he will get more and more de-conditioned.

473

His pancreatitis is back and he has needed a lot of red blood cells transfused. On the brighter side his BUN is down to 97. Still "critical" since normal is 0-20 but improving every day. AND – today while doing his leg exercises with him I asked him to help and he pushed his right leg. I asked him to do it a second time and he did it again. Later he moved his left thumb when I asked him to move his fingers and just a bit ago he helped with the right leg exercises again. These are little things but they are so wonderful to see.

He's chilling out now listening to his ocean Beethoven CD. Of course, it is not really HIS. He will probably scold all of us when he can talk about making him listen to so much classical music at night.

Monday, October 29, 2007 1:01 PM

So many people have asked what they can do to help. Anyone who knows me knows that my usual response is nothing. But believe it or not I do have a request for those of you who are non-sewing challenged (unlike me. I am completely deficient in this area!) Would anyone would be willing to make a hospital gown for Zachary? If a few people want to each make one that would be very cool. I don't know if there is a pattern out there (I told you I don't sew AT ALL) but I think it would be a very simple thing to cut. The sleeves need to be made so that they open up completely and can be closed with Velcro or snaps. The back can either be tied shut or closed with Velcro or snaps. His size would be about the same as extra small or small adult. It should be long enough to go to his knees.

The hospital has gowns, of course. However, the patterns and colors are boring and girly. And they seem to have forgotten that there are kids between the size of a 10 year old and a 20 year old. What boy wants to wear lavender pajamas? What15 year old kid (boy or girl) wants to wear pants that are made for a 20 year old?

Zach has always been adamant about NOT wearing hospital pajamas while inpatient. I always pack his clothes from home. The only time he wears the hospital stuff is when we need quick access to his chest – like when he goes to surgery or after his thyroid operation or now. I don't think he is going to be too happy once he wakes up and realizes that he is wearing the same ugly blue gown every day. I do think he'd feel better (and look less sickly) if he had hospital gowns that showed things he is interested in.

I looked online to see about buying stuff but there is not anything that he would like and very little for his size anyway. Then I remembered that Sam's little friend Samantha had a whole collection of gowns that her family and friends made for her when she was in he ICU a few years ago. After Samantha passed away, her mom gave the gowns to Sam and Sam loved them. He had Blue's Clues and many different holidays and Scooby doo and who knows what else. They were awesome. But Zach is too big for them and anyway – I don't think he wants Blue's Clues on his gown. So if anyone is willing to make him one or if multiple people want to each make him one please let me know. I will reimburse you for the fabric and also the shipping cost if you do not live in the Milwaukee area.

Regarding Zach – he is definitely waking up. We've been reading a little and he is very attentive. He is still moving his legs a little bit. This morning when his nurse was in the way of his Justice League movie he moved his head. I guess we just had to find the right incentive. I asked if we could consult rehab and the team agreed. The rehab doctor is awesome – we've worked together on resident education and personally he has helped with wheelchair stuff for both boys. I am anxious to see what he has to say – and what things he thinks we can do to help Zach.

We're going down to IR (interventional radiology) today which is a big venture out of the unit given he is intubated. But he needs a new J tube put into his intestine because the current one is not working very well. All of his medicines that go into the J tube are leaking out.

Darth Vader had another accident this morning. Last night his nurse taped him to the ceiling by the head so that he was not hanging from the curtain rod. That was great until his primary doctor walked in and Darth suddenly dropped down to the floor. Dead? Nope not quite. The ENT revived him by picking him up and tucking him into the curtain rod. Only thing is that now he looks beheaded. Not sure which is better. Darth hung or beheaded?

Sorry for taking a few days to write. Each day is so busy even though it does not seem like we should still be this busy with Zach's care. Life in the hospital is marked by all these events which seem so little and yet are important and seem to mark the day just as much as breakfast, lunch and dinner. AM Rounds with the ICU team, individual conversations with each specialist and his primary doctor, therapy, radiology test, etc. In between there are little things that end up taking hours: turning him every 2 hours, making sure his plan is followed and making sure that nothing wrong is happening, bathing him, dressing changes, suctioning…and the moments that matter most: talking to Zach when his eyes open, reading to him, orienting him and reminding him of all the wonderful things he has done and all the things he likes and all the people who love him.

Basically, we are in a relatively "do nothing" phase which is hard for everyone – including me. I have to remind myself that the choice to do nothing is actually doing something. It's hard to be patient but I think the best thing we can do right now is to let Zach's body heal with only as much intervention as he shows us he needs. Not anymore. This is not typical in the ICU but they team has been great about making sure this happens.

His bleeding has improved a lot. That is ½ the battle for extubation. The other ½ is making sure that he clears any clots he has made to stop that bleeding. Clots in his airway will bring us to the same dismal point if we try to extubate with them there. The plan now is to take him to the OR on Monday afternoon to look and clear out anything as non-traumatically as possible. I don't think they will try to extubate that day but we still need to talk about the specific plan for OR.

He is taking all of his own breaths now 24 hrs/day. He does have positive pressure assisting him – similar to his BiPAP that he has at night when home. But every breath is his. We started doing two 2 hr periods of this earlier in the week and then two 3-hour periods. He did so well we decided to leave him on it all the time. So for now his lungs remain healthy. Small, but working as well as they did before the code.

We are weaning down many of his medications – pain medications and sedatives. We have to be very cautious with this because he has proven to be extraordinarily sensitive to the slightest change.

He has been awake more and more. It is nice to see. He is bothered by specific things which is also a good sign. He has a good cough and gag which will be crucial once he does not have the ET tube to help him breathe. On only a few occasions has he moved his arms of legs, he does not yet squeeze a hand or wiggle fingers/toes. These are certainly concerns but he has a pre-existing weakness which complicates his recovery. He also has had a left arm bleed and a right lower leg bleed which has made those limbs very heavy. Even so, last night he did lift his left arm a few times. At times he will turn his head. He has already gotten further than many thought he would and we think we just need to let Zach show us what he can do in his own time. No one seems especially concerned at this point. The ICU doctor said she thinks he may just be very de-conditioned. He is getting PT and OT and I try to follow up with exercising him a few more times/day.

He is getting his IVIg over 10 days and he is on day 6. He is definitely struggling with it even at this slow rate. However, I am confident that it will help him once we get it into him. He also continues to struggle with pancreatitis which can be very painful. I think he's well covered with pain meds but we'll watch carefully.

Thank you to everyone who has offered to make a gown for him. I think this will be so neat for him – not just having the coolest gowns at CHW but also knowing that people all over have given their time to this. I am overwhelmed with so much generosity. Thank you!!!!

Sunday, November 4, 2007 9:01 PM

Yesterday the ENT specialist and anesthesiologist said they planned to extubate Zach in the OR on Monday if everything looked good. However, Zach has pretty significant pancreatitis that has worsened each day. This morning his Lipase was 5600 (normal 23-300) and it may not be prudent to extubate him under these conditions. His abdomen is bloated and firm which pushes up on his lungs and makes breathing that much harder. Although he continues to take all of his own breaths (with pressure support to make them more effective), he is definitely working harder. He is retaining a lot of fluid again and his CVP (central venous pressure which looks at how "happy" his heart is) has been high since Saturday. None of this is ideal.

We started a new continuous IV infusion today called phentolamine. This was a drip that we gave to Sam. It helps decrease blood pressure and can help improve heart function. We also increased one of his diuretics but it does not seem to be helping yet.

His OR time is still reserved for 1 Pm but his primary doctor, the ENT, the anesthesiologist and I are meeting about noon to discuss whether or not he should go to OR and if he does should it just be an exam and not an attempt at extubation. I am so sad to see him do poorly again when he has come so far. I am trying to remind myself that he is a long way from where he was right before his first heart arrest and those first weeks when he was in the ICU. He is strong – so strong. He is definitely the person I strive to be.

Grandma got Zach a "book on CD" of his favorite book called *The Cay*. He read this in 5th or 6th grade and he talks about it a lot. He seems to remember all of it so I thought he might like to listen to it. I have been reading him a book called *Witches* by Ronald Dahl and also a Star Wars book called *A New Hope*. He seems to listen though it is hard to know for sure. He may just be very impressed that his mom is saying words like Luke Skywalker and Storm Trooper.

Thank you to everyone for continuing to think of Zach. He is so well loved.

Monday, November 5, 2007 10:57 PM

Well... Zach did not get extubated today. I think we made the right decision but it was very hard to have the day for extubation pass once again. In the last 4 days he has retained about 5 liters more than he has taken in. That means he has gained about 5 Kg. He looks considerably swollen and we can take that as a measure of the degree of swelling they would likely find in his airway. This would make it really hard to breathe on his own given his de-conditioned state. In addition his abdomen is very swollen and firm - pushing up on his lungs. His lipase jumped to about 7000 today so his pancreatitis is far from over. His kidney function has worsened in the last 48 hours and his CVP (which shows us how well his heart is working) is still too high.

None of this would worry us excessively in a different situation as he has dealt with it all in the past – many many times. But if we are asking him to breathe on his own then it is only fair to give him the best chance possible to prove to us that he can. As a group (ENT, anesthesiologist, intensivist, Peter and me) we agreed to wait a week until he "de-swells" and gets back to some sort of equilibrium that we are all happy with. At this point we have tentatively planned to send him to OR for probable extubation on Monday Nov 12.

We recognize that there may never be a perfect time to extubate him but this was definitely not the day to try given how many things are amiss. We also decided to take him off the "auto" mode of the vent which had him taking all the breaths on his own. If he is sick then he should not be spending so much energy working to breathe with his swollen abdomen. There is no reason not to give him a rest so he can devote all his energy to fixing the other parts of his body that need help right now.

On the good news front, he continues to NOT bleed and we decreased his cryoprecipitate infusions from 2x/day to 1x/day. If all goes well we may decrease his platelets to 1x/day or perhaps his Factor 7a drip.

AND, it was just a few hours after we decided not to take him to OR today that he started to improve. At this point he looks like he will end up taking less fluid in then he puts out – which is to say he will be "negative" and negative is a really good thing when you are 5 liters "positive." I hope he keeps this up so that his swelling decreases as fast as it happened. His electrolytes are a bit of a mess with all the fluid shifting but we're addressing it as it happens. It's the least of my concerns at the moment.

He has been so incredibly sleepy the last few days and today was no different until about 4 PM. At that time he woke up and he looked like he would have stayed awake all night. At 9 PM we turned down the lights and put on the softer music (that I know I will hear about when he can tell me what he thinks of it). He had no choice but to close his eyes and sleep since the room became pretty boring. When awake we read his *Star Wars* book, talked and he watched a few movies. He looked so attentive and interested. It was the best gift of the day to see him look so awake and aware.

479

Brittany plans to come home this weekend which I know he will love. He likes when I talk to him about Brittany, Sammy, Abby and his friends at school. I keep reminding him about all the things he has to look forward to and all the people who care about him.

I'm going to try to sleep a little. It's a bit hard to sleep in an ICU room versus the IICU room he has on 4 west but I am starting to sleep for a few hours at a time without waking up. He has had awesome nursing care so that makes it a bit easier.

Monday, November 12, 2007 10:08 AM

Zach is on the OR schedule for this afternoon. He is an "add on" so I do not know an exact time. Drs. Berens and Robey will take a look at things and make a decision about extubating him. This will depend on swelling and bleeding.

We started him on decadron – a steroid – this morning which should help decrease swelling in his airway as long as it is not terribly bad. He will get that every 6 hours if we extubate him for the first 24 hours. His hematologist has written out a plan for extra blood products before he goes to OR and then afterwards in case anything gets scraped or cut during extubation. The plan is as before – to remove the breathing tube and put him on BiPAP using a full face mask. BiPAP gives assistance with taking and exhaling those breaths. This is what he uses at home during the night. However, it does not initiate the breaths and it does not give as good support as a ventilator. So we will have to see what he does and if he can maintain his oxygenation levels in his blood.

He has had 2 nurses all weekend because it was impossible for one nurse to do alone. I could have predicted this but what do I know. The nurses themselves said they cannot care for him alone. It's not that they are incapable of performing the skills needed to give his care. The issue is there is so much to be done with him being intubated. On a perfect day with absolutely no additional things required, someone who knows his care well can do it alone if they do not eat lunch or take time to critically think and if I help them – which I cannot stay up all night to do. That's not sustainable. Hopefully, he'll get extubated and go to Intermediate ICU soon and this will be a non-issue.

The weekend was quiet. As the residents and fellows say, "boring is good." Brittany was home but her visit was fairly short. Zach had been awake most of Friday night so unfortunately he was very tired all day Saturday and she did not get to see him with his eyes open very much. Sunday he was very awake but mostly after she left to go back to school.

I have been reminded that I never updated about his thyroid pathology. I guess it was so secondary that I forgot. As it turns out the mass was not malignant. This is good news on one hand although the oncologist points out it would have been easier to treat than what they found. Pathology found that the mass is a lymphatic malformation which is unheard of in the thyroid. This means that the liver masses are likely lymphatic malformations as well. This problem with his lymphatic system is a chronic problem – he will continue to develop lymphatic "masses" – they will appear as the thyroid one did and then stay the same size.

They are benign but the problem is they can grow anywhere. Depending where they grow it could be very serious if they impact what needs to happen in that part of the body. For example the one on the thyroid was likely pressing on his parathyroid glands and that led to bone destruction (because the bones were getting the wrong signal to continually release calcium to the point of utter depletion). I don't know that we can do surgery to remove them every time – I suppose it would depend where it is and what havoc it is causing. There may be other ways to treat but the oncologist said we can talk about this when he is better. We will not do anything for now. The good news is that without the mass of his thyroid his bones are now getting the "right message." They seem to be keeping calcium inside and hopefully he can rebuild some bone and that will give him less pain over time. So that is the result we have. It sounds good to not have a malignancy but from what I am told – it might have been better to have the malignancy. Time will tell.

Monday, November 12, 2007 10:44 PM

Zach was extubated about 2 PM. At 5:15 PM one of the doctors that extubated him said he had gone 3 hours longer without needing to be re-intubated than he had anticipated. One of his doctors called a

481

bit ago and asked "Is he still breathing?" and right after that a second doctor called and asked "Is he still extubated?" Blunt but truthful sentiments that ought to tell you how precarious things are at the moment.

He is very very weak and having trouble moving his tongue out of the way. So he obstructs A LOT when he breathes. He has an oral airway which is a tube in his mouth that holds things open so he can breathe more effectively. On top of that he has a full face mask to give him BiPAP. He looks like he is on a tilt table with his head up and feet down. Of course he keeps sliding down the bed in this position. He also has his head positioned up as if he is sniffing the ceiling. With all of that he can compensate pretty good but none of it will last long term. The oral airway is too rigid to leave in past tomorrow. So if he cannot breathe without it they have already told me they will reintubate. I think it could go either way.

It sounds like many in the OR would not have let him come out extubated based on how hard he was working without BiPAP. Dr. B and Dr. R thought it was very important to give him a chance. I am not a gambler so my first thought when they brought him back breathing so hard was that I could not believe they would bring him back like that. My second thought was that they better not leave. They did but checked back often until he started working less to get a breath in.

His 4 PM and 8 PM blood gasses looked really good. Surprisingly good. But then again Zach and Sam have always been great compensators. They can compensate until they can't and then they go downhill in the blink of an eye. So although the good gases are comforting, the only thing I am really looking at is how hard he is working.

He is definitely scared and that is hard to see. He gets a very frightened look in his eyes when he has trouble breathing. I can only imagine what is going through his head. He may well remember having trouble and going down the night of the code. So we just reassure him that he is doing great. That we know it is scary to work hard to breathe but he has loads of people surrounding him who will help him and not let him get sick. His only 2 jobs are to rest and to cough. Coughing is so tough but the more he can do it the better off he will be. He seems to calm when we talk to him and conversely he

482

easily picks up on any fear from any of us when he is not doing well. So we have to be very careful of that. Star Wars 5 saved the day this afternoon as he finally relaxed when I put it on and gave him his head phones.

More tomorrow....hopefully to say that he did well and was able to remain extubated. He could use all the prayers and love and thoughts and wishes and hopes that all of you can give to him.

Tuesday, November 13, 2007 10:34 PM

Hanging in there...one hour and sometimes one moment at a time. We added chest PT but very gentle given his bleeding. More than anything he needs to start coughing more and get stronger. As long as he is not coughing we need to suction him frequently to prevent the near catastrophe we had this morning when he had a blood clot stuck in his airway. Zach's hematologist added a few things to see if it gets the post nasal bleeding to stop. He is not strong enough to clear out that drainage on his own.

We as a group feel that the more we can get him to sleep well when he falls asleep the better he will do and the less likely it will be that he needs to be reintubated. To that end we try to touch him as little as possible when he falls asleep and when awake we try to keep things calm and quiet. I think I have read 5 chapters of Star Wars A *New Hope* today to him because it seems to consistently bring his sats up and calm him when I am reading. He has one of our favorite Respiratory therapists tonight so that makes me feel very comfortable.

Tuesday, November 13, 2007 10:04 AM

Zach is struggling a lot more than we would like to see. He does okay for a time and then he suddenly drops his oxygen saturation level. He sounds awful at these times and he is working too hard.

During the night the oral airway was removed. The doctors are talking about trying to put that back in or reintubating him. I think he is very close to needing this.

He scared us this morning as he was not moving air very well and was obstructing with his tongue. His sats dropped into the 70's (which they did last night too) and this alarmed everyone. The respiratory

483

therapist worked with Peter and Zach's nurses to suction him as Zach is so tired that his cough is not good. His cough was much better last night when I went to bed and is almost non-existent now. Finally they did suction out a clot. However, he looked to have quite a bit of "fresher" blood. Not new but not too old either.

He is scared but distracts relatively easily. He is listening to *The Cay* right now (his book on CD). I wish I could do this for him. I cannot imagine the feeling of fighting for every breath. Right now he is more relaxed but that changes fast.

The doctors added 2 more breathing medicines to help loosen things up so that hopefully he will be able to cough out some of his secretions.

Fine line between letting him get used to this and struggle in the process in the hope he will get over this hump versus allowing him to work too hard so that he gets exhausted and cannot compensate anymore. No one knows where that line is or how much latitude we have before he falls off.

It's just heart breaking to watch this. I hope with all my heart that this struggle is worth it and he does not end up reintubated.

Wednesday, November 14, 2007 9:37 PM

Still extubated.

Last night he did amazingly well. He sounded so good when we listened to his breath sounds this morning. He looked so peaceful at rest – more peaceful than he has been many nights even before this ICU admission. His many doctors were happy. Morning rounds were optimistic.

By mid-day he looked awful. Terribly labored breathing. Never opened his eyes – probably because all of his energy is devoted to breathing. He could not get comfortable and the more everyone tried to make him comfortable the worse he got. He was very distraught about getting suctioned and this made him work even harder. His heart started showing increased stress (higher CVP), his kidney function worsened and he started retaining fluid again.

On top of that we made too many drug changes and he is having withdrawal symptoms. We turned his sedative drip off on Monday. It was a very low rate by then and it needed to be turned off but he never

484

does well with any medication change. Then Tuesday we decreased his narcotic drip because he needed to wake up a little. We have learned not to make too many changes in such a short time but in this case we had to do it. He'll be okay in terms of the withdrawal in a day but it has been hard on him today.

Evening rounds were dismal. We were back to whether or not we should reintubate him tonight. It is hard to believe things can change that fast and then change again in the blink of an eye. He looks slightly better now but working harder than he should. We have made changes on his BiPAP settings and I hope they help. He needs to sleep desperately and that sleep needs to be restful and not a result of labored breathing. I truly believe that had he not had such a great night on Tuesday he would have been reintubated by mid-day today. The fellow on tonight is an anesthesiologist who is finishing his critical care fellowship. I have known him since Zach was much younger and he is a very careful thinker. So at least there is a small bit of comfort in knowing that if we have to reinsert the breathing tube he will do it. Still....I hope we don't go there tonight.

His bleeding did stop with the extra Factor and platelets last night. Very thankful for this. Very thankful for a hematologist who does not take chances or the "wait and see" approach with Zach in this situation.

Friday, November 16, 2007 10:18 PM

Sorry for the lack of update yesterday. The last 2 days have been so incredibly busy. I looked up on Wednesday. and it was close to 5 PM and I had not eaten and yesterday I never ate the lunch I bought until 4 PM. Everything has been so minute to minute. Good moments and scary times. Food seemed like an afterthought. Mountain Dew, on the other hand, is always a priority.

I think (and I hope this is true) that Zach has turned a corner or at least started to round the bend. Things have improved since yesterday afternoon. In talking with the anesthesia fellow, she told me that if Zach had been any other kid they would have intubated him on Wednesday night/Thursday morning. She echoed what I have heard from everyone and what I feel myself. It is just so hard to watch him work for every breath. All we want to do is to take that work away

485

from him and see him go back to being more peaceful and comfortable. And one way to do that is to put the breathing tube back in for him. It's that easy. We all agreed that we did not want to intervene prematurely. But the fear we all had was that we would fail to recognize his Zach specific signs that we had crossed the line of no return, or worse, that he would not show any signs – either of which would lead to an emergency intubation which he may or may not have survived.

Rounds Thursday morning centered on how re-intubation is always looming and how every time they get called to Zach's room they wonder if this will be the time they need to reintubate. What a cheerful way to start the day. His chest x-ray report followed….his right lung had worsened and was reportedly close to collapsing. At the same time his very weak cough had stopped all together, likely from exhaustion. I talked with one of the fellows and asked him if there was not something we could do to give him a fighting chance. He agreed we could do more so we added IPPV which basically is a cough assistance technology…I won't even try to explain it except to say it's done every 4 hours and helps elicit coughs. We also ordered a bed with percussion to assist him in coughing.

By Friday morning he was coughing spontaneously and his right lung looked more open. It is still not good but so much better. He has successfully been off BiPAP (but on a non-rebreather mask so he does not retain CO_2) on 2 occasions today. Many of his doctors are hopeful although the new ICU doctor that started today reported off to the night people that he might need to get reintubated. I'm almost to the point of being bored with the speech 2x/day.

His kidneys decided to behave today after taking a little hiatus with his heart this week. That is encouraging too. He has still not really been awake since Tuesday but if you or I had to work as hard as he had to breathe then we'd be sleeping too. Only today has he had some truly peaceful periods with minimal respiratory effort. For the most part he is still working more than he should.

Hopefully this will all remain true through the weekend. We so need to have some good and BORING days around here.

Today has been a good day in many ways. Zach was able to have the non-re-breather mask a few times and did well. He opened his eyes for longer periods of time which he has not done in many days. He watched a good portion of *Fantastic Four* and enjoyed visits from family. I asked him to arm wrestle me and I could see his muscle tense up and then feel him push against me. So that means he won and I told him so. He got his hair washed and looks great.

He did appear to have a few "panic" moments. His eyes flew open and he was forcing his mouth shut against the Bipap as if he was trying to hold his breath. This is typical for kids his age who have been in the IC for a long time. It is part of what is called "ICU psychosis." I don't think he quite has that but it would not surprise me if he had a touch of disorientation, fear, etc. This comes from the constant stimulation of this environment. Hopefully, this will not progress. We agreed to start holding his middle of the night respiratory treatment except for the medication that goes through his BiPAP. The goal is to give him a block of time for about 7 hours of uninterrupted sleep if at all possible.

I am worried that we have seen more blood today when he has been suctioned. It's unclear where it is coming from. My hope is that it is dripping down from his nose but it seems more likely it is coming from his throat or even further down in his trachea. He really only has it after his IPV treatment (the "cough machine"). We had planned to cut his cryoprecipitate to once/day today but our fellow just came in and after some discussion we decided that was not a good idea. So he will remain on 2/day cryo still.

He is also having sudden drops in his oxygen saturations. This may oddly be a sign of improvement but they are scary. He does this during and sometimes after his IPV treatment. The theory that we have gone with right now is that the treatment mobilizes all the "stuff" that has been stuck in his lungs so that he can cough it up. This is a good thing as we want it out of his lungs. Unfortunately, when he coughs it up, there is so much that it temporarily impacts his ability to breathe effectively until we suction it out. And the suctioning is an issue too as the more it is done the more he needs it. The ICU nurses are used to suctioning until a kid sounds good but this is just not the right thing

487

for Zach. So the fellow and I just talked with the staff about that and I think we all agree that he should only get suctioned to the point of unblocking any obstruction and not any more than that.

The doctors feel it is realistic to think we can get Zach out of the ICU this week. I agree as long as the above does not get worse. Basically we have said that when he is ready for one nurse and his respiratory care is every 6 hours instead of every 4, he can go to 4 west. There is nothing the 4 west nurses cannot do that the ICU nurses cannot do so if he only needs one nurse he may as well have that in the intermediate ICU. That would be the best Thanksgiving gift of all.

I did run out to Barnes and Noble tonight to get him some new CDs for night. While there I picked up *The Little Prince*, which is a book I loved as a kid. Later in nursing school I had an instructor that would read us a chapter every week during one of our labs for she felt it was something that would be good for us all to hear. I have wanted to read it to him but the only version I have at home is in French (since I had to read it in French class years ago). It will be fun to read it with Zach, though I am sure he will still prefer reading Star Wars.

Monday, November 19, 2007 10:48 PM

Yesterday (Sunday) and this morning were not good days in terms of his desaturation events. He does just fine but then very suddenly his oxygen saturations drop, he needs 100 percent oxygen and sometimes assistance with his breaths and suctioning. It requires two people because one person has to take care of his oxygenation and one person has to do the suctioning. It would not be a big deal if he did not go down so fast and so often. After about mid-day he is so tired he cannot cough effectively enough and things get worse and worse and eventually he is so exhausted he is not coughing at all.

This is why he needs 2 nurses at all times and this is why he is still in the ICU. If it was predictable and there were signs it was about to happen he could go to the 4th floor but we are not there yet. At least we defined the ICU discharge goals today which are to decrease the amount of respiratory care and assistance he needs and to need only one nurse. If we accomplish the first goal then that will satisfy the one nurse goal and he can go to 4 west. Now I did give them a deadline that we need to be out of the ICU by Friday or I am taking him home.

To address the exhaustion we have started a new protocol of giving him a big bolus of dextrose (sugar) before his last evening respiratory treatment and then a slower infusion of D 25 (25 percent dextrose) for the next 3 hours. At the same time we have insulin infusing. The theory is that the burst of sugar will give his body some extra energy when he needs it at night so that he can continue to cough and clear his lungs out. This is a therapy that a friend who has mito, used last year when she was very weak and needed energy to get through rehabilitation. Peter and the ICU team were very willing to try it but they felt it would be far more effective if they added the insulin because that would help assure that the dextrose gets into the cells where it can be used to make energy. We started tonight and so far he did great. His sugar level in his blood is not too high and best of all he coughed up a storm so that we could suction it out and he was resting peacefully by 9:30 PM which is far earlier than the last four nights. The fellows on tonight are intrigued and we are thinking about using it on and off through the day for other things like physical therapy, etc. Time will tell if it remains a good thing for Zach.

My family will be coming into town this week for Thanksgiving. Hard to believe it is that time of year. We have been here 9 weeks and in the ICU for 7 of those weeks. Time flies though I cannot say we're having fun. Anyway…it will be nice to see my family and nice to have Brittany at home. I miss her and I miss seeing my Abby every day. I am lucky to have two wonderful girls. And lucky to have my 2 wonderful boys.

Thursday, November 22, 2007 10:41 AM

Zach was doing quite well but took a dramatic turn for the worse on Wednesday morning. His kidneys have taken a terrible nose dive, for reasons we do not entirely understand, and in the last 24 hours has had only 156 cc of urine output. He is terribly acidotic and his blood PH is quite abnormal. In fact his entire blood gas has gotten very bad. This morning his lungs sound worse and on x-ray they look "more wet" given he is retaining so much fluid. It looked like he might be turning around slightly earlier this morning but we are not so sure now.

489

The ICU doctors wanted to do some dramatic things last night such as start him back on epinephrine. I understand their desire to do this as this is what they might do for every other patient with Zach's concerning labs and clinical change. I had deep concern, however, about getting that aggressive with Zach. On the one hand it could be viewed as proactive, which is the perspective that the ICU team has. Better to intervene earlier than have him go through another cardiac arrest. From a different perspective it could be too much – somewhat like beating a lame horse. That is my perspective. We have always treated Zach proactively but with careful consideration in light of his poor energy delivery to his cells. If Zach is getting by the wrong thing might be to give him a drug (epinephrine) that makes his heart work harder than it has the capacity to do right now. On the other hand maybe getting by is not ok......no one knows, least of all me. All I have is gut feelings and they may not always be right. So we had this conversation several times through the night.

The ICU doctor was respectful and willing to defer to me but he worried that if my decision was wrong (not to put Zach on epi) then I would bear the burden of that responsibility. I said he was exactly right but the thing about being a mother is that I will bear that responsibility even if I am right. If I choose the wrong thing I'll never get over it. But if he chooses the wrong thing, which makes me right, yet I went along with it against my better judgment then I will never get over that either. No matter what anyone says, and no matter that I always make the best decisions I can, no one can control how I feel. I am not sure I can even control it. I wonder if any mother can get to a place of not feeling responsible, even if she did the best she could.

There has not been one doctor that feels they know what to do for him. Yet all have good hearts and want to help. The problem is that they fall back on what they know to do -naturally. And the question for me is whether it will be the very wrong thing for Zach. They know so much more than I do and they have so many ideas. They take the time to brainstorm and Zach is lucky to have people care that much. They are smart – some are so incredibly smart it makes my head spin. And yet...I know much more about Zach than they do. I know his labs and his patterns and his history; it is etched in my brain. Somehow we have to put their global knowledge and vast experience together with my very specific knowledge and experience with Zach. It gets hard

490

when they have conflicting ideas. It is likewise hard because Zach is often so paradoxical that even a simple thing like holding an antihypertensive (blood pressure lowering medicine) for low blood pressure could be very wrong because sometimes those medicines actually improve his heart function and increase his blood pressure.

For now he is getting mega-dosed with diuretics in case he has gotten resistant to them. We changed his antibiotics in case he is infected. He is getting stress doses of steroids. He will get a bolus now of dextrose (sugar water) with insulin to help bring energy to his cells. We have drawn cultures from his blood and urine to see if he has an infection. He is getting back to back transfusions to help give him energy. He is getting a lot of bicarbonate to help correct his severe acidosis. We turned down one of his cardiac/blood pressure medicines which might help and might be lethal. All of this is supportive for the most part. We don't know anything else to do.

I am heartbroken that just when he was doing better he took such a bad turn for the worse. It is hard to know it is a holiday and he does not know it and probably does not care. I am trying to gain perspective and remember that no matter where we are and what our circumstances are there are always things to be thankful for. That is hard – I am not Pollyanna, but I am trying.

When I think back on this past year I am thankful for our trip to San Diego. Zach was so well there and he enjoyed so many different things.

I am thankful that after he did so poorly this spring and we thought he had dropped to a new and lower level of function he improved and was better than ever this summer.

I am thankful for my girls and their love for their family, their resilience despite their circumstances, their humor, their patience and their compassion.

I am thankful for supportive family, friends, school district, employer and colleagues and community.

I am thankful for every person, whether they work in the lab or they are a doctor, who has had a part in giving Zach each day he has had at home.

I am thankful for my sweet Sam who makes me laugh when I remember him and who I think of every day as I try to be the person he believed me to be.

I am thankful for Zach's primary doctor and for his hematologist who have taken time every day since this admission started to help Zach and to help me.

I am thankful to the nurses and fellows and residents from both the PICU and 4 west who have taken such good care of Zach.

There are so many other things I could list and I hope to be careful to always remember despite the many things that I wish I could change

Saturday, November 24, 2007 9:52 AM

Zach has had a very rough time since Thanksgiving evening. His acidosis, while not worse, did not improve despite aggressive treatment. His heart showed more signs of dysfunction. There were a series of med changes that may have been good but too late to help or they may have been what pushed him completely over the edge. The timing of his rapid decline fits pretty near exactly with when those drugs wore off but we will never know for sure.

The culmination was a very sudden onset of hypoxia, (poor oxygen delivery to the body), loss of blood pressure and pulseless electrical activity (his pacer worked but the heart could not respond to the pacing). He was resuscitated. He is now intubated and on several cardiovascular drips – epi and vasopressin. He is on high ventilator support settings but his lungs are very filled with fluid as is the rest of his body. His kidneys are working a little but not enough. I do not know what today will bring.

What I do know is that I love Zach with all my heart.

Sunday, November 25, 2007 6:25 PM

Zachary is hanging in there but still his status is quite critical. He remains on incredibly high doses of epinephrine though we did take him off the vasopressin today. His ventilator support is up on some parameters and down on others so it's a wash. His lungs are filled with fluid and he continues to retain most of what we have put into him. It's really quite concerning that he is not eliminating fluid via his kidneys except for a very small amount. This absolutely has to change - his kidneys need to start working and they need to work soon - it's about as simple as that.

492

I am worried that the drip of epinephrine is part of the problem and I am further worried that he needs his Labetalol and that without it he will not recover. Unfortunately, the labetalol will not work with the epi and the epi cannot simply be stopped. So I hope they take it down as quickly as possible. Epinephrine is a great lifesaver but it makes the heart work too hard – especially if using the dose Zach is on. The ICU doctors tell me they have never seen such a high dose used in man – and they are referring to today's dose which is 50 percent of the dose he was on Friday night (and about 30 percent of what he was on in October).

Zach is peaceful and not in any pain. He got his hair washed today and one of his new PJ gowns. He looks very spiffy despite the extra fluid weight he continues to gain. He is a strong boy and we continue to tell him that. We were going to move to the 4th floor ICU where he could have a bigger and quieter room. BUT…the ICU doctor is not happy about that. He thinks it is dangerous to move because of the doses of epi that Zach is on. So for now we will stay in our smaller room in the noisy ICU. I was dragging my feet about going anyway since I can't take the fellows with me and at this point they know Zach enough to know they can't predict anything and that they have to be very careful. It definitely would have been nice to have the better room though and it would just psychologically feel like a step out of the ICU but today won't be the day to do that.

As one of my doctor friends told me, this is between God and Zach, and unfortunately the things we do will not be what ultimately makes him better or worse. Zach's own doctor said that we need to listen to Zach and what he tells us he can do and what he cannot. He is right and so we try to look for that. Zach has pulled through a lot – he has surprised all of us many times and there have been many miracles. I hope that his life will continue to be filled with those miracles but sadly I do not have the power to make that happen. So I sit here and just plead to God, to the stars and to anyone who listens – please let him recover. Please give me more time with Zach –funny, courageous, thoughtful and compassionate Zach.

Monday, November 26, 2007 10:39 AM

Zach's lungs sound remarkably good for someone as fluid overloaded as he is. Everyone is impressed with his ability to stay on the same vent settings given the situation. His face actually looks less swollen despite the fact that he is not getting rid of the fluid. It is nice to see it look a bit better since last night.

Last night his output dropped to 3-5 cc/hour which is terrible. We gave many different diuretics on top of the ones he already gets. Nothing helped. Today we are going to try the drug he received a few hours of 2 months ago – Conivaptan. This is a different type of diuretic that might help his kidneys out some. It's scary to everyone because his first arrest was about 5 hours into getting this drug. At the time they told me that the drug had nothing to do with his arrest. But still…we worry. But there are no steps left before dialysis right now so we feel the risk is one we should take and can be careful about.

The difference this time is he has an epinephrine drip on board and we can increase it quickly if his pressure drops. He is on a closely monitored unit with instantly available physician support. We did not start it on night shift because we wanted a full staff in place. Also this morning Zach's anesthesiologist put an arterial line in which will give us the ability to monitor blood pressures constantly. I had refused one on Friday night which is totally against ICU practice but in this setting I think it is necessary and we cannot get away without one.

Zach blinked a few times responsively last night so it is more than a little annoying to hear the ICU team say he is comatose. Apparently if they do not see it they do not believe it even though all his nurses saw it as well. He gave a definite blink when I told him I have his Christmas music CD. He loves his Christmas music!

We continue to have such a wonderful team of nurses, pharmacists and doctors. Zach is well cared for. Last night about 2 am his nurses, the attending on call ICU doctor and a transport nurse and me were staring at flow sheets and brainstorming ideas for Zach. I can't say we had any bright ideas but the time of day and the thought that went into that discussion make it clear how much everyone wants to help him.

That's all. We'll start the drug about noon so that we have a full hospital staff for some time yet today.

494

Monday, November 26, 2007 10:53 PM

We started the Conivapan at noon as planned. His pressures have been fine. No improvement in kidney function yet but that is not surprising. The loading dose will not be in until midnight and then he'll have about 3 more days of it. We should see a positive effect by tomorrow if it is going to work.

Hoping for kidneys to wake up – hoping and hoping and hoping...

Tuesday, November 27, 2007 9:29 AM

My precious Zachary passed away early this morning. Despite being quite ill, his sudden downward spiral last night was unexpected for the staff and of course for me. He could not oxygenate his body and his heart is so tired that it could not compensate anymore. There will be an autopsy because no one can understand what happened. I have a feeling that in typical "Zachsam" fashion there will not be clear answers.

Zachary was not in pain and it all happened so quickly that I do not believe he had time to feel any fear. I was with him and he was surrounded by his longtime 4 west nurse, 2 of his primary ICU nurses, his pharmacist, the fellow that saved his life in October and the ICU doctor that knew him the most. I hope he knew how much love and hope was in the room with him.

Zachary Ryan Juhlmann - the one and only
This is how Zach introduces himself
And he is the one and only - the bravest, kindest, most positive, most compassionate, most resilient....he is my one and only Zachary.

I do not know anything about arrangements. I will post it on here when I do.

Thank you for loving Zachary. Please carry him in your hearts as so many of you have continued to carry Sam.

Wednesday, November 28, 2007 10:18 PM

Zachary's obituary and information about the memorial service will be in both the *Waukesha Freeman* and the *Milwaukee Journal Sentinel* starting Friday through the weekend.

Zachary had such a love for Thanksgiving. He so looked forward to his aunts, uncles, grandparents and assorted friends spending the day with us. In the last two years he especially looked forward to his big sister, Brittany, coming home from college for the holiday.

He had two favorite things about the holiday. One was playing board games as a family with our extended family. We'd usually play

497

games as teams and he was sure never to be on Mama's team because Mama was never as good at those games as his uncles and aunts.

Zach's second favorite part of Thanksgiving was baking pumpkin bread with me - and of course eating it. It saddened me that he did not get to celebrate Thanksgiving this year in the way that he is accustomed to. I always thought that when he was discharged we would make a big batch of pumpkin bread.

Zachary's love for Thanksgiving – a holiday without all the fanfare and gloss of Christmas – speaks to my favorite thing about this child of mine. His Joy - Joy found in the simplest of things. Even if it had turned out that he was not able to sit or swallow or talk I think we would have found a way to bake together and find joy in that process. No matter what the illness had taken from Zach it is impossible for me to believe that it ever took his joy.

In honor of Zachary we will be serving pumpkin bread after his memorial service on Monday night. (Don't worry – there will also be sweeter things to snack on!). If anyone would like to make a loaf of pumpkin bread for Monday please let me know by Friday evening so I can give an accurate count to the wonderful women who will be baking for Monday.

Sunday, December 2, 2007 3:05 AM

Thank you for the many messages. I remain somewhat in a state of shock which I am sure will go away when the funeral is over and the house is still. Until then we have my Mom, Frank, brothers and sister here and my Dad flew in today. My friend Janet and her husband Neil flew in from Georgia on Wednesday. My friend Kathy came from Tennessee (the land of guns and knives) Friday. They have all been of invaluable help in preparing for Monday. I am beyond lucky to have such caring friends and family.

Below is Zachary's obituary. It hurts to even write that word. I miss him profoundly. His death still seems impossible.

Juhlmann, Zachary Ryan Of Waukesha, died Tuesday, November 27, 2007, at Children's Hospital of Wisconsin at the age of 15. The funeral service will be held at 6:30 PM, Monday, December 3, 2007, at RiverGlen Christian Church, S31 W30601 Sunset Dr., Waukesha,

498

with a prior visitation from 2:30 until 6:30 PM at church. The burial will be held on December 4 at 10:00 AM, at Salem Cemetery in Wales, WI. Zachary was born on April 20, 1992 the son of Louis and Anne (Fischer) Juhlmann.

He attended Banting and Bethesda Elementary Schools, Butler Middle School and most recently began his freshman year at Waukesha West High School.

Zach, joyful in hope and positive in all circumstances, loved his life, living it deeply and fully. Never desiring special treatment, Zach relished attending school, especially his art, science lab and personal finance classes and socializing with his friends. Zach, known for his sense of humor and "best" laugh resounding down hallways, schemed jokes to play on his nurses, doctors and family and relished April's Fools Day. With his vivid imagination, Zach wrote amazing stories, created impressive art pieces and invented spicy and elaborate recipes. He favored watching movies, especially "Star Wars", loved all things Nintendo and saved his money to purchase electrical items at his favorite store, Best Buy. He delighted in making presents for people and winning chess. The synergy of Zach's joy, profound compassion, optimism and perseverance left a lasting impression on all who met him, leaving this world a brighter place.

Zachary joins his "best brother," Samuel Juhlmann, who preceded Zachary on March 3, 2005. Zachary is lovingly remembered by his parents, Louis and Anne; two sisters, Brittany and Abigail; grandparents, Louis and Sharon Juhlmann of New Jersey, Mary Jo and Frank Balistreri of Genessee, WI and John and Patty Fischer of Florida; aunts and uncles, Mike and Elaine Fischer, Maribeth Fischer, Sean Russell, David Cieri, James (Clarie) Juhlmann, Darren (Debbie) Juhlmann, Sarah Juhlmann, Alex Fischer and Matt Fischer, as well as a large extended family.

Zachary's family expresses deep appreciation to blood donors, Home Care Medical, Waukesha School District, the community and Children's Hospital staff who continually went above and beyond allowing Zachary to have the best life. The family is especially grateful to Dr. Peter Havens, Zach and Sam's primary care doctor, for his excellent care of and passionate dedication to the boys.

Tuesday, December 4, 2007 3:16 PM

Zachary was buried this morning, next to his best brother and best friend, Sam. It is impossible to believe that this is real. I know I am a mother - always - to four children but it stings to know that on Earth I have only half of the children present with me that I had once upon a time. I feel lost and disoriented, without any purpose and if I did not feel my heart beating right now, I would think it was dead. I know time lessens some of this...but I also know that time does not lessen it as much as everyone thinks and hopes. And unlike my brave son, I am having a hard time finding the courage to do this again. I will do it - for the boys and for my daughters - but never with the grace that Zach displayed his entire life.

I loved taking care of Zach -just reading and talking, playing games or teasing him... and caring for his physical body. I know that many think this was a hardship for me but it honestly never felt that way to me. I would not have wished it on him, but I always felt lucky that I could do the little things I did that allowed him to stay as healthy as possible.

As horrific as the last 10 weeks have been, it was a gift to have that time with Zachary minus any other distractions. The time in the ICU does not justify or explain or make it all okay. But given that we were handed the circumstances of an extended ICU stay, I treasure that I was able to make my world him. Everyone says how much that must have meant to him and I know it did. But it may have meant more to me.

I also am thankful that the last 2 or so months brought to light, as never before, how much Zach is loved. I never did hang up all of his cards because I was sure that we would be leaving the ICU "any day now." But he had hundreds of cards. I was inundated with visitors from our own hospital. People in radiology, dietary, lab, blood bank, OR, etc., etc...all touched by this child of mine. Messages in the guest book, visitors, and phone calls, handmade gifts...including the most wonderful collection of pajama gowns. The nurses and I had fun picking out a gown for him each day and they reminded others of who he was and is. His hematologist visited most every day to see him and make me laugh. His primary doctor, so beloved by Zach, gave inordinate amounts of time to us and walked me through the darkest places I have ever been. Our residents and fellows and nurses cared for him, visited him and held such hope for him. Friends and family looked out for me so that I never doubted that many held us close.

The house is so still now. Except for my mom and Frank, my family had to leave today. My friends, Janet and Neil and Kathy, had to go home to their own children. Brittany left to go back to college a little while ago. It is just Abby and me at home. Tomorrow she will go to school, which she wants to do. For the first time in 15 + years I have no idea how I will fill an hour, let alone a day. I cannot go back to work right now…though I will eventually.

Another day I will share the text of what his sisters said about him at the memorial service. He was so blessed to have two beautiful hearted sisters - and he knew this.

Wednesday, December 12, 2007 10:06 PM

"I believe the wolf is innocent because the wolf didn't try to blow down the house. The wolf wanted sugar. The third pig didn't know what the wolf wanted."

Zach defending the wolf…Not sure what grade this is from but I guess the kids were asked who they believed – the wolf or the 3 pigs.

The days seem to go by fast but the nights are long. I think this is what happened to Zach initially when he was in the ICU – he had his days and nights reversed and now I do too. "Would've, Could've Should've" must be the name for the special hell made just for parents. I know I made the best decisions that I could have at the time but it is easy to identify every wrong twist and turn with the aid of hindsight.

Zach's homebound teacher stopped by today with a cookie that he loved to make with her. They are called Oreo cookies but they are definitely not like the Oreo cookies we buy in the store – not even the double stuffed ones. They are amazing cookies. It was nice to talk with her and good timing too. Right before she came I had a little melt down.

I was actually being productive today and paying the myriad of bills and filling out forms – all having accumulated for months. I wanted to transfer money from the bank to Abby's school cafeteria account and set it up for "automatic replenish." This eliminates the

6:30 am scramble for lunch money. So I took care of that but then thought I would see how much money Zach had left and inquire about how to transfer it to her account. Only he did not come up on my list. So I did the "find student" search, typing in his name and school. "Student not found" was the reply I got. I tried putting in his middle school but he was still "not found." Just like that – wiped out of the system as if he never existed. It just made me sick. I know that realistically his name must be removed from the school district roster and I don't care really about the money itself. I can straighten that out someday. Finding not a trace of his precious name is what hurt. It was unexpected – one of many reminders that I will continue to get that he is not here.

Yesterday was a snow day for the kids in our district. This was good as Abby needed a day off from school. She is exhausted. I am sure Brittany is too. They are both working so hard to catch up on their school work.

I promised to write about the visitation and the memorial service. I was overwhelmed with the sheer numbers of people who made it a point to come. His PT and OT from when he was just a year old along with teachers and aids from early childhood (preschool) came. The fellows, residents, attending doctors and nurses from his last weeks of life came. And everyone from the many in between years came. Family, friends, teachers from nearly every year, health care providers, administrators, kids and young adults and their families who my kids have grown up with…I tried but in the end did not talk with everyone. Zach touched many lives and I felt so honored that people went out of their way to be there that afternoon and night for him.

I will include part of the service tonight but not all of it.

Celebrating a Life

Prior to the service my brother played the piano as people walked into the church. My brother's name is David Cieri and he is an amazing musician from New York City.

The service opened with Angela Mangold, a friend of one of Zach's nurses singing the Billy Gilman song, "My Time on Earth." David accompanied her on the piano. Angela has a beautiful voice.

Kyle Turner, who is Zach and Abby's youth minister, welcomed everyone.

Gramps (my Dad) - <u>Isaiah 40:31</u>

"But those who trust in the LORD will find new strength. They will soar high on wings like eagles. They will run and not grow weary. They will walk and not faint.
He then read the words from the song "Eagle's Wings."

Abby – "Commemorating My Big Brother"

Zach was with me since the day I was born. Once he got over his jealousy of Mama's new baby, he adored and protected me like a good brother does. We would play doctor or surgeon, put together crazy numbers of puzzles, or crawl around together.

My mom moved me into Zach's room when I was a baby. We stayed there for a long time together, just loving waking up to each other each morning and talking to each other until we fell asleep each night. I can remember so many games we invented, so many art projects we dove into, so many TV shows we watched together over the years.

Zach and I didn't have a perfect relationship. We fought SO much about ridiculous things. We grew older and we grew apart. I was always so frustrated he couldn't play any sports or stay up late to watch a movie. I was jealous of my friends that complained about their brothers for stupid reasons. In the beginning of 8th grade,, I finally started to realize that none of that mattered. That any amount of time I got to spend with Zach was a great privilege. Not because of time, but because of what a wonderful, positive person Zach was, how much I could learn from him. Zach loved his life more than any of us will ever be able to imagine. He loved me with all of his heart; loved to see me and play a game with me and just be with me. He worked hard for me.

I may have been invited to more parties. I may have been able to run outside and stay up late and eat delicious food that he could not. But he has already exceeded the best life I could ever live. He lived and lived and lived. And I will forever celebrate him for that. I am so, so proud of him. My brother. Forever and for always.

Tuesday, December 18, 2007 2:24 AM

I hate grief. It makes one feel like they are in perpetual postpartum mode. Some days I cry at everything…food in the pantry, a dirty sock of Zach's in the closet, his pictures and school notebooks. I have taken to watching late night sappy Hallmark and Lifetime movies on T.V. and then I cry at all the predictably sad moments. This, of course, is pathetic. If I watched more than an hour of TV a week before Zach passed away that was unusual for me.

Other days I feel like a cold hearted non-human. I feel as if I am not me and in fact am watching me with awe from a distance. "Look. She is shopping at the mall and looks normal." Or "Did you see that? She decorated the tree with Abby and did not shed a tear." I have no idea why some days I am so non-emotional. Maybe it is a self-preservation biological thing. The heart can only bear so much. The pain of missing my boys is so physical that it is hard to imagine that if I had a cardiac echo (ultrasound of the heart) that it would not show a heart that has lost significant function, slowly pumping blood, tired, boggy and over stretched. Of course I know my echo would likely look just fine but it is one of the things I wonder about. Are the days when I feel virtually nothing -stone-like really - a protection of my physical heart? Storing it up for days when I cannot move because my heart hurts so badly?

Well enough of that musing…. Friday I got a call from the high school health room staff person. She took it upon herself to inquire about the balance in Zach's lunch account, acknowledging that she knew that was never the point to me. At any rate, he had about $4 and she transferred it to Abby's account. She also said that even though he is apparently not a student according to the lunch/cafeteria record keeping system – he IS still in the computer for the school district. And, in fact, Sammy is too. I was so touched that she did this for me. It meant so much to me. Of course I cried.

504

The staff at West High School also want to open up their semi-annual blood drive in March to the community in memory of Zachary. I love this idea. I love that his memory can be used to bring better awareness and most of all the gift of life-saving blood to others who need it as desperately as he and Sam did.

The teacher in charge of yearbook also contacted Abby and asked her to talk with me about having a page dedicated in the yearbook in memory of Zach. I am honored and touched by this request. Naturally we said yes.

Meanwhile the kids at Butler Middle School have been busy. This is where Zach and Abby went for 7th and 8th grade – where they graduated from in June. Here are some excerpts from an email I received from Zach's former teacher. She said she wanted me to know how special Zach still is to Butler.

"We wanted to do a Coin War for the dance in honor of Zach. The kids, mostly 8th graders but some 7th graders, helped me organize and collect money. The students raised a little over $1300. In the last two days they collected $962."

"Beyond collecting money many students asked about Zach and students who didn't know Zach asked a lot of questions and were proud to be a part of remembering him."

"We are going to donate $1000 of the money to Children's Hospital and use the rest to purchase a tree to plant at Butler in memory of Zach."

"To go even further, several 8th graders came to me and asked if Friday could be wear Zach's favorite color day to further remember him. We are asking people to wear purple in honor of Zach tomorrow."

I am amazed at the generosity of these kids. While Zach may have known some of the 8th graders (they would have been in 7th grade when he was there), it is doubtful that he knew more than a handful of 7th graders. Yet they wanted to do this. If only we could find a way to grow hearts like those of children and transplant them into adults who become cynical, cold and selfish. Not to say all adults are like that. Yet it is true that many could learn a thing or two from these children.

So now there is a tree at Bethesda Elementary for Sammy and one at Butler for Zach. It's a beautiful thing to think about.

Finally, Donna, Sam's 1st grade teacher wrote a note in the guest book about how she was thinking about Sam and how he laughed so much at the reading table. I love that memory. He caused such a disturbance during his group time but Donna handled it well. They had their own little jokes and routines and he was so proud to be part of that reading group. He was always so excited when he could read a word – practically bouncing off his chair to tell her that he recognized something. What a perfect 1st grade teacher for Sam.

Continuing with the service…This is the sonnet my mother wrote for Zach and read at his Celebration of Life.

Sonnet for Zachary

Until I trod among the forest trees,
I did not hear their sigh of letting go
Or see the happy sailing of those leaves
To sow new life: to darken and to grow.

Eyes alone deceive for there is more
As earth receives those leaves and trees pull back.
Creation is at work though we deplore
The striking loss, the frost of Winter's lack.

As I look at you, your quiet change
And lose you in the only way I know
I think like seasons, plans must be long-range
And summer will return to what lies low.

Though at first I may not know your sign,
I will not give to death the final line.

Mary Jo Balistreri--November, 2007

Thursday, December 20, 2007 1:16 PM

On Tuesday afternoon I had to go see Dr. Fein. I didn't understand why I needed help, because it seemed to me that you <u>should</u> wear heavy boots when your dad dies, and if you <u>aren't</u> wearing heavy boots, <u>then</u> you need help. But I went anyway because the raise in my allowance depends on it."

506

--Oskar in the book *Extremely Loud and Incredibly Close* by Jonathan Safran Foer

I read this book shortly after Sammy went away and I love it because it is so real. Oskar is a little boy – maybe about 9 or so if I remember correctly. His Dad has just died. He is sad and that weighs heavily on him (hence the "heavy boots") , but as is typical in our society, he is sent for therapy so that he does not walk around with those "heavy boots." Oskar, at a very young age, is learning that grief makes everyone uncomfortable.

This is from a column in the *Milwaukee Journal Sentinel* today.

Focus shifts to boys' lives, not deaths
Written by Laurel Walker

A beautiful tree, sometimes decorated by small hands, grows outside Bethesda Elementary School in Waukesha. It was planted to remember a little boy named Sam Juhlmann. He died 2 1/2 years ago, then a 7-year-old first-grader, of a disease that sapped the energy and life from his small body.

When the snow is gone and the hope of spring is back, another tree will be planted, but this time at nearby Butler Middle School, this time for Zach Juhlmann, Sam's 15-year-old brother. He succumbed to the same assault of mitochondrial disease on Nov. 27.

How can any family survive such sadness, such overwhelming loss?

The boys' mother, Anne Juhlmann, said the Waukesha family - she, her husband, Louis, and their daughters Brittany, 20, and Abby, 14 - finds a way.

They survive on their memories of the boys' lives. They survive by knowing that others remember, too.

Speaking of her son Sam, Anne Juhlmann said Wednesday, "The only way to deal with it, and I'm not saying I did this perfectly - I had stopped trying to figure out why he died and what I could have done, and I focused on why he lived."

Now, with Zach's death barely three weeks ago, "I'm back at step one," she said.

Students and teachers at Butler Middle School are helping to focus on Zach's life.

They remember, especially the eighth-graders, even though Zach was a year ahead of them and a freshman at Waukesha West High School. For the past three years, the students have raised funds in Zach's honor.

Once the donation paid for a laptop with computer games for the floor at Children's Hospital of Wisconsin where both Sam and Zach spent so much time all through their lives. Last year, donations went toward DVD players on the same floor.

Last week, the seventh- and eighth-graders who know of Zach's valiant fight waged a fight of their own - a spirited "coin war" with each grade challenging the other to add to Zach's cause.

When they were done, said Marianne Petruzzello-Kirsch, a special-education teacher who knew Zach well, they'd collected a record $1,300 in four days. It will buy that tree for planting, a plaque to memorialize him, and a $1,000 check headed to Children's Hospital.

Anne Juhlmann, a nurse who teaches in the special needs department at Children's, said the money will go toward a project that teaches pediatricians in training how to care for children with special health care needs.

Mitochondrial disease attacked virtually every part of the brothers' bodies. Mitochondria is the part of the cell that makes energy from food and oxygen. When it doesn't function, the cells and the organs those cells support begin to die. Zach was diagnosed at age 6, and his baby brother at age 15 months.

In a journal about her children, Anne Juhlmann wrote of Sam: "He was a child with big brown eyes who was tiny for his age, though his presence was enormous. He loved to tell jokes - none of which were funny. Yet to hear his uninhibited laughter at his own jokes was a stop into the sunshine from the shadow, so we asked him to tell the jokes again and again."

About Zach, she said Wednesday, "The word I use to describe Zach was equanimity. He just had this beautiful way of accepting whatever life tossed at him and making the most of it, not letting it depress him or using it as a crutch. He was very hopeful . . . very creative. He had a wonderful sense of humor and was just very wise beyond his years."

Teacher Petruzzello-Kirsch said, "He never quit." Even on days when his energy was low, he wanted to do everything other kids did. He worked hard. He was always open, willing to answer students' questions about his backpack of drugs and food that were administered through tubes.

Zach, Petruzzello-Kirsch said, was "one of those kids who changes who you are, who makes you re-evaluate."

He was, in other words, unforgettable.

Friday, December 28, 2007 1:02 AM

I realize that it is now after midnight but today is still here for me -and today it is December 27th – a month since Zach's death. Many people have asked how I am doing or simply expressed the hope that I am okay, have found comfort in memories or in the knowledge that my boys are happy and together. I appreciate the kindness, support and shared sorrow that I know is the true author of those words. However, I have not answered the many messages, letters and calls I get because I am living a reality that most people really don't want to know. You can choose to stop here…or you can read on, knowing that nothing I write tonight will be sugar coated or inspiring.

How am I doing? As much as I love words and the history of words, I have yet to find anything that comes close to truly expressing how much I hurt. I am sad. I cry. I miss Zach. I miss his doctors, nurses, therapists, home care providers, pharmacists, lab techs and on and on. I even miss being in the ICU and inanimate objects like his IV pumps. I want to help him with his homework and finish reading the *Star W*ars series to him. I want to tuck him at night and hear him laugh.

I am comforted by some of my memories, while others haunt me. I relive his death. I re-think my decisions constantly and wonder if I had chosen what was behind door A or B would we not have inadvertently opened death's door? I am exhausted because I cannot sleep at night. I love remembering the happy times. I love hearing people tell me stories about him and I laugh sometimes just thinking about him…like yesterday when I found $407 hidden in his mini

ATM machine. He did love "personal finance." Then – and inevitably - tears fall on the very memories that console me, for Zach is not here…Sam is not here…and I will never have new memories to treasure in my heart.

Am I comforted by the fact that my boys are in heaven and this has somehow fulfilled God's perfect plan? No – I am simply not that faithful and trusting – and certainly not that unselfish. I want my boys and I want them now.

Paul Celan, a Romanian Holocaust survivor penned the following: "Rise up against multiple meanings. Trust the trail of tears and learn to live." My friend's priest told her that - her only 2 children have left this earth courtesy of mitochondrial disease. She, in turn, sent it to me after Sam passed away. In essence it means that it is folly to look for answers. We need to feel the grief and somehow learn to live with it.

The pastor who spoke at Zach's funeral spoke of the importance of grieving. He reminded us that of the shortest sentence in the bible – "Jesus wept."

The truth is that I see neither meaning nor hidden blessing in either of my boys' deaths. Their deaths feel so senseless and no matter where they may be – whether together, happy, cured, warm, safe - I do not feel they should be anywhere but with me. The "multiple meanings" Celan referred to can never explain or justify this for me. I am honestly just fighting -not very well most of the time - to have trust that if I learned how to live again after Sam died – albeit as a different person – then perhaps I will learn to live once again as a still different version of myself. But for now I am weeping. If Jesus could weep than surely I can too.

I never knew how much Zach was the glue that held me together after Sam's death. I never knew how much he was the "wind beneath my wings" and my hope…..

More on that another day....

Tonight Zach's homebound teacher, Donna, and her son Will came over. Will made guacamole - which was excellent. Donna made enchiladas -also awesome. I was not sure how I would do but we talked for hours and it was good for me. Donna, of course, is like family to me...as so many who supported Zach and Sammy with school came to be over the years.

510

2011

Thursday, February 10, 2011 5:43 AM

Thank you for checking to see if I have updated.

I miss Sam and Zach. I can't write about anything new they have done but I have not finished writing about all that they did in their too short lives...I have not finished writing about all the ways they touched people...about how they continue to teach me....about the things people say to me to let me know that Zach and Sam continue to be part of their lives.

I am not done telling their story. I'm not sure I will ever be.

In August a doctor asked me a normal question: "Where are you going for fun this summer?" I answered that we could not take a vacation this summer. He changed the question. "Well than what are you doing for fun?" I was silent. I could not think. He looked at me and asked, "What exactly are you doing for you that's fun?" I just stared at him. I felt so disconnected and confused....I tried to answer but there wasn't an answer. He didn't stop. His next question was, "Are you still writing?" All I could do was shake my head no. "Why not?" he asked. I'm sure you can guess by now what my answer was. Silence. The doctor was my doctor at the time (he has since moved away); he had been the boys' doctor from the time they were each a baby. There was a lot I didn't say but he didn't need me to. "Promise me that you will write. Find a time. Make a time. But within the next few months promise me you will write again." I promised....and I have been writing but not online. The things I have been writing are not suitable for an audience. They have simply helped me process and gain my bearings when i feel most lost.

So I come here simply to say please don't give up on me - on us - please continue to remember Zach and Sam. I can't tell you how much would love to take an hour each week to write stories about them. I can't do that right now. The good news is that for the first time in a long time i see some light at the end of the tunnel.

This past year has been one of the most difficult I have ever had. Difficult in a very different way than the first year after Sm died or after Zach died. Physically, emotionally, socially, professionally...it has been hard and eye opening and challenging on virtually every level. I have felt powerless to help myself and to help my daughters through their own struggles. I have felt alone and have learned the

512

incredibly harsh realities of being a person with a chronic illness that is not readily visible.

Living life, loving and learning and maintaining hope, is the only thing I know to do if I want to continue being a mother to not only my 2 boys but my girls as well. To turn my back on life, or worse become apathetic and uncaring is to be untrue to everything I told my children I believed in; it's an affront to what I both taught and yet also learned from all four of them.

I re-read a speech I gave at a memorial in the fall of 2006. I spoke of the months after Sam died...how I had to find one thread to hold me to earth because I did not have the will to live. I had to hold that thread with all my strength and trust that if I acted my way through the day, that eventually I would feel a desire to live. The thread I held on to was my 3 surviving children. Then, as now, my love for them as the only thing I could feel. So I trusted that and held on. I made a commitment to live. The only thing I knew to still be unwaveringly true was my love for my children -I trusted it more than I trusted myself.

Sometimes that's all we can do: blindly trust. Not blind in the sense that we know not what or who we trust. We know and it is precisely because we trust in that person or feeling that we can walk--blindly--unsure of every step we take. That is how I have felt for almost a year. So seeing some light through the blindfold is a wonderful and hopeful thing. I hope it gets brighter and in time I can see the landscape more clearly and feel as if I know who I am, where I am, what I am doing, where I have come from and where I am going. Right now I still feel very lost.

Thank you to my landmarks - which is to say thanks to all of you. You give me perspective and help answer some of those above questions when you visit the boys website despite that i don't write; you call, stop me in a work hallway, email, come to my home, send a card. You've told me about your own struggles, your babies about to be born, your new jobs, deaths in your family. I barely answer if it's an email and yet you have patience and continue to tell me about your lives...I cannot tell you thank you enough. It grounds me. That may not make sense and I am too tired to explain it...I will try to someday. For not just accept my thanks and know that in sharing your lives with me you have helped me keep walking--blind as I may be.

513

Please keep sharing what is going on in your lives with me. Please keep telling me when you think of the boys. That is what has helped the thread become something stronger. I still have days when I feel that I am holding on to a piece of thread and I am petrified that it would be so easy to let go--or that it could break -and the fall would be fast. Most days I have more confidence that I am anchored with yarn and some days even rope. I can breathe without thinking so hard about it. I can see light and dark and feel cold and warm. I am not constantly telling myself to hold on.

In a few weeks it will be March 3rd. I don't have the courage to write how many years it has been since March 3rd 2005. I will think of it when the day comes but for now I simply can't. In that same speech I said that the moment of Sam's death can never be compared with the entirety of Sam's life. I believe that is true. What scares me is that I have come to learn how faulty memory is. That has been an enormous lesson for me in the past 6 months. I don't want to ever forget anything about Sam (or Zach) and yet I know, even as I write those words, that I have probably forgotten many things. So I have a request...please tell me a memory you have of Sam -either something you experienced with him or something that I told you. Or you could tell me something you learned from Sam, or something you will never forget -even if it is that at the tender age of five he mooned me at the kitchen table. (I'd like to know if anyone would have kept a straight face while telling him that big boys don't moon their moms at dinner time).

I can see Sam. I can hear him and feel his spirit and joy still. Lately I have been writing things furiously about him....as I did when he first died. So that is my request as we approach March 3rd. if you have memories to share please leave them in the guestbook or email them to me. Help me celebrate his life on March 3rd and not his death. curling up, as I have wanted to do, and quitting life would allow his death and Zach's death to win. Letting go would allow the struggles my girls have had over shadow the lives that have led up until now. Please tell me about Sam: who he is, what he did, what has changed because of him, what reminds you of him, what your favorite story is of him.

Before I close I will briefly share that our state continues to move forward with improving emergency care for children like Sam. We just got another grant funded...and within a year we should have kits for parents and doctors and others to help them plan for emergencies. I feel blessed that I am paid to be part of that effort. It helps me focus on something other than my incessant *what if, should have, would have* and *could have*. It reminds me that even as Sammy died, he taught our entire community a lesson. His death feels so wrong, so needless, so unfair and I don't' think I will ever accept it as anything but wrong. Sam impacted emergency care in Waukesha. That does not feel like a fair trade. It's not even that comforting. Still, there is a measure of solace as we move forward with our grant, working to improve emergency care for kids with special health needs. We are moving at a snail's pace but like my own past year -I appreciate that we are at least moving. And every step is a vote for life...a vote for the life that Sam lived and the lives he changed.

April 20, 2011
HAPPY BIRTHDAY ZACHARY

My pregnancy with Zach was somewhat difficult. I was hospitalized early due to several scares during which I wondered if my baby would be born alive. Of course I did not know Zach was a he then. I always wanted to be surprised. It was only with Sam that I knew ahead of time. I made it through the first trimester and eventually I started feeling better.

I was excited about the life growing inside of me but during the holidays, I suddenly felt a strong sense that something was not right – that my baby was going to be born sick. It was not based on anything but it persisted for weeks. Then at 28 weeks, while working, I had sudden onset of terrible pain. I was terrified that it meant that my sense of something being wrong was accurate.

I was working night shift and one of the residents offered to do an ultrasound. I agreed but was terrified of what he would tell me. We ended up laughing at the results. Nothing dire had occurred. Rather my baby had been kicking so hard that I was bleeding and bruised. Looking back, I wonder about the accuracy of that explanation from a first year pediatric resident but at the time it was welcome news during a very bittersweet time of my life. Now I had proof that I had

515

a strong and healthy baby. I bragged to everyone about how my baby had kicked me hard enough to cause bruising

The previous winter my friend's daughter Callie had received what was then a death sentence – she was HIV. By autumn it was clear that Callie would not live to see her second birthday. Times were different then. There was little in the way of treatment and she was deemed too sick to go home. She lived most of her life in the hospital. I'd known her dad long before she was born which made witnessing his pain especially hard. I felt helpless and inadequate as I watched life slowly drain from her little body month after month.

The caterpillar dies so the butterfly could be born. And, yet, the caterpillar lives in the butterfly and they are but one. So, when I die, it will be that I have been transformed from the caterpillar of earth to the butterfly of the universe-- John Harricharan

A few weeks later while working on Valentine's day I found time in the middle of the night, as I usually did, to scoop my little Callie up and rock her. But that night was different. As I rocked her she began to slip from this life to the next. Her heart beat slower. I called someone to wake her dad up. We sat on a cot holding her. The resident and a few others sat on the floor or on the cot with us. We had known this moment was coming all week but it didn't stop anyone's tears as she slipped further and further away. The decisions had been made long ago and so there was nothing for us to do but bear witness with her father. As her heart beat slower and slower Zach began to kick harder and harder. By the time her heart beat for the last time I could have sworn he was doing somersaults. Even then I felt that part of her life infused into his during those final moments.

I went into preterm labor within a day. The official opinion was that my preterm labor was directly related to Callie's death - my body's way of raging against the unfairness of a beautiful little girl's life being snuffed out before she had even started to live. Heartbroken, I agreed, at the time. I have since come to see it differently. I think the preterm labor was a gift from Zach to me. I realize that the notion of an unborn baby having the sensitivity and ability to give his mother the gift she needed most sounds incredibly insane and ridiculous. Perhaps, but after knowing Zach for 15 ½ years, nothing will ever

516

convince me otherwise. The preterm labor was his gift to me -his way of affirming life and reminding me of its joy. Perhaps it was the many months he was with me caring for Callie. Whatever the reason I am very sure that he understood even then that life is a gift.

I was admitted to the hospital and with the help of medicine the preterm labor was stopped eventually. I took the medicine until I was 38 weeks pregnant. My doctor told me to expect that the baby would be born as soon as the medication levels dipped in my blood. That was on April 1st. Zach was due on the 12th. He was not born until April 20th. Is it any wonder that April Fool's Day was his favorite holiday? I should have known then that when he got older he would declare the entire month of April open wide for April Fool's Day jokes. The baby who was constantly doing something to buy his mom a few nights in the hospital – who kicked his mom so hard she bled - who wanted to be born so much that his mom had to be on bed rest for two months - was ultimately born 8 days late. I would guess he was laughing that great big laugh of his. What a good joke to play on Mama.

May you live all the days of your life-- Jonathan Swift

Zach was a beautiful baby. I doubt he'd appreciate my choice of adjectives but there is no other way to describe him. He was simply beautiful. And healthy! He was so strong that he could life his head up before he was a week old while lying on his stomach. I temporarily forgot about my fear that he had a chronic illness. Instead I reveled in showing him off to everyone.

By the time he was five weeks old it was evident to me that he was not as healthy as he seemed. Initially the doctors agreed and we were capitulated into a world of tests, procedures, specialists, hospitalizations and an ever growing list of diagnoses he did not have. In the end he was not diagnosed until he was 6 ½ years old. By then all four of my children were born and Sam was already 15 months old.

During his last 8 years I watched the disease relentlessly attack one organ after another. During the last two years of his life he had so many life threatening moments that I lost count. An incredibly intelligent child, I watched pain medication and disease interfere with his learning. My little boy who can be seen jumping off the bottom 3 to 4 stairs in a movie he made during the days after Sam died lost the

517

ability to walk upstairs and often relied on a wheelchair by the time another year passed. While his mind remained creative and brimming with ideas for art projects his hands often failed to cooperate. I watched him work so hard to learn to write his name in cursive only to watch his hands become so weak that he could not write small enough to fit his signature on a piece of paper. Those are just a few examples of what I watched -and hardly the worst examples. His life and his life message cannot be found in those examples which is why I don't want to dwell on them.

My life is my message-- Mahatma Gandhi

In the end we found ways to deal with any loss that disease threw at us because Zach never lost his love of life. That love of life was his message. He is not unique in his love of life but I do think he is unique in that he was born that way. I cannot take credit for it nor can I attribute it to his experiences or other factors. He simply understood that life was precious and not to be taken for granted before he was born. It makes me wonder sometimes if I gave birth to a very old soul housed in a baby's body.

He accepted his challenges but he never became resigned to them. I know that there is a tendency to turn dead people into saints. Well, I am not going to insult Zach by doing that. He was not a saint or anything close to perfect. He did naughty things, disobeyed at times and annoyed his sisters on purpose. But those are the very things that underscore his innate ability to accept and embrace life without being resigned to his challenges or allowing them to limit his hopes, dreams and outlook.

This past year has been a very hard year for me. I find myself thinking of Sam and Zach more than ever. Zach, especially comes to mind, because at his age he was old enough to choose to whine, feel sorry for himself or revel in pity. Yet he chose none of those. It seems to me that the harder things looked to us from the outside, the harder he fought to truly live - to have "normalcy" - to love unconditionally and to always find a way to laugh. I saw that every day and I knew he did it intellectually. Yet, only this past year have I started to truly comprehend what a feat that was. I have sadly learned how prevalent and insidious discrimination and low expectations of the chronically ill are. While I think it's typically unconscious it does not make it feel any better. It has been equally difficult to realize that we live in a world where chronic illness is seen as a weakness that lowers one's value and even worse -makes a person invisible.

Zach was not unaware of these things. But I can count on one hand the times he broke down about them. Mostly he quietly lived within that reality and found a way to truly be happy –to truly have faith that his worth and the value of his life were not to be determined by others. I think about this nearly every day. I \typically feel very inadequate when compared to Zach and Sam. But I remind myself that Zach would say that the only person I need to measure up to is me. He understood that and drew strength from it as a baby as far as I can tell.

April 20th is Zach's birthday - a very bittersweet day. I miss him terribly. At the same time I feel more thankful than ever for the lessons and example he showed me. I often complain that I don't have a compass, GPS, tour   guide or directions. I forget that if I listen to the soundtrack of Zach's life (as well as that of my other three children) I have the best guide to life possible. My children have taught me so much more than I have taught them.

Fly free and happy beyond birthdays and across forever, and we'll meet now and then when we wish, in the midst of the one celebration that never can end--Richard Bach

Happy Birthday my sweet boy!

Yes, I know you would cringe outwardly but I also know that you were so proud of how close we were. Our last vacation in San Diego frames one of my most cherished memories: you said I was the best friend you ever had . I admit that at the time I was incredibly touched and thought you were the sweetest boy in the world. (that word again!) But Zach - I don't think I realized that you were one of the best friends I have ever had too. And you still are. I wonder if you know how much you have helped and guided me in the past year. Your birthday is so hard without you here but a life that does not include you just looks black.

This year your big sister surprised me and I think you would have approved. I was feeling sad and trying to make myself start cooking

519

some chili for you. I thought she was at work, Abby was babysitting, and the house was quiet. And then she walked in with grocery bags filled with ingredients to cook a spicy dinner in your honor. Not only that but she had assorted ingredients to make smoothies! The only rule was we had to make something up – no recipes to follow. She and I put just about every ingredient into ours. I'm guessing you would have done the same only added in some tobacco sauce or something like that! As it turns out she is pretty sick and could barely sit through dinner but she wanted to do that for you.

Abby is busy and will graduate soon. I hate to tell you this but prom is coming up and most of your friends are taking girls! Tomorrow she is going to see George Winston in concert. Try not to be too jealous! I hope you will be able to see the yearbook because Abby asked me to make a special surprise for it this year. She misses you and wanted to make sure that everyone remembers you are supposed to graduate with her -with all of your Bethesda and Butler friends. Oh – and she was voted most likely to be the president. Don't worry –If she becomes president I will make sure that everyone remembers she is still your LITTLE sister!

We love you Zachary! Please take good care of Sammy for me.

Thursday, November 11, 2011 3:51 AM

I have gotten a lot of emails asking if I am ok -are we ok. I have not known how to answer that so I have not. It's pretty much the same reason why I have not updated. I have always been able to see the stars at night. And it has been really important to me to point them out to others...not because I want to prove I can be the best Pollyanna out there. No, the reason is that so many times writing and talking about it made those stars even brighter.

When the boys were alive that was true and it remained true after they left. I deeply believe there are always stars and we owe it to ourselves - if no one else -to find those stars and share them with others. I believe that seeing and sharing the stars is why Zach and Sam lived as long as they did. You see, along the way I learned that when we take the time to point out a beautiful star we see, we suddenly develop a little following. **Before long the light of one star - sometimes one that is incredibly dim to the human eye -reflects**

and radiates from one person to the next. Sometimes it felt as if the sky itself had opened up and all this warm and amazing light was raining down on us. It is as if there is a wonderful energy - Zach and Sam energy - wrapping itself around all of us. When they were alive it gave me such a sense of community and shared purpose--it inspired me to never stop looking for the stars. And after they died it gave me the same.

So I hope it is clear that I am committed to star gazing. But I also must be honest and say I am working really hard to see stars and have been for some time. It's too late (or early depending on how you view 3:51 am) for me to explain and I am unsure that I even comprehend it myself. All I know is that I felt--and in many ways still do -wrong about saying this on the boys' website. I have always been honest when I write here and tried to say exactly how I feel. I have shared my fear and despair and joy and everything in between. Naturally I am not completely at peace and happy all of the time and it would have seemed disingenuous to pretend otherwise.

Yet somehow I got it in my head this summer that I had to wrap every word I said in beautiful paper and explain my life in the past 12 or so months as something other than what it is. And yet I am committed to the truth and for that reason could not reconcile the 2 things. How do I say something makes sense to me when it clearly does not? How do I say I can't find the stars...I have been looking for hours tonight and I just can't see them? Can I even say that? That's what went through my head every time I got an email asking how I am - and each time I considered updating their site I ran into that same wall. My story just did not seem worth telling anymore and even if it was I did not know how to tell it when the pages were increasingly smudged by rain and dimmed by clouds.

You want to know if I am ok. I don't know how to answer that. I am ok in that I am here and that's always a good thing. I am ok because I know it could be worse. But...I am also not ok. Not at all. I am not ok for all the usual reasons: health and poor response to treatment, the discovery that we are forgotten quicker than we want to imagine, the awful helplessness of not being able to fix things for my kids, a deep sense of fear about the future, strained relationships, professional/work place challenges, grief and other emotional pain, too much to do and not enough sleep.

521

I feel I am slipping backwards and it is a very disconcerting feeling. It's been 5 1/2 years since I held Sam and almost 3 since the night Zach died...I really don't understand why the littlest thing stops me in my tracks - why now and not in the first years after they died? It's like super duper post traumatic stress that did not start for years after the fact. I'm not sure there is such a thing but that is how it feels. I hear a code called and want to run out of the hospital and drive as fast and far as I can. I see an ambulance and freeze. I read that *Toy Story 3* is out on DVD and I feel as if the air has been sucked out of me.

Please do not feel sorry for me. It is what it is. As Zach would say, "Life's not fair Mama! Get used to it!" He is right. Life is not fair. I guess I am struggling with the get used to it part. That's not a bad thing.... I have learned a lot about people and friendships and what matters and what is real in the past year. I am still growing and as long as that is the case then in a sense I really am ok.

But keeping it real also means saying that I don't feel ok most days. I'm just not sure how to make it better. I hope that makes sense and at least lets everyone know that I am alive and not lying in a hospital bed....from what I can gather that seems to be the most common concern. Please know that all of your messages have meant a lot to me. All of your acts of kindness have touched me. In a sense there have been days when so many of you have wrapped my star up and handed it to me. You have given me days when I don't even have to look for a star because you shared yours with me.

Thank you.

Anne Fischer Juhlmann worked as a Family Program Coordinator as well as a Pediatric Case Manager in the Family Resource Center at Children's Hospital of Wisconsin, teaching other parents how to advocate for their children with special needs and disabilities. Based on her unique perspective as a health educator who lived daily with the realities of mothering two terminally ill children, Anne founded at Children's a unique education program for the hospital's residents. TEAM (Together Everyone Achieves More) training included course work that Anne created, along with home visits, for Anne believed passionately that doctors must see children with chronic and debilitating illnesses in *their own surroundings* -- not only in a hospital bed--in order to fully appreciate the non-medical challenges that also impacted--enormously--the child's well-being. The program, initially a requirement for third-year residents, was soon required of second-year residents as well. For her efforts, Anne received the Pediatric House Staff Outstanding Educator Award in both 2007 and 2008.

Just a month after Sam's death, Anne was the keynote speaker at the Wisconsin Make-A-Wish Foundation's annual banquet, sharing with others her hard-earned and heartbreaking wisdom. She held numerous fundraisers for Make-a-Wish, gave presentations at the United Mitochondrial Disease Foundation's Annual Conferences, and was more than anything, a passionate advocate for the Blood Bank of Wisconsin, often writing in the online journal of the anonymous donors who "give so that my child may live." Still, as she wrote in the journal, being a mother to her two brave sons and her talented and generous daughters was her most important role.

50912218R00319

Made in the USA
Charleston, SC
11 January 2016